The Northern

STUDIA IMAGOLOGICA

AMSTERDAM STUDIES ON CULTURAL IDENTITY

10

Series editors
Hugo Dyserinck
Joep Leerssen

Imagology, the study of cross-national perceptions and images as expressed in literary discourse, has for many decades been one of the more challenging and promising branches of Comparative Literature. In recent years, the shape both of literary studies and of international relations (in the political as well as the cultural sphere) has taken a turn which makes imagology more topical and urgent than before. Increasingly, the attitudes, stereotypes and prejudices which govern literary activity and international relations are perceived in their full importance; their nature as textual (frequently literary) constructs is more clearly apprehended; and the necessity for a textual and historical analysis of their typology, their discursive expression and dissemination, is being recognized by historians and literary scholars.

The series STUDIA IMAGOLOGICA, which will accommodate scholarly monographs in English, French or German, provides a forum for this literary-historical specialism.

The Northern Utopia

British Perceptions of Norway in the Nineteenth Century

Peter Fjågesund and Ruth A. Symes

Rodopi

Amsterdam - New York, NY 2003

Published with financial support from The Research Council of Norway, The Norwegian Tourist Board, and Telemark University College

Cover artwork:
David Hockney
"The Valley. Stalheim" 2002
Watercolour on paper (6 sheets)
72 x 36"
© David Hockney

and

Richard Lovett: Norwegian Pictures (1885)

ISBN: 90-420-0846-6
©Editions Rodopi B.V., Amsterdam - New York, NY 2003
Printed in The Netherlands

CONTENTS

ACKNOWLEDGEMENTS

This project began during the academic year 1996–1997 when the two authors were working at the Norwegian Study Centre at the University of York, England; Peter Fjågesund as the Resident Norwegian Director and Ruth A. Symes as a Lecturer in British Culture and Director of Studies. The Centre – a satellite of the Department of English and Related Literature – provides the opportunity for Norwegian students to undertake short courses in English whilst immersing themselves in British culture. For staff and students alike, this allows for the exploration of the many similarities and differences between the two cultures within their contemporary context.

In the summer of 1997, the authors, both of whom had interests in literary and cultural history, made the fortuitous discovery of a passage from the mid nineteenth-century travel volume *Through Norway with a Knapsack* (1859), in which William Mattieu Williams described the 'national filial tie' between Britain and Norway. They were inspired to wonder whether other commentators had expressed similar views and before long had discovered the work which would be seminal to the project: Eiler H. Schiötz's *Itineraria Norvegica: A Bibliography on Foreigners' Travels in Norway until 1900* (1970–1986). This invaluable source proved that there was a huge interest in Norway in the nineteenth century; and indeed, about one third of all foreign travelogues from the period were published in Britain. Schiötz's work gives publishing details, lists of the places visited by each traveller and, on occasions, brief biographical details of the writers. Although they benefited from a number of other bibliographic sources, the authors are especially indebted to the thoroughness of Schiötz's work, which quickly enabled them to identify material and generate research questions.

Throughout the project, the authors have been helped by many professional organisations on both sides of the North Sea. In the first instance they would like to thank the Norwegian Study Centre for giving them the opportunity to initiate and pursue a subject of mutual interest. Furthermore, they thank Telemark University College and the Norwegian Non-Fiction Writers' and Translators' Association for granting funding for study leave; and Telemark University College, the Research Council of Norway and the Norwegian Tourist Board for financial support towards the publication of this book.

The project has involved many hours of hands-on examination of primary and secondary sources in British and Norwegian libraries and archives. In some cases, the authors have been greatly helped by individuals working in these institutions who have pointed them in the right direction or searched on their behalf. They would like to thank: The Bodleian Library, University of Oxford; The British Library, London; Colindale Newspaper Library, London; G. W. Oxley, Archivist, Hull City Archives; Helen Roberts, Archivist, The University of Hull, Brynmor Jones Library; John R. Hodgson, Co-ordinating Archivist, The John Rylands Library, Manchester; Miss Pat Southern, Librarian, Literary and Philosophical Society of Newcastle-upon Tyne; The National Library of Norway, Oslo Division; The Portico Library, Manchester; Brigitte Istim, Punch Library, London; Ms Yvonne Sarrington, The Royal Geographical Society, London; the Faculty of Arts and Sciences Library, Telemark University College, Bø; Chris Jones, Senior Lecturer, University of Wales, Bangor; David Whiteford, Senior Librarian, J. S. Battye Library of West Australian History; Alison McCann, Assistant County Archivist, West Sussex Record Office; Stephen Forbes, BBC Information; and the University of York Library.

For information on individual travellers to Norway, there are a number of dedicated persons and organisations that deserve special mention. For information on Edward Wilson Landor, the authors contacted Mrs Jean Field, The Landor Society, Leamington Spa, Warwickshire, and on Landor's Norwegian adventure, Sven Gøran Eliassen, Director of Borgarsyssel Museum, Sarpsborg. Fascinating details on William Ewart Gladstone's interest in Norway were provided by Patsy Williams, Librarian, St Deiniol's Library, Hawarden, Flintshire and by Elizabeth Pettitt, Archivist, Flintshire Record Office; Sue Gates, Librarian, The Tennyson Research Centre, Lincolnshire advised on Tennyson's trip to Norway. Andrew Laing, Adviser on Pictures and Sculpture at The National Trust, very kindly provided a typescript of the unpublished memoirs of his ancestor, Samuel Laing, a British resident in Norway in the 1830s. Finally, Morten Harangen, journalist, NRK Vestfold, provided useful

The unusual subject of British travel to Norway prompted some questions that could only be answered by those outside the traditional realms of academia. The following people have provided information from their own areas of expertise: Kate Langstrøm Nordahl, Information Officer, British Embassy, Oslo; Naomi Symes, Naomi Symes Books, Warrington; Hugh Meller, Historic Buildings Representative, The National Trust, London; Dave Tylcote; John Phythian Tylecote; Tim Youngs, Editor, *Studies in Travel Writing*, Nottingham Trent University; Hannah Kay, Curator, Rhodes Museum, Bishop's Stortford, Hertfordshire; Gwyneth Jones, House Manager, Capesthorne Hall, Cheshire; Vidar Skiri, Manager of the Bromley-Davenport estate in Romsdal; Torfinn Arntsen, Press and Cultural Attaché, Royal Norwegian Embassy, London; and Paul Smith, Archivist, Thomas Cook Archives, London.

A number of fellow academics gave guidance to the authors in the early stages of the project. The cross-cultural work of Inga-Stina Ewbank, Emeritus Professor at the University of Leeds, provided an Anglo-Scandinavian academic precedent, whilst Professor T. C. Smout of the Institute for Environmental History, University of St. Andrews, Scotland, and Professor Bjørn Tysdahl of the Department of British and American Studies, University of Oslo, read and commented on the early stages of the manuscript. Similarly, in the later stages of the project, Associate Professor Ellen Schrumpf, Telemark University College, read chapters 2 and 3, giving valuable advice on the presentation of Norwegian history. We are grateful for their candour and encouragement.

At the end of the project, the authors must thank those who have helped transform it from manuscript to published page. They are grateful to Professor Joep Leerssen, Leerstoel Moderne Europese Letterkunde of the University of Amsterdam, who recognised the potential of the book for the Rodopi Press series devoted to imagological studies. They also thank Marieke Schilling at Rodopi for her advice on the technicalities of the manuscript, and Trond A. Lerstang of the Copying Centre at Telemark University College, who not only painstakingly transformed the manuscript into camera-ready copy, but also scanned the large majority of the illustrations.

In many senses, the book has been a joint project carried out via electronic correspondence across the North Sea. Both authors have been involved in all aspects of the process from searching archives and organising material, to writing and editing. Nevertheless, each author has been primarily responsible for distinct sections of the book; Peter Fjågesund is the author of chapters 1, 2 and 4; Ruth A. Symes is the author of chapter 3 and has contributed sections to chapter 2. The experience of discussing and co-operating on the manuscript has been a mutually enjoyable and enriching one.

Finally, the book is dedicated to two important sources of inspiration. First to Frank Kendall, who is a devoted twentieth-century traveller to Norway and a friend of the Norwegian Study Centre. Over many years, Frank has repaid the hospitality he has received in Norway many times over by welcoming literally thousands of Norwegian students into his home in Yorkshire. He has shown a keen interest in this project. Secondly, the book is dedicated to Ruth's father, William Symes, whose unfailing encouragement and interest helped to spur on the project in its early stages and whose continuing influence has been felt throughout, despite his death in November 2000. It has been completed, in part, for him.

INTRODUCTION

This is my third expedition to the north;
it is a strange whim to get in love with
deserts, with ice and with snow.

Andrew Swinton, 1792

In an article entitled 'The Viking Road', the writer and broadcaster Magnus Magnusson sees the daring engineering skills required for the modern oil installations in the North Sea as an echo of the equally adventurous spirit and the maritime expertise represented by the Viking longships more than a thousand years ago (Magnusson 1990, 1). In both of these historical epochs the North Sea, one of the world's most treacherous and inhospitable stretches of water, has played a crucial role as a highway between, as well as a barrier against, two different cultures. For the British, islanders gradually developing into cosmopolitans, it represented a northern frontier against the Outside, the Unknown, or, as Edward W. Said and other critics have aptly termed it: 'the Other'. Over the centuries, the Britons' encounter with their Nordic neighbours – be they friends or foes – had a marked impact not only on how they viewed themselves within their own national borders; it also exerted a radical influence on the ways in which they saw themselves in relation to the outside world.

The present study attempts to take a closer look at how the British, during the turbulent and eventful period of the nineteenth century, cultivated and developed their relationship with one of their closest neighbours, namely the Norwegians. Probably the most striking characteristic of this relationship was the apparently overwhelming incongruity of the two countries. Britain was beyond doubt the world's leading power in military and commercial as well as industrial terms; it was indeed, during most of the century, the one global superpower, commanding a position greater than that of the United States today and spearheading virtually every field within modern culture, science and technology. Norway, on the other hand, was a peripheral country in most senses of the phrase – hardly a nation in its own right – with a tiny population, consisting primarily of traditional farmers and fishermen. Nevertheless, there developed, in the course of the nineteenth century, strong and intimate bonds between the two countries that were only further strengthened in the twentieth. In the light of the fundamental incongruity already mentioned, the nature of these bonds, as perceived from a British perspective, deserves a closer examination.

One country's perception of another is necessarily a complex and many-faceted phenomenon; at the same time, any attempt to describe such a perception is bound to resort, sooner or later, to general characterisations. In order to demonstrate that these are supported by a sufficiently diverse spectrum of evidence, this study employs a large number of different primary sources, including travelogues, prose fiction, poetry, newspaper reports, articles from journals and magazines, letters, tourist brochures and handbooks for travellers. But it also includes articles from contemporary encyclopedias and other examples of factual and purportedly 'objective' prose. Additionally, this wide spectrum of primary sources is brought into a dialogue with modern critical writing, all of which together will contribute to a new perspective both on the history of Anglo-Norwegian relations, and on the more general history of British self-perception in the nineteenth century.

The issue at stake, then, is how the national character of Norway and the Norwegians was perceived by British commentators from the late eighteenth through to the end of the nineteenth century. It is suggested that this character is not simply *reflected* in the range of texts under investigation, but actively formulated through them. This assumption – that discourse, and, in the wider sense of the word, literature, articulates and shapes a pattern of cultural identifications – was first formulated as part of a research agenda by that specialism in Comparative Literature known as *Imagologie* or 'Image Studies'. After a promising start in the mid-twentieth century it was, for a while, marginalised within the field of literary studies, and kept alive mainly by the efforts of Hugo Dyserinck and his 'Achen Programme'. Dyserinck himself maintained in his comparatist handbook (1991) and in numerous articles (1966, 1982; and Dyserinck and Syndram, 1988, 1992) that the role of stereotypes and images was central to the comparative study of cultural encounters and exchanges, and that the role of literature was crucial in the formulation and dissemination of such stereotypes. These insights have gained fresh currency and relevance over the last two decades, as genres like travel writing have come to attract more attention from specialists in literary and cultural studies, and as the formative influence of mental constructs, perceptions and attitudes in human affairs has been more widely recognised in the rise of the new cultural and literary history (cf. Leerssen 2000).

From this theoretical standpoint, the validity of the commentators' observations of Norway – that is the material and therefore ultimately indeterminable facts about exactly what Norway was like and how it differed from Britain – is of less interest to this study than the reasons for which such observations held credence at the time they were produced, and the ways in which they were expressed. Or, as the Dutch critic Joep Leerssen puts it: 'even though the belief is irrational, the impact of that belief is anything but unreal' (Leerssen 2002, 1).

This investigation thus asks rather different questions from those traditionally posed by empirical historians. First, it identifies and explores the many interconnected discourses that circulated around the concept of Norway in the nineteenth-century imagination. At issue here are the political, social, ethnic, literary, religious, aesthetic and – to a lesser extent – biographical contexts that gave rise to the viewpoints expressed in the many published texts on Norway. Whilst individual accounts are undoubtedly shaped and differentiated by the particular writer's regional origins, class status and gender, as well as by his or her personal idiosyncrasies of style, it is the similarity and unity of the writers' claims that are their most distinctive feature. What inspires and intrigues is the fact that the image of Norway – contradictory though it may at times be – is a shared phenomenon created by what the writers had in common, namely a country of origin and an historical epoch. How Norway *appeared* in the eyes of these travellers and commentators, and what *seemed* to be its differences from Britain, are the objects of this investigation, not least because through the expression of these *appearances* and *seemings* we can glimpse the fermenting whirlpool of ideas that constituted the British consciousness in the nineteenth century.

Secondly, it is suggested here that representations – in this case of a country and its people – may be deconstructed through the skills of literary and linguistic scholarship. As suggested above, perceptions of Norway are filtered through and shaped by the structures of a wide register of genres, each offering different representational possibilities. On a micro-level, the idea, for instance, of Norway's cold vastness and lofty magnificence is constructed through lexical choice, its differences from Britain delicately achieved sometimes through syntactical balance, and sometimes through the juxtaposition of unfamiliar ideas and the careful arrangement of paragraphs. Moreover, the texts are approached not simply as repositories of information, but as dynamic constructs which offer different kinds of relationship with their readers. As such, considerations of audience, purpose, voice and tone are seen as integral to the examination of content. Bringing together as it does both materials and methodologies from the fields of literature and history, this study does not see texts as a mere illustration of history, nor does it see history as a mere background for literature; rather it considers texts to be powerfully constitutive of histories.

Among the highly varied source material, however, there is no doubt that the travelogues deserve particular mention. From the last decades of the eighteenth century to the end of the nineteenth, British travellers to Norway published around two hundred travel accounts, describing in varying detail their Norwegian adventure. A large majority of these were in the form of books, usually published soon after the travellers' return to Britain, but some were also published as articles in journals and magazines. Undoubtedly, the travelogues constitute the largest and most comprehensive source of information about the British view of Norway in the period. Obviously, it should be kept in mind that the travelogues formed only one element in a great intertextual cycle of information on Norway, whereby non-writing travellers as well as travel writers, journalists, novelists and poets supplemented and modified each other's observations, thus together producing the multifarious and sometimes contradictory British 'image' of Norway. Nevertheless, as opposed to much of the other material, the travelogues – at least the large majority of them – are based not on second-hand information, but on first-hand experience of the country and people in question.

During the last couple of decades travel literature has become the subject of an intense and fascinating academic study, frequently involving cross-disciplinary methodologies and thereby providing insights ignored by more traditional approaches in such fields as literature, history and anthropology.[1] But this diverse use of the

---

[1] For a list of central works in this field from recent years, see Morgan 2001, 230n.

travelogues has also necessarily raised some fundamental questions about their status as sources of information about the past. First, what kind of 'mental blinkers' or culturally conditioned preconceptions should a modern reader expect to find in these observers of well over a century ago; or, from an imagological perspective: to what extent did 'the conventions and commonplaces inherited from a pre-existing textual tradition (...) overshadow the experience of reality'? (Leerssen 2002, 2). Second, in what ways did external factors, such as the book market, influence the writers' representation of the Other, in this case Norway and the Norwegians? And third, a large and complex question, triggering several more: how did the writers perceive their own role and their relationship to their audience? Where did they place themselves on the scale between the objective and the subjective, the scientific and the personal, the factual and the fictional? These questions, all of which ultimately revolve around the credibility and the information value of the travelogue, will be tentatively discussed in the following, but will also surface again and again throughout the book as a whole.

The presence of what could be called a national bias or preconception on the part of the observing Briton becomes particularly evident in the way that several writers underline the gulf that exists between themselves and the Other. This concerns in particular the contrast between what is presented as the excessive civilisation of Britain and the corresponding primitive nature of the foreign destination. As a result, and despite the geographical proximity of the two countries, British travelogues from Norway constantly remind a modern reader of texts about other and far more distant places, such as the interior of Africa. Some accounts even make this connection more or less explicit and attempt to explain it. In his book *The Oxonian in Thelemarken* (1858), for instance, the Oxford don Frederic Metcalfe discusses the popularity of travel literature and makes the following observation:

> Indeed, the avidity with which books of travel in primitive countries – *whether in the tropics or under the pole* – are now read, shows that the more refined a community is, the greater interest it will take in the occupation, the sentiments, the manners of people still in a primitive state of existence. Our very over-civilization begets in us a taste to beguile oneself [*sic*] of its tedium, its frivolities, its unreality, by mixing in thought, at least, with those who are nearer the state in which nature first made man (viii; italics added).

The common denominator between 'the tropics' and 'the pole' is clearly their primitive nature, which comes across as the main contrast to the strains of 'our very over-civilization'. This particular perspective of the over-civilised Briton observing a primitive Other – incidentally, the term 'Other' is equally applicable to both people and landscapes – seems to have a decisive effect on the point of view and indeed the lexical choices adopted by most of the travel writers in question. In the following passage from Thomas Forester's *Norway and Its Scenery* (1853), virtually every other word suggests the author's emphasis on the uniqueness of his Norwegian experience, thus exemplifying a point underlined by Leerssen, namely the essentially *contrastive* relationship between the familiar and the Other:

> [T]he true character of the scenery of Norway, and of its *simple* and well conditioned people, can only be learnt by *scaling* its snowy Fjelds, *penetrating* its *secluded* valleys, and following the windings of its Fjords into the *depths* of the mountain ranges, by *cross-roads and paths* sometimes all but *inaccessible* even to the *pedestrian* traveller. Those, however, who are disposed to embark in such enterprises, should well count beforehand the cost of the undertaking. It will try the *mettle* of the most *hardy, resolute, and enthusiastic* lovers of nature in her *wildest* aspects (49; italics added).

The message is clear: the narrator depicts himself as a hero who has successfully tackled challenges and obstacles that only a select few are able to endure, and he emerges as a character of nearly superhuman stature. In other accounts this sense of undergoing an extreme ordeal is tinged with unintended comedy. Thus, the somewhat pompous Charles B. Elliott, in *Letters from the North of Europe* (1832), gives the following alarming report, not from isolated and mountainous wastes, but from the centre of Bergen – a town of more than 20,000 inhabitants – in the summer of 1830: 'It has struck one o'clock in the morning, and my companions are asleep. The jackals and wolves are striking up a second to the air of the watchman, who is passing under my window singing his usual chant (…)' (145). In *Sketches in Holland and Scandinavia* (1885), the celebrated travel writer Augustus Hare succumbs to the same temptation of spicing his narrative with wild and furious beasts: 'Wolves seldom appear except in winter, when those who travel in sledges are often pursued by them. Then hunger makes them so bold that they will often snatch a dog from between the knees of the driver' (132). The above examples clearly suggest a narrator who –

like a modern war correspondent – bravely puts his life on the line in order to report to his readers. In his *Scenes of Travel in Norway* (1877), Joseph Phythian ruminates even more explicitly on this feeling of being a solitary representative of civilisation in a savage environment. Walking through the crowd at a local fair at Vossevangen together with his fellow traveller, the author reflects:

> We walked on, two Englishmen, as everybody knew. Our nationality is our pride sometimes. I have often felt it an honour to belong to England, for the name, 'Englishman,' is grander than that of 'Roman.' We scarcely realise this at home, but in a distant land, looking, some way, more broadly upon the world, the fact has more significance. The feeling is not that I, as an individual, am above these other people, but that my country, of which I am a part, is above theirs. And this is particularly the case in Norway, where the distance is greater than in many countries. The position of England is a commanding one. No doubt her wealth is one of the principal sources of homage, but let us hope that the high national character for various excellencies is also an element of power (122).

The passage offers a rare and direct insight into the self-perception of the nineteenth-century Briton and of the self-confidence, mixed with a sense of moral and cultural superiority, with which he regarded the world around him. No wonder, then, that the same author later in the book exclaims: 'Surely Norway has been made as a playground for the people of other countries, but especially for Englishmen' (113-14)! His compatriot, the 'unprotected female' Emily Lowe, similarly asks rhetorically 'who but English' [*sic*] would dream of travelling into the Norwegian wilderness. Interestingly, she must admit that a certain Ida Pfeiffer, the daughter of a Viennese industrialist, has also performed the same feat, 'but she confesses to being skinny and wiry, and was able to wriggle about unmolested; the English or Americans are rarely of that make, and so generally blooming and attractive, that it must be a certain inborn right which makes them nearly always the first to penetrate into the arcana of countries triumphantly' (227). Thus there is no doubt that the travellers' consciousness of themselves as Britons contributed strongly to the way in which they viewed Norway and the Norwegians – a point that will be underlined in the following chapters.

A second aspect that could be seen as having an influence on the credibility of travelogues is the possibility that their form and content may have been influenced by market demands. Despite Bourdieu's groundbreaking discussions around the complexity of 'cultural production' and 'the literary field' (Bourdieu 1999), relatively little research has been conducted in this very complex area, but it still seems possible to mention some, albeit tentative, factors that may have had an impact on the finished product. First, the main motive for the large majority of the *early* travel writers was not necessarily to make a profit from the sales. According to Mark Davies's study *A Perambulating Paradox: British Travel Literature and the Image of Sweden c. 1770–1865* (2000), the relationship between the publishers and the travel writers of the period was a gentlemanly one conducted between equals, and, he adds: 'While the desire to be published could be strong, I believe its fulfilment answered far more to social/academic ambitions than plain economic necessity' (31). As an example, he mentions a writer from the 1820s, Arthur de Capell Brooke, who 'may well have considered the profit motive as unbecoming a man of his rank (captain) and station in life. This would account for the absence, in Murray's publication ledger, of any mention of copyright fee or profit-sharing in regard to A *Winter in Lapland and Sweden* (1826). His only recompense appears as twenty copies (of a 750 edition); presumably more palatable, albeit their three-guinea retail price, than hard cash' (31–32).

Another point that Davies underlines is the fact that travelogues from Scandinavia represented a relatively minor part of the overall market for travel literature, and he concludes that 'very small editions – generally 500–1000 copies – were typical for "serious" travel literature on the North in the 1800s' (44). He quite correctly adds, however, that, despite obvious parallels, Norway and Sweden were not immediately comparable, and although the popularity of Sweden increased from 1875 onwards, it was 'not to the extent of neighbouring Norway' (34). This is confirmed from a list of the publication dates of British travelogues on Norway: not only is there a larger number of travelogues from Norway overall, but out of the close to two hundred texts used as primary material for the present study, seventy-five percent were published in the second half of the century, and more than fifty percent in the period 1870–1900. Thus the popularity of Norway, which will be discussed in more detail in chapter 1, evidently increased radically in the last decades of the century. It should also be mentioned, with respect to the low print-runs mentioned by Davies, that nearly twenty-five percent of the texts used in the present study went through two or more editions in the course of the nineteenth century, and some, like the works by Clarke, Coxe, Lord Dufferin, Lowe, Williams and the anonymous *Three in Norway by Two of Them*, together with novels by Corelli, Martineau and Lyall, must have meant good business for writer and publisher

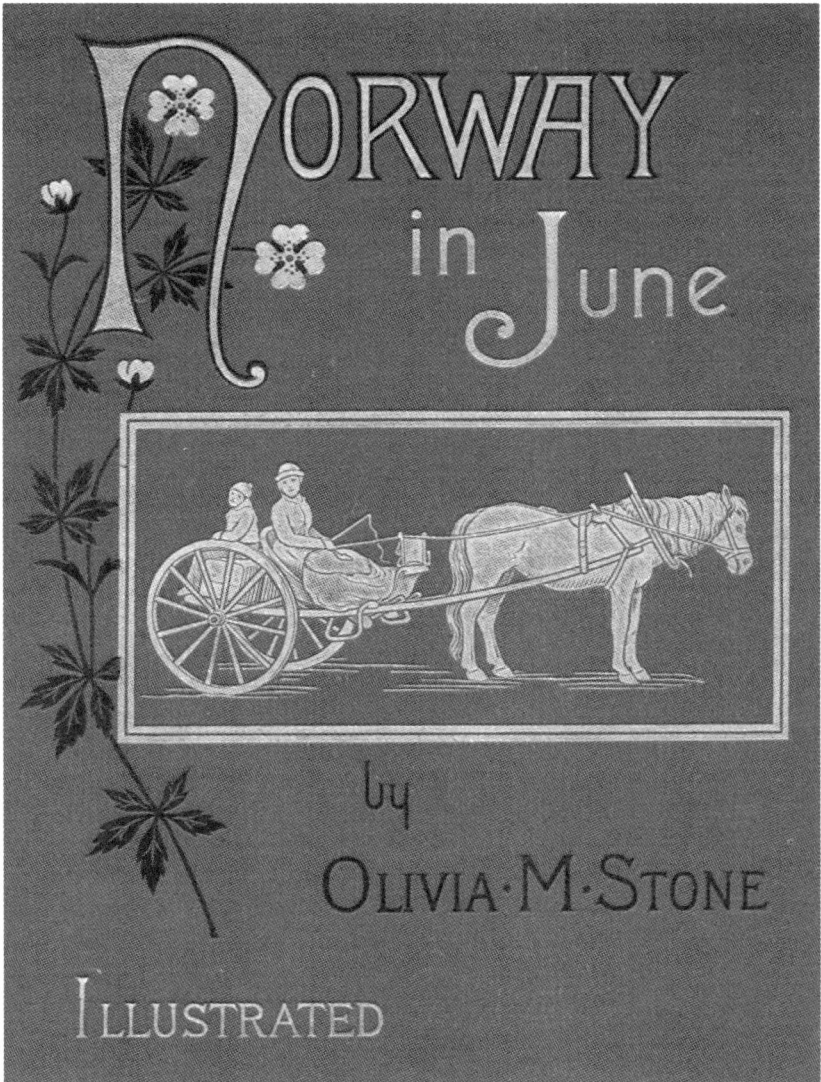

The cover of Olivia M. Stone's *Norway in June* (1882). A second edition of the book came in 1883, and a third in 1889.

alike. Finally, it is tempting to mention Paul du Chaillu's two-volume work *The Land of the Midnight Sun* from 1881. Admittedly, Du Chaillu was a French-American explorer, but having previously published extensively on Africa, he was well known to the British public, and in Harper's *New Monthly Magazine* of November 1881 John Habberton says that du Chaillu's book was 'published simultaneously in America, England, Germany, France, Sweden, and Denmark – an incident unparalleled in the history of publishing' (882). Clearly, such an ambitious publishing venture – the publisher was John Murray – suggests that not just the writer but also the subject appealed to a considerable audience. Against this background, and together with the gradual professionalisation of the publishing industry, it seems reasonable to conclude that the profit motive may have been more evident among both writers and publishers in the second than in the first half of the century. It is, moreover, likely that this consideration, accompanied by increased competition within the market for travelogues, may have encouraged individual writers to underline and exaggerate even further the spectacular, the unique and the extreme aspects of Norway, that is the contrastive elements mentioned above.

A third question with regard to the credibility and reliability of the travelogues as historical sources is how the writers in question perceived their own role as narrators and the validity of their accounts. In his book *Travel Literature and the Evolution of the Novel* (1983), Percy G. Adams argues that the origin of the novel is largely to be found in the travelogue, and in doing so also shows how the travelogue contains unmistakable elements of fiction: 'Throughout history [travel] literature has been a combination of the objective and the subjective, of details of setting, history, and customs to go with the traveler's own experiences, adventures, and reflections' (108). Still, the fact remains that travelogues generally have a somewhat seductive appearance of objectivity. With regard to those of the nineteenth century, this may have to do with the fact that their immediate predecessors were the so-called topographical accounts of the seventeenth and eighteenth centuries, which more than anything focused on the tangible facts of the countries described. In his book *Loneliness and Time: The Story of British Travel Writing* (1992), Mark Cocker also claims that the majority of accounts from the nineteenth century are concerned with 'the events of real life': 'The idea that the travel book was a work dealing with real facts – an impression often confirmed by index, footnotes and bibliography – rather than an imaginary world, has led to a perception of it as a literature closely associated with geography or history or some other scientific discipline' (5–6). Although this is undoubtedly a correct observation, Barbara Korte seems to achieve a more balanced picture in her description of nineteenth-century travelogues:

> Many Victorian explorers appear in their accounts as heroes every bit as courageous and enduring as the protagonists of the contemporary adventure novel; moreover, the travelling heroes offered their readers the thrill of adventures which had actually been experienced. Their accounts not only have an exciting travel plot, but they also make the travelling persona an interesting character within this plot (Korte 2000, 88–89).

Still, this does not mean that the eighteenth-century legacy has disappeared from the genre entirely:

> Despite the obvious elements of adventure in their texts, the majority of Victorian explorers were nevertheless also committed to imparting information (…). In this manner, the explorers of the nineteenth century continued in the tradition of earlier writing of exploration and scientific travel, even if they generally displayed a more marked concern with the travel plot (ibid., 89–90).

Other critics, however, suggest that the arrival of the subjective element and the marked presence of the narrator's persona may have started even earlier than the period indicated by Cocker and Korte. In *Imperial Eyes: Travel Writing and Transculturation* (1992), Mary Louise Pratt discusses – with a reference to Laurence Sterne and his contemporaries – how the so-called sentimental traveller had become a relatively standard element in travel writing from as early as the 1760s onwards. Thus by the time Mungo Park's famous travel book *Travels in the Interior Districts of Africa* was published in 1799, the average reader was already well acquainted with the kind of writer who 'wrote, and wrote himself, not as a man of science, but as a sentimental hero. He made himself the protagonist and central figure of his own account, which takes the form of an epic series of trials, challenges, and encounters with the unpredictable' (Pratt 1992, 75).

One of the earliest accounts from Norway – Andrew Swinton's *Travels into Norway, Denmark, and Russia in the Years 1788, 1789, 1790, and 1791* from 1792 – gives a good example of the transition from this apparently facts-oriented account to the more subjective and individualistic account generally associated with the following century. In his book Swinton passes a rather caustic remark on the later Archdeacon of Wiltshire William Coxe's well-known work

Travels into Poland, Russia, Sweden, and Denmark, published two
years before, but based on a journey, which included Norway, in
1784:

> He has given us many accurate and useful details concerning
> manufactures, commerce, population, public revenue, military establish-
> ments, and the ceremonials observed in various interviews with which he
> was honoured by Nobles, Princes and Kings. These, together with
> historical extracts from a great number of Writers, with multiplied
> experiments on the congelation of mercury, made by different
> Philosophers, at different times and places, *swell his volumes to a
> respectable size as well as price.*
>
> It is not, however, long details, biographical, historical, or
> philosophical, that are expected by every Reader to inform the principal
> parts of books of travels. What the Traveller himself observed, inferred,
> suffered, or enjoyed – but above all, manners, customs, dress, modes of
> life, domestic economy, amusements, arts, whether liberal or
> mechanical, and, in a word, whatever tends to illustrate the actual state
> of society, and that not only among the great, but the body, and even the
> very lowest of the people: all this, in the opinion of those who read rather
> for amusement, than the study of either politics or natural philosophy,
> should enter into those narratives which are supposed to hold a kind of
> middle rank between the solidity of studied discourse and the freedom of
> colloquial conversation (v-vii; italics added).

From the point of view of a modern reader, this is interesting
information, because what Swinton is doing is to introduce his
readers to an open discussion both about his own role as a narrator of
travelogues, and about the expectations of his readers, and in the
course of this discussion he emphasises the importance of the
traveller's subjective experience of his journey. This, he claims, is
what contemporary readers would like to see, because they read
'rather for amusement' than for the study of 'politics and natural
philosophy', and are, consequently, not interested in the 'long details'
of Coxe and others. To simplify, the Romantic – but apparently also
pre-Romantic – focus on the individual and the individual experience
draws a new degree of attention to the very voice of the narrator, and
in the nineteenth century travel writers increasingly reveal an
awareness that they somehow find themselves under scrutiny from
their readers. In his Norway book from 1829, the Rev. Robert
Everest, for instance, shows very clearly that he is not entirely
comfortable with his role as a travel writer:

The writing a volume of travels seems to be generally considered an easy task, but any one, who has made trial, will find that it is not so. He will feel that he has undertaken the part of an historian, and that too under considerable disadvantages. He must, at all events, tell a long story, of which he is himself to be the hero; and the odds are not in his favour that he will come off tolerably successful, with two such awkward circumstances against him. Perhaps, the perpetual recurrence to self, the detail of what he ate and drank, of whom he talked to, and who talked to him, of the inns he put up at, and the bills he paid there, may be as loathsome to him as it would be to some of his readers; and, in that case, he has only to glean up the scanty materials which the tract he passes through may afford him. He is to describe not the past, but the present, where his own observations, and not the previous labours of others, are to be his only records to refer to (vii–viii).

Everest, then, shows a considerable amount of uncertainty regarding how to project himself and his role. He is discussing, in short, his own self-representation as a writer, which again is a feature closely connected with the whole image of the romantic artist. Apparently, he faces further obstacles when contemplating the fact that his account is from the barren North:

The North (…) has no classic recollections, no ruined monuments of former splendour, no fantastic, and gorgeous superstitions. He who goes there must be content with seeing mankind in a simple, and happy state, and Nature in her sternest form. Of such enjoyment there is plenty. He will probably quit its shore with a better opinion of his fellow-creatures than he had when he landed on it. And that is something gained (ibid., viii–ix).

The North, it seems, throws the narrator back on the subject of himself even more forcefully than areas abounding with the great and admirable monuments of human achievement. In this empty wilderness, there is hardly anything that can be safely categorised and contextualised within the established conventions of continental culture and thus placed within a common frame of reference. Everything the traveller to Norway experiences is, in a sense, new and will have to be filtered through his or her own individual consciousness before being transformed into a narrative and presented to the reader. Clearly, such a strong element of subjectivity could be seen as undermining the documentary value of the accounts.

***

Among the many nineteenth-century British accounts from Norway, there is one that exemplifies this ambiguity with striking and peculiar clarity, and that therefore deserves a more comprehensive treatment. Edward Wilson Landor, a younger cousin of the writer Walter Savage Landor, visited Norway in the summer of 1835. According to R. H. Super, one of Walter Savage Landor's biographers, Edward was 'in his early twenties' (277) at the time. It is not known whether he suffered from the same violent and unpredictable temperament as his more famous cousin, but in the following year he published a two-volume work, *Adventures in the North of Europe, Illustrative of the Poetry and Philosophy of Travel*, which – at least in parts of the narrative – appears to entice the reader into a no-man's-land between fact and fiction. The first indication of the work's somewhat ambiguous status appears on the very first page, in an introduction entitled 'To the Reader', where Landor confesses that 'I wish only to account for having forsaken the common track of travellers, and thrown an air of romance over incidents which, notwithstanding, are literally true' (1: iii). The sentence, which is not just paradoxical but even self-contradictory, is typical of the way in which Landor deliberately draws a veil around himself and his function as a narrator. He even offers the reader some candidly material reasons for his choice:

> Quite aware that in the well-trampled field of literature I had no chance of making an impression as a sober, plodding traveller, I imagined that by creating a more interesting wanderer (...) who should follow the path I had myself pursued, I might, perhaps, win over a few readers who would have taken no pleasure in a mere matter-of-fact, laborious narrative. And I was not the less willing thus to humour (as I thought) the taste of the public, since it left me more at liberty to employ those colourings, and to indulge in those speculations, which will be found, perhaps too numerously, to pervade the ensuing pages. We sympathise with a fictitious character in the expression of thoughts that from a real personage we should scarcely tolerate (ibid., v).

However, as soon as the reader has more or less accepted the fictional character of the work, Landor throws another smokescreen, when he concludes: 'Every incident, in short, may be unhesitatingly relied on, except such as are on the face of them fictitious – as "the Pastor's Story," &c. in the second volume' (ibid., vi). Having thus played cat and mouse with the reader, Landor has – in a way worthy of his more famous cousin – achieved at least one of his goals, namely that of creating suspense, by making the reader assume a 'willing suspension

A NORWEGIAN STOREHOUSE, WITH A DISTANT VIEW OF GOUSTA.

J.Coleman del.

Pub. by Saunders & Otley, Conduit S. London June 15. 1836.

F.Rosenberg Sc.

The frontispiece from Edward Wilson Landor's *Adventures in the North of Europe* (1836). The picture is unusual in that it shows the actual encounter between the traveller and the local inhabitants. The scene is from Telemark and shows both the characteristic local architecture and the famous Gausta mountain in the background.

of disbelief'. As a result, he also arouses the reader's curiosity concerning the one part of his narrative that is purportedly purely fictitious. The question, then, is how and why this particular story is different from the rest of the account. It is necessary, in other words, to take a closer look at Landor's pastor.

Having described his journey from Denmark and up the Swedish coast, including for good measure an interesting essay on 'The Poetry and Philosophy of Travel' (which will be discussed in ch. 1), Landor enters Norway, and soon after Frederikshald (now Halden). So far, *Adventures* has not been noticeably different from the majority of other travelogues, and the reader has no apparent reason to raise an eyebrow at the fact that Landor, who intends to go to Christiania, takes a wrong turn at Frederikshald and walks for a couple of days before reaching the southern bank of the river Glomma, on which side he continues. Along the way he passes a waterfall, which is in all probability the one at Sarpsborg described by Mary Wollstonecraft and several other travellers, whereupon, on the third morning, he hears church bells. And this is where 'the Pastor's Story' begins.

The narrator enters the church and takes a seat together with 'a congregation of about twenty respectable peasants' (1: 235). He does not understand the sermon, but is struck by the appearance of the officiating minister:

> [H]e seemed to be about fifty years of age, his black hair was streaked with gray, his eye dark and sparkling, but sunk in his head from wasting sickness rather than deeply set by nature; his countenance was noble and engaging, though bearing the traces of ineffaceable sorrow, and his hair and deportment dignified and reverend (1: 235–36).

After the service, the two men engage in conversation. It soon appears that the pastor is half English; his name is Ernest Vormensen, and he invites Landor to stay at the parsonage for a few days. The pastor gradually takes the traveller into his confidence and finally confesses to him a terrible secret he has kept to himself for many years. As a young man the pastor, on a visit to England, had become involved in a tragic love affair. In a fit of jealous fury he had murdered his rival, and immediately returned to Norway, never to be arrested. On his return he had fled into the mountains, where he had spent the whole summer. Here he met a perfect female spirit or nymph (Norw. *hulder*), with whom he fell in love. The two lovers having met regularly for some time, the nymph's father insisted his daughter ended the relationship, and she finally departed, leaving him a ring. The pastor then shows Landor the ring, which he wears on his finger, as proof of the truth of his story. Later the same evening both Landor and the pastor go to bed, in separate but adjacent rooms. In the middle of the night Landor is woken by a violent commotion in the other room, and on entering finds that the pastor has had a fit. He soon recovers sufficiently to be able to tell Landor that the nymph has just returned and told him that she will come back for the ring on a specific day later in the week. He also predicts that he will die on that same day. Weak and partly unconscious, the pastor is then nursed for the next few days by his servants at the parsonage, whereupon he dies on the day he had predicted. Landor notices that the ring is no longer on the pastor's finger, but despite a major investigation among the servants, the ring is not found. Landor then stays for the funeral, and continues his journey with not so much as a comment on the fantastic story he has just related.

As suggested earlier, Landor admits that 'the Pastor's Story' is a product of his imagination, but granted his almost consistent attempts to obscure the difference between fact and fiction, the reader will inevitably speculate as to whether the story is one or the other. This leaves the possibility of at least two different readings.

The story undoubtedly contains a convincing array of fictional elements. First, Landor creates a clever Chinese-box effect of frame narratives that looks surprisingly modern, with the travelogue itself as the first level, the narrator's story about the pastor as the second, and the pastor's own story as the third. Furthermore, his story contains such standard features from Victorian fiction as a sudden and unexpected legacy (not included in the above summary); at least two striking and highly unlikely coincidences; a duel; and the fairy-tale element of the nymph. In addition, the pastor's story carries some rather striking similarities to Mary Shelley's novel *Frankenstein* (1818). Just like Frankenstein's friendless monster, the pastor, having committed an unsolved murder, roams the unpopulated wilderness in the hope of finding a woman capable of giving his life meaning and purpose. In the same way that the monster offers his heartbreaking confession to Frankenstein, the pastor describes – over several pages – his God-forsaken loneliness to the English stranger:

> The awful silence weighed upon my heart; my knees smote together, and I paused and leant upon my staff. I was a *murderer*, and *something* told me with terrible distinctness that God had forsaken me, and left me a prey to the bears of the forest, or the relentless demons that pervade it. (...) I felt that I was doomed to wander through life companionless,

pitiless, joyless, – without an object that could afford me interest, or a
thought that could give me pleasure (2: 26–30).

It might be speculated that Mary Shelley's interest in the North and
the Arctic, where an important part of her novel is set, also indicates
the inspiration she undoubtedly drew from her mother's – i.e. Mary
Wollstonecraft's – travelogue from Norway, which also includes a
description of the waterfall at Sarpsborg, in the immediate vicinity of
the pastor's parish. Considering the few books available to Landor
about Norway and the relative fame of *Frankenstein* (the single-
volume third edition had been published in 1831), it is reasonable to
assume that both Shelley's novel and her mother's travelogue had
formed part of Landor's background reading, or even of his reading
matter on the journey itself.

Despite these unquestionably fictional elements, however, the
story also carries features that make it tempting to investigate
possibly *factual* sources. First, the narrator distinguishes strongly
between his own story and that of the pastor; as soon as the latter has
concluded his story, the narrator very quickly undermines its
credibility both by a series of rational arguments and by drawing
attention to the pastor's 'excited imagination' (2: 49). The effect of
this is interesting, because although it reduces our faith in the pastor's
tale, it increases our faith in that of the narrator. We are, in other
words, led to believe that Landor during his journey met a Norwegian
pastor who told him an utterly peculiar story, but thanks to Landor
himself we are provided with a healthy scepticism towards that very
story (although he himself draws attention to the ring, which he
claims to have seen, and which provides an interesting link between
the pastor's tale and that of his own). Second, Landor leaves just
enough information about his whereabouts to enable the reader to
actually follow his footsteps. He even makes the reader aware, in a
footnote, that when he describes distances he uses the word 'miles' in
the sense of *Norwegian* miles. Also, he insists that during his
wanderings before meeting the pastor, he stays on the southern side
of the Glomma, but still close to the river. In this way it is actually
possible to establish that the church he comes to is almost certainly
Varteig church, which at the time was part of Tune parish.

An investigation into the history of the parish shows that the vicar
at the time, actually from 1820–1859, was Johan Nielsen Vogt. Thus,
there was no pastor dying under mysterious circumstances in 1835,
when Landor visited the area, but there may still be interesting
parallels between Vogt and Landor's pastor. First of all, the names

Vormensen and Vogt both begin with the same letters, a not uncommon way of concealing a real identity. Landor furthermore describes the pastor as around fifty years old. Vogt was born in 1783 and was then fifty-two during Landor's visit. More important, however, is the fact that Landor's rather detailed description of the pastor's appearance and personality is strongly reminiscent of that of Vogt. While an active and forward-looking member of the community, Vogt was known to have a strikingly powerful exterior, but was at the same time disturbingly sombre and melancholy. Sven Gøran Eliassen, the historian of Tune and director of Borgarsyssel County Museum, even suspects that he may have been suffering from manic depression.[2]

Another feature, in the border area between fact and fiction, is the possibility that the pastor's unhappy love affair may be connected with Landor himself. Although very little is known about his life, some information can be gleaned from the more abundant material about his cousin, Walter Savage Landor. In particular, in Malcolm Elwin's *Landor: A Replevin* (1958) it emerges that Edward in 1835, that is the same year that he visited Norway, developed an affair with his cousin's daughter, Julia, during a visit to Walter Savage's house at Fiesole near Florence. Edward was then '[a] somewhat unsatisfactory young man of twenty-six' (304),[3] and Julia only fifteen. Edward's feelings were reciprocated, and Mrs Landor was in favour of the match (Field 2000, 96), but the lovers were hardly looking forward to broaching the subject with the formidable and unpredictable Walter Savage, and the affair dragged on for two years, until Edward's letter to his cousin, asking for his consent to their engagement, was brusquely and decidedly rejected. Thus it is perfectly plausible that Landor, while writing his travelogue between the summer of 1835 and its publication the following year, could personally identify with the pastor's unhappy love affair, and that this could be seen as one reason for introducing this peculiar parenthesis into his otherwise matter-of-fact account. It would even be tempting, considering Walter Savage's temper, to read the nymph's uncompromising father as Edward Wilson's wry portrait of his cousin.[4]

As the above discussion has demonstrated, perhaps the most intriguing aspect of Landor's story about the pastor is the way in

---

[2] Mentioned in a telephone conversation with P. F. March 2002.

[3] Super, above, claimed he was in his 'early twenties'. As he was born in 1811, he was actually twenty-four at the time.

[4] Julia's and Edward Wilson's letters from January and February 1837 to Walter

which it moves with almost imperceptible fluidity in and out of the worlds of fact and fiction. As readers we are, in other words, largely the victims of an arbitrary and sometimes rather imaginative narrator, who is in effect a creator of his own reality.

***

Thus, so far this introduction may be read as a cautionary tale about the general *un*trustworthiness of the travelogue as a source of credible information. To sum up, it suffers from stereotyped and nationally conditioned preconceptions; it is subject to the unpredictable forces of the market and the literary field in general; and it is not to be trusted in its distinctions between the factual and the fictional. Furthermore, these caveats apply, of course, even more to the use of poetry and fiction as historical source material. In the context of the present study, however, it is important to keep in mind that the main concern is not primarily with the hard facts concerning Britain's relationship to Norway, but with the far less tangible phenomenon of the kind of image that British travellers passed on to their countrymen. This is, in other words, not primarily a study of facts, but of perceptions, and these perceptions are, by definition, strongly coloured by a subjective, and sometimes even a creative, element. But this does not make them less relevant as a source for understanding nineteenth-century Britons' view of the world around them. On the contrary, these aspects, which have traditionally been of minor interest to the political historian, are not just a necessary

Savage Landor, asking for his blessing, still exist in the Warwickshire County Record Office (letter dated 4 February 1837, in CR 1908/276/1-4). They reveal the girl's desperate plea to her father and the young suitor's bold defence of his actions and his very forthright criticism of the man who had earlier accused him of baseness. There is also a poem, in fifteen stanzas, from Edward to Julia on the occasion of the broken engagement. It begins as follows:

Ah! fear not that I should upbraid thee
    For the course thou art driven to pursue;
Thy kindred and friends have betrayed thee,
    But ne'er shall I call thee untrue.

Though thy lips may be forced to discard me,
    Thy heart shall not pass to another;
Still, still art thou doomed to regard me
    With emotion I would thou couldst smother.

supplement to more factually based descriptions; they may indeed
provide us – as a number of image studies have demonstrated – with
a more comprehensive understanding of the past than a more
conventional approach is capable of doing. Also, if one chooses to
regard the travelogues as essentially fictional rather than factual
works, they often represent, as in the case of Edward Wilson Landor,
an insight into the world of non-canonical writers and their works that
may also throw new light on the established names.

As suggested above, the last few years have seen a remarkable
output of academic investigations using travel literature as a source
for an understanding of the growth of a national British identity, but
the large majority of these studies have used primary sources either
from the Empire beyond Europe or from the traditional British
destinations around the Mediterranean. Northern Europe, and
especially Scandinavia, has been strikingly absent, even in such
recent and general studies as Marjorie Morgan's *National Identities
and Travel in Victorian Britain* (2001). No comprehensive study of
British-Norwegian relations based on this kind of material has so far
been published, and consequently most of the source material has
also been lying dormant for well over a century. As a result of this it
has been necessary to allow the primary sources themselves to speak
as much as possible. The main ambition of the present work, then, is
to open up the field, point to a number of its main features, and
encourage colleagues to make use of this fascinating and plentiful
material for further studies. This obviously means that a number of
areas have either been ignored or subjected to little more than a
passing comment. In particular, hardly anything will be said about the
significance of the Norwegian and Scandinavian contribution,
represented by Henrik Ibsen and others, to the literary and cultural
debate in Britain towards the end of the century. There are at least
three reasons for this choice: it is a subject large and complex enough
to merit a separate investigation; although such a comprehensive
study has not yet been written, the general field has been covered
from various perspectives, that is in the large critical literature on the
central figures and their work; and finally, the ultimate impact of this
movement on the general public is more of an early twentieth-century
than a late nineteenth-century phenomenon.[5] Also, with respect to
Ibsen in particular, Burchardt rightly points out that 'the attention
which he attracted in England was of a purely intellectual,
cosmopolitan character (…)' (193), which hardly served to modify to

---

[5] For an early account of this movement, see Burchardt 1920, 113–95.

any significant extent the British view of Norway and the Norwegians.

In the thousands of pages written about Norway and the Norwegians, British travellers and commentators obviously touched upon or discussed in depth a wide spectrum of issues. Consequently, in this study a lot of thought and experimentation have gone into structuring the material in a workable way. From the beginning, however, some key areas emerged as central points of focus around which clusters of related topics tended to assemble. In their very basic forms these are tourism, history, society and nature, each of which is awarded a separate chapter. Seen as a whole, these individual approaches to Anglo-Norwegian relations exemplify a number of major and frequently conflicting forces vying for supremacy in the great debates of nineteenth-century European society. The most conspicuous feature is perhaps the fundamental debate, intensifying as the century progressed, about the usefulness, value and unfortunate side-effects of progress. This particular debate is also characterised by a conflict between two very different approaches to contemporary society: one looking back to a simple and supposedly harmonious past; the other looking forward to a future of even more daring achievements. Then, closely related to this overriding tension are topics such as the country and the city, nature and culture, health and disease, the individual and the masses, and the north and the south. The essentially dialectic or binary quality of these central issues is further underlined by the fact that the primary material in question has been assembled and composed by writers who were acutely aware of crossing a boundary between the familiar and the Other. Similarly, this dual focus has been constantly present in the composition of this study, whose various drafts have been travelling – although electronically – back and forth across the North Sea, between the authors, living in Britain and Norway respectively.

In conclusion, the comparative element ensures that a wide range of issues concerning a distant, under-developed country on the fringes of civilisation are seen not – as one might expect – as irrelevant to, but rather as intimately connected and interwoven with the issues of a country at the very hub of progress and modernity. Paradoxically but also encouragingly, therefore, a study of contrasts and opposites between nations and cultures may well produce the conclusion that ultimately the differences between the Other and the familiar are less striking than the fundamental similarities.

1. 'MORE THE RAGE EVERY YEAR':
THE INFLUX OF BRITISH TOURISTS AND TRAVELLERS

> Wrapping my great coat round me, I lay down on some sails at the bottom of the boat.
>
> *Mary Wollstonecraft*, 1796

Despite the ancient links between the countries around the North Sea, there is no doubt that the level of contact between Britain and Norway went through a process of gradual deterioration from the time of the Renaissance onwards. British interests turned towards the south of Europe and, during the age of discovery, towards a rapidly expanding world of new and distant continents. As a result, from a British point of view Norway and the Nordic countries were perceived, for at least a quarter of a millennium, largely as a political, commercial and cultural backwater, fading out of focus and leading their own and isolated existence far away from the contemporary field of action.[1] Thus, the meagre entry on Norway in the first edition of the *Encyclopædia Britannica* (1768–1771) provides an embarrassingly representative summary of the British perception of Norway at the time. In its entirety it gives the following frugal information: 'Norway, a kingdom of Europe, situated between 4° and 30° east longitude, and between 58° and 72° north latitude, bounded by the Atlantic ocean on the north and west, by Swedeish [*sic*] Lapland and other provinces of Sweden on the east, and by the sea called the Categate and Schaggeric on the south. It is a cold barren country, subject to Denmark' ('Norway'). The last sentence, in

---

[1] For a summary of British descriptions of Norway and the Norwegians from the Viking age to the eighteenth century, see Burchardt 1920, 3–16.

particular, which conveys with impressive brevity both the unambiguous geography of the country and its miserable political status, seems more like a dismissal than a bait for prospective visitors.

It is hardly surprising, therefore, to find that travellers, for several decades to come, turned to the ancient image of *Ultima Thule* to describe either Norway as a whole or certain parts of it, especially Telemark (*Tele-* and *Thule* were assumed to be etymologically connected). Andrew Crichton and Henry Wheaton, in their *Scandinavia, Ancient and Modern* from as late as 1860, refer to the Greek traveller Pytheas, who visited the northern regions ca. 320 BC and asserted that 'the Ultima Thule of the classic authors was neither Orkney nor Iceland, as is generally believed by modern writers, but must have been the southern part of Norway (...) '. And, they add, 'he represents the higher districts as wild and uncultivated, and peopled with savages, who subsisted by hunting and fishing' (21). The Oxford don Frederick Metcalfe similarly claims two years earlier that 'Thelemarken is the most primitive part of Norway; it is the real *Ultima Thule* of the ancients; the very name indicates this (...)' (Metcalfe 1858, x).

Alongside these long-held misconceptions of Norway, however, a new view was materialising. This view would ensure that by the late nineteenth century the British view of Norway was radically different from that of a hundred years earlier. In order to acquire a better impression of the various elements that constituted this transformation, it seems natural to turn, first of all, to British attitudes to travel in the eighteenth century, and then to how these attitudes were gradually modified, in the first decades of the nineteenth, by various cultural and political movements. With a surprisingly rapid change of focus, the qualities associated with Ultima Thule came to be perceived as no longer irrelevant to travellers and commentators, but on the contrary as embodying the very dreams and visions of a new and alternative generation.

British Travel in the Eighteenth Century

In the British context, 'The Grand Tour' is frequently used as a generic phrase, encompassing the foreign travels of young and wealthy people throughout the eighteenth century. This may at times be misleading, because such a general label tends to ignore the fact that British travel abroad had already gone through some major changes by the time of the fall of the Bastille. These changes concerned not only the number, but also the social background of the travellers. 'The Grand Tour proper', according to Donald Low, 'was an experience restricted to a social elite – a typical traveller was Horace Walpole, the Prime Minister's son, who paid both for his own journey and for that of his companion, the future poet Thomas Gray, like himself an old Etonian and Cambridge undergraduate – and to the male sex' (Low 1977, 173). Walpole and Gray, both in their early twenties, toured France and Italy from 1739 to 1741, acquiring – or intending to acquire – the finishing touches on an education shared with but a tiny and highly privileged segment of young Britons at the time. This on-the-road university course had at least a twofold ambition: to acquaint young men with the ancient and Renaissance heritage to be found primarily in the Mediterranean countries of Italy and France; and to provide them with contemporary knowledge about such matters as geography, politics and commerce.

As the century progressed, however, these tours, which were elitist in both financial and cultural terms, were gradually overshadowed by the peregrination of considerably larger numbers of travellers, whose chief ambition was not primarily to broaden their mental horizons, but rather to *voyager pour voyager*. In his article 'Tourism and Cultural Change', Jeremy Black points out that travel for pleasure was on the increase in the eighteenth century, and in an attempt to explain this change, he emphasises the importance of fashion:

> The eighteenth century was at the higher social level increasingly a consumer society affected by fashions; news of the latter spread by the growing number of ephemeral publications and the literature of social manners. Travel became fashionable as a means of finishing the education of youths, as a source of social polish, and as a pleasant and desirable way in which to spend periods of leisure. A linked reason of great significance was the cosmopolitan nature of European society during the period that has been described as the Enlightenment. (...) Furthermore, the sense of a common European cultural inheritance was no longer obscured by an awareness of hostility. To British tourists Rome was now an ancient source of cultural inspiration, Paris the present forcing-house for European culture and ideas (Black 1990, 185–86).

As a result of this, in the second half of the century, 'Continental tourism became both less socially exclusive and more varied in type. In place of aristocratic youths' travelling for two or three years, it became more common both for people to travel later in life and for them to go abroad for shorter periods' (ibid., 192–94). Thus, what can be characterised as a modern mode of travel was already in place before the French Revolution. As a consequence, the political crisis of the 1790s and the ensuing wars effectively brought British travel on the Continent to a halt for two decades, and caused an accumulation of *Wanderlust* which initially had to be satisfied by armchair travel. 'Magazines and reviews of the period were full of articles describing journeys overseas or the customs of other lands' (Low 1977, 174). It would seem that the urge to travel rather suddenly became a real possibility when the borders were reopened in the post-Waterloo years. James Buzard, in his book *The Beaten Track: European Tourism, Literature, and the Ways to 'Culture' 1800–1918*, claims that 'after 1815 Britons seemed to explode across the Channel, heading abroad in greater numbers than ever before (…) (Buzard 1993, 19). And with respect to the Victorian period in general, Maria H. Frawley claims that '[t]he number of Victorians travelling at leisure increased steadily (…) as a rise in wealth and a decrease in the cost of travel made foreign vacations possible for even the lower middle classes' (Frawley 1994, 20). It should be remembered, however, that even though the number of travellers increased, foreign travel for leisure remained the preserve of a relatively small minority, whereas for the rest of the literate population books and illustrations remained the only source of information, even after 1815.

With regard to the discovery of more far-off places such as Norway, there were also other elements worth keeping in mind. First, it should be emphasised that among the British, the attraction of the Continent was always ambivalent and uncertain. Although, as Linda Colley shows, the British elite, even after Waterloo, spoke the French language, read French literature, imitated French cuisine and so on, there was still a deep-seated scepticism about everything French (ref. Colley 1996, 177–78). According to Jeremy Black, this scepticism originated from a British 'sense of cultural unease' (Black 1990, 186): 'For many, Britain was less sophisticated, urbane, attractive, and fashionable than France, the indigenous culture less rich than the Continental counterpoint of classical restraint and baroque exuberance. (…) Lockean philosophy, deistic religion, and the English cultural inheritance could not compete successfully with Continental culture' (ibid., 187–88).

Second, it should be remembered that less visited countries had their own distinctive appeal – particularly those which were perceived to boast the attractions of nature. As will be discussed in greater detail in ch. 4, the qualities concerning man and nature, generally associated with the early decades of the nineteenth century, were deeply rooted in the art and the thinking of the previous century. H. Arnold Barton thus correctly notes in his book *Northern Arcadia: Foreign Travelers in Scandinavia, 1765–1815*, that throughout the eighteenth century there was

> a sentimental counterculture to Enlightenment rationalism and utilitarianism, which in time came to be personified by Jean-Jacques Rousseau. In his native Switzerland, Rousseau found a new Arcadia, where a sturdy peasantry, uncorrupted by the evils of civilization, lived simple and virtuous lives amid natural surroundings inspiring in their awesome grandeur (Barton 1998, 3).

This counterculture, which had matured during the years of revolution and war, and which also partly regarded the events in France as indications of a failing civilisation, clearly expressed a powerful ideological shift. In terms of patterns of travel, the early nineteenth century sees a growing distinction between what are usually designated the 'traveller' and the 'tourist', a distinction closely connected with the search – prevalent to this day – for places whose freshness and otherness had not already been spoiled by the presence of others. As James Buzard argues, 'the authentic "culture" of *places* – the *genius loci* – was represented as lurking in secret precincts "off the beaten track" where it could be discovered only by the sensitive "traveller", not the vulgar tourist' (Buzard 1993, 6).

Third, in her book *English Travel Writing from Pilgrimages to Postcolonial Explorations*, Barbara Korte points out that after the discovery of Australia, 'there were no more continents to be found. (…) In the absence of completely "new" landmasses, the explorers now directed their efforts to the interior of "old" continents which were still largely unfamiliar to Europeans – the Arctic Regions, South America, Australia and, most significantly, Africa' (Korte 2000, 87). Admittedly, there was probably a large majority of Britons who continued to visit the traditional sites on the Continent, but there is no doubt that a steadily increasing number sought out alternative destinations. As will be seen, this is amply confirmed in the case of Norway, but also by other countries situated on the periphery of Europe. For instance, in a study of British travellers in Greece in the nineteenth century, Helen Angelomatis-Tsougarakis concludes – possibly stretching the point slightly – that '[t]he tour of France and Italy was given up and travels in Greece, Albania and Turkey, which were part of the Ottoman Empire, became fashionable' (Angelomatis-Tsougarakis 1990, 1).

Norway and the Continent

Reading nineteenth-century British travel accounts about Norway, one is invariably left with the impression that, though geographically close to Britain, this land of the fjords and the Midnight Sun was generally perceived as being distant, or as Thomas Forester puts it in 1850: 'Though the coast of Norway lies within a few hours' sail of the northern shores of Britain, that country is less generally known than many which are divided from it by the broad ocean' (iii). With the background outlined above, together with improving communications, this clearly contributed to making the country more attractive. The geographical proximity made Norway more readily accessible to a growing number of travellers, whilst the perception of distance was necessary to retain that element of otherness which had come to represent the main appeal of any destination. Travel writers, eager to sell their books, and travels agents, eager to sell their travels, both emphasise a set of relatively specific qualities associated with Norway, some of which have survived into the holiday industry of the twenty-first century:

One of the early travellers, Arthur de Capell Brooke, visited the country in the summer of 1820, and in the first lines of his introduction he informs his readers that the object of his book is 'to introduce to the notice of the numerous travellers, who daily leave our shores, a country little known, though interesting alike from its natural features, and the manners of its inhabitants' (Brooke 1823, v). He then goes on to draw a rather peculiar comparison between Norway and 'the South':

> While the South has continued the great centre of attraction, it appears no way strange, that the northern parts of the European continent should hitherto have excited so little attention. Veiled, according to the general notion, in almost continual darkness; and fast bound for the greater part of the year in chains of ice; the possibility of a summer has hardly been contemplated, or that such a country should possess any attractions, likely to repay the labours of the traveller. Such even is the chilling influence of cold over the imagination, that the bare mention of the Arctic regions is sufficient to repress its wandering; and the idea of crossing the Polar circle operates with tourists in general, as a sufficient obstacle to their proceeding thither (ibid., v–vi).

Paradoxically, it is precisely the aesthetic qualities which have hitherto made Norway *unattractive* to British travellers that are being used to rouse the curiosity of the readers. Brooke seems aware, in other words, that the taste of the British travelling public is in the process of changing, an assumption which appears to be confirmed by the fact that many later travellers, having read his work, refer to Brooke as an authority on Norway. Another writer from the 1820s, the Scottish solicitor William Rae Wilson, adds a different, and less tangible, dimension to the quality of the north. 'It has been remarked by an eminent author', he says (a footnote identifies this author as Lord Woodhouselee), 'that the mind of man is more perfect as one moves northwards; a penetrating air seems to produce penetrating souls, and wind and weather, the keener they are, appear to give the sharper edge to the human understanding' (Wilson 1826, 130).[2]

That Norway was presented as a new and intriguing alternative to the more well-trodden paths is also evident from some rather derogatory remarks about its most obvious competitor, namely the Alps. According to Thomas Forester, Switzerland had become too much of a tourist trap: 'the traveller passes from day to day through the stereotyped stages of an Alpine tour' (Forester 1853, 48). And in the novel *Vivians: A Family in Victorian Cornwall*, which was published as late as 1935 but set in Cornwall and Norway in the 1840s, the view of the Telemark mountains inspires a discussion between the two English sisters Mary and Tony about the difference between Norway and Switzerland. Mary quotes Coleridge's lines about the vales of Chamonix, but Tony responds: "'Sovran Blanc! What can that neat little land-locked Switzerland be in comparison with our grand Norway?'" (Hughes 1935, 51). Charles B. Elliott even goes so far as to suggest that Norway offers 'a succession of richly-varied landscapes rivalling those of the Alps and the Himala [*sic*]' (Elliott 1832, vii).

Mary Wollstonecraft adds another dimension to this picture. From the historical and aesthetic perspective of the 1790s, she arranges various travel destinations in a kind of hierarchy, the full appreciation of which requires that each new destination is approached in a specific order. And regarding Norway as a society that still had a long way to go in terms of cultural progress, she claimed that '[i]f travelling, as the completion of a liberal education, were to be

---

[2] Another side to this argument is of course that it may be read as a British assertion of an intellectual superiority over the traditional and *southern* heartland of European culture, or even as a Scottish disparagement of the English.

adopted on rational grounds, the northern states ought to be visited before the more polished parts of Europe, to serve as the elements even of the knowledge of manners, only to be acquired by tracing the various shades in different countries' (Wollstonecraft 1987, 173). Interestingly, a Thomas Cook travel guide from 1890, i.e. a century later, draws exactly the opposite conclusion, stating that Norway is not for the novice:

> I really cannot tell what is the great charm of Norway, nor do I think the nameless charm is the same for each. Perhaps those who are old travellers enjoy Norway most. It is well known that in order to do the whole duty of travel, an apprenticeship must be served, by no means an irksome one, on the contrary, full of delight; nevertheless it *is* an apprenticeship, and until it has been served, no man can pass as a member of the travelled community. The curriculum includes a knowledge of Paris, of the Rhine, of Switzerland, and a dozen regular rounds. When these have all been 'done', then comes Norway as a land of pure delight to the traveller (Cook 1890, 5).

Without drawing too far-reaching conclusions on the basis of these two statements, one might safely argue that this contrast between the preferences of the 1790s and those of the 1890s offers an interesting insight into the changing perception of the value of travel which had taken place in the course of a century: Wollstonecraft still firmly believes that this value consists in the acquisition of knowledge and culture, whereas according to the Thomas Cook guide, the ideal traveller is a connoisseur of untouched landscapes. In between, of course, lies a process of cultural conditioning – not least with respect to the view of nature – which had a formative and lasting impact on the traveller's taste.

However, the contrast between Norway and the Continent also manifested itself in more particular areas. One is the emphasis by many travellers on the fact that Norway was virtually without what could be called a material cultural history. As has been suggested above, the Grand Tour was an exploration of culturally predefined destinations; its chief value lay in making young aristocrats acquainted with the best and most illustrious achievements of European civilisation. Whether associated with political history, religion, architecture, philosophy or art, these achievements were almost invariably to be found in an urban setting, and they were typically enjoyed and admired in the form of public monuments, libraries, galleries and buildings (frequently ruins). In Norway, on the other hand, the traveller encountered hardly anything he or she would naturally categorise as manifestations of culture and civilisation. Thus, the Norwegians were perceived as living in an almost timeless natural state. The obsessive angler William Bilton gives a clear suggestion of this in his book *Two Summers in Norway*, from 1840:

> If they were swept away from the face of the earth, the Norwegians would leave behind them no monument of human skill, or labour, or intellect, to tell another generation that a great people had so long tenanted the wide extent of Scandinavia. Nature's monuments would indeed still remain: Norway's Fjelder and Fjords would still claim the homage of the admirer of the sublime and beautiful. But no work of public utility or ornament – (its two or three cathedrals can scarcely be reckoned an exception) – no achievement in Science or Literature, wherewith the human mind of one period holds converse with the mind of all times, would exist to excite the regrets and admiration of the future wanderer on these shores (Bilton 1840, 2: 224–25).

This impression is confirmed by Alfred Elwes, who gives an interesting indication of the shift in priorities that had taken place among travellers from the 1700s to the 1800s: 'It is nature, and nature alone, that we learn to admire in these remote regions, no castle, no ivied fane, speaks to us of the feudal baron or the sandalled monk: the peaked rock, the green slope, and the lofty fir, meet our view and tend, from the total absence of man's labours, to raise our thoughts to a higher Intelligence' (Elwes 1853, no pag.). Whereas an eighteenth-century traveller would have avoided 'these remote regions', simply because they did not contribute to elevating the human mind, the travellers of the 1850s are attracted precisely by this very absence of civilisation, and find in it a reminder of the 'higher Intelligence'.[3]

It is tempting, at this juncture, to digress briefly and mention a similar viewpoint but from a diametrically opposed perspective to that of the British travellers. From the spring of 1862 to the summer of 1863, the Norwegian writer Aasmund Olavsson Vinje travelled through major parts of Britain, studying the country in much the same way that Britons were observing Norway at the same time. In 1863 he then published a book in Edinburgh, entitled *A Norseman's Views of Britain and the British*, in which he comments, from a Norwegian

---

[3] A relatively rare exception to this rule is H. J. Whitling's article 'The Architect in Search of the Picturesque, in Norway' (1850), which, despite its title, underlines *not* the country's natural attractions but rather the need to preserve the many ancient treasures and remains that bear witness to the country's cultural and historical significance.

point of view, on this very question.[4] 'Old baronial castles, and
strongholds of the middle ages, are numerous throughout the
country', he says, but then adds significantly: 'but I did my best to
eschew all feelings of romance when I visited them. To me they
looked like mouldering bones sticking half out from the graveyard of
history' (149). Thus, both the British travellers in Norway and the
Norwegian traveller in Britain are writers who have in common a
Romantic scepticism about civilisation and an urge to avoid it. This
is in line with the argument of Anne Janowitz, whose *England's
Ruins, Poetic Purpose and the National Landscape* discusses
precisely how landscapes containing ruins and other man-made
constructions from the past can be read as messages of political and
cultural conflicts. For instance, one and the same ruin may suggest
conquest and victory to one observer, and humiliation and defeat to
another. With Romanticism, however, the ruin is increasingly seen as
nature's re-conquest of man-made, cultural artefacts. The
achievements of civilisation, in other words, which the young men of
the eighteenth century were taught to admire, are returned, in the
Romantic obsession with ruins, to the Great Mother. The past, then,
becomes according to Janowitz, 'an idealized "pastness" which
submits the circumstances of history to a flawless and mild
uniformity' (Janowitz 1990, 59). In the British context, Janowitz sees
this development in connection with the process of nation building,
and the need to create a 'homogenous society', in which the conflicts
of the past are buried. Against this background, it is only to be
expected that British travellers would regard Norway, or perhaps seek
to regard Norway, as a country free from the burdensome conflicts of
the past. With nothing but an endless supply of untouched nature,
made naively pure and innocent by Romantic philosophy, Norway
represented an uncomplicated utopia which easily lent itself to both
sympathy and admiration.

Along with this fortunate absence of material reminders of the
past, Norway also had another quality which distinguished it from the
beaten tracks of the Continent: it offered resistance to the traveller by
being inaccessible. For the business traveller this was obviously a
drawback rather than an advantage, and a letter from 'Mr. F. John',
printed in *The Times* on 17 March 1814, but dated Arendal 25
February, shows exactly how inaccessible Norway could be,
especially in the winter:

[4] According to the Foreword of the Norwegian edition, the book was received in
Britain amid considerable controversy. *The Times* called Vinje 'the mad Norwegian'.
Nevertheless, it is claimed that the book has been reprinted several times.

I left Harwich on the 30th of January, in the *Albion* packet, for
Gottenburgh. The *Albion*, after the mail of the 28th of January, and two
passengers, were put on board the *Diana*, set sail back to England, her
leaky condition not allowing her to beat the seas in these latitudes. Our
Captain (M'DONOUGH) expected that a gale might free the Swedish
coast from the enormous quantities of ice, that stretched from 12 to 15
miles out to sea, which floating about in huge masses rendered it
extremely dangerous to approach: in consequence he determined to
cruise in the Sleeve between Marstrand and the Skaw, the northern point
of Jutland. My own impatience, together with the importance that
naturally attached to 10 mails, which our packet and our companion the
Lark had on board, led me to hope that the merchants of Gottenburgh,
who must have been informed of our arrival off the coast, would contrive
to send off an ice boat for landing the bags and passengers. However, no
prospect of relief being held out to us from any quarter, after a cruise of
nine or ten days, we prevailed upon the Captain to make the coast of
Norway, where in consequence of the late peace, the pilots might be
expected to come out.

But for the traveller of leisure, things were different, and again one
has to look for explanations in the Romantic philosophy of travel.
According to James Buzard, this stated that

> travel offers us channels for those energies that must remain pent up in
> our domestic rounds. It stimulates active imaginative impulses and
> invites us to indulge them before returning home: we multiply events
> *innocently*, and set out on adventures 'as it were' Travel, in sum, has
> become an ameliorative vacation, which like the emerging nineteenth-
> century concept of culture, promises us a time or imaginary space out of
> ordinary life for the free realization of our otherwise thwarted potential
> (Buzard 1993, 102–3).

The object of travel, in other words, became adventure, discovery,
exploration and a kind of self-realisation that was beyond reach in a
civilised setting. This required not comfort, careful planning and the
company of fellow travellers, but rather a one-man journey beyond
the pale of civilisation, as in Mary Shelley's *Frankenstein* (1817),
where the unfortunate hero climbs alone to the summit of Montanvert
in Chamonix, because the presence of another would destroy the
solitary grandeur of the scene' (Shelley 1992, 94). As Mark Davies
remarks in his book on British travellers in Sweden, only in this way
could the travellers present 'themselves as expert interpreters of this
mysterious "otherness"' which their destination represented (Davies

2000, 60). Similarly, Mark Cocker claims that

> travellers thrive on the alien, the unexpected, even the uncomfortable
> and challenging. In fact, the more difficult the journey and the more
> circumstances are stacked against them, generally the fuller the travel
> experience. This element of opposition, of having to react to the places
> and people encountered, is at the heart of travel. The constant need to
> refocus and recreate permits a sense of renewal and an almost endless
> impression of freedom (Cocker 1992, 2).

In her recent study *Pleasure and Guilt on the Grand Tour*, Chloe
Chard even introduces the word 'transgression' to describe this urge
to go beyond the familiar (Chard 1999, 16). Statements confirming
such attitudes can be found in a large number of the travelogues in
question. The Scotsman Henry David Inglis, who published his
account under the *nom de voyage* Derwent Conway, makes it
expressly clear that Norway is not a land for the weak and the meek:
'On three sides, she is surrounded by a boisterous ocean, and girded
too, by a barrier of rocks; and, on the other, mountains rugged, and
snow-capt, shut her out, like the valley of Rasselas, from the rest of
the world (…)' (Conway 1829, 41). Joseph Phythian similarly insists
that his choice of holiday 'had not fallen on Norway without due
consideration. I had looked the map of Europe over, and there seemed
little untrodden ground' (Phythian 1877, 1), and on entering the
interior of Telemark, he proudly claims that it seemed 'our expedition
were one of exploration in a strange land' (ibid., 16). Still, it is hardly
possible to find a travel writer who more fully confirms this active
search for opposition than the artist Edward Price, who during his
visit to Norway in 1826 wanted to travel from Christiania to Bergen,
which would require the traveller to cross the wild and uninhabited
mountain plateau of the Hardangervidda. In his book, typically
entitled *Norway, Views of Wild Scenery*, he relates the complications
of his planned itinerary in the following way:

> I endeavoured whilst in Christiania to obtain information respecting the
> country; and many were the dissuasives to prevent me from going to
> Bergen; very figurative language prevailed respecting the mountainous
> region between Christiania and Bergen; an habitual and hereditary dread
> pervaded those with whom I conversed. It was described as a land of
> savage heights and unfathomable depths, where wild beasts were
> ravenous, and starvation would assuredly meet the traveller. (…) I
> listened with unqualified satisfaction to the respective narrations, and my
> pulse beat quicker, and enthusiasm rose to its highest point, when full

evidence was before me that Norway in its mountainous region bore the impress of sublimity (Price 1834, 18).

Furthermore, Thomas Forester, who two decades later included Price's journal in his own book *Norway and Its Scenery* (1853), appears to regard this fondness for an inaccessible landscape as a typically British – or rather English – characteristic. In the survey chapter 'English Travellers in Norway – Progress of Discovery', he notes that 'the unsophisticated inhabitants' in various parts of Norway found it incredible that an Englishman would travel for other than utilitarian reasons:

> The idea of any one undergoing the difficulties of penetrating into such districts from curiosity, or for recreation, could scarcely be comprehended.
>   Under these circumstances it has very much fallen to the lot of English travellers to open out the way to some of the most interesting points in Norwegian scenery, before unknown and unvisited. In some cases these have been as much objects of discovery as if they had lain in the heart of Africa, or the wilds of New Zealand, instead of, at farthest, a few days' sail from the shores of England (Forester 1853, 2–3).

In the same chapter he also describes the first travellers to Norway, who turned aside from the splendid 'allurements' of the Continent, 'to bend their steps to a land whose rugged paths had yet to be trodden out, and whose only charm was to be found "in her dim mountains, her silent forests, and her lonely lakes." To the solitary wanderings of some of these travellers, we are indebted for fresh discoveries, which guides and hand-books had not yet heralded' (ibid., 15). As a result of this attitude, one could almost argue that the travel guides, which were published in increasing numbers as the century progressed, were regarded by the genuine travellers primarily as guides for where *not* to go. As several critics have pointed out, the struggle for *authenticity* made the genuine travellers – or rather those who perceived themselves as genuine travellers – shun the recommended sites and instead discover their own. '[T]he place that is endangered by ease of access', according to James Buzard, 'is a sacred precinct in danger of violation; its vanishing or soon-to-vanish quality of being "untouched" becomes a subject for elegiac travellers' reveries' (Buzard 1993, 40). As a result, travel is transformed into a paradoxical race for taking possession of the many unravished brides of natural quietness before the hordes rush in and disturb the peace. The demand for *originality* is as uncompromising to the Romantic traveller as to the Romantic artist.

A final contrast between Norway and the Continent is given a striking expression by the Edward Wilson Landor (ref. Introduction). In his *Adventures in the North of Europe* (1836), there is a chapter called 'The Poetry and Philosophy of Travel', where Landor shows himself to be a product both of the Enlightenment and of the Romantic period. His point of departure is the eighteenth-century idea that travel is not only a leisure activity whose only purpose is to pass the time in a pleasant manner; on the contrary, the purpose is to *improve* the traveller. However, he is fundamentally critical of the Grand Tour model:

> To roll over Europe in a closed carriage, with guides and attendants, and interpreters, brings no improvement; – all roads are alike, when paved with gold. The traveller must be buffeted to be instructed; the luxurious must encounter privation, the imperious contradiction; the powerful must be taught his weakness, the learned his ignorance, the wealthy the vanity of riches. Difficulties and hardships are wonderful refiners; by them we are sifted and tried; the little good we possess is made apparent; we are shown the dregs, and may cast them away if we please (Landor 1836, 1: 81).

In effect, then, Landor literally recommends the path of most resistance, just like his colleagues quoted above. But in doing so, he makes use of a metaphor, which deserves attention from a literary point of view, and which is also particularly applicable to the Norwegian context. In the book *Travel Literature and the Evolution of the Novel* (1983), Percy G. Adams spends an entire chapter on literary motifs connected with the coach and the inn and claims that the so-called 'closed coach motif' is 'one of the closest bonds between the established travel book and the evolving novel' (214). Though moving, and therefore suggesting an element of freedom and adventure, the closed coach is clearly seen by Landor as typical of the outdated, eighteenth-century style of travel. Being closed, it also turns a blind eye on the qualities of the landscape through which it travels, and serves only as a means of transporting the traveller from one established site to another. Furthermore, the closed coach was made for two or more passengers and consequently created a group experience which was not compatible with the Romantic ideal of the solitary traveller.[5] Landor's powerful metaphor is particularly

---

[5] For a fascinating discussion of the *nineteenth-century* closed coach, see Sartre's discussion of the claustrophobic passage in Gustave Flaubert's *Madame Bovary*, where Léon and Emma travel through the streets of Paris in a horsecab with curtains drawn. Ref. Sartre 1971, 2: 1275-86.

The Courtyard, Victoria Hotel, Christiania.

Most travellers either bought or rented a carriole for the journey in Norway. Despite initial scepticism, they almost invariably came to the conclusion that it was the only vehicle suitable for the Norwegian roads. This picture from Pritchett (1879) shows a traveller ready to depart from the courtyard of the Victoria Hotel, Christiania.

relevant in Norway, where the open carriole (frequently spelled
cariole), made for one passenger only, ensured precisely the
individual experience and immediate contact with the natural
surroundings, advocated by Romanticism.[6]

But Landor's passage may also help explain on a deeper level why
the elitist and comfortable Grand Tour was gradually exchanged for
the ideal of 'roughing it'. His perspective reveals that he is hardly a
member of the aristocracy. On the contrary, there is a possibly class-
conditioned disgust in his statement that 'all roads are alike, when
paved with gold'. Landor, in other words, comes from the relatively
new and increasingly affluent middle or upper middle class – his
father was a physician – whose Puritan and frugal work ethic is more
or less perfectly in tune with Landor's own philosophy of travel. Like
the Romans, he holds up the banner of *Per aspera ad astra*: success
is ensured not through inherited wealth and an idle enjoyment of it,
but through hard work. As he puts it himself: 'Difficulties and
hardships are wonderful refiners.' In a post-revolutionary Europe,
this also gives added significance to the closed carriage, which could
be interpreted as an image of an aristocracy that journeys on in
traditional style, oblivious to the changed reality around them.
Travelling in Norway, on the other hand, clearly required both an
individual effort and an acceptance of toil and hardships.

Tourist versus Traveller

Landor's philosophy of travel also raises another question, which has
been briefly mentioned above, namely that of the long-lived tension
between the tourist and the traveller. Even though the exclusivity of
the Grand Tour gradually came to an end, it would be misleading to
assume that it was simply replaced by a general democratisation of
travel. In the period after Waterloo, travel indeed became both
simpler and less expensive, and was consequently made available to
new and steadily broader segments of society, but that did not
necessarily remove its traditional elitist associations. With the
Romantic search for originality and authenticity, travel came to be
seen as an integral part of the individual's self-realisation. As a result
the genuine traveller developed a mortal fear of becoming associated
with the mob or the masses. It does not come as a surprise, therefore,
that a distinction is introduced between the two categories tourists

[6] See further discussion of the carriole pp. 90–91.

and travellers, and that complaints about the perpetual presence of tourists become a commonplace in the travel literature of the period. According to James Buzard, this negative use of the word 'tourist' does not just go back to the mid nineteenth century, as claimed by the *Old English Dictionary*. It rather goes all the way back to William Wordsworth, whose poem 'The Brothers', from the 1800 edition of *Lyrical Ballads*, begins with the 'homely priest of Ennerdale' sighing irritably: 'These Tourists, Heaven preserve us, needs must live / A profitable life!' (Wu 1998, 332). But it is only after Waterloo that this negative use of the word comes into common use:

> The topical literature of the years following the Napoleonic Wars is full of hyperbole about British tourists' deluge, invasion, or infestation of the Continent, an onslaught marked chiefly by suddenness, liquid formlessness, and deafening noise. The *Westminster Review* remarked in 1825 that 'immediately after the peace' of 1815, 'the inundation of Britons, like a second irruption of the Goths, poured down upon Italy (...)' (Buzard 1993, 83–84).

What this clearly indicates, is that the eighteenth-century class division in connection with foreign travel has perhaps been removed, but at the same time it has been replaced by a division of a different kind, one more closely connected with the romantic and largely bourgeois aristocracy of spirit than with that of birth. Thus phenomena such as refinement, culture and true taste are – at least on the surface – detached from name, wealth and social connections, and made into qualities associated with the unique and socially free-moving individual. Admittedly, there are to be found among the travelogues on Norway some remarks which treat these dividing lines with easy-going irreverence, but significantly they tend to be written by non-Britons. Thus, it is tempting to quote the American J. Ross Browne who, in the July 1862 issue of *Harper's New Monthly Magazine*, admits without a blush: 'After twenty years' experience of travel by land and sea, I now frankly admit that the governing motive of my wanderings is to get out of one country and through another with the least possible delay' (Browne 1862, 146). It should come as no surprise that his article is entitled 'A Flying Trip to Norway'!

One Briton who shows at least a degree of tolerance towards different categories of visitors is John George Hollway who, in the preface to his book *A Month in Norway*, explains what is the aim of his account:

It is addressed to the fagged and weary literary man, politician, professional man, teacher, 'et id genus omne;' for whom, after working hard and close at head-work the major part of the year, and sick of 'breathing the breaths and thinking the thoughts of other men in close and crowded cities,' it is good to rush far away for their short holiday to fresh fields and pastures new, where they can refresh both mind and body and nerve themselves for the next year's inevitable struggle (Hollway 1853, iii–iv).

He then goes on to claim that Norway is not just interesting to the wealthy sportsmen, but also to people of less extravagant means who can only afford a few weeks' holiday:

I do not mean to say that Norway is never visited in this way now, but I think it has hitherto entered into the heads of comparatively few that it was worth while to go to Norway unless for three or four months' salmon fishing and shooting, or perhaps yachting. But there must be hundreds of men who, although they have no yachts, and neither time nor skill to fish the rivers, or stalk wild reindeer on the Fjelds, would nevertheless find much in a four weeks' tour in Norway deeply interesting to them (ibid., iv).

So far, Hollway comes across as a representative of the new and numerous groups of foreign travellers, i.e. a representative of what the aristocratic travellers of the eighteenth century would have called the mob or the masses. But it soon becomes clear that Hollway in no way sees himself as a member of the faceless crowd. During his comparison of the Alps with Norway, he acknowledges that the former can offer even greater scenery:

But to me, in much of the certainly glorious scenery of more Southern Europe there is always one great drawback: it is now made such a regular exhibition of. Every mountain is, as it were, labelled, – every waterfall ticketed – every place is a show place – and all its beauties methodically inventoried; you are not allowed to form your own impressions, you must take those of other people, which are already most plentifully provided for you. Heaps of guide-books, troops of guides, are your inevitable tyrants; the latter demons relentlessly environing you, and howling in your ears, when you long to stand before the glories of nature, silent, thoughtful, and alone (ibid., 38–39).

Armed with Romantic ideas of enjoying nature in silence and solitude, Hollway launches a full-scale attack on the loud and vulgar legions with whom, when in the Alps, he is forced to share his sacred communion with nature. As the passage very strongly suggests, he sees himself as an individual separated out from the rest; an aristocrat, not of birth, but of sensibility, equally unique and different. As a result, he feels the intrusion of howling guides more or less as a personal insult, and he goes on with an increasingly shrill voice:

> I don't want to know the exact height of the mountain, or the accurate depth of the lake; to be told where to stand, and how and what to admire; and because pre-eminently attractive scenery, by drawing thousands of real admirers, and thousands more of sham ones who come to see what others have praised must at last be degraded in this way, it is that one has greater satisfaction among less striking scenes, where at least one is allowed to find the beauties for one's self, and where the great Temple of Nature is not profaned by swarms of these self-ordained priests that stand, with outstretched hand and greedy eye, between her and her worshipper.
>
> Beauties enough you will indeed find among the wild glens and rock-bound fiords of Norway. It is not too much to say that, for hundreds of miles, every turn of the road, every winding of the fiord, discloses a picture which would repay the traveller for having journeyed hundreds of miles to see (ibid., 39–40).

Norway, then, emerges as Hollway's only possible cure. But even here he is not safe; the enemy tracks him down, and while discussing the building of a Norwegian road, he concludes in a way which says very little about Norway, but all the more about his own views of the social situation back home: '(…) we may perhaps hope that the major part [of the road], which avoids the terrific hill, will be open when our grandchildren come to visit this, by that time, vulgarised and cockneyfied country' (ibid., 115). Such statements are far from unique in the travelogues of the nineteenth century. The later MP and expert in old real property law Charles Elton (1839–1900), for instance, remarks in 1864 that 'Norway (…) is as yet unspoiled by Cockneys …' (Elton 1864, 1), and in the article 'The British Tourist in Norway', in *Blackwood's Edinburgh Magazine* for July 1872, the anonymous author, who 'prefixes reverend to his name' (318), gives the following description, containing ample doses of social prejudice:

> The inevitable Cockney is of course present, fitted out as if he had gone to take possession of a newly-hired preserve. I met one of these beside an upper feeder of the Hardanger. He was prepared for anything that might turn up – bear, wolf, boar, reindeer, capercailzie, or ptarmigan. He permitted himself to be seduced for some days into regions still more remote from 'the luxuries of the Saut Market', than that where I found

him. He complained that he had not been successful, and admitted, on cross-questioning, that he had got sight or trace of no living thing save his conductors. I suspected that people had been playing tricks on his intellect touching the merits of my geological hammer, for he came forward at once to meet me with an inquiring interested face, and, 'Well, sir, have you had any success?' He was a very pure specimen of Cockney breed, except that he had not that assumption of superiority generally claimed by those who also assume the privilege of inverting the aspirates. The more academic class of his fellow-tourists had bestowed on him the name of 'The Arditer,' on account of his efforts to make it known that his rifle was 'a hard hitter'(ibid., 326).

'Cockneyfication', however, should not primarily be read as a reference to the London dialect in particular or for that matter to the working class. When John Keats, many years earlier, was attacked, also by *Blackwood's Magazine*, for his 'Cockney' style, it appears that the word contained primarily an accusation of 'vulgar pretentiousness'. Thus it seems to have been used as a general term to label anyone lacking the required degree of sensibility, a quality which could often be perceived as being intimately associated with both accent and class. Other travellers, however, refrain from such explicit expressions of social prejudices; instead, they promote the idea, only slightly less transparent, that Norway is a special place that only certain groups would know how to appreciate. Olivia M. Stone's book *Norway in June* (1882), which was printed in three editions in seven years, makes it clear that

> Norway possesses few attractions to those comprising the class who are accustomed to place themselves under the charge of Mr. Cook. In the sense they understand it, travelling in Norway has not yet been made easy, and I must candidly own to hoping that things may long continue as they are now. The typical tourist so inseparably connected with Switzerland and the Rhine seems to avoid splendid scenery when coupled with what to him would be scant personal comfort. What would he do without his six or seven courses at table d'hôte, obsequious waiters, electric bells, and all the various et ceteras that are comprised in the establishment of a well-regulated hotel! (Stone 1882, 99)[7]

Emily Lowe, another lady traveller and author of the famous *Unprotected Females in Norway*, takes leave of Bergen and Norway with a wish that it remain a well-kept secret among the initiated few:

---

[7] For a detailed discussion of the role of Thomas Cook, see Buzard 1993, ch. 1.

| 100 | PUNCH, OR THE LONDON CHARIVARI | [SEPTEMBER 9, 1876. |

JOHN BULL AND HIS GUIDES.

HE pilgrim of Britain, | Learns to like and to
His track fain to fit | look
in | By his Guide or his
Rule spoken or writ- | Book,
ten, | Be it MURRAY or COOK;

The same thing's left undone, | All their "selves" glad to merge,
The same by each one done, | Through the same gap must surge,
'Twixt Thule and London. | Like the sheep of Panurge,

As COOK bids, on they scurry; | With his own eyes once looked: | To be grave or rejoice; | Trots and halts in a band,
Or tractably hurry | Now he likes his routes Cooked, | Till his voice is COOK's voice, | Likes, dislikes, second hand,
At the order of MURRAY. | His opinions Red-booked, | And his choice is COOK's choice. | At the word of command.

JOHN BULL once had a "willy," | His thoughts run in a mould— | COOK's tariff his steady care: | And regains his own shore,
And also a "nilly;" | Calf's-foot jelly-like, cold— | His taste ruled by ready care | His travelling o'er,
Loved to dally or dilly— | Laughs or sighs, as he's told | Of MURRAY or BAEDEKER. | The same BULL as before.

The polarisation between tourists and travellers is a leitmotif in all travel literature, here illustrated in the 9 September 1876 issue of *Punch*. Blind to anything but the stereotyped information of the guidebooks published by Murray, Baedeker, Cook etc., British tourists swarm abroad: John Bull 'With his own eyes once looked: / Now he likes his routes Cooked, / His opinions Red-booked, / His thoughts run in a mould / […] Till his voice is Cook's voice, / And his choice is Cook's choice.'

> Farewell! sweet, bizarre Bergen! Queen of the North! long may you
> preserve your own individuality, and those granite isles keep innovation
> from you, and be break-waters to stem the tide of modern assimilation!
> May the soft wave gently float to your shores those alone who will
> acknowledge your supremacy; the innate traveller, not the tourist (Lowe
> 1857, 176–77).

It is an interesting paradox that these aristocrats of sensibility, the
large majority of whom were undoubtedly also comparatively well
off in material terms, made an ideal of denying themselves comforts
that they could easily afford, while at the same time criticising those
who were probably less affluent but who still preferred the luxury of
modern tourism. For both groups, however, the holiday represented a
welcome contrast from the daily routine.

In the large majority of travelogues, then, there is a fairly
consistent tone reflecting a view of Norway as a haven as yet
unaffected by the discontents of civilisation. Undoubtedly, this
discontent has its roots in the general scepticism against civilisation
launched initially by Rousseau and other cultural critics of the pre-
Romantic and Romantic periods. But it should also be seen as directly
related to the contemporary political scene in Victorian Britain, which
constitutes the immediate context of most of the accounts in question.
Although the travellers to Norway came from a gradually broadening
social spectrum, the majority still represented a relatively
homogenous group. W. Mattieu Williams, who travelled *Through
Norway with Ladies*, gives the following description of his fellow
passengers from Britain to Norway, focusing rather conspicuously on
those of his own sex:

> Most of the passengers were good specimens of modern English
> manhood; members of the Alpine Club, col-climbing clergymen,
> yachtsmen, and sportsmen of the vigorous type who hunt their game as
> well as kill it. The majority were young men born and reared in what a
> fine writer would call 'the lap of luxury,' and sufficiently sated thereby
> to rejoice in turning their backs upon Mayfair, in order to refresh their
> souls and bodies by wholesome struggle with the invigorating hardships
> of Scandinavian sport and travel (Williams 1877, 3).

Eight years later, in the article 'Our Tour in Norway' from *The Girl's
Own Paper*, 'Two London Girls' make the following observation on
board the steamer from Hull to Bergen:

> Then there are four fine men in knickerbockers, armed to the teeth with

pickaxes, alpenstocks, and nailed boots; a 'little Yankee' and his dame, who snugly recline in big American hammock chairs (the lady's diamond earrings are worthy of remark); a delicate-looking doctor and pleasant wife; 'Paddy from Cork,' a tall, shy man in a new blue serge suit; a clergyman, who shouts fearfully; his wife and sister; a stately naval commander, and others ('Our Tour in Norway' 1885, 285).

This picture is largely confirmed by Jean A. Mains's unpublished MA-thesis *British Travellers in Norway During the Nineteenth Century*, where she comments on the social background of the travellers:

> Both sexes belonged to the professional, middle or upper class, the aristocracy and royalty. As might be expected in their day and age, the women had led a purely domestic or social life apart from a few writers like Edna Lyall or Lady Wilde. Occupationally, the men were more diversified – artists, authors, bankers, civil servants, clergy, diplomats, doctors, gentlemen of leisure, lawyers, officers (army and navy), poets, politicians, schoolmasters, scientists, statesmen, students and academics from Oxford, Cambridge, Edinburgh and St Andrews (Mains 1989, 22).[8]

Although 'more diversified', these groups still belonged to the more or less well-educated urban middle class, i.e. a class which in relative terms enjoyed a sheltered and privileged existence, and which, with the Reform Bill of 1832, had acquired a significant share of political power. However, Victorian society was throughout the period in a state of constant and radical change, and consequently ripe with fears of conflicts which might threaten the uneasy social and political equilibrium. Matthew Arnold's dramatically entitled *Culture and Anarchy* (1869), for instance, which divided the population into Barbarians, Philistines and Populace, reflected precisely how Victorian society was characterised by profoundly conflicting interests. Furthermore, the jealous guarding of interests, which frequently characterises groups which have recently come to power, is also typical of the average traveller to Norway, and may help to explain the almost aggressive attempt to keep Norway 'uncockneyfied'.

Cockney, then, served as a label for that vulgar element of the population who surrounded the supposedly more sophisticated traveller in his native environment, and from whom he tried to escape

---

[8] For more detailed information on individual writers, see 'Biographical Information', pp. 347–66.

through foreign travel. But he was also faced with another challenge, a near relative of the Cockney, namely the Yankee. E. J. Goodman gives a good example of this in *New Ground in Norway* (1896). Travelling by boat on the recently opened Telemark Canal, he visits Hotel Dalen, a new and palatial tourist machine with electric light and other modern conveniences. Goodman quickly concludes that Dalen, which because of the Canal has become transformed within a few years, has nothing to offer the traveller. He therefore returns with the boat to the even smaller hamlet of Kviteseid (which he calls Kirkebø), and here he finds his largely untouched 'little paradise' (Goodman 1896, 89). On board the boat, however, there is also a group of Americans:

> [T]here was a large party of Americans, of the most typical 'globe-trotting' sort, who were 'doing' Europe at the top of their speed. How those Yankees travel! They had been through France, Germany, Switzerland, Spain, Italy, in the course of a few weeks, and were now flying through Norway and going next to Russia. They boasted that they had never stayed more than a day at any one place, and 'calculated' that they would be travelling in this way for about eight months (ibid., 85–86).

Still, the traveller's contempt for the tourist is not unique to the Victorian period. In Tim Moore's recent travel book, *Frost on My Moustache: The Arctic Exploits of a Lord and a Loafer*, which describes an attempt to duplicate the Icelandic and Norwegian journey of Lord Dufferin in 1856, the author takes the typically Victorian prejudice and magnifies it into burlesque proportions when he witnesses the arrival of a new group of tourists at Spitzbergen: 'These were cosseted tourists, little people, idiots, scum. I, and I alone, was the Explorer' (Moore 1999, 275). The obvious irony saves the author's face, but the remark still shows that this contempt for the tourist – whether acknowledged or not – has become an established part of the mental luggage of travellers everywhere.

Women Travellers

From a modern point of view, there is a rather striking similarity between the way in which the majority of nineteenth-century British travellers preferred not to encounter other travellers than those of their own class, and the way in which the same travellers expressed a fundamental scepticism with respect to the idea of British women travelling to Norway. Both these forms of protectiveness reflect a society that was strongly divided in terms of both class and gender roles. Against this background, it is particularly interesting to examine the answers from the many male writers to the perennial question of whether women ought to travel to Norway at all. As will emerge from the passages below, some of the considerations mentioned are of a purely practical and understandable nature, but just as often they reveal as much about men's attitudes to themselves as about their attitudes to women.

In his first book – *Norway in 1848 and 1849* – Thomas Forester shows a surprisingly liberal attitude:

> If I were asked whether English ladies could be recommended to undertake a tour in Norway, I should be disposed to reply, that much of its most interesting scenery may be visited, not only with perfect safety, but without any particular privations or grounds of apprehension, by such as are not very fastidious on the score of accommodations, have a reasonable share of courage and enterprise, and are prepared to place implicit confidence in their conductors (Forester 1850, 95).

In his *Norway and Its Scenery*, which came out three years later, however, it is almost as if he feels obliged to correct his former recklessness, because here he enters into a long discussion, gathering support for his now considerably stricter views by quoting Alfred Smith, the curate of Poulshot in Wiltshire, who had published his *Sketches in Norway and Sweden* in 1847:

> How far is it practicable for ladies to travel in Norway? It is a very natural question, and it may perhaps occur to some of a class of our readers to whose gratification we should greatly wish to contribute, whether ladies can be advised to travel in Norway. (...)
>
> Let us see what experienced travellers have said on this subject. The Rev. Mr. Smith, in the Introduction to his beautiful Plates of Norwegian Scenery, remarks: 'I am not ignorant of the indomitable spirit, energy, and courage with which English ladies will surmount the greatest difficulties, and brave the utmost peril. I can easily believe many would scamper with fearless intrepidity on Norwegian ponies down the almost perpendicular cliffs of a fjord, and through trackless rocks and dismal forests; but I doubt if they will be so easily persuaded to entrust themselves to the rough arms of a Norwegian boatman, redolent with finkel, repose their delicate limbs on a shaggy bearskin in some Norwegian barn, or wrap their cloaks around them, and spend the night in a dreary forest, with a stone for a pillow and heather for a bed.' (...)
>
> For ourselves, we agree with Mr. Smith that the want of suitable

accommodation is the main obstacle to females undertaking a tour of any extent in the remoter districts of Norway, where all the finest scenery is to be found. No one who has not been an eyewitness and personal sufferer can form any idea of the disgusting annoyances to which travellers are exposed who have to seek their *gîte* where they can find it on unfrequented roads. The time is not come when even the great highways to Bergen and Drontheim are open to female tourists. The resting-places where decent accommodations can be obtained, are still of rare occurrence. For a lady to undertake such a journey – of three or four hundred miles – in a carriole, a vehicle which carries only one passenger, and is not much more roomy than a park chaise, with equal exposure to the weather, would be preposterous (Forester 1853, 79–81).

Forester's passage is interesting first of all because it confirms an impression touched upon above: it is important for the male travel writer to convey the impression that Norway is primarily a place where none but men of mettle may survive. Consequently, the conditions that the traveller will have to endure are dramatised so as to convince the reader – especially the female reader – that Norway is beyond a woman's physical and mental capacity. If the warning of a 'night in a dreary forest' and 'a stone for a pillow and heather for a bed' is not sufficiently alarming, the Rev. Smith adds to the burden the effective contrast between the 'rough arm' of the finkel-smelling Norwegian boatman and the 'delicate limbs' of the English lady, finally throwing in the 'shaggy bearskin' for good measure. John Bowden chooses a similar approach to the question of whether ladies ought to travel in Norway. Again, with a relatively obliging gesture, he claims that 'it is quite safe for them to do so, but not very expedient.' But he then adds: 'If ladies have strong constitutions and good nerves, know how to drive a spirited pony, are not very nice in their eating and drinking, and, above all, can undergo fatigue, they may safely venture to undertake a tour in Norway' (Bowden 1867, 243). There is an unmistakable rhetorical quality about Bowden's series of conditions. In effect, he asserts, though it is wrapped up in a conditional form, that only those women who could not justifiably be called 'ladies' would find travel in Norway endurable.

Equally interesting is the discussion of whether women can possibly travel alone or whether they will need a male escort. Thomas Forester is once again adamant: '(...) we can on no account recommend them to undertake the journey unless they are accompanied by a gentleman already experienced in Norwegian travel, and in some degree acquainted with the language, or unless the party is attended by a courier who has been well recommended, and

who speaks both languages, English and Danish' (Forester 1853, 83).[9]
John Hollway is largely of the same opinion:

> I see no necessity for *men* to take with them an interpreter or courier, if
> they choose to take the little extra trouble of informing themselves before
> starting of a few essential particulars. Where ladies are of the party, an
> intelligent and experienced *tolk* (interpreter) will be found of course a
> great comfort, if not exactly a necessary [*sic*]. With ladies perhaps it
> would be desirable to take one; but a party of two or three men will find
> themselves more independent, more in the way of coming into personal
> contact with the peasantry, see more of their hospitable customs, and
> learn more about them and their ways, by picking up beforehand a little
> of the language, and acting as their own tolks (Hollway 1853, 14).

First of all, Forester and Hollway seem to take it for granted that men
by nature are more competent communicators, or learners of foreign
languages, than women. Secondly, women are presented as incapable
of taking 'the little extra trouble of informing themselves' about a few
'essential particulars' before leaving. As a result, an interpreter
becomes essential. But the second part of the passage is even more
striking: whereas women will need an interpreter, men are actively
discouraged from having one, because it would reduce their
independence and their opportunity of seeing, learning and coming
into 'personal contact with the peasantry'. This passage, in other
words, offers an excellent example of how Victorian society
consistently prevented women from developing their own
individuality, experience, knowledge and, as in this case, their own
voice. Whereas the men 'will find themselves more independent'
without an interpreter, the women will need one, literally because
they cannot – like the speechless Bertha Rochester in *Jane Eyre* –
speak for themselves.

There is, however, one solitary woman traveller to Norway who
undermines so effectively all male warnings about women visiting
the country without male escort, that she can hardly be counted as a
representative member of her sex. Furthermore, it is striking that so
little is mentioned in the numerous British travelogues from the
1800s about the woman who was perhaps the most notable of all
female travellers to Norway, namely Mary Wollstonecraft. In fact,
besides Thomas Forester, who in his summary 'English Travellers in
Norway – Progress of Discovery' mentions Wollstonecraft in a

---

[9] For a further discussion of the question of language, see ch. 3, pp. 254–60.

footnote, there are few references to her other than in a translator's note in the English editon of 1813 of the famous work *Travels through Norway and Lapland* by the German traveller and scientist Leopold von Buch. Thus, when von Buch's translator claims that the Norwegian landscape in Wollstonecraft's account drew 'some of the most beautiful specimens of description in the English language' and describes the lady as 'the celebrated Mary Wollstonecraft' (von Buch 1813, iii), he is hardly in line with the great majority of Victorian travellers, unless by 'celebrated' he refers to her sexual reputation, which left her largely ignored for the entire nineteenth century.[10] When reading Wollstonecraft's account, however, one is overwhelmed not only with the book's literary qualities but also with the accuracy of observation and the impressive display of journalistic craftsmanship in gathering information about Norwegian society at the time. All in all, she does a more convincing piece of research in the course of a few weeks' stay in some sheltered towns on the south coast and a brief visit to Christiania than most of her male followers after as many weeks of 'independent' travel. Consequently, her book, to which we will return in greater detail in ch. 4, did not conform to the image of female inadequacy that the average Victorian male traveller preferred to convey. Travelling alone under very rough conditions and doing a man's job in terms of representing her American lover's business interests, Wollstonecraft portrays herself in an impressively unheroic fashion, in considerable contrast to many of the rather boisterous male writers.[11]

The typically male Victorian attitude discussed above is also thrown into relief by the following passage from Emily Lowe's teasingly entitled book *Unprotected Females in Norway*, which, though published pseudonymously, presents a woman well capable of looking after herself. Touring Norway together with her mother, whom she rarely mentions, she passes a verdict concerning women travellers that would probably make Forester and Hollway wince with embarrassment:

---

[10] One more text concerning Wollestonecraft's trip to Norway should me mentioned, however, namely *The Wanderer in Norway*, a ninety-page poem by the Scottish poet and Professor og Moral Philosophy Thomas Brown (1778–1821). The poem, published in 1816, offers a rather oversentimental account of her journey and of her relationship with her American lover in Paris, and is apparently based more on Wollstonecraft's own account (and other writings by her) than on Brown's knowledge of Norway.

[11] For a fascinating account of the reasons for Wollstonecraft's journey to Norway, see Richard Holmes's Introduction to Wollstonecraft 1987, 9-43.

LADIES ON HORSEBACK.

Emily Lowe's book *Unprotected Females in Norway* (1857) paid little heed to the countless warnings from male writers about the insurmountable problems that female travellers in Norway would encounter. Illustration from the book.

> We two ladies (...) have found out and will maintain that ladies *alone* get
> on in travelling much better than with gentlemen: they set about things
> in a quieter manner, and always have their own way; while men are sure
> to go into passions and make rows, if things are not right immediately.
> (...) The only use of a gentleman in travelling is to look after the luggage,
> and we take care to have no luggage. 'The Unprotected' should never go
> beyond one portable carpetbag (Lowe 1857, 3).

Lowe's irony and condescension are perfectly understandable, but
Victorian society had a wide and varied register by which the male
supremacy was efficiently upheld. It is not surprising, therefore, to
find Lowe's book treated with considerable scepticism by other
writers. Thus for instance *Norway in 1858, Lindesnœs to the
Midnight Sun*, published two years after Lowe's book, employs yet
another manipulative technique against non-conforming women.
Ironically, the book is written by husband and wife, John Benjamin
and Sarah Popplewell (Schiötz 1970–1986, 1: 377), who clearly
indicate that Miss Lowe's account of her stay in Norway has not
passed unnoticed:

> Mr. A— saw a good deal of Miss Lowe (the unprotected female) in
> Christiania, and told us many amusing things about her. There is no
> doubt her book is an entirely made-up thing, and she writes of many
> things as having happened to herself which had been told her by fellow-
> travellers, some of them having taken place years ago. Mr. A— took her
> to dine with a friend of his in Christiania. The gentleman said of Miss
> Lowe, 'Well, I am very glad indeed to have spent an hour with such a
> woman, it is quite a treat, but heaven defend me from such a woman as
> a wife!' (Popplewell 1859, 36).

As appears from the quote, two accusations are brought against Miss
Lowe, both of them indicating defects of character that would
severely undermine her credibility. First, her book, which is probably
no further from the truth than most other travel accounts, is presented
as entirely a piece of fiction; second, and more seriously, her qualities
as a woman are questioned with a wry sense of humour.

In her study *A Wider Range: Travel Writing by Women in
Victorian England*, Maria H. Frawley describes the aim of her project
as ascertaining 'how travel and writing functioned together in
nineteenth-century England to enable women to cross physical and
ideological distances, to expand institutional and psychological
borders' (Frawley 1994, 15). As has been shown above, women
travellers to Norway crossed similar barriers and, as Frawley puts it,

the travel accounts of adventure, in which category the Norwegian travelogues most naturally belong, 'challenged assumptions about the female need for protection that were underwritten by their culture's binary organization of sexual difference' (ibid., 107–8). But by challenging these assumptions, Victorian women were also faced with the prejudices of their time and of their fellow male travellers. One of these prejudices was the 'tendency to associate women with the creative rather than with the rational and analytical' (ibid., 33), a tendency that necessitated the intervention of a controlling male. Thus when Mrs Alec Tweedie – note the form of her name – books her and her sister's tickets before leaving for Norway in 1892, she is hardly surprised when 'the booking-clerk laughed at the idea of two ladies undertaking such a journey …' (Tweedie 1894, 1). Despite this fundamental scepticism about women travelling on their own, however, 'the large majority of Victorian women travellers travelled alone' (Frawley 1994, 23), which in itself is a powerful indication that the male qualms were largely unfounded. In her article 'Mr. Gladstone in Norway', however, Lady Brassey suggests a practical compromise which, towards the end of the century may have become relatively common, namely several women travelling together. During a visit to Odda, the Brasseys make an excursion to the 'Laathefos' (Låtefossen) and the 'Buerbræ Glacier' (Buarbreen): 'While we were at lunch several carioles had passed us *en route* from Christiania to Odde, including one procession of eight of these vehicles, seven of which were occupied by as many women, who would have been "unprotected" females, but for the occupant of the eighth, their "tolk," or escort-guide, who brought up the rear' (Brassey 1885, 487).[12]

Increasing Popularity

The nineteenth century witnessed a radical, though gradual, increase in the number of British travellers to Norway. There is little comprehensive statistical evidence to support this claim, but as will be seen in the following, there is no doubt that the discovery of Norway as a destination of leisure travel can be dated roughly to the 1820s. Clearly, the political events of 1814, which will be discussed

[12] The above discussion of British women travelling in Norway may be usefully compared with that in ch. 3 (pp. 207–28) of British – male and female – views of Norwegian women.

in the following chapter, contributed strongly to the British awareness of a country which had hitherto been largely ignored by other than merchant travellers. Thus, whereas *The Times* had only sixty-five articles about Norway in the ten-year period 1804–13, it had as many as 125 in the year 1814 alone. The effect of this new interest then became apparent in the following decade. Robert Taylor Pritchett, writing sixty-five years later and looking back on the first visitors, even fastens on a particular year: 'English visitors commenced about 1824; Lord Lothian, Lord Clanwilliam, and Lord H. Kerr, 1827; the Marquis of Hastings, 1829; and in 1830 we have Elliott's account of Norway' (Pritchett 1879, 6). Further evidence, largely confirming that of Pritchett, is found in the references in several travel accounts to various kinds of guest books signed by the travellers at stations and inns. William Rae Wilson, who travelled in the south-eastern part of Norway precisely in 1824, relates that on entering Norway through one of the main routes into the country (Frederikshall; now Halden), his landlord asked him to write his name in such a book: 'On looking over the list of travellers, I was surprised so few of my countrymen were to be found who had visited this spot' (Wilson 1826, 84). Similarly, on the way from Bergen to Molde, John Barrow Jr. in 1833 finds a '*Livre des Etrangers*', that is

[a] book in which travellers insert their names. It commenced in the year 1821; but there were scarcely any names entered in it, and not one of our own countrymen among the number. This led me to examine all the books carefully as we travelled onwards, and the result was, that not one Englishman appeared to have been upon this route for very many years, if ever, as some of the books, afterwards met with, began with the year 1795, and the greatest number of names contained in any one of them did not exceed forty, that is to say, one stranger in the year (Barrow 1834, 282–83).

When he arrives in Molde, Barrow also checks the so-called travellers' book, which contains many more names, 'but still I could not trace one of our own countrymen among them' (ibid., 328). However, Robert Bremner, travelling in 1836, finds a guest book at Bolkesjø in Telemark containing information about quite a number of other Englishmen who had visited during the previous fifteen years:

At first scarcely one English name occurs; indeed, for whole years together there are few travellers of any description. In 1826, two English names appear. In 1827, the Rev. Mr. Everett [i.e. Everest], author of a work on Norway, records his transit. In 1828, the Marquis of Lothian,

Earl Clanwilliam, and an illegible Englishman, seem to have been the only visitors; in the following year Lord Villiers and Lord Craven present themselves, accompanied by a Reverend friend, also raised to the peerage by the native servant who had entered the names. Of late years, however, there are at least eight or ten English visitors every summer, nearly all of them noble (Bremner 1840, 2: 130).

On his way to the Rjukanfossen in 1848, Thomas Forester comes to the station at Dal – also in Telemark – and finds documentation to support Pritchett's choice of 1824 as the year in which the migration of travellers started:

> In looking over the *Dagbog* at Däl [*sic*], which in Norway is an official document, the first names of English visitors discovered were in 1824. None afterwards appeared till 1827, when those of Lords Lothian, Clanwilliam and H. Kerr occurred in one party. The following year there were three visitors. Then came, in 1829, the Marquis of Hastings; and, in 1830, eight English names are inscribed, including those of Mr. Elliott, who published an account of his journey, and Mr. Shore. For fifteen succeeding years there seems to have been hardly a single visitor. In August, 1845, the Rev. M. W. Mayo was here, accompanied by the Rev. Alfred Smith, who has lately given to the world a splendid volume of drawings sketched during this tour. Since that time it appeared that we were the only English visitors, except, be it recorded to their honour, some ladies of the name of Vivian (Forester 1850, 95).[13]

The writers quoted above, all of whom write in or about the first half of the century, are unanimous in describing the first travellers of leisure to Norway as belonging to a small and highly exclusive segment of British society, and as being correspondingly few in number. Against this background, a statement from 1840, by Robert Gordon Latham, poses certain problems:

> Plenty of people go there [to Norway], for pleasure as well as for business: high and low, titled and untitled; some to fish, and others with the vain hope of shooting bears. Of all these, nine out of ten take the same route, at the same season of the year, and go to the same inns. If two Englishmen are in Norway, at the same time, the chances are that they will meet each other (Latham 1840, 1: 32).

---

[13] The Vivianses were a wealthy mining family from Cornwall, and in 1935 Molly Hughes, a member of the family, wrote the romantic novel *Vivians: A Family in Victorian Cornwall*, which is a portrayal of her mother and aunt, who, in the 1840s, travelled to Norway to visit friends in Telemark.

In order to consider whether Latham can be regarded as a trustworthy witness with regard to the extent of British travel to Norway, it might be worth looking more closely at his account. Although Latham, who was a linguist and ethnologist, later became Professor of English Literature at University College in London and the translator of Esaias Tegnér's *Frithiof's Saga*, he was only twenty-one during his journey to Norway, and his travelogue was not published until seven years after the actual event. Furthermore, a modern reader might suspect that his general enthusiasm for the young and democratic Norway, fuelled partly by his friendship with Henrik Wergeland, provided him with a personal interest – expressed in the parlance of tourism – in marketing Norway as a destination not just for the titled elite, but also for the less wealthy. On the other hand, one should also take into account that Latham, in 1840, may have been influenced by an awareness that the number of visitors had been steadily increasing since his own visit seven years earlier.

Regardless of how one chooses to interpret Latham's description, however, the fact remains that Norway during these very decades was experiencing a steadily growing attention from abroad, imparted not just through the printed word but also through an expanding market for pictures, especially of natural scenery. S. C. Hammer, who in 1928 published a general introduction to Norway, points specifically to this phenomenon when explaining the discovery of Norway by British travellers:

> In the course of the 'forties as well as in the course of the 'fifties this propaganda for making Norway known in England and on the Continent enjoyed a fresh impetus through a number of lithographic plates and works with illustrations in colour, which were published in London and Paris, all bearing on various types of scenery in Norway. From the latter period also date the first volumes on sport and fishing in this country, another characteristic evidence of the increasing popularity of Norway as a holiday country (Hammer 1928, 6).

Still, the visitors of the first half of the century found a country virtually unprepared for the business of accommodating foreign travellers. Those who came – and in the first decades many of them limited their journey to the coastal areas – found something akin to hotels only in the major towns, and even here the standard was not up to what a British officer and gentleman would reasonably expect. Arthur de Capell Brooke, in 1820 a major in the army and later a baronet, is far from impressed with the accommodation he is offered in the capital Christiania: 'At the hotel where I lodged, the only one, I believe, in town, the accommodations were of the very worst description; and when on my departure my account was presented, the charges quite confounded me' (Brooke 1823, 95). In the rest of the country, and particularly in the interior, private accommodation was the only alternative and was frequently of a very spartan standard indeed.

As has been indicated, however, a change was taking place around the middle of the century. It was only then that what might be called the Norwegian tourist industry slowly came into being. This divide is conveniently illustrated by the fact that in 1850 the Englishman Thomas Bennett opened the first travel agency in Norway. Having arrived in Christiania two years earlier simply to 'see Norway', he very quickly saw the business possibilities that were opening up in connection with the steadily growing number of visitors who needed help and advice. From 1850 onwards, there is hardly a British travelogue that does not mention Bennett, usually accompanied by profuse expressions of praise and gratitude. Even J. MacGregor, the Scotsman who brings to Norway the new and peculiar naval creation called a canoe – it is actually a kayak – acknowledges Mr Bennett's generous assistance in finding suitable rivers for his journey:

> The traveller's friend in Norway is Mr. Bennet [sic], who knows everything and helps everybody. He fills several posts of duty and honour, has an office full of maps and books, and a yard full of carioles and carriages, and a desk full of outlandish bank notes for shillings; and if you wish to journey safe and fast over Norway, and with big fish to the rod, and big bags to the gun, it is well to talk first with Mr. Bennet. He had aided me there ten years ago; but now it was an utterly new line to be catechized upon by the first English traveller mad about boats, and so he was fairly nonplussed (MacGregor 1867, 8).

Bennett's long and successful career – he died in 1898 and his travel agency still exists – is inextricably linked not only to the growth of Norwegian tourism but also to the close ties between Britain and Norway in the nineteenth as well as in the twentieth century. According to Mains, 'Bennett's epitaph is written into the records of his church [in Christiania]: "He was the father of the British community (...), an honour to the land of his birth, a blessing to the land of his adoption"' (Mains 1989, 40). At the same time, his work constitutes a useful Norwegian parallel to such British tourist operators as Baedeker, Murray and Cook, and in that particular respect it should be noted that at least one writer gives Bennett precisely the same treatment to which these were regularly subjected, making it very clear that he regards himself as a traveller rather than as a tourist. The anonymous author of the article 'The British Tourist in Norway' in the July 1872 issue of *Blackwood's Edinburgh Magazine*,[14] begins by admitting – though with a touch of irony – that the traveller may well 'put himself under tutelage or direction, and leave the responsibility of laying out the whole scheme of his labours and his enjoyments to a master-spirit' (37). However, he has himself been careful to avoid such assistance:

> This organisation of all the offices that minister to the wants and weaknesses of the tourist – connecting guides, drivers, and valets with a sort of hierarchy, or army under a general – is one of the sublime ideas conceived from time to time by the great minds of the world. It is likely that to many he has proved the guide, philosopher, and friend; and if he has also been their master, owner, and driver, it were pity to disturb them, good souls, unconscious in their happy slavery. ... Bennett is, on the whole, evidently a magnanimous despot, showing himself so in the many shapes in which he offers to the British Tourist the means of helping himself. He seems to say, If you can get on without me, do so by all means, and here is no end of guiding literature to help you (ibid., 37–38).

The mid-century transition from Norway as a virgin territory or even a 'heart of darkness' to a 'destination', is also illustrated by a charming passage from one of the great advocates of Norway, namely the Oxford don Frederick Metcalfe, author of the travel books *The Oxonian in Norway* (1856) and *The Oxonian in Thelemarken* (1858). An acknowledged authority on Old Norse, he also wrote *The Englishman and the Scandinavian; or, A Comparison of Anglo-Saxon and Old Norse Literature* (1880). Although published in the late 1850s, Metcalfe's travel accounts read as if they were written some decades earlier; he is most decisively an old-style traveller, or rather wanderer, who seeks out remote and unvisited areas on foot. One day at the end of July in 1857, he is sitting in his rooms at Lincoln College, listening to the rats in the cupboard. The 'Oxford Long Vacation' has just started, and he does not know how to spend his summer:

> Norway! and why am I not there? It is too late this year to think of it. I must write to that friend, and say I can't keep my promise, and join him thither. No, I must be content with a little trout-fishing in Wales or Scotland. At this moment a tap is heard at the door. An ingenuous youth,

[14] The same author was quoted above on 'Cockneyfication'.

undergraduate of St. Sapientia College, and resident in the
neighbourhood, had brought a letter of introduction from a common
friend, begging me, as one deep in the mysteries of Norwegian
travelling, to give the bearer some information respecting that country, as
he thought of taking a month's trip thither.

    As I pulled out Munck's [i.e. Munch, P. A.] map, chalked out a
route for the youth, and gave him a little practical advice on the subject,
a regular spasm came across me. I was never plagued by that malicious
gadfly, or 'tsetse,' so much as I was for the rest of the day by an
irresistible desire to be off to the old country (Metcalfe 1858, 2: 67–68).

In a sense, this is a meeting between the old traveller and the young
tourist. Whereas Metcalfe has acquired a highly individualistic
experience of Norway, the student who asks for his advice will meet
a gradually more professionalised and standardised system. Another
account from the same year, Lord Thomas Allnutt Brassey's *Journal
of a Voyage through the Western Isles of Scotland and along the
Coast of Norway*, confirms that the time of 'solitary travel' had
passed. On board a steamship entering the Sognefjorden, he
complains that '[t]he number of Englishmen whom we met was quite
amazing. At each of the numerous stations at which we stopped some
fellow countrymen came on board, and joined the increasing throng'
(Brassey 1857, 47–8). The American traveller Charles Loring Brace
also reports in 1857 that Christiania

> is evidently a great resort for travellers. All the principal shops are for
> strangers – filled with prints, or characteristic Norwegian objects; others
> are crowded with accoutrements for carriole-travelling, and salmon-
> fishing. English is spoken everywhere, and Englishmen throng in every
> hotel. Our landlord (in the *Hôtel du Nord*) says he sent off fifteen English
> sportsmen yesterday up the country, each in his carriole (Brace 1857,
> 2).[15]

Nine years later, however, in May 1866, a supplement to Cook's
Excursionist and Home and Foreign Tourist Advertiser reproduces a
letter from 'an English gentleman in Norway', who can only be Mr
Bennett. Here he warns prospective travellers to Norway that
facilities are still not up to scratch:

> I beg to inform you that it is not so easy to make Excursion Tours in

[15] For more on the extent to which English was spoken in Norway, see ch. 3, pp.
254–60.

Norway as in Switzerland, Germany and other parts of the Continent, because there are so few towns in the interior of the country for the accommodation of large parties. If more than ten or twelve come to a station to sleep at night, it is a question whether beds could be procured. I think, however, small parties might be arranged for (Cook 1866, 10).

Still, in the course of the next couple of decades, there is a sharp increase in the number of visitors, and correspondingly of travelogues. 'Sixty-One', the pseudonymous author of the book *A Trip to Norway in 1873*, characterises Norway as 'that land that has been described, and crossed and recrossed, and camped, and touristed, and knapsacked ad infinitum' (Sixty-One 1874, ix). W. Mattieu Williams, who travels *Through Norway with Ladies* in 1876, similarly emphasises, though with a note of sadness, the changes which have taken place since his first visit twenty years earlier:

> The very great development of tourist traffic throughout Norway during the last twenty years has, of course, effected considerable innovations upon the old primitive simplicity of tourists' accommodation.
>
> On all the leading highways the stations have lost more or less of their old farmhouse character. The traveller does not now share the supper of the bonder and his housemen in the heavy timbered smoke-stained kitchen, but is provided with special apartments built on purpose for his accommodation, and fitted up as luxuriously as the ideas and means of their peasant proprietors admit.
>
> The tourist who would now repeat my experiences of 1856 must step quite aside from the beaten tracks. By doing so, he may still find the primitive Norwegian habits unaltered, and enjoy magnificent scenery that is even now almost unexplored (Williams 1877, 353).

An interesting piece of statistical information in this connection is provided by S. Golder, one of the first cycling tourists and the author of *A Tandem Tour of Norway*, who during his visit to Bergen the previous year stayed at Smeby's Hotel. In the three-month period from 1 July to 1 October 1887 this hotel had as many as 559 English and Scotch visitors, 119 Norwegians, nine Germans, seven Australians, four Danes, three Dutchmen, two Russians and two Cubans: 'This shows', according to the author, 'that the English are, as usual, to the fore' (Golder 1888, 89). In *The Adventures of Five Spinsters in Norway*, Edith Rhodes, Cecil Rhodes's elder sister, also relates that she visited the 'Picture-Gallery' in Bergen, and '[t]here is a book here of the people who have visited the gallery; we were so amused to see a lot of names we knew' (Rhodes 1886, 48). And in Sande, a small village in the county of Sogn og Fjordane, she finds

English newspapers: 'the *Field, Graphic, Daily Telegraph*, which is a refinement I have seen nowhere else' (ibid., 119). But also the names of hotels give a strong indication of the nationalities to which they were primarily catering. The main hotels in Trondheim, according to 'Three Girls', seem to be the Britannia Hotel and the Hotel d'Angleterre, the latter presumably offering French cuisine to British visitors! The same names appear in Christiania, together with the Victoria Hotel.

Finally, in the accounts of the 1890s, one almost senses the advent of the twentieth century. At Haukeliseter, in the virtually unpopulated part of Telemark, Edward J. Goodman encounters people 'from Bayswater and Kensington, from Manchester and Liverpool' (Goodman 1892, 307). One also senses the outline of a Norway radically different from that which met the first travellers a hundred years earlier. John Bradshaw, in *Norway: Its Fjords, Fjelds and Fields*, gives expression to the change that has taken place:

> Slow though the process has been of opening up Norway, there is now abundant evidence that a new order of things is reigning. Sleepiness is being aroused from its slumber, more life, more vigour, a bolder spirit, and a keen insight into futurity is being manifested. Where, a little more than a decade ago, there was practically nothing in the way of accommodation in the country districts, except of the scantiest, most limited and most primitive kind. Now, there are new hotels springing up in every direction. (…) There can be no doubt that the Norwegians are at last awakening to the fact that they have got something to offer to the public which cannot fail to be appreciated at its proper value, providing they themselves do something towards procuring proper facilities and increased comforts. This the Norwegians appear to be striving for, with an earnestness and determination that does them infinite credit.
>
> Improvements are now in constant operation, and in a few years time there will, as compared with a few years ago, be quite a transformation scene. Older travellers in these parts will marvel at the greatness of the change, and the comparative ease with which they will be able to get over the ground, to say nothing of the improvement in hotel catering and accommodation – a very important matter these days. This all-round improvement must necessarily continue, for the trip to the Land of the Vikings is fast becoming one of the most popular of summer tours (Bradshaw 1896, 49–50).

In 1893, Miss L. Vickers similarly describes a scene that would have been unthinkable a few decades earlier. Travelling, in modern fashion, together with a group of fourteen other tourists on board the 'Albano', she relates how the party, on their way back to England, are photographed in traditional Norwegian costumes:

> When the photographing was finished, there was an auction on deck, and
> a large collection of articles were put up for sale, including a Hardanger
> ladies' dress, a spinning wheel, many framed Norwegian views, which
> had before adorned the saloons of the vessel; also little curios, deck
> chairs, novels and periodicals, for which their owners had no further use
> and various other articles (Vickers 1893, 140).

Norway had literally become a packaged commodity or product,
which was marketed and sold by professional operators whose image
of the country was bound to be very different from that of the free-
wheeling traveller. On a less cynical note, there is no doubt that these
operators also contributed strongly to a wider awareness of Norway
amongst the British public, especially towards the end of the century.

This awareness also spilt over into the areas of literature, art and
popular culture, and there is, not surprisingly, a close correspondence
between the increase in the number of travellers and that of novels,
poems, articles and other material connected with Norway in the
latter decades of the 1800s.

In the area of pictorial arts, the attention naturally focused on the
Norwegian landscape, both because this constituted the primary
attraction of Norway and because the landscape picture was in vogue
at the time. The main channel through which Norwegian scenery was
made available to the British audience was, again, the travelogues. In
the early decades of the century, there were published a few large-
format works of plates, containing little or no text, the most famous
being *Boydell's Picturesque Scenery of Norway* (1820), a large two-
volume publication with eighty full-page colour aquatints by John
William Edy; Edward Price's *Norway: Views of Wild Scenery* (1834);
Views in Norway (1849) by Michael Biddulph; and James Randell's
Views in Norway from Original Pictures (1854). Naturally, these
works were expensive and printed in very limited editions. Far more
important, therefore, for the dissemination of a visual impression of
Norway, were the ordinary, small-format travel accounts, a large
majority of which were illustrated, frequently by competent artists.
These illustrations, then, were bound to reach a far broader audience
than the more exclusive works of plates.

In addition, there were also a number of professional painters who
contributed to a wider interest in and knowledge of Norway. Few of
these are now known by name, but Olivia Stone mentions in the early
1880s that

English landscape-painters avail themselves of Norway far more than Norwegians, and each year the Royal Academy, Dudley, the Water-Colour, and other galleries, hang more Norwegian subjects than I should think were ever seen in Christiania. One can only hope that in future the art of Norway may be worthy of her nature (Stone 1882, 433).

One of these painters was the Bristol-based William West (1801–1861) who was for a long time more famous for his contributions to Clifton's Camera Obscura and the Clifton Suspension Bridge than for his paintings. However, according to the art historian Francis Greenacre, he 'was soon to earn the title of "Norway West" and from 1847 he exhibited many views in [sic] Norway' (Greenacre 1973, 195). Greenacre does not indicate the whereabouts of West's pictures, but adds that '[t]he watercolours of Norwegian rivers imitate Ruisdael in their composition and are of poor quality' (ibid.). Similarly, it is not known whether West ever visited Norway or whether he found inspiration from other artists.

The latter is no doubt a possibility, because at least one of West's paintings has been wrongly attributed to a contemporary of his, also based in Bristol, who is known to have visited Norway. Francis Danby (1793–1861) probably came to Norway for the first time in the summer of 1825, only to make a second visit in 1840, and during this period produced several pictures inspired by the Norwegian landscape, the most famous being the dark and monumental oil painting 'Liensfjord, Norway' (ca. 1835), which is now in the Victoria and Albert Museum in London. In his study of Danby, Eric Adams claims that he 'had done something new by adding Norway to the Alps and the north of England as a source of romantic landscape' (Adams 1973, 54). Furthermore, there are close similarities, which did not pass unnoticed by critics, between Danby and his more famous contemporary John Martin. Accusations of plagiarism were launched against Danby, but also by Danby against Martin. Adams comments that

Danby's critics frequently noticed that while his more extravagant fantasies resembled those of Martin, they were more closely based on observation of natural effects, and it is plain that his conception of the *Sixth Seal* owed something to his familiarity with the high mountainous wastes of Norway, which he recorded in drawings like the *Cascade in Norway*, and adapted for the purpose of biblical illustration in *The Israelites Led by the Pillar of Fire by Night* (ibid., 56).

It is possible, then, that the dramatic landscapes in some of Danby's major works, and perhaps in some of Martin's, may at least in part be attributed to an inspiration from the west coast of Norway, which Danby is known to have visited.

Just as painters and print makers turned their eyes to Norway, so too did authors of popular novels. 'Three Girls' – i.e. Violet Crompton-Roberts – states in the Preface to her book *A Jubilee Jaunt to Norway* that 'there really *does* seem to be a demand for light reading on Norway' ('Three Girls' 1888, v), and one of her friends adds: "'I have written to Mudie's, to ask him to send me books on Norway; as, like all the world, we mean to be in fashion, and go there this autumn; and I can't get any'" (ibid.). Whether 'I can't get any' suggests that there never were any books on Norway or whether they had all been borrowed remains a mute point, but later in the same book it is stated with emphasis that 'Norway is becoming more "the rage" every year' (ibid., 92), and with respect to light reading it is not surprising to find that the 'Three Girls' also mention Marie Corelli's vastly successful novel *Thelma: A Society Novel*, which had been published the year before, and whose subtitle in later editions was *A Norwegian Princess*.[16] In addition, at the back of *A Jubilee Jaunt to Norway*, there are excerpts from various newspapers, one of which claims that books on Norway 'are nowadays in demand by many tourists who flock every summer to the fjords' (*The Scotsman*, 27 August 1888). Mention should also be made of a considerably earlier novel, namely Harriet Martineau's *Feats on the Fiord: A Tale of Norway* which, though first published in 1841, continued to be reprinted for the rest of the century and into the first decade of the next. Martineau (1802–1876), a public figure of some note and a friend of the Wordsworths, should not be underestimated as a promoter of Norway among British readers. Then in the years around 1890, there were published a series of fictional works, such as Edna Lyall's *A Hardy Norseman* (1889) and Durham Griffith's *An Arctic Eden: A Tale of Norway* (1892), together with several collections of short stories by George Egerton, all of which involve contemporary British and Norwegian characters and settings in addition to

---

[16] According to Mains, *Thelma* went through as many as fifty-six editions (Mains 1989, 129). The change of subtitle from *A Society Novel* (in the first edition) to *A Norwegian Princess* may in itself be seen as an indication of the marketing potential of everything Norwegian at the end of the century. More curiously, and possibly as an indication of the novel's literary qualities, it may also be mentioned that *Thelma* was translated into Urdu as late as in 1972! See further discussions of the novel in chs. 2 and 4.

intercultural love stories, emphasising and implicitly encouraging an intimate relationship between the two countries. On an advertisement page of an American edition of *A Hardy Norseman*, the author, whose real name was Ada Ellen Bayly (1857–1903), is described as 'one of the best of the new novelists. Her portrait will appear in the May number of the *Fashion Bazar*' (not paginated).

Despite the contemporary praise of Edna Lyall and the fact that *A Hardy Norseman* even to a modern reader displays a number of literary qualities, she never really acquired a place in the top division of writers, and even though a biography was published immediately after her death (see Escreet 1904), her name soon faded out of view in the changing literary landscape of the new century. Paradoxically, George Egerton (1859–1945) suffered a similar fate, despite being closely associated with the burgeoning Modernist movement. Like Lyall, Egerton published her books pseudonymously. Her real name was Mary Chavelita Dunne, and her connections with Norway purely coincidental, in the sense that she eloped to Langesund on the Telemark coast together with her lover, Henry Peter Higginson, in 1887, apparently without any previous contacts with the country. While in Norway, Egerton 'read avidly the works of Ibsen, Bjørnson, Strindberg and the young Knut Hamsun' (Stetz 1982, 5), and in 1893, after a number of rather enigmatic encounters with Knut Hamsun (ref. Fjågesund 2002), she published her first collection of short-stories, *Keynotes*, which became a rather formidable success, selling more than 6,000 copies in the first year. This was followed in 1894 by *Discords* and in 1897 by *Symphonies*. All of these three collections contain stories set in Norway, as does her epistolary novel *Rosa-Amorosa* (1901), which is based on the author's love affair with a Norwegian student in Christiania in the autumn of 1899. It should also be mentioned that Egerton translated Hamsun's first novel *Hunger*, which was eventually published in London in 1899, nine years after the original.[17]

As indicated above, despite experiencing a sudden leap to fame, enjoying the somewhat mixed pleasure of being caricatured in *Punch*, and being generally, though in her opinion unjustly, associated with the assertive type of the 'New Woman', Egerton was not for long in the public eye. Still, she serves as a useful reminder of an important cultural and intellectual movement which is closely associated with the 1880s and 1890s, and in which Norway and Scandinavia in

---

[17] For a discussion of Egerton's significance for late nineteenth-century literature in general, see Bjørhovde 1987, 129–67.

general played a crucial role. In the standard work *Modernism 1890—1930* (1976), the editors Malcolm Bradbury and James McFarlane emphasise that '[i]n trying to pin Modernism down – tentatively and crudely – in terms of men, books and years, attention is first drawn to Scandinavia (...)' (37). Even though this was not a broad, popular movement, it still forms an important element in an attempt to explain the British awareness of Norway and Scandinavia at the time, especially because Britain, in this particular context, was in the unusual position of receiving rather than giving these fresh cultural impulses. The main Norwegian representative of these ideas in Britain, however, was not Hamsun. Whereas in Germany he acquired a large and popular appeal from the early 1890s onwards, in Britain he was somewhat crudely subsumed within the group of avant-garde writers of the Decadent movement, as Tore Rem has shown (see Rem 2002). It is rather Henrik Ibsen who is the great Norwegian standard bearer in what Bradbury and McFarlane call 'the Modern Breakthrough'. This is not to say that Ibsen plays any significant role in the British travelogues of the period. On the contrary, he is conspicuously absent. Considering the fact that the majority of travel writers came from the segment of society that could safely be called the Establishment, it is perhaps not surprising that they would prefer to ignore a man who 'was asserting that individual fulfilment depended upon deciding for oneself – and, if necessary, deciding in defiance of every established social norm' (Biddis 1978, 149). Whilst it may not have been appreciated by the British Establishment at the time, the cultural challenge that came out of Norway during these decades suggested very strongly that the country was standing on its own feet and was capable of independent and critical thinking.[18] And so, incidentally, it proved that it possessed those very qualities of rugged individualism that the British liked to celebrate in themselves as a legacy of their Viking ancestors. And indeed, the Viking age formed an important background for a large number of popular novels, children's books and poems which established a significant point of contact between nineteenth-century Norway and the distant past. This, however, will be discussed in more detail in ch. 2.

---

[18] The related subject of the reception of Norwegian literature in Britain in the late nineteenth century is beyond the scope of this book, but may be studied in some detail in Brian W. Downs's article 'Anglo-Norwegian Literary Relations 1867–1900' (1952), which also provides a good catalogue, and chronological survey, of English translations of Norwegian works.

Health and Sport

Like all travellers' destinations, Norway in the nineteenth century
represented a number of different attractions which, put together,
encouraged thousands of Britons, who meant 'to be in fashion', to
visit the country. Some of these attractions have already been touched
upon and others will form the topics of the following chapters. There
are, however, some more specific pull factors which form integral
parts of the image of Norway that was presented to the British public.
A common denominator for all of these is that of healthy, outdoor
activity, i.e. an activity closely connected with individual freedom
and absence from the hustle and bustle of civilisation. It is interesting
to note, however, that many travel accounts do not make it clear
whether Norway is primarily a remedy for the stresses and strains of
modern life or for a general sense of *ennui* (after all, there is no doubt
that the massive growth of tourism in the nineteenth century was in
various ways connected with the fact that larger segments of the
population acquired more spare time and, as a consequence, more
'time to kill').

There are certainly indications that Norway was used either as a
place which would prevent illness, or as a place of recuperation from
it. In Edna Lyall's novel *A Hardy Norseman*, the young woman Cecil
Boniface, who has lost two sisters and herself has a 'consumptive
look' (Lyall 1890, 54), is sent with her brother 'to healthy old
Norway, to gain there fresh physical strength and fresh insights into
that puzzling thing called life (...)' (ibid., 6). Somewhat surprisingly,
however, it is primarily the professional tourist operators late in the
century who, supported by scientific evidence, recommend Norway
as a place for the sick. A Thomas Cook brochure from 1897 claims
that

> [t]he rapid increase of balneology in Europe during the beginning of our
> century, aided by the development of chemistry and the foundation of
> hydro-therapeutics, also extended to the northern countries; and as this
> movement happened contemporaneously with the revival of the nation to
> an independent life, it was natural enough that its earliest manifestations
> included the establishment of the first proper Norwegian health-resort,
> namely the seaside baths of Moss in 1835, and the sulphur baths at
> Sandefjord, 1837 (Cook 1897, 37).

And later in the same article:

Everywhere the quietude and perfect rest so beneficial to the invalid is found. Even the most restless mind will after a short stay begin to feel the soothing influence of the calm and placid surroundings of such a retreat. Entirely removed from the enervating excitements inseparable from the popular health-resorts and watering-places of the outside world, there is nothing to disturb the progressive restoration of health. There is no restraint, no fear of trespassing anywhere. Nobody interferes, and the stranger is undisturbed in his contemplation of arcadian harmony. (…) Everything contributes to give rest and peace to overwrought brains and nerves. An eminent English therapeutist has made the characteristic remark that 'The whole art of the physician consists in procuring rest for the patient.' No place can be more suitable for that purpose than Norway (ibid., 39–40).

According to Alan Wykes, precisely the same argument was still being used in a 1913 edition of Thomas Bennett's guidebook *Norway* (Wykes 1973, 39). This confirms James Buzard's claim that travel had become 'a medicine for the troubled mind' and 'a tonic all the more necessary in a utilitarian world that stultifies the deepest sources of imaginative life' (Buzard 1993, 102). Still, Jean A. Mains argues that relatively few came to Norway explicitly for reasons of health:

The fortunate came to Holmenkollen, then one of the best hospitals in Europe. A few miles north-west of Oslo, the sanatorium stood on a hill with a southern exposure at an altitude of 1000 ft. (…) The exhalations of its surrounding pinewoods were believed to be therapeutic. In these optimum conditions, the sanatorium specialised in the treatment of asthma, bronchitis, lung diseases, heart conditions, mental disorders, insomnia and general convalescence (Mains 1989, 19).

Thus, for the large majority, the primary object of going to Norway was the 'free enjoyment of the scenery of this romantic country' (Forester 1850, iv), or as Edith Rhodes puts it: 'To any one fond of out of doors I say, Come to Norway if you want a month of perfectly free, sunshiny, healthy life' (Rhodes 1886, 106). That there is an element of escape in this celebration of life in the open wild is evident from Robert Pritchett's account, where he even admits to an urge to get away not just from the place but also from the time in which he lives: 'Our delight is to live out of the present century in fresh air and simplicity' (Pritchett 1879, 13).

Fishing and hunting were perhaps the most important elements in the marketing of Norway as the place for the active sportsman. There is a considerable literature on and by British salmon-fishers in Norway, but as these accounts are of a relatively limited interest to anyone but the angler, they will be dealt with only in passing here. A central work is *Field Sports of the North of Europe*, which was published as early as 1830 and reprinted several times during the century. The author was Llewellyn Lloyd (1792–1876), the son of a wealthy London banker, who travelled extensively in Norway in 1823. Three years later he moved to Sweden, where he lived until his death. *Field Sports*, whose subtitle in later editions was *A Narrative of Angling, Hunting, and Shooting in Sweden and Norway*, probably contributed strongly to the awareness in Britain of the opportunity for sport – in the nineteenth century sense of the word – in Norway.

At the same time, i.e. from the 1830s onwards, Norwegian salmon rivers such as the Alten (now Alta) and the Namsen were discovered by the so-called 'salmon lords'. The obsessive angler William Bilton's account from 1840, *Two Summers in Norway*, is one of the early examples of this sub-category of travelogues. Bilton, who rather quickly concludes his comments on Norwegian history and society in order to turn to the 'piscatorial capabilities' of the country, appears to have visited the Namsen both in 1837 and 1839. Like a child let loose in a toy shop, he lists his catch with an enthusiasm that for the non-angler may appear rather monotonous: 'None but Salmon of the largest size were moving: I killed five, which together weighed 117 pounds, an extraordinary average; and I besides rose seven others of at least equal calibre. One the biggest [*sic*] (of twenty-four pounds) being hooked foul, gave me great trouble to land' (Bilton 1840, 1: 258). And a few pages later:

> It will be seen by the list appended to the second volume, that I fished parts of thirty-one consecutive days, on the Namsen, excepting Sundays: four of these proved *blank*, owing chiefly to the Seals and the weather: but in the remaining twenty-seven days, I caught 106 Salmon, which together weighed 1558 pounds; besides twelve white trout, thirty-six pounds. Nine of the Salmon weighed thirty pounds and upwards; thirty-three, or nearly one third of the whole, weighed twenty pounds and upwards, each (ibid., 277).

The chaplain at the British consulate in Christiania, the Reverend Mourdant R. Barnard, on the other hand, gives a far more informative – and entertaining – description in his *Sketches of Life, Scenery, and Sport in Norway* from 1871, by providing insights into the changing social background of the anglers. By this time, the salmon fishers are no longer just an exclusive group of lords who had bought the rights to entire rivers for next to nothing, but men – and even women – from various walks of life. While ignoring the focus on the weight and

The Stige-steen, or Ladder Rock.

One of the many 'salmon lords' who came to Norway from the 1830s onwards. Several of them developed close and permanent ties to the country, coming back on an annual basis, and buying property and shares in salmon rivers. Illustration from Pritchett (1879).

numbers of the salmon caught, he relates instead how this particular obsession even has an impact on the social life in London itself:

At a certain season of the year, we usually miss sundry of our acquaintances from town. Just as symptoms of a shady side to Pall-Mall become apparent – just as white hats come in, and we begin to wonder whether or no one could relish a snug little feed at the Star and Garter, or at the Crown and Sceptre, fellows seem to drop out of society, as it were, most mysteriously. The well-known piccadillies no longer grace the windows or portico of the Rag, and the halls of Poole cease to echo their familiar tones. For a week or two previously you might meet De Browne rushing in and out of Fortnum and Mason's as though he had taken long odds against his doing it a certain number of times in a certain number of half hours; while, if you drop into Fitz-Smythe's rooms, you are labelled with his ancient and noble patronymic, deal boxes of a most preposterous length compared to their disproportionately narrow dimensions, which are commingled somehow with a vile smell of new macintoshes; and the lively O'Flaherty's den will be choked probably with a huge canvas concern that looks all over like emigration and Robinson Crusoe combined. A week or so after, and, 'Where's De Browne?' 'Gone to Norway, salmon-fishing.' – 'What has become of Fitz-Smythe?' 'Oh! he's off to the Namsen.' – 'Who knows where O'Flaherty is?' The sheriff of Middlesex isn't regarded in the Loffodens, and the Caucasian race never can face the Arctic Circle, so O'Flaherty's safe for two months to come.' – 'And who's seen – ?' 'Oh! she's off to the Tana, too, with Charley Naughtiboy. He's rigged her out in knicker-bockers and a garibaldi, and she makes a capital man – wouldn't know the difference! haw, haw! No end of fun. I'm going with a yacht-load of fellahs next week. Make one?' Such and such conversation betokens the now annual rush of Englishmen, &c., to Norway, in search of what O'Flaherty calls 'diversion.' (Barnard 1871, 139–40).

This diversion frequently consisted – at least for those who could afford it – of a combination of fishing and hunting. Lord Garvagh, member of an old Irish salmon-lord family who had visited Norway for three generations, is a typical representative of this particular kind of traveller. In October 1872, this twenty-year-old 'B.A. Christ Church, Oxford, Member of the Alpine Club' (Garvagh 1875, title page) arrives in Bergen and takes a boat to a place he names Urland (probably either Urnes or Aurland), deep into the Sognefjorden, where he intends to fish salmon and hunt reindeer. Equipped with snow shoes and assisted by local helpers who have been 'in the service of the family for many years' (ibid., 155), he climbs up to one of the mountain cabins which his father has had built specifically for reindeer hunting. Bad weather drives the group back down to the valley, but Lord Garvagh's account in *The Pilgrim of Scandinavia* (1875) still gives a good indication of the kind of rough out-door life pursued by many travellers in Norway.

Barnard also comments on the opportunities for hunting, and mentions in particular Bratsberg Amt (i.e. the present Telemark County) as a superb area for bear hunting: 'Bears are numerous throughout the province; the average number killed being 33 $^{11/15}$ per annum; and I would almost recommend any one desirous of enjoying some bear-hunting to select this Amt in preference to any other in the whole of Norway' (Barnard 1864, 68–69). He also provides interesting statistics for the whole of Norway for the period 1846–1860. During these fifteen years there were killed on average 230 bears, 120 lynxes and 3,230 eagles every year. At a time when Britain was rapidly exhausting its areas of wildlife, Norway thus must have seemed a virtual paradise for hunters.[19] Although conditions changed fairly dramatically towards the end of the century, especially regarding bears, which became very nearly extinct, Frederick Metcalfe's chart of 'wild animals destroyed in Norway' in the 1848–1850 period fully confirms that Barnard's information can be trusted:

	Bears	Wolves	Lynxes	Gluttons	Eagles	Owls	Hawks
1848	264	247	144	57	2,498	369	527
1849	325	197	110	76	2,142	343	485
1850	246	191	118	39	2,426	268	407

Communication

'Without this commodity it is impossible to get on in the northern parts; and the quantity of it that was consumed during my tour is almost incredible' (Brooke 1823, 216). This matter-of-fact remark – on brandy – by Arthur de Capell Brooke goes to show that travel does not just consist of breathtaking scenery and memorable views of buildings and people; it also has a very practical side. For instance, in Finnmark, which is what Brooke means by 'the northern parts',

---

[19] It is only typical that Dickens, in his description of Mr. Headstone's pursuit of Eugene through the streets of London in *Our Mutual Friend* (1864-65), creates an ironic and highly urban version of the British obsession with hunting, the 'British sportsman', and 'the pleasures of the chase' (Dickens 1997, 533).

brandy appears to be what petrol is these days: a necessary commodity for getting from one place to another.

Brooke's remark is also a useful reminder of how different the conditions for travel were in the nineteenth century in comparison with today. This was true particularly in the first few decades of the century, but also later in certain parts of the country. Furthermore, it should be remembered that these difficult travelling conditions also had a bearing on the structure and form of the travelogues themselves. In his book *That Sunny Dome*, which primarily deals with Regency Britain, Donald A. Low points out that

> most of those who wrote about their journeys had covered at least some part of the ground they described on horseback or on foot. As a result, they knew intimately the land which their readers wished to learn about, and the human scale of their experience is reflected in their writing. It was the last age of the horse, and of relatively unhurried travelling. With the coming of steam, those who published *Tours* and diaries of their travels would rely more on hastily made notes and on secondhand information, less on thorough familiarity with the villages and fields lying between places large enough to have railway stations (Low 1977, 175–76).

The nineteenth century, then, offers a fascinating transition from one mode of travel to another, and Norway, being behind Britain and the Continent in the development of modern means of transport, stands out yet again as different from the European norm. It is perfectly possible, therefore, that the nostalgia for the past, which is clearly one of the main reasons for Norway's appeal, was partly connected with the fact that this country offered a traditional mode of travel. This was then again associated with qualities that were popular at the time, such as simplicity and closeness to nature.

This ideal is perhaps most clearly expressed in the Romantic and Victorian celebration of the peripatetic. Whereas in the eighteenth century walking had been regarded as socially degrading, primarily because associated with poverty and vagrancy, the nineteenth century – inspired by Romantic philosophy – had a keen sense of the quality of man's direct contact with the elements. In *Walking, Literature, and English Culture: The Origins and Uses of Peripatetic in the Nineteenth Century*, Anne D. Wallace underlines how nineteenth-century writers elevate walking into a sort of meditation:

> Essays by William Hazlitt, Henry David Thoreau, John Burroughs, Robert Louis Stevenson, and Leslie Stephen, although differing in detail,

all argue that the natural, primitive quality of the physical act of walking restores the natural proportions of our perceptions, reconnecting us with both the physical world and the moral order inherent in it, and enabling us to recollect both our personal past and our national and/or racial past – that is, human life before mechanization. As a result, the walker may expect an enhanced sense of self, clearer thinking, more acute moral apprehension, and higher powers of expression (Wallace 1993, 13).

As might be expected, these qualities are primarily associated with the individualistic and slow-moving traveller – or on this case wanderer – as opposed to the tourist, whose restless roaming from place to place requires a fast and efficient means of conveyance. As Wallace points out, this new and nostalgic attitude to walking is naturally inconceivable without precisely the transport revolution which took place from the end of the eighteenth century onwards. It was only when public transport had been made available to virtually everyone, that walking again could be made, in a sense, exclusive. There is, in other words, something deliberately backward-looking or conservative about this popularity of walking, which Wallace also regards as a protest against the enclosures and the destruction of the natural landscape of the late 1700s and early 1800s, 'for English common law provides that public use itself creates public right of way. Thus walkers on a public footpath were, by means of walking itself, unenclosing that path, reappropriating it to common use and preserving a portion of the old landscape against change' (ibid., 10). Thus Wordsworth is very much in line with contemporary fashion when in the thirteen-book *Prelude* of 1805 he says: 'A favourite pleasure hath it been with me / From time of earliest youth to walk alone / Along the public way (...)' (Wordsworth 1995, Book iv, ll. 363–65). A similar point about the quasi-democratic and quasi-egalitarian aspect of walking is made by Rebecca Solnit in her book *Wanderlust: A History of Walking*: 'By the late nineteenth century the word *tramp* as both noun and verb was popular among the walking writers, as was *vagabond* and *gypsy* (...), but to play at tramp or gypsy is one way of demonstrating that you are not really one' (Solnit 2001, 123–24).

It is perfectly in line with this overall attitude to walking that a number of the early travellers to Norway cheerfully accepted that they had come to a country where public communication was non-existent, and where roads – at least in the interior – were only fit for the most primitive vehicles. Charles B. Elliott, for instance, appears to have walked across most of southern Norway, including the

Hardangervidda, in the summer of 1830, and during his stay in Bergen it is with enthusiasm rather than frustration that he describes the plans for his arduous journey:

> The scenery of this country is indescribable. (...) I had intended to proceed from Christiania to Stockholm, but Norway possesses a power of fascination which has proved irresistible. (...) There are no diligences, and comparatively no travelling; for the towns of this country have far less communication with each other than with foreign states: and the journey from Bergen to Christiania, which I hope to commence on Monday, is undertaken by scarcely a dozen people in a year. A Norwegian resident of this town has just told me that he does not remember to have seen here more than one English traveller during the last five years (Elliott 1832, 99–100).

As the reader soon learns to expect from Elliott, his walking is presented as a unique and solitary feat, in splendid isolation from the collective throng of others. Again, it is interesting to note that this is a decade or two after British roads had been made subject for the first time to the modern road-building techniques of Thomas Telford and John McAdam. Elliott, in other words, appears to have made a conscious choice to seek the most out-of-the-way wilds of a country which, at the time, was famous precisely for its inaccessibility. But even a couple of decades later, travellers like Frederick Metcalfe and W. Mattieu Williams sought out similar areas, the latter also suggesting the element of walking in the title of his frequently reprinted book, *Through Norway with a Knapsack*. Besides, Williams's itinerary left few other options than going on foot:

> Start for a rough walk over the Haukelid Fjeld into the Tellemark, the most uncivilized region of Norway. (...) There is a rudimentary road for about a mile out of Röldal which gradually degenerates into a track about a foot wide, and presently to mere shoe-wearings upon the rock; and even this track is lost altogether at the crossing of every bog, of which there are many (Williams 1859, 254).

However, the most spectacular proof that walking was not beneath even the most elevated is provided by Lady Brassey, who in *The Contemporary Review* of October 1885 reports on the Norwegian journey of the seventy-five-year-old Prime Minister William Gladstone. When the party arrived at Eidfjord in the Brassys' yacht in order to visit the famous Vøringsfossen, Gladstone and some of the men decided to walk up the steep and inaccessible Måbødalen rather than go in a carriole. At 8.30 p.m., according to Lady Brassey, they were back on board, having walked eighteen miles to see the waterfall:

> [A] hardish day's work for any one, but really a wonderful undertaking for a man of seventy-five, who disdained all proffered help, and insisted on walking the whole distance. No one who saw Mr. Gladstone that evening at dinner, in the highest spirit, and discussing subjects both grave and gay with the greatest animation, could fail to admire his marvellous pluck and energy (…) (Brassey 1885, 491).

Romantic notions about walking, however, did not mean that most travellers were uninterested in the standard of Norwegian roads. On the contrary, it is an omnipresent topic, but one that still leaves the modern reader somewhat puzzled. There are at least two prominent and trustworthy witnesses from as early as the 1790s to the effect that the roads were of a perfectly acceptable quality. Having published his famous *Essay on the Principle of Population* in the previous year, Thomas Robert Malthus in 1799 made a rather extensive journey through the eastern part of Norway, visiting Christiania and Kongsberg before going north to Trondheim. In his *Travel Diaries*, which were only discovered and published in the 1960s, he remarks on the journey through Gudbrandsdalen: 'The road for the two or three last stages had still continued very good, tho with some steep pitches. It must have been formed in many parts at a great expense. I understand that the present road has not been finished above 7 or 8 years. It was almost impassable before' (Malthus 1966, 130). Similarly, Mary Wollstonecraft comments that the roads between Larvik and Tønsberg 'were very good; the farmers are obliged to repair them; and we scampered through a great extent of country in a more improved state than any I had viewed since I had left England' (Wollstonecraft 1987, 98).

It should be noted, however, that both Malthus's and Wollstonecraft's comments refer to main roads in relatively central parts of the country.[20] From Kongsberg further into the interior of Telemark, for instance, the accounts generally concur that the roads

---

[20] Incidentally, Malthus's characterisation may be compared to that of his travel companion, Edward Daniel Clarke, concerning the road to Kongsberg. In his multi-volume *Travels in Various Countries of Europe, Asia and Africa* (1824), which is partly based on Malthus's own diaries, he states with conviction that '[t]he roads were very bad, and at this season of the year rendered almost impassable by the depth of the mud which covered them' (Clarke 1824, 10: 415–16).

are hardly worthy of the name. William Henry Breton, travelling in 1834, claims that this is 'one of the very worst public tracks in Norway' (Breton 1835, 325). Also near Tyrifjorden in the late 1830s, William Bilton encounters another recurring problem in a country full of unruly waterways:

> The floods, which are usual in the early part of the summer, is [sic] consequence of the melting snows, had carried away most of the bridges, and torn up some of the road: so that we were frequently obliged to make our way, as best we could, across fields, and through intricate places, which nothing but the lightness of our vehicles joined to great labour and perseverance, enabled us to surmount (Bilton 1840, 1: 141).

Even as late as the 1870s, a number of areas, and in particular Telemark and the far north, were regarded as close to inaccessible, thereby paradoxically increasing, as has been suggested earlier, their attractiveness as mysterious regions begging to be explored. However, this was not a view shared by all travellers. Augustus Hare, clearly not enjoying his too close encounters with the Telemark landscape, gives a vivid picture of his dramatic journey in 1878:

> But what roads, or rather what want of roads, lead to Tinoset! – there were banks of glassy rock, up which our horses scrambled like cats; there were awful moments when everything seemed to come to an end, and when they gathered up their legs, and seemed to fling themselves down headlong with the carriage on the top of them, and yet we reached the bottom of the abyss buried in dust, to rise gasping and gulping and wondering we were alive, to begin the same pantomime over again (Hare 1885, 111–12).

A few years later, and in the same area, M. Paterson complains that '[r]oad there was none over this tract, but a mere scratch upon its obdurate surface, and the cariole made its way up the steep and slippery ascent, across broad white sheets of rock, sometimes so slant in cross-section as to tilt it to an angle, which, had I been inside, might have been alarming' (Paterson 1886, 283). Coming from the Britain of the 1850s, where roads and railways were cutting through Tennyson's 'scarpèd cliff and quarried stone' and crossing valleys in the form of enormous bridges, John George Hollway regards the Norwegian roads with the eyes of an impatient modern engineer and with a pronounced sense of irony:

> In ordinary engineering, difficulties are avoided if possible – if

impossible to avoid, overcome; but in Norwegian road-making it would actually seem as if difficult places were sought for, not to overcome, but to come over. The directions for laying out a true Norwegian country road would run somewhat in this way: – 'To make a road from A to B. – Select, if possible, somewhere between the two places, a range of hills (if not directly between the given termini, but a little out of the way, so much the better); take one of these hills (the highest for preference), and conduct your road over the extreme top of it: – care should be taken in selecting the hill that it should be one the sides of which are as rocky and uneven as possible; this will give a pleasing variety to the levels of the road, and will allow the traveller time to appreciate the scenery, by detaining him on his way about twice as long as need be' (Hollway 1853, 41–42).

Against this background, S. C. Hammer is not far from the truth when he claims that '[d]own to the middle of the nineteenth century, the conditions of travelling in Norway as well as the means of conveyance were in all essentials the same as they had been since the Middle Ages (…)' (Hammer 1928, 3). But it is also true that major changes were taking place precisely at this time. Thus, the following passage from Thomas Forester's *Norway in 1848 and 1849* can be regarded as representative of the age:

Soon, then, the silence of those untrodden forests will be broken by the ringing stroke of the woodman's axe; and those passes, through which we toiled with so much difficulty, will be rapidly threaded by the light carriole. But if future tourists should find their progress through scenes which must always be eminently attractive thus facilitated, we, their pioneers, may perhaps rejoice in having drawn attention to them, and shall ourselves assuredly long retain the vivid impressions which our rambles in these wild districts, and our intercourse with the inhabitants, in their unfrequented and primitive state, are calculated to make (Forester 1850, 21).

Interestingly, Forester is aware that he finds himself at a watershed from which he can look to the past as well as to the future. The challenge and resistance posed by the wild Norwegian landscape is now, in 1850, an object of sentimentalism and nostalgia as it is disappearing under the march of progress, represented by 'the woodman's axe'. At the same time, however, he also regards the same scenes as becoming 'eminently attractive thus facilitated'. The same ambiguity is evident in Olivia Stone's observation from 1882 that the new roads are excellent, 'reducing the discomforts of road-travelling to a minimum; but', she adds significantly, 'we frequently found that

THE NÆRÖDAL.

The extensive road-building in the latter decades of the century made modern tourism possible, especially in the inaccessible parts of Western Norway. However, several travellers deplored the march of progress. This picture shows the Stalheimskleivi in Nærøydalen, in the Sognefjorden area. It was built for horse and carriage as early as 1840 and is still in use. From Lovett (1885).

the old roads led through by far the more beautiful and picturesque scenery, and passed houses older and quainter than those on the new' (Stone 1882, 316–17).

As the roads improved, walking and to some extent riding became less and less common, and the carriole, which in the early decades could only be used on the main roads, became the standard means of conveyance virtually all over the country. Regarded as a characteristically Norwegian invention, and frequently met with a considerable amount of initial scepticism, the carriole – a small open carriage for one person – is discussed in some detail in almost every single travelogue of the period. Lord Brassey, who later travelled in Norway with Gladstone, gives the following description, full of admiration for the ingenious little vehicle:

> The cariole would be a most comfortable conveyance anywhere; but it is impossible to conceive anything more perfectly adapted to meet the peculiar difficulties of the Norwegian roads. So light, so well balanced, and provided with an excellent substitute for springs in its long shafts, it glides over hills and through dales with the greatest ease and comfort (Brassey 1857, 65).

The female traveller S. H. Kent, author of *Within the Arctic Circle*, even goes so far as to claim that '[o]f all kinds of European travel (…) I am inclined to consider Norwegian cariole-driving as the most delightful mode of travelling (…)' (Kent 1877, 18). Waxing lyrical about the vehicle's simple but skillful construction, the journalist Edwin Arnold also makes an interesting comparison:

> There is something singularly akin in these same solitary conveyances to the melancholy and reserved dispositions of the Norwegians. Completely separated from your companions, you are forced in upon your own thoughts; and these often take their character, as is natural, from the lonely and sombre mountains through which you travel; while if you make any attempt at conversation, the wind or some thundering cataract allows but half your remarks to be heard – 'The rest disperse in empty air' (Arnold 1877, 44).

The carriole, in other words, represents not only an image of the personal characteristics of the Norwegians; it is also the perfect conveyance in which the romantic and solitary traveller, exposed to wind and weather but still protected by the narrow, coffin-like box, can commune with the natural surroundings. It could almost be seen as the perfect compromise between the ideal of walking and Landor's detested closed carriage, mentioned earlier.

The unanimous praise of the Norwegian carriole is also extended to the horses, which are invariably described as patient, sure-footed and generally superbly adapted to the variable and demanding topography of the country. Wollstonecraft remarks that 'indeed I have never met with better, if so good, post-horses, as in Norway; they are of a stouter make than the English horses, appear to be well fed, and are not easily tired' (Wollstonecraft 1987, 98). George Matthew Jones, a captain who travelled in Norway in the early 1820s, similarly claims that the Norwegian horses 'are a much finer race than those of Sweden, small but willing, generally of a light brown, with a black mark on the back. When at speed, they can only be stopped by a noise of the lips, which they obey in a moment (…)' (Jones 1827, 106). And Samuel Laing, in his highly influential *Journal of a Residence in Norway During the Years 1834, 1835, & 1836* (1837), regards them as 'beyond all praise': 'they scamper down hills as steep as a house roof, and in going up hill actually scramble. They make no objection whatever, if you have none, to any path or any pace; they are the bravest of horse kind' (Laing 1837, 25).

Thus, up to the middle of the nineteenth century, those who chose to travel in Norway were essentially performing what the critic Guglielmo Scaramellini calls 'picturesque voyaging', which comprised walking, horseback trips or journeys 'in carriages of animal traction; these modalities offered the opportunity to see the landscape in a manner that Wolfgang Schivelbusch refers to as "panoramic travelling"' (Scaramellini 1996, 50).[21]

As the century progressed, however, this mode of travel, which in the rest of Europe had already been on the wane for some time, also began to lose ground in the central parts of Norway, primarily due to the introduction of faster and more efficient means of transport. The first railway line opened between Christiania and Eidsvoll in 1854, nearly three decades after the Stockton & Darlington Railway in the north of England. British engineers were instrumental in planning and building the railway, and the whole operation, which took three years, was supervised by Robert Stephenson, the son of George Stephenson himself. The distance from the capitol to Eidsvoll was about forty miles; the journey took about two and a half hours, and with the steam ship on the sixty-mile long lake Mjøsa, about one third of the distance to Trondheim could now be travelled not only much

---

[21] For a more detailed discussion of the picturesque and the travellers' view of the Norwegian scenery, see ch. 4.

faster than before, but also in relative comfort. The success of the railway was soon apparent, and in the following decades a network of new lines was planned and built in various parts of the country, facilitating the transport of goods as well as of people. The critic Sir Edmund Gosse, for instance, reports enthusiastically in 1874 that

> in the summer of 1872, the very important railway connecting Christiania with the great timber port of Drammen was opened, and in 1873, the Storthing voted the expenses for a stupendous labour of engineering, the formation of a railway between Lillehammer, on the great central lake, and Trondheim, which, as a glance at the map will show, will throw the north and centre of the country open to trade in an extraordinary manner (Gosse 1874, 176).

A similar development took place with regard to travel at sea, but contrary to what one would expect in a seafaring nation, the Norwegians were slow to exploit the opportunities offered by the steam engine. The first two steamships, built in London, were in operation on the south coast from 1827 onwards, but up till the 1850s they were owned and run by the state, at a loss. In fact, the peak year for Norwegian sailing-ships was as late as 1880, when 7,761 vessels of this kind were registered, and the Norwegian merchant navy was the third largest in the world, after Britain and the United States (Berggren et al. 1989, 313). This may partly explain why there seems to have been hardly any commercial traffic of passengers, at least from the Norwegian side, between Britain and Norway before roughly 1850. Until then, the only possibility of going by boat to Norway had been to go via Gothenburg or one of the German Hansa towns in the Baltic, or travel directly from Britain on a cargo ship. It was only when the steamships arrived, with accurate and predictable departure and arrival times, that regular crossings could become a reality. This coincided, of course with the fast-growing supply of Britons who wanted to visit the country. Thus, Thomas Forester's remark in *Norway and Its Scenery* (1853) that there was a steamer going directly from England to Christiania around 1850, probably indicates that this was one of the first of its kind. Nearly two decades later, the former chaplain of the British Consulate in Christiania, John Bowden, reports that the standard has risen dramatically:

> Messrs. Thomas Wilson, Sons, and Co., despatch a passenger steamer weekly from Hull to Christiansand and Christiania. These boats are well known for their comfortable accommodation and the regularity of their passages. The well-known John Smith, steward of the steamer

Scandinavian, belonging to Messrs. Wilson, is still in their employ. (…) Messrs. Dunkerley and Co., of Hull, despatch a passenger steamer thence every ten days direct to Stavanger and Bergen, on the west coast of Norway. (…) Messrs. Breslauer and Thomas, of 9, Gracechurch Street, E.C., despatch a passenger steamer direct from London to Christiania, calling at Christiansand, once a fortnight during the season (Bowden 1867, 249–50).

From then until around the turn of the century, British travel to Norway appears to have experienced a period of considerable growth. This is demonstrated with particular clarity by W. Mattieu Williams, who in 1876 published a 'new and improved edition' of his travelogue from 1859, *Through Norway with a Knapsack*, enabling him to draw a useful comparison:

> During the twenty years that have elapsed since my first visit, the development of tourist traffic between England and Norway has been very remarkable. Instead of a vessel of notorious unfitness for passenger traffic, such as that in which I sailed from Hull in 1856, there are now some excellent vessels sailing from that port to the same destination. Instead of carrying six or seven saloon passengers and two in the fore-cabin, they are now all crowded at every trip during the summer. This is especially the case with the *Angelo*, a splendid passage ship of 1600 tons, 262 feet long, 33½ feet broad, with separate dining saloon, drawing room, reading room, state rooms, special promenade, and dormitories for seventy-four first-class passengers. This or other vessels sail weekly between Hull and Christiania, and *vice versâ*. Besides there are packets between Hull and Bergen, Hull and Trondhjem; between London and Christiania, Leith and Christiania, Newcastle and Christiania and Bergen, and quite a multitude of indirect routes, such as *viâ* Gothenburg, Copenhagen, Hamburg, Kiel, &c. Tourists who are victims to sea-sickness may now cross to Calais and do the rest by railway (Williams 1876, 17–18).

Thomas Cook brochures from the early 1890s confirm that the popularity of Norway continued to grow. In 1892, prospective travellers are informed that the tourist season in Norway even extends to as late as the middle of November:

> It will be seen that we are again devoting especial attention to Norway, &c. ,Tours. Although the season for visiting these fascinating and romantic districts is comparatively short, the facilities for reaching Norway are yearly increasing.
>
> Our thirteen days cheap tours to Western Norway and the Fjords will be continued weekly until November 13th, and on page 7 will be

seen a list of splendid Yachting Steamers sailing from various ports in England to the Norwegian *Fjords* at frequent intervals, by all of which we book and berth passengers (Cook 1892, 1).

With respect to the modernisation of travel, it is also tempting to include a passage from the 1892 publication *To Christiania, Stockholm, and Gothenburg* by George Clementson Greenwell. Though he does not demonstrate a particularly keen eye for Norwegian scenery, Greenwell reserves his powers of observation for the technical subtleties of a brand-new ship which apparently promises a wholly new dimension in terms of speed and comfort:

> *July 5th. [1890]*—The *Tasso*, which has only made four trips to Norway, is an iron screw steamer of 1,328 register tons. The engines are triple compound; the cylinders being 22½, 37 and 61 inches in diameter, with a stroke of 42 inches; the steam pressure being in the two first 160 lbs. per square inch respectively, and in the third 10lbs. per square inch with 25 inches of vacuum. The pitch of the screw is 18½ feet. The consumption of coal is 24 tons per day, when the revolutions of the screw are 74 per minute, which should give a speed of 13½ knots per hour (Greenwell 1892, 1).

An important element in the modernisation of sea travel within Norway was the building of the Bandak Canal, which was finished in 1892. This vast undertaking, which created comfortable access for steamships to the interior of Telemark at an altitude of nearly 240 feet and through eighteen locks, gives an interesting indication of the arrival of modern tourism even in remote and hitherto inaccessible areas. At Dalen, a tiny village at the upper end of the canal, surrounded by towering mountains and more than sixty miles from the coast, a new and magnificent hotel was built and equipped with electric lighting generated by a nearby waterfall.[22] From this inner station a new road then took the tourists across the Haukeli to Odda on the west coast, thus establishing a new, faster and more comfortable main route from east to west. *The Field*, on 20 October 1894, enthusiastically describes the canal and the road as 'marvels of ingenuity', giving special attention to the magnificent series of six locks at Vrangfoss: 'hewn out of the solid rock, [they] are unequalled in Europe, if not in the world' (*Tourist-Guide* 1895, 28). In all the reports on the Canal, the feats of modern engineering are duly

---

[22] After suffering decades of negligence, the hotel has recently been restored to its original glory and continues to receive guests who arrive on the ships sailing on the Canal.

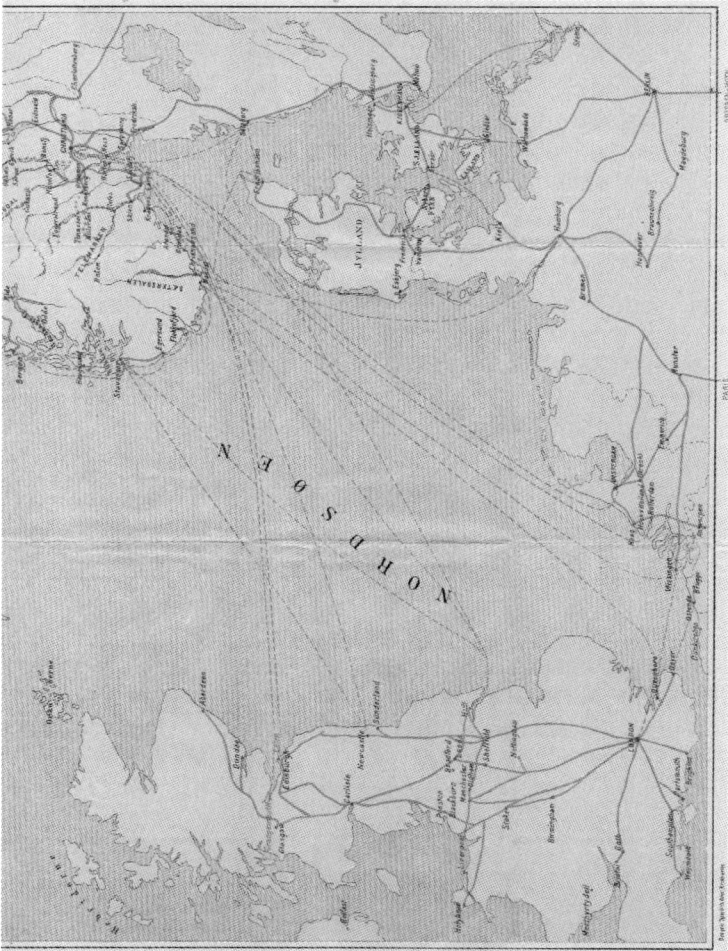

This map from 1898 shows the extensive network of routes to a wide range of Norwegian destinations at the end of the nineteenth century. The fact that it was published by the Norwegian Winter Tourist Association also suggests that many of the routes were in operation throughout the year. From Somerville (1898).

celebrated, thus underlining the ways in which the development of modern tourism was closely connected with and dependent on the nineteenth-century progress in areas such as science, engineering and communications. The *Daily Telegraph* of 29 October 1892 praises the Canal as 'the greatest triumph that Norwegian engineering skill has as yet accomplished' and foresees that it 'will become one of the most favourite routes for tourists in the whole country' (ibid. 27). The large-format magazine *The Graphic* similarly claims on 23 September 1893, in an article supplemented with three illustrations, that 'Norwegian engineers have never before had such a task allotted to them, but by their skill and energy they have triumphed over every obstacle, and left this crowning monument to their enterprise and ability' (402). Thus the Canal, though built primarily to facilitate the transport of goods and timber, also became essential in the development of the tourist industry at a time when Norwegian scenery was more popular among foreign travellers than ever before.

It should be remembered, however, that this is also the period of the second large wave of emigration from Norway to America. This paradoxical situation, in which well-to-do travellers and tourists discover in Norway the leisure land of their dreams while at the same time thousands of natives place their dreams in another land and travel in the opposite direction, is suggested by a brief but significant remark by the 'Three Girls' in *A Jubilee Jaunt to Norway*, published in 1888, during one of the main waves of emigration from Norway. The remark concerns a large number of their fellow passengers on the way back to England: 'The *Hero* had brought as many as 300 Norwegian emigrants to Hull, the first stage of their way to America' ('Three Girls' 1888, 8). Olivia Stone, a few years earlier, makes a similar observation:

> During part of the voyage home the monotony was agreeably broken by watching two of the emigrants [to America]. These were Telemarken peasants – two women in costume; I suppose they were only girls; they appeared young; but they were veritable Amazons. One may prophesy a wealthy future to such a massive amount of limb and breadth of shoulders in a country where these qualities are invaluable. The dress increased their masculine appearance. They wore knitted petticoats, or dresses, that only reached to the knee, so displaying to full advantage their very substantial understandings, encased in thick woollen stockings and wooden clogs, pointed and turned up at the toes like Chinese shoes (Stone 1882, 434).

Stone's comments underline how individuals, caught – perhaps painfully and helplessly – in the whirlwind of historical forces, can become the subject of a tourist's sentimental gaze, and also how the encounter between the observer and the observed opens up for a wide register of different and frequently conflicting perceptions. This is especially the case as long as the observer's conclusions, as in this case, are based not on communication and exchange of viewpoints with the Other, but purely on a one-way view.

Having considered how Norway was 'discovered' in the 1820s, and gradually became a major destination for British travellers towards the end of the century, it is now time to turn to more specific areas which caught the travellers' interest and which, with the benefit of historical hindsight, serve as interesting comments on nineteenth-century preoccupations in Britain itself.

2. 'BACK TO HIS FOREFATHERS' HOUSE':
A COMMON PAST REKINDLED

> From Captain Cook to Lévi-Strauss
> the traveller reports on the sensation
> of coming face to face in a remote
> place with the apparent past of the
> human race in its pristineness or
> menace.
>
> *Dennis Porter*

Contemporary Revolution and Heroic Tradition

On a stormy October day in 1788, William Thomson, who wrote under the pseudonym of Andrew Swinton, approached Norway on his 'third expedition to the north'. In a letter written during the blustery crossing, he says: 'On the third day after we left the shores of Britain, the rocks of Norway appeared, heaving their rugged precipices awefully above the waves that foamed underneath. I renewed my acquaintance with every hill and mountain, and hailed the ancient domains of our conquerors' (Swinton 1792, 5). There is a touch of the Promised Land about these mysterious contours that rise out of the turbulent sea on the third day. Also, while carrying with it the salty air of Viking conquest and memories of old connections between Britain and Norway, the passage concludes with a respectful bow from the conquered to their conquerors. Thomson's letter, written a year before the French Revolution and published in the middle of revolutionary turmoil, thus serves as a useful introduction to and a foreshadowing of the ways in which Norway in the decades to come was to acquire a special role in the British consciousness, a role intimately connected not only with turbulent contemporary politics but also with the distant past.

As was demonstrated in chapter 1, it was only from the 1820s onwards that the number of British travellers to Norway started to rise to a significant number. There are, therefore, relatively few contemporary British comments on the process leading up to Norwegian independence (or semi-independence) in 1814 and on its immediate aftermath. The majority of travel writers regard these events as an historical backdrop against which they discuss later nineteenth-century concerns and issues. Moreover, as the fascination with the Vikings and the distant past is primarily a Victorian phenomenon, in itself influenced by the events of 1814, it seems appropriate to consider the Viking question at a later stage in this chapter, thus following the order in which these issues were presented to the British public. This requires, first, a general understanding of Britain's attitude to nationalist liberation movements, and second, a more specific knowledge of Anglo-Norwegian relations in the decades before and after the fall of Bonaparte.

At the beginning of the nineteenth century, the implications from the political earthquake of 1789 were still felt throughout Europe. First the Revolutionary and then the Napoleonic Wars affected all corners of the Continent. Furthermore, in 1776 Britain had suffered the loss of the American colonies, thereby experiencing what were to prove the first rumblings of a series of nationalist liberation movements which would eventually result in the dismantling of the entire Empire. Both the first and the second generation of Romantic poets and artists gave their enthusiastic support to the ideas of freedom and independence. During the first decades of the century Wordsworth, for instance, produced close to a hundred *Poems Dedicated to National Independence and Liberty*, and such second-generation Romantics as Shelley and Byron both contributed in various ways to the Greek war of independence against the Turks. Political thinkers were equally engaged in heated debates about the fundamental principles of power and government as well as the rights of the individual. The verbal volleys of Edmund Burke and Thomas Paine in the 1790s, together with equally radical statements by writers such as Mary Wollstonecraft and William Godwin, underlined how profoundly British society was divided between tradition and reform. At the same time, the country was undergoing major social changes. The process of industrialisation was already well underway; the new century witnessed an accelerating exodus from the countryside to the urban centres; and in the process new groups of the population demanded a degree of political influence corresponding to the social and economic position they had acquired. Thus, William

Cobbett, who in 1763 had been born into a rural community apparently impregnable to radical change, found it hard to believe, during his rural rides of the early 1820s, that the population had nearly doubled during his lifetime, because he witnessed only a depressed and depopulated countryside (Cobbett 1967, 79). The years prior to Waterloo, in other words, were a period during which the political stability of Britain was severely shaken, due to events both inside and outside the country's borders.

This general background is essential for an understanding of the British perception of Norway throughout the nineteenth century, not least because both countries were directly involved in and affected by the attempts to reassemble the European map after the Napoleonic upheaval. As it turned out, these events – despite setbacks – not only confirmed an old sense of kinship; they also pointed forward to a future relationship of unusual strength and durability, in times of peace as well as war. Undoubtedly, the large number of British travellers to Norway during the nineteenth century contributed strongly to reinforcing these good relations, which were – almost literally – crowned in 1896, when Prince Charles of Denmark, who was later to become King Haakon of Norway, married Queen Victoria's granddaughter, Princess Maud, thus placing the resurrected line of Norwegian monarchs on a secure, Anglo-Scandinavian foundation.

1814 and Norwegian Independence

In 1813, John Black, the English translator of *Travels through Norway and Lapland,* written by the famous German geologist Leopold von Buch, complained in a preface that the British knowledge of Norway was 'extremely unsatisfactory', and 'in truth merely sufficient to whet our curiosity' (von Buch 1813, iii). In the light of the turbulent political situation at the time, however, he ventured to predict that Norway 'will in all probability soon become the theatre of a bloody war, in which the British nation are pledged to co-operate' (ibid.). Black was proved wrong, a fact which should come as no surprise considering the constantly shifting power game played by the European powers prior to the final fall of Bonaparte. Although this is not the place to recapitulate this process in its entirety, it nevertheless seems necessary to give a brief sketch of the respective roles of Norway and Britain in the period leading up to the severing of the union between Denmark and Norway – a union of several hundred years' duration – and the establishment of the new union with Sweden in 1814.

For a number of years after their outbreak in 1792, the Revolutionary Wars did not represent any significant threat to the Norwegian merchant navy, whose existence depended entirely upon open borders and free access to foreign markets. Although involved in skirmishes with the warring nations, the Twin Kingdoms of Denmark and Norway were on the whole successful in retaining their neutrality. The Wars even provided Norway with a golden opportunity for extra profits. According to the historian T. K. Derry, '[t]he nineteenth century opened propitiously with seven fat years, in which the towns sold Britain about three-fifths of a record output of timber, exported with additional profit in Norwegian vessels' (Derry 1973, 2). In 1807, however, the British navy having unceremoniously appropriated practically the whole Danish fleet, Denmark-Norway was thrown into the hands of Napoleon. The ensuing British naval blockade not only meant a breakdown in communications between Denmark and Norway; it also cut Norway off for a number of years from essential corn supplies and – equally important to the Norwegian economy – profits from shipping. Meanwhile, after the Russo-Swedish war of 1808–1809, Sweden was forced to cede Finland to Russia, whereupon the new Swedish crown prince Charles John (Norw. Carl Johan), a French marshal whose original name was Jean-Baptiste Bernadotte, turned his eyes on Norway as a suitable compensation. At the treaties of Åbo in 1812 and Stockholm in 1813, Russia and Britain respectively promised to support Sweden's claim. Then, at the Treaty of Kiel in January 1814, the Danish King Frederick VI accepted, under threat of a Swedish invasion, the loss of Norway to Sweden. The terms of the treaty, however, were not met with approval in Norway. Inspired by the revolutions in France and America and by strong nationalist sentiments, the Norwegians were unwilling to allow others to decide their fate. Instead, they were determined to achieve full independence. Furthermore, there was a general assumption among the Norwegians that 'the British people, who had figured as the champions of liberty against Napoleonic despotism in Spain and elsewhere, would support them if they rose against the imposition of an alien master who had served Napoleon' (Derry 1973, 5). Against this background Prince Christian Frederick of Denmark, whom the King had sent to Norway the preceding year, summoned the assembly at Eidsvoll in April 1814. Its mandate was both ambitious and daring, namely the writing of a constitution.[1] At the same time he sent the wealthy merchant and landowner Carsten

Anker (1747–1824) to London to gather support for the Norwegian cause.[2] Anker's arrival at Gravesend on 17 March, that is well before the assembly convened at Eidsvoll, was duly recorded the following day by *The Times*, whose article quotes a lengthy passage from the *Edinburgh Courant* 'of Monday last'. This had been written in connection with Anker's initial landing in Scotland and reflects the British uncertainty about the general sentiment in Norway:

> There has been much speculation respecting the feelings of the Norwegians on being transferred to the dominion of Sweden. Some accounts have represented the inhabitants as extremely indignant at the late treaty, by which they are disjoined from Denmark; while others state, the population as very well satisfied with an arrangement, by which they become so nearly connected with a country, of which, from situation, they should form so natural a part. All doubt upon this subject are [*sic*] put an end to by the arrival of a Deputy from Norway to this country. Baron ANKER, as an accredited agent, or in some other official capacity, with his suite, arrived at Leith on Saturday evening, on a special mission to the PRINCE REGENT and Government of this country, from a provisional Government established in Norway, in consequence of the transfer of that country to Sweden. The exact nature of the mission cannot, of course, at present be divulged; but we understand, that the inhabitants are decidedly hostile to the late measures by which they are separated from Denmark, and determined to resist the execution of the treaty. They, no doubt, wish the interference of Great Britain, but this must be a most delicate point in the present crisis of Continental affairs.

The point was indeed delicate; despite a generally sympathetic attitude and the fact that Anker was personally acquainted with the Foreign Secretary, Lord Castlereagh (Østvedt 1968, 6), the Tory Prime Minister Lord Liverpool made it clear, during his only interview with Anker on 26 March,[3] that Britain would stand by her obligations in the Treaty of Kiel, and the motion put forward by the Whig opposition 'in support of the Norwegian cause was eventually defeated by a 3:1 majority in both houses of parliament'.[4]

---

[1] The inspiration did not only come from the United States and France; Spain had also acquired its own liberal constitution in 1812.

[2] The Ankers had close commercial connections with Britain, and Peder Anker (1749–1824), Carsten's cousin, received many of the British travellers to Norway at Bogstad outside Christiania, including Mary Wollstonecraft, William Coxe, Edward Daniel Clarke, and his more famous fellow traveller Thomas Malthus.

[3] Taylor 1974, 197. According to Riste (2001), the interview took place the day before.

[4] Derry 1973, 7. A detailed presentation of 'English sympathies' and the

Nevertheless, according to the historian Colin Lucas, Liverpool reminded Anker that 'the British had inserted into the Treaty of Stockholm a clause in favour of the people of Norway and the British could assure the Norwegians that the King of Sweden had no intention of incorporating Norway into Sweden, but "that he would consider Norway as an annexed kingdom and was ready to preserve to the inhabitants their Property, Constitutions, Laws and Privileges"' (Lucas 1990, 274). However, as the historian Olav Riste makes clear in his recent book *Norway's Foreign Relations – A History*, 'Norway's sovereign independence was not yet negotiable' (Riste 2001, 46). In his book *Excursions in the North of Europe* from 1834, John Barrow Jr. looks back on the British handling of the crisis, and quotes from Lord Grey's long and eloquent defence of 'the glorious cause of Norway' in the House of Lords, in which he asked:

> 'And what people is it whose fate you are thus to decide? – a people who have never done you any wrong, who have never injured any of your interests – a people who are known to you only by their virtuous character, by their meritorious services, by their interchange of good offices, by the extension of your commercial relations, and by their constant and unremitting discharge of all those duties which constitute the moral greatness and happiness of a nation.'[5]

Fifteen of the 112 representatives of the Eidsvoll assembly were meanwhile making rapid progress on a draft constitution, and on 17 May, after a week of plenary discussions, the full assembly passed the Constitution, electing at the same time Prince Christian Frederick King of Norway. The British blockade had already been reimplemented, and as the news of the events at Eidsvoll spread, the Swedish regent Charles John reacted with speed and determination. First of all, he tried a diplomatic manoeuvre, whereby the other powers behind the Treaty of Kiel were encouraged to put pressure on Christian Frederick to step down. These attempts proved futile; in July, the Norwegians even tried to send another delegation to Britain, which without further ado was expelled upon arrival (Lucas 1990, 276). Then, at the end of the month, Charles John attacked. The military operations, which resulted in only a small number of

parliamentary debates, very much from a nationalist Norwegian point of view, is found in Wergeland (1897). See also Leiren (1975).

[5] Barrow 1834, 333. Barrow would probably also have first-hand knowledge of these events from his father, Sir John Barrow (1764–1848), who was Second Secretary to the Admiralty at the time.

casualties, were concluded after less than two weeks, with the Swedish forces proving far superior to those of Norway. At Charles John's initiative, negotiations were opened, and in August the Convention of Moss was signed, under whose terms Christian Frederick promised to relinquish his power and leave Norway, while Sweden accepted the Eidsvoll Constitution, thereby going a long way towards endorsing Norwegian independence.[6] Then in October Charles John was duly elected the new king by the Norwegian Storting, whereby Norway formally entered into the union with Sweden, a union which, according to *The Times* on 5 November, 'seems to promise mutual benefits to both countries.'

As it appears from the above summary, there was a certain ambiguity about the British reactions to the dramatic events during the spring and summer months of 1814, an ambiguity which reflected tensions within early nineteenth-century Britain herself. Obviously, this had most immediately to do with the delicate strategic dilemmas with which the country was contending during the final stages of the Napoleonic Wars.[7] But also in the great debates about democracy that were to characterise the early part of the century, Norway would be seen by many other European countries as a model to be emulated. Thus for instance Madame de Staël, 'voice of the liberal French opposition', had written to Charles John on 12 July 1814 strongly urging him to accept the Constitution (Riste 2001, 50). Furthermore, thanks to this document of 110 brief paragraphs, Norway had passed from the hands of Denmark, 'an uncontrolled and absolute sovereign power' (Laing 1837, iii) into the hands of Sweden. In the process, she had managed to maintain an unprecedented amount of freedom and independence and to extend the right of representation to a relatively wide spectrum of her population. It would seem, in other words, that viewed in the context of the great ideological battle between Burke and Paine two decades earlier, the Norwegian solution might have offered a compromise acceptable to both parties. But in 1814 there was no neutral ground, and Britain was irrevocably implicated in the changing fortunes of Norway. On the one hand, she had been instrumental in the hand-over to Sweden; on the other, enlightened commentators were aware of Britain's obligation to make sure that the liberties of Norway were preserved.

---

[6] The declarations of Christian Frederick and Charles John were both printed in *The Times* on 7 October.

[7] For a discussion of this political balancing act, see Colin Lucas (1990).

Britain was thus in the peculiar position of supporting Sweden's claim to Norway, whilst also apparently welcoming the independence and ensuing democracy of the new Norwegian state. There is no doubt that in a period so soon after the loss of her American territories and the drama of the French Revolution, the British government was uneasy about the implications of the Norwegian Constitution. Any emulation of Norwegian independence by Britain's many colonial territories, and any extension of political representation within Britain herself, were viewed as threats to the continued progress of the Empire. Colin Lucas describes Britain's graceless role in the handover of Norway in the following way: 'The British contribution seems to have been essentially to have refused the Norwegians any glimmer of hope and to have blockaded their infant independence out of existence' (278); whereas his colleague C. B. Burchardt, in his now somewhat dated study, less sternly comments that whilst the British *government* supported the dominance of Norway by Sweden, the British *people* were far more inspired by the possibilities of the Constitution (Burchardt 1920, 20). And the people in this case comprised not just the Opposition and the liberal press, but also a fair number of conservative politicians.

This popular enthusiasm for the Norwegian cause found several outlets. The poet, critic and editor Leigh Hunt (1784–1859), for instance, who together with his brother had been sentenced to two years' imprisonment in 1813 for liberal against the Prince Regent, continued to publish the *Examiner*, a Sunday weekly, from Surrey Gaol. During August and September 1814, the paper's leading article 'dealt with the Norwegian question for eight consecutive weeks', including scathing attacks on Charles John and on the British government for leaving the Norwegians gracelessy in the lurch (Leiren 1975, 373 and 381n).

At the same time, the Welsh poetess Charlotte Wardle published her poem 'Norway' (1814) – 160 lines, mostly in heroic couplets – 'respectfully inscribed' to the 'Prince of Denmark'. The poem begins, and continues, with dauntless ardour and energy:

> Bright from the arid regions of the north,
> Her genius bursts, he breaks his icy chains!
> One bright Phænomenon he shineth forth,
> The northern light! the light of freedom reigns!
> Hail, brave Norwegian! Son of freedom hail!
> Oh! may your cause, your sacred cause prevail;
> And may no hand of rude oppressive pow'r,
> Crush the bright offspring of this anxious hour –

Dim the Aurora that in splendour throws,
The beam of freedom o'er your gelid snows (ll. 1–10).[8]

It then concludes, with a reference in the penultimate line, to the new-won freedom of America, a reference that even in 1814 may have caused a sting of wounded pride in a number of British hearts:

The beams of freedom gild her mountain's crest,
The beams of freedom warm her natives [sic] breast,
And blest with freedom – will her sons be blest!
Then shall the rude Atlantic's utmost tide,
The coasts of freedom lave on either side,
From that fair land 'neath sable Labrador,
To rugged Norway's rude and arctic shore! (ll. 154–60)

In another poem, published in the *Star* on the very 17 May, that is necessarily before the news of the signing of the Constitution had reached Britain, an unknown poet appeals to the British government to support Norwegian independence rather than hand the country over to Sweden:

O! let not history stain her honest page,
Bright with the triumphs of the present age,
With the sad tale, that Britain drew her sword
To bend Norwegians to a foreign lord.
That she, who fought, all Europe's realms to free,
Uplifts her arm – to murder liberty (Mains 1989, 249).

That the British stance towards the terms of the Treaty of Kiel was seen as an act of treachery against the principles of liberty, is also confirmed by the sonnet 'The Fate of Norway', by Sir Aubrey De Vere (1788–1846), the father of the Victorian poet of the same name. Published in 1842, but most likely written a number of years earlier, the poem asks what happened to the spirit of liberty 'when Norway fell, / Spurned by the Free, by Despots bought and sold?' (De Vere 1842). Similarly, both the well-known Felicia Dorothea Hemans (1793–1835) and Emmeline Stuart-Wortley (1806–1855) wrote poems entitled 'Old Norway', which in their descriptions of the old Norsemen also seem to echo the more recent but equally heroic struggle for independence.[9]

---

[8] For more information on Wardle and her family background, see 'Biographical Information', p. 365.

[9] Mains (1989, 248–49) debates whether Hemans's poem 'Old Norway' has an

Thus, in the *poetic* treatments of 1814, there is an unambiguous celebration of the ideals of the American and French revolutions. In several of the travel accounts from the following decades, however, a modern reader senses a slightly different tone. There is no doubt that the great majority of nineteenth-century travellers, looking back on this *annus mirabilis* of Norwegian history, express considerable empathy for what Norway had achieved, and in particular for the peaceful way in which it was achieved. But one can also hear an unmistakable note of caution, which may indicate, first, that the revolutions and popular unrest of the late eighteenth and early nineteenth centuries were causing general and growing concern; and second, that the majority of travel writers were largely members of the moderate, but far from radical, middle and upper-middle classes, as discussed in the previous chapter. Steeped in a Burkean conservatism, which above all emphasises gradual change rooted in the historical tradition, several of the accounts in question make a point of the connection between 1814 and the ancient Norwegian heritage.[10] It would appear that it is important for them to underline that the changes in Norway were made possible by particular national conditions that were not necessarily equally present in Britain. Another approach is to play down the implications of the events in Norway and give an overall impression of stability despite the upheavals the country had been subjected to. Thomas Forester, for instance, in his preface to *Norway in 1848 and 1849* – written, incidentally, soon after the renewed revolutionary drama of 1848 – claims that 'of all the states of Christendom, this northern kingdom appeared almost the only one exempt from the desire or the apprehension of change' (Forester 1850, v). Along similar lines he then goes on, later in the book, to insist on Norway's unique position

historical background, and ultimately dates it to 1829. Although this may be correct, it seems probable that the theme of stubborn independence points back to the events of 1814. It appears to have been first published in *National Lyrics and Songs for Music* (1834). The first of the three stanzas goes as follows:

> Arise! old Norway sends the word
>   Of battle on the blast;
> Her voice the forest pines hath stirr'd,
>   As if a storm went past;
> Her thousand hills the call have heard,
>   And forth their fire-flags cast.

[10] The question of the social, and regional, background of the various commentators on Norway will be discussed in more detail in ch. 3.

in relation to other European countries:

> Compared with other newly created constitutional states, – Spain, Portugal, Naples, – Norway stands out in highly favourable contrast. The revolutionary spirit which has recently convulsed almost the whole of Europe, has found no echo there. Standing in this position, and pointed to as a model for other countries, it might be wondered from what quarter arising, and founded on what grounds, any apprehensions can be entertained of the stability of her constitutional system (421–22).

Against the background of repeated outbursts of violent revolts and sudden changes both in Britain and other countries, it comes as no surprise that most British commentators find Norway a peaceful haven, and that they express a desire to return to an alleged past when political changes, as recommended by Burke, occurred gradually and undramatically. Lord Dufferin, high-flying diplomat, negotiator in hot-spots around the world and 'one of the most admired public servants of his time',[11] thus typically underlines the enviable qualities that characterise Norwegian nationalism, while at the same time reminding the reader of the turbulent contemporary scene:

> Noiselessly and gradually did a belief in liberty, and an unconquerable love of independence, grow up among that simple people. No feudal despots oppressed the unprotected, for all were noble and udal born; no standing armies enabled the Crown to set popular opinion at defiance, for the swords of the Bonders[12] sufficed to guard the realm; no military barons usurped an illegitimate authority, for the nature of the soil forbade the erection of feudal fortresses. Over the rest of Europe despotism rose up rank under the tutelage of a corrupt religion; while, year after year, amid the savage scenery of its Scandinavian nursery, that great race was maturing whose genial heartiness was destined to invigorate the sickly civilization of the Saxon with inexhaustible energy, and preserve to the world, even in the nineteenth century, one glorious example of a free European people (Dufferin 1857, 388).

As indicated above, however, this did not mean that British observers like Dufferin necessarily recommended that the Norwegian model be emulated back home. William Bilton, in *Two Summers in Norway*

---

[11] *Encyclopædia Britannica*, 11th ed., s.v. 'Dufferin and Ava, Frederick Temple Hamilton-Temple-Blackwood'. See also 'Biographical Information', p. 353.

[12] 'Bonders' is an anglicised version of the Norwegian plural form *Bønder*, i.e. farmers. The Norwegian singular is *Bonde* (in the nineteenth century nouns were capitalised in Norwegian).

(1840), for instance, admits that Norway has acquired a number of institutions and political traditions that provide a relatively radical degree of democracy and 'equalization of property'. Nevertheless, he argues that such solutions would not work in Britain, and supports his claim by insisting that in Norway some of the changes have also contributed to creating a country of intellectual poverty (263–64).

'A Suitable Past': Echoes of Tudor Harmony

The history of the building of a national identity is largely a history of myth making. In the nineteenth century both Britons and Norwegians were engaged in creating such national myths as parts of large-scale nation-building projects. Some of these myths were unique to one of the countries, whereas others had common roots in the distant past. There is no doubt that British travellers and other commentators from the 1820s onwards were fascinated by Norway's small and recent but surprisingly successful attempts to create national myths designed to sustain a burgeoning national identity. The most obviously symbolic act the traveller could perform in order to show his or her respect for the national struggle was to visit Eidsvoll, which, very soon after 1814, was turned into a national shrine. Most prominently, the later ethnologist and linguist Robert Gordon Latham, travelling as early as 1833, spends several pages on the 'Constitution House', which incidentally was owned by an English merchant at the time. He visits the building together with the poet Henrik Wergeland himself, on whom he also spends an entire chapter.[13] Looking back on the visit a few years later, Latham's prose rises into a lyrical celebration of Norwegian nationalism:

> Such is the Norwegian Constitution, of which every man, woman, and child in the country knows the import and the value. The poems of Homer were not more in the mouths of the young Athenians, than are the clauses of the Grundlov (*Ground-law*) in those of the Northmen. The whole Constitution is printed upon a single sheet. I never went into a farm-house of the better, and rarely into one of the humbler sort, without seeing it glazed and framed, hanging against the wall like an ordnance map, or a family picture at home. (...) Happy (...) are the children of the North! that have a Constitution as portable as a pocket-handkerchief.

[13] Henrik Wergeland (1808–1845), more than anyone else, contributed to establishing the tradition of 17 May (i.e. the day of the passing of the Constitution in 1814) as a day of national celebration, a tradition that is still very much alive.

Such a copy is now lying before me; far away, indeed, from its black-letter brethren, the freedom-breathing children of the press at Christiania, but still treated with all due honour, as a noble, and a worthy exile (Latham 1840, 2: 102).

Two decades later, John George Hollway pays a similar tribute as he passes Eidsvoll on his way north:

It was in this house that the men who framed the eminently successful Norwegian constitution met in the spring of the year 1814, after the Norwegian nation had declared its independence, and then set to work to draw up what has hitherto proved the most successful and most lasting of all constitutions ever turned out on a sudden, spick and span new as this was. (...) The conference or council wherein this great and successful work was accomplished sat just four days! In four days a meeting of practical and earnest men created what learned philosophers and theoretical statesmen have invariably miserably failed in producing, a lasting working constitution (Hollway 1853, 142).

Both Latham's and Hollway's passages actively participate in the Norwegian celebration of Eidsvoll as a place of worship and reverence, thus nourishing and sanctioning the national myth. Incidentally, they also contribute to the development of Eidsvoll as one of the few Norwegian tourist attractions that are not primarily concerned with untouched nature. But while not necessarily recommending the Norwegian form of democracy in Britain, their encounter with and interpretation of Norwegian national identity also trigger comparisons with national myths deeply embedded in their own consciousness. One such myth, frequently referred to by travellers, is that of 'Merrie England'. In her recent study *Myth and National Identity in Nineteenth-Century Britain*, Stephanie L. Barczewski discusses the various ways in which the legends of King Arthur and Robin Hood were mobilised in the 'conflicts in nineteenth-century Britain over inclusion and exclusion in the nation' (Barczewski 2000, vii). As Barczewski points out, these legends were used as a reservoir from which ideals from the past were mobilised in the context of the contemporary political scene. As a result of the Romantic celebration of rural values, this 'suitable past' was frequently deployed in a marked anti-urban campaign to convince city-dwellers to return to the land:

In this period, 'country life' came to represent order, stability, and naturalness, values which its urban counterpart seemed to be rapidly annihilating. As a corollary to this idealization of the rural, the historical came to be highly valued as well. (…) '*Merrie England*' [was] a cultural ideal which located the remedy for the evils of modern life in a golden age found sometime in the late-medieval or Tudor era. Then, it was argued, English society had been from top to bottom wholesome, prosperous, and healthy (ibid., 105–6).

These attitudes are frequently reflected in travelogues from Norway, and, as will be discussed in subsequent chapters, many of them regard the farmers and the rural communities in general as utopian models of fellow-feeling and social harmony. In 1824, basing his description on a journey from as early as 1799, Sussex-born Edward Daniel Clarke returns over and over again to the many parallels with 'Old England':

Old ballads pasted on the wall – story-books of witches and giants – huge heavy carved work upon the cupboards and furniture – rows of shining pewter-plates and earthenware – brown mugs for beer – hog's puddings and sausages dangling from the roof – these, and all the amusements of their fire-sides, carry us back to 'the golden days of good *Queen Bess*' (Clarke 1824, 10: 323).

Samuel Laing similarly comments appreciatively on the 'primitive old-fashioned household ways' of what he calls the Norwegian gentry: 'The family room is what we may fancy the hall to have been in an English manor-house in Queen Elizabeth's days' (Laing 1837, 157). Furthermore, in the descriptions of Charles Boileau Elliott and John Barrow Jr., both from the early 1830s, the comparisons are more explicitly associated with the political climate in Britain. The former's account reflects on the 'curious spectacle' of the Norwegian Storting (Parliament), which the author has been to see:

Some of the members are dressed in coarse woollen cloth like blanketing; with hair hanging profusely over the shoulders, broad-brimmed hats of various shapes, and boots of a certain size. The whole costume, as well as their humble mode of speaking, or rather reading their opinions, attests to the unsophisticated simplicity of these worthy sons of our northern ancestry. They tell a tale of days once known in England, before the progress of luxury had introduced abuses which call for a corrective hand; the hand of a moderate, judicious, and Christian reform (Elliott 1832, 189–90).

Writing in the year of the Reform Act, Elliott is somewhat hazy with respect to his political stance, but appears to take for granted that his readers will share with him a general concern that the pace of change in Britain is too fast. Barrow, on the other hand, is more explicit in his criticism of the great changes that have taken place in the British countryside in connection with the enclosure acts of the previous decades. His view of the Norwegian peasants is that they are 'very much like what the peasantry of England might have been in former days, before manufacturers and large farms had destroyed all semblance of agricultural equality by reducing the small farmers and peasantry (…)' (Barrow 1834, 324). Like William Cobbett, witnessing the depopulation of the British countryside in *Rural Rides* (1830), Barrow airs an aristocratic dislike of the rising class of traders and industrialists, and ruminates nostalgically but somewhat curiously on a past of alleged 'agricultural equality'.

For the large majority of British commentators, however, there was a more distant past that served as the most powerful link between the British and the Norwegians, namely the period of the Vikings, who, in a larger context, were regarded as one of several Teutonic tribes. As will be shown, this intense and multifarious preoccupation with the early history of the British nation was an important ingredient in the construction of contemporary nineteenth-century society and in the visions of an even brighter imperial future.

Forefathers Across the Sea

Britain, for the British, seemed to occupy the highest plane of nineteenth-century civilisation in terms of culture, politics, industrial wealth and imperial aggrandisement. As Paul Langford has remarked in his study of visitors' views of England in the period up to 1850, 'the highest compliment that could be paid to foreigners was to regret that they were not English or even to tell them to their face that they deserved to be English' (Langford 2000, 314). Concomitantly, from the sixteenth century onwards, a growing interest in Britain's Teutonic heritage had arisen 'in response to complex religious and political needs, and [had] matured over the succeeding three centuries in step with England's rise to imperial status' (MacDougall 1982, 2). From the late eighteenth century onwards, the British had been engaged in an enthusiastic search for their national origins, a search that involved a rigorous interest in ancestry and inheritance. If the

British characteristically exhibited xenophobia in the nineteenth century, they were, by contrast, highly complimentary of foreigners from certain nations thought to have historical connections with Britain. In short, Britons differentiated themselves from most other nations and cultures, but also sought antecedents through whom they might strengthen their own claims to world ascendancy. As an example, in her study *The Eve of the Greek Revival: British Travellers' Perceptions of Early Nineteenth-Century Greece*, Helen Angelomatis-Tsougarakis makes an interesting observation with respect to Greece that also appears to be relevant to Norway. Towards the Greeks, she claims, British travellers generally 'assumed a very aloof and patronizing attitude', but they also 'seemed to think that they could legitimately consider themselves to be the real descendants of the ancient Greeks' (Angelomatis-Tsougarakis 1990, 23). In a constantly changing and expanding world, where the British played a leading role while at the same time being exposed to a large range of different peoples and customs, it is not surprising to find that this country in particular felt a need to emphasise certain cultural and ethnic roots over others, and that these preferences were characterised by an attempt to safeguard traditional connections. Thus, despite the significance, even in a world context, of the classical, Mediterranean culture, there was an unmistakable trend towards a focus on a culture nearer to the people of the home soil and their history.

It is against this background that there was a marked desire, from the late eighteenth century onwards, to trace Britain's Teutonic heritage. The antiquarian Paul Henri Mallet's *Northern Antiquities*, translated into English by Bishop Percy in 1770, explained the importance of the Viking as well as the Anglo-Saxon heritage of Britain. The Vikings had invaded England in successive raids since the eighth century. In addition, they had invaded Northern France and given rise to the Normans.[14] The Normans, in turn, had invaded England in 1066, thus giving the English a double Teutonic ancestry. There were many ways in which the British utilised their knowledge of their Teutonic inheritance in the nineteenth century, but for the traveller to Norway, the most obvious appropriation of the idea was in the recognition of physical and psychological similarities between the Norwegians and the British. By the mid-nineteenth century, these

---

[14] Thomas B. Willson, in his article 'Some Norwegian Characteristics', from *The Girl's Own Paper*, refers to a prayer frequently used in Northern France at the time: 'A furore Normannorum libera nos, Domine' ('Deliver us, O Lord, from the fury of the Northmen'; our translation) (Willson 1887, 530).

characteristics were conceived as biologically rather than socially determined (Langford 2000, 8–9). The shift to a biological understanding of nationality is important to an examination of the commentaries by British travellers on the Norwegian people. As the century progressed, what were at root biological similarities between the British and the Norwegians were seen as giving rise to other similarities in manners and morals.

The Teutonic type of Norwegian (as opposed to the Sami) was recognised by many commentators. The fourth edition of *Encyclopaedia Britannica* (1801–1810), a rare public source of information about Norway at that time, commented that 'the Norwegians are generally well-formed, tall, sturdy, and robust, brave, hardy, honest, hospitable and ingenious; yet savage, rash, quarrelsome, and litigious. The same character will nearly suit the inhabitants of every mountainous country in the northern climates. Their women are well-shaped, tall, comely, remarkably fair and obliging' (s.v. 'Norway'). I. A. Blackwell, who edited Bishop Percy's translation of Mallet's *Northern Antiquities*, similarly defines the physiology of what he terms 'the Teutonic race' as follows:

> Fair complexion, fair, often flaxen, reddish, golden coloured smooth hair, commonly not curled; large blue eyes, broad high brow, skull larger and rounder than in the Celtic variety, bones thicker, chest broader, so the hips, legs straight, heels and ankles strong, feet often large, even clumsy when compared with the Celtic variety; greater strength of muscle, tallness of figure, above what is called the middle size; skull and face a form that approaches nearer to a half circle, to which the thinner end of the oval is added; disposition to become corpulent (Mallet 1847, 33–34).

In keeping with these definitions, commentators invariably mentioned the strength and good health of the Norwegians. Arthur de Capell Brooke, in *Travels through Sweden, Norway and Finnmark to the North Cape*, painted a lively picture of the athleticism of the locals who, he remarks, 'may be said to be in a constant state of training; and their activity in consequence is so great, that they keep up with ease by the side of your carriage, at full speed, for the distance of ten or twelve miles' (Brooke 1823, 107). This dramatic account of the rude health of the Norwegians is substantiated by those travel accounts which *explicitly* make the Viking and Norman connections between Norway and Britain. Visiting Christiania in 1857, Charles Loring Brace in *The Norse Folk* (1857) commented that 'there is nothing in the city to especially distinguish it from other European cities, except the appearance of the peasants. These are

A DESCENDANT OF THE OLD SEA-KINGS.

The British aristocracy, largely of Norman descent, retained a profound admiration for their Scandinavian ancestors, and many travellers were eager to point out the striking similarities between themselves and their Norwegian 'cousins'. It is hardly a coincidence that this farmer and 'descendant of the old sea-kings' probably also could have passed for a member of the British gentry.

marked-looking men and women – usually blonde, with ruddy complexion, regular Norman features, light hair, and faces expressing a certain reserved and sober strength of feeling. They have, most of them, powerful frames' (2).

In the nineteenth century it was important for Britain to articulate her Teutonic kinship with Norway. This articulation was conducted through many channels, but crucial to its continued acceptance and popularity were the evident physical similarities – of colouring, stature and physiognomy – between the inhabitants of the two nations. The eighteenth-century historian Paul Henri Mallet's description of these typical Teutonic characteristics has been mentioned already; equally important is his description of the *mental* attributes thought to necessarily arise from the physical. His comments below might equally well apply to the British as to the Norwegians:

> Temperament: sanguine, nervous and phlegmatic prevailing. Psychological character: Slowness, but accuracy of perception; general slowness, but depth and penetration of mind; not brilliant for witticism like the Celtic variety, but distinguished by acuteness, fondness for independence, it being valued more highly than equality of condition or rank: provident, cautious, reserved, hospitable, but not sociable on a large scale with aristocratic conservative tendencies; respect for women, without assuming the Celtic character of frivolous flippancy; sincerity, forgetfulness of received injuries, adventurous, distinguished for cleanliness (Mallet 1847, 34).

Whilst such characteristics were by no means universally favourable, they served to distinguish the Norwegians, and the British who had descended from them, from the Celtic peoples and also from other, more geographically distant, races. Even on those rare occasions in travel accounts where the Norwegian character is adversely criticised, the commentators tend to gloss the description with an approving tone, as here in William Bilton's account in *Two Summers in Norway* (1840):

> Perhaps, it is not without justice, that the Norwegians are accused of slowness in their ideas, equally as in their corporal movements: and from their isolated position they are necessarily contracted, more, however, in their information than their mental capacity. They do not seem readily to comprehend any thing out of the sphere of their limited experience; and exhibit inordinate wonderment and admiration at every thing strange or new to them. On the other hand, they show considerable intelligence

with respect to the things within their reach; and if not gifted with much
original genius, are excellent followers and imitators (87–88).

Such commentary indicates that what pleased the British more than
anything was the idea that the Norwegians were an educable race,
similar and yet inferior to the British. It is hardly reading too much
between the lines to assume that Bilton hoped that the Norwegians
would be 'excellent followers and imitators' of the British. In the
same book Bilton also voiced a similarly rather superior approbation
of the Teutonic way of life and cast of mind: 'Our habits of living, and
of thinking, amalgamate much better with the Teutonic than with
either the Gallic or Italian character: and of all the Teutonic races, the
Norwegians seems to sympathise with us most readily' (54).

By the mid-nineteenth century, commentaries on Teutonic
appearances and psychology were starting to show signs of a new
discourse, the pseudo-science of phrenology. One nineteenth-century
phrenologist described phrenology as teaching 'that talents,
dispositions, capacities and adaptability or non-adaptability (...) can
be inferred from the form of the head' (Morgan 1871, 8).
Increasingly concerned with preserving the purity of the English race,
some of the advocates of phrenology were quick to construe the
urban poor, prostitutes, criminals and the insane 'as degenerate types
whose deformed skulls, protruding jaws, and low brain weights
marked them as "races apart"' (Stepan 1985, 98). Phrenology did
more than simply differentiate between temperament types and
between racial types; it came to ascribe a strict intellectual and moral
hierarchy founded on physical characteristics. A brief example of the
racial superiority inherent in the phrenological discourse can be seen
in the following commentary on the Caucasian variety of head from
Nicholas Morgan's popular textbook of 1871:

> The head of this race is large and oval-shaped, with an elevated and
> amply developed forehead, and a well-proportioned face. The hair is in
> general fine in texture, and the skin fair. They present the finest
> specimens of symmetry and beauty, and the highest state of mental
> endowment and intellectual culture. Amongst them, liberty, literature,
> refinement, the arts and sciences, and everything that tends to ennoble
> man, have reached the highest point of cultivation in the present age, and
> genius has attained it mightiest results. They are destined to be the
> conquerors and sole inhabitants of the world (9).

It can be seen here how descriptions of physical characteristics lead
almost imperceptibly into dangerously flawed evaluations of society.

As far as such racial theorists were concerned, the Norwegians, like the British, fitted quite conveniently into the same Caucasian group, and indeed within its same Teutonic branch. Association with the Norwegians, including, it might be imagined, intermarriage and procreation, would not be a problem in the eyes of these theorists.

As is always the case with theories about identity, the physiognomy, psychology and latterly phrenology which linked the Norwegians and the British were predicated to some extent on a discussion of their opposites. As has been mentioned already, the Teutonic characteristics of the Norwegians and the British were delineated in marked contrast to the qualities of other nations, in particular the Gauls, Latins and, perhaps most frequently, the Celts. Like travel to Scandinavia, travel within Britain to its 'Celtic periphery', that is Wales, Scotland and Ireland, was popular in the nineteenth century, and here the British – or most often the English – increasingly saw themselves as different from and superior to this Celtic stock. Murray G. H. Pittock comments that the status of the Celtic became recognisably aligned over the course of the century to other colonial perspectives, such as Orientalism. As a consequence, Celticism was associated with such qualities as emotionalism and feminine weakness (Pittock 1999, 60), which again resulted in a condescending attitude by the British. The Vikings and their modern descendants, on the other hand, were considered to be profoundly masculine, and thus worthy of both respect and pride at traditional bonds.

Norway was praised for her lack of Celtic contamination, but there were one or two interesting exceptions to this. Those areas of Norway traditionally seen as dangerous or more than usually primitive, attracted some comparisons with the Celtic fringe in Britain. As a later section will show, the Sami population engendered some such commentary, so too did the inhabitants of Telemark, one of Norway's least accessible regions. Here is the Rev. Robert Everest in *A Journey Through Norway, Lapland, and Sweden* (1829) on the inhabitants of this anomalous district:

> They are tall, brawny men, with long disordered hair, and reminded us of what we had heard of the wild Irish. Perhaps it might be from fancy, but we thought the Irish cast of countenance predominant among them. Certainly there is a difference between them and the rest of the Norwegians, who are mostly of smaller persons (26).

Of course such descriptions of apparently marginal groups within a predominantly Teutonic country served only to strengthen the British feelings of kinship with Norway. Norway's relationship with her 'Celtic' elements could imaginatively be seen as similar to England's relationship with the problematical Irish in particular. In this way the Norwegian people, as fellow Teutons, were implicated in complex ways in the whole business of constructing a British identity in the nineteenth century.

The impact of Teutonomania on the reading public of Britain should not be underestimated. Andrew Wawn's major study *The Vikings and the Victorians* starts out by outlining the impressive literary output that came to colour so strongly the later (that is the twentieth-century) perception of the period. From a very modest beginning around the time of Queen Victoria's ascension in 1837, this literary output developed into a flood of material: 'poems, plays, pious fables, parodies, paraphrased sagas, prize essays, published lectures, papers in learned journals, translations, travelogues, scholarly monographs, and entries in encyclopaedia [*sic*]' (Wawn 2000, 3). According to Wawn, however, this does not mean that the Vikings were presented with one particular image; on the contrary, there was a 'wide variety of constructions of Vikingism':

> [T]he old northmen are variously buccaneering, triumphalist, defiant, confused, disillusioned, unbiddable, disciplined, elaborately pagan, austerely pious, relentlessly jolly, or self-destructively sybaritic. They are merchant adventurers, mercenary soldiers, pioneering colonists, pitiless raiders, self-sufficient farmers, cutting-edge naval technologists, primitive democrats, psychopathic berserks, ardent lovers and complicated poets (ibid., 4).

This multifarious and frequently contradictory picture served, paradoxically, as a powerful catalyst in the great British nation-building project. The flexibility of the Viking image was almost unlimited and could be employed – as will be shown in the following – by conservatives and liberals alike. In his book *Racial Myth in English History*, Hugh A. MacDougall comments that '[b]y the mid nineteenth century, most Englishmen uncritically accepted the basic tenets of Anglo-Saxonism [a term which MacDougall uses as synonymous with Teutonism]. At the height of Victorian imperialism it seemed abundantly manifest that England's triumph grew out of its blessed inheritance' (MacDougall 1982, 3). It was a postulation supported by numerous great British historians and writers, including Charles Kingsley, James Anthony Froude (who, as will be shown, also visited Norway), Sir Charles Wentworth Dilke and J. R. Seeley.

As we shall see, however, not all segments of the British population were necessarily credited with the honour of this biological bond.

Among British commentators writing about Scandinavia, the word 'Teuton' was frequently substituted by the word 'Viking'. This term was then used in what, with the benefit of hindsight, appears like a great propaganda effort to weld together a sense of British nationhood, leading to a justification for imperial expansion. It is of course a considerable paradox that these bands of merciless invaders and plunderers – as they were often seen – from a thousand years earlier were so effectively recast as representatives of Britain's proud and ancient heritage. To a large extent, however, it is precisely such a complex and many-faceted picture that emerges.

The awareness of the Viking connection is very much present among British travellers, and in the second half of the century especially there is scarcely a single travelogue that does not mention it in one way or another. John F. Keane, for instance, whose lively account from 1887 describes a trip in a merchant ship to take on board ice in Kragerø, reveals in his first encounter with local fishermen outside the Norwegian coast how the historical dimension echoes loudly in his mind. Having commented on how difficult it was 'to keep clear of the poor fellows' drift-nets', he remarks: 'What a race of bearded giants those fair Norwegian fishermen are, in their odd-looking decked boats, cutter-rigged, and as round as apples! (…) There were half a dozen of them in the boat, five stalwart young Norsemen, and one old Viking with a voice like a bull' (178–79). Charles Loring Brace and Charles Elton both give similar reports from Tofte at Dombås, a farm whose history is said to go back to King Eystein in the early twelfth century. Here Brace appears to have trouble finding the right words, having first met the host at the station, and then Mr Tofte himself:

There was something very notable in [the host's] appearance; he was not exactly a 'gentleman,' in the usual acceptation, not a man of the world, but he impressed you as a kind of natural prince; tall, strong, with commanding features and long, black hair, and an air of genuine dignity. (…) The host (…) returned, and brought with him an old gentleman with a still more noble and patriarchal air. This one welcomed me in the same dignified manner, and told me in a few words that he was a direct descendant from one of the old Norwegian kings, HAROLD HAARFAGER. (…) I know not how to express enough my sense of the courtesy and the intelligence of this Bonder landlord. With our limited means of understanding each other, he showed such a quickness and keenness – such an appreciation of the point of every question – that I was surprised how much we communicated in so few words. Then everywhere, he manifested such a true and manly courtesy, that I left him feeling the country was fortunate that possessed such a class. They are evidently the muscle and bone of Norway; and when greater enlightenment and modern enterprise shall reach them, we shall see what a nation this vigorous old Norse people can yet make (Brace 1857, 28–31).

Elton, who accepts uncritically the view of Carlyle and others that Odin was a man turned god, is similarly impressed by Mr Tofte's family tree:

> Mr. Tofte is a well-known character in Norway, and his claim to be descended from Harald Haarfagre, and, *par consequence*, from Odin, is allowed to be just. The family are accordingly immensely proud of the distinction, and take precedence of the other farmers in church, &c.; nor will a Tofte ever marry out of his own family (Elton 1864, 258).

Also, when he comes to the Sognefjorden, Elton learns of fascinating genealogies among the locals: 'It is said that many of the peasants on the Sogne Fjord can trace their pedigrees to the soldiers who went to Jorsala (Jerusalem) with Sigurd, and can tell legends of the Eastern luxuries and wealth, which were brought home' (ibid., 74).

But more interestingly, the majority of travellers are not content with simply pointing out similarities between present-day Norwegians and their Viking ancestors. Rather the observations in Norway are used to acknowledge deep family ties between the two nations. A romantic and sentimental version of this sense of kinship is found in the sonnet 'Welcome', from the collection *Orellana and Other Poems* (1881) by the Scotsman James Logie Robertson , 'a popular and prolific writer of his day' (Mains 1989, 257):

> Was it the filial instinct of a child
>> Yearning to visit the ancestral home
>> That drove me o'er the furrows and the foam
> To Norway northward of the ocean wild?
> Meseemed at least from fell on fell up-piled
>> Streamed voices – Now at last, though late, ye come;
>> Here is your parent land, no longer roam:
> And the scenes grew familiar all, and smiled.
> But who was he, this worshipper of Thor?
>> Or, likelier, Odin would the genius suit
> Of a bold-cruising Viking ancestor –
>> Some scale-mailed Eric, or chain-shirted Knut!

> – Vainly I questioned welcoming breeze and torr,
> The winds were silent now, the mountains mute!

Charles Elton furthermore remarks that to Englishmen 'this country should possess a peculiar charm, as the mother of so many families, the colonizer of so many counties in England' (Elton 1864, 3). The anonymous author of an article in the July 1872 issue of *Blackwood's Edinburgh Magazine* also proudly asserts that '[w]e have among us men like these Norwegians – tall broad-shouldered, abounding in muscle, blood, and bone', whereupon, with a rather less pleasing air, s/he adds: 'but unfortunately we have beings of another kind in the slums of our cities, and also in the huts of our agriculturalists' ('The British Tourist in Norway' 1872, 313). Against this background it seems justifiable to conclude that the nineteenth-century celebration of the Vikings contains a very obvious element of social prejudice: the bloood connection between Britain and Norway is reserved not for the nation as a collective unity, but for particular and privileged segments of the population. When Olivia Stone sits opposite 'a fine-looking Norwegian gentleman', she 'might readily have mistaken him for an Englishman', but not just any Englishman: 'so like was he to one's conception of a "fine old English gentleman, one of the olden time"' (Stone 1882, 3). And when later in her book she witnesses a gathering of people in Hardanger who have come to the quay to see the steamer, they remind her of 'what a picked number of our own countrymen would be like' (ibid., 322). The mountaineer William Slingsby also admires the Vikings – in a rather self-congratulatory fashion – because they became 'the progenitors of the finest race in the world' (Slingsby 1904, 14). But again, this 'finest race' encompasses only 'the best blood which we possess' (ibid.).

In a number of travelogues, the Anglo-Norwegian blood bond is even appropriated and thereby monopolised by the narrow elite of British royalty and aristocracy. 'The Northmen', according to Thomas Forester in *Norway and Its Scenery*, 'gave kings to England, and dukes to Normandy (...)' (Forester 1850, 43), and even though he describes the 'amalgamation' that took place between the two countries, he soon returns to the upper orders of society:

> In the course of two generations, the rude bearing of the piratical Viking merged in the chivalry of the Norman Baron; and the fierce worshippers of Odin became the devout sons and defenders of the Church. (...) The descendants of the Northmen soon lost all traces of their descent from the Sea-Kings of Norway; but many a peer proud of his Norman lineage, if its annals could be carried two generations beyond the Conquest, would

have to admit a real though remote kindred with the independent Bonder of certain districts of Norway (...) (ibid., 45).

In the article 'The Norwegian Fjords', from *Longman's Magazine* in December 1882, the historian James Anthony Froude sets out on a pilgrimage in a steam yacht visiting, among other places, the ruins of Rolf or Rollo the Ganger's castle in the Romsdalsfjorden. Here he finds not only historical but also contemporary evidence of connections among the highest orders:

> It was there that Rolf, or Rollo as we call him, set out with his comrades to conquer Normandy, and produce the chivalry who fought at Hastings and organised feudal England. This was not to be missed; and as little, a visit which we had promised to a descendant of one of those Normans, a distinguished Tory member of the House of Commons, and lord of half an English county. He had bought an estate in these parts, with a salmon river, and had built himself a house there (Froude 1882, 209).[15]

As will be discussed in the following chapter, *simplicity* was one of the central features that British travellers noted among the Norwegians, and while in Norway this lord of half a county and connoisseur of the genuinely Rousseauesque life, enjoyed the rustic simplicity of his forefathers:

> We found our Englishman. His house is under the Horn at the bend of the valley, where the ancient fjord must have ended. (…) The house itself was simple enough, made of pine wood entirely, as the Norway houses always are, and painted white. It contained some half-dozen rooms, furnished in the plainest English style, the summer house of a sportsman who is tired of luxury, and finds the absence of it an agreeable exchange (ibid., 210).

Froude's aristocratic friend, in other words, has gone full circle and returned not only to the geographical origin of his forefathers, but also to their way of life, now back in vogue.

The travellers' keen eye for aristocratic blood among the

---

[15] Froude's distinguished friend was General William Bromley-Davenport (1821–1884), who had visited Romsdal since 1849 and who bought the farm Øvre Fiva in 1862 together with a fair share of the river Rauma. He owned Capesthorne Hall in Cheshire and was a Tory MP for West Warwickshire from 1864 until his death. His descendant William Arthur Bromley-Davenport still owns both the farm and the stretch of river in Romsdal. The above information has been received from Bromley-Davenport's Norwegian estate manager, Vidar Skiri.

Norwegian farmers is also evident in an incident reported by William Mattieu Williams in his book *Through Norway with a Knapsack*. There is no doubt that the author has been severely affected by this encounter with a Norwegian beauty on the road near Otta in Gudbrandsdalen:

> On looking up I was startled by a strange apparition. A tall, elegant, and most beautiful girl, about eighteen years of age, was standing before me; (...) She (...) was the personification of absolute pride – of innate, unassuming pride – a pride that is unconscious of its own existence, that makes no effort at dignity, and has no thoughts of dignity, but is instinctive dignity itself. (...) She was a perfect specimen of what we regard in England as the high Norman aristocratic type of beauty. Her face was a long oval, of geometrical perfection; her eyes were deep blue; her forehead was high and white; her nose, long and straight; every feature, in short, was unexceptional in form and symmetry. Her hair was flaxen, and her complexion clear, with very little colour. She was dressed with much care and neatness: a clean kerchief smartly tied over her head, and a black cloth jacket closely fitting her beautiful figure (Williams 1876, 197–99).

However, in a later work, *Through Norway with Ladies* (1877), Williams takes his enthusiasm for aristocratic blood connections one step further. Just as Brace and Elton met a descendant of Harald Hårfager at Dombås, Williams and his six women companions are granted an audience with another near-royal at Hjerkinn (Williams's spelling is 'Jerkin'), only twenty miles further north. This is 'the old man, Jerkin of Jerkin'. Williams, who describes himself as a chemist and thus a man of the modern world, makes a humble bow in front of the aging majesty and reports:

> The worshippers of pedigree should all stand uncovered in the presence of Jerkin or any of his family. If our aristocracy are blue-blooded because their ancestors came over with the Conqueror, the blood in the veins of Jerkin and the neighbouring farmers must be ultramarine, for they are of the same stock as William the Norman himself, only that their connection is with the elder branches of the old family, while the Conqueror descended from a younger son, who had to seek his fortune abroad; his elder brother holding the family estates somewhere hereabouts (Williams 1877, 222).

If the Gudbrandsdalen farmers capitalised upon their alleged pedigree – with tongue in cheek – to market their services to gullible tourists, this apparently did not occur to Williams. On the contrary, he intimates that the blood of the Gudbrandsdalen farmer is not only the same that flows in the veins of the British aristocracy, but that it is even of better quality: whilst William the Conqueror descended from a younger son, old Jerkin is the product of the first-born sons through countless generations. Against this background, it comes as no surprise that Williams, in the 1876 edition of *Through Norway with a Knapsack*, gives his enthusiastic support to a continued mixing of blood in the form of intermarriages between the royal families of Britain and the Scandinavian countries. In a note at the very end of the revised edition, he comments of the wedding that had taken place in 1863 between Prince Edward and Princess Alexandra of Denmark:

> When writing the above more than eighteen years ago, I was strongly tempted to express my firm opinion on the desirability of an union between the royal families of Great Britain and Scandinavia, but abstained from such expression, feeling that it would be a personal impertinence on the part of a private subject like myself to make such a suggestion. With such decided feelings on this subject, I need scarcely tell my readers how heartily I participated in the national rejoicings that hailed the marriage of our genial and hearty British Prince with the elegant and accomplished daughter of Denmark; and although it is not the fashion now-a-days to suppose that royal alliances have much political effect, I do hope and believe that this will have considerable influence in the direction above indicated (Williams 1876, 308).

A similar attitude to Anglo-Scandinavian unions permeates several fictional narratives from the last two decades of the century. In Marie Corelli's novel *Thelma: A Norwegian Princess* (1887), Edna Lyall's *A Hardy Norseman* (1890) and Durham Griffith's *An Arctic Eden: A Tale of Norway* (1892), the relationship and eventual marriage (in Lyall, a double marriage!) between a Briton and a Norwegian is not just a main element in the plot; it is also implicitly encouraged by the narrator in a way which harmonises with Williams's general attitude.[16] In Corelli and Lyall, this motif is furthermore presented in combination with strong references to the Viking past. Corelli rather spectacularly conjures up a late nineteenth-century Norwegian girl whose father is a full-blooded heathen Viking, a Finnmark *bonde* who

---

[16] The same basic theme, but with a Danish girl, is used in William Hurton's dramatic sea story *The Doomed Ship: or the Wreck in the Arctic Regions* (1856). Here the young Englishman and the girl, who comes across as the epitome of the Victorian madonna figure, are the only survivors from a ship that sails from Tromsø in Norway and ends up stranded in the Arctic. Needless to say, they marry on their return to civilisation.

at the end of the novel is buried in traditional style, in a burning ship sent out to sea. The young English baronet, Sir Philip Bruce Errington – 'the wealthy and desirable *parti* for whom many matchmaking mothers had stood knee-deep in the chilly though sparkling waters of society ' (Corelli 1894, 9) – thus meets in Thelma not just a true aristocrat of his own calibre and consequently a perfect match. More significantly she represents – not unlike Jane Eyre in relation to Mr Rochester – a healthy and redeeming force for a man gone astray in a decadent and overcivilised London.[17] Edna Lyall's male hero, Frithiof, is similarly named after the hero of the *Frithiof's Saga*, which had been made enduringly popular in translations both of the original saga and of the rather stream-lined and somewhat freely adapted version by the Swedish bishop Esaias Tegnér from 1825. In the novel, part of the action is also set in the Sognefjorden, which is the original setting of the saga, and constant references to the story of Frithiof provide a significant backdrop for the contemporary Anglo-Norwegian relationships in the novel.[18] Stephanie Barczewski largely confirms that endorsements of the renewal of the blood connection between Britain and certain other countries formed a part of the British nation-building project and of the attempt to construct a national identity. In the chapter '"Our Fathers Were of Saxon Race": Robin Hood, King Arthur, and the Rise of Anglo-Saxon Racialism', which surprisingly does not refer to the Viking or Scandinavian element, she mentions similar examples of nineteenth-century fiction that sanction the combination of, for instance, Norman and Saxon blood (Barczewski 2000, 135).

Into this approval of specific ethnic categories, it is possible to read a profound connection with the widespread fear in Britain of social dissolution, physical degeneration, and national decadence. This is especially the case in the latter part of the century. The combination of Darwinian insights, imperial encounters with 'the primitive', and profound worries about the urban masses produced a powerful undercurrent of cultural pessimism which counteracted the more official faith in continued progress and Britain's global supremacy. Some of this sentiment was also expressed in the context of Norse mythology. James Logie Robertson, for instance, in his collection *New Songs of Innocence* (1889), turns to the Norse vision

---

[17] The name Errington is hardly coincidental. For a thorough presentation of Marie Corelli's life, her enormous popularity and her place in the late nineteenth-century literary landscape, see Federico (2000).

[18] For a full discussion of the remarkable popularity of the *Frithiof's Saga* in the Victorian period, see Wawn (2000), ch. 5.

of the final apocalypse, the so called Twilight of the Gods, to describe
the prevalent late nineteenth-century fear of approaching disaster.
The title of the poem, 'Ragnarök', is the Norse word for this terrible
event, which is characterised by raging wars and furious monsters
accompanied by natural disasters that eventually lead to the ravaged
earth disappearing into the sea.

> So wildly the clouds are wedded
>   In conflict fiercely dumb,
> It seems that the hour long dreaded
>   Of Ragnarök is come!
> The gods are fighting yonder,
>   The evil with the good –
> Ah, Willie, watch and ponder –
>   Will the evil be withstood?
>
> There's a Ragnarök, my Willie,
>   For many a human heart:
> The winds of doubt blow chilly,
>   The hopes of spring depart.
> From Thor the strength is riven,
>   And Baldur the loved is dead,
> And Odin grows old in heaven
>   And hangs his heavy head (ll. 9–24).

As Daniel Pick points out in his study *Faces of Degeneration* (1989),
these fears were also vividly brought to the surface in such popular
novels as Richard Jefferies's *After London* (1885), Robert L.
Stevenson's *Dr Jekyll and Mr Hyde* (1886), George Gissing's *The
Nether World* (1889), Oscar Wilde's *The Picture of Dorian Gray*
(1890) and H. G. Wells's *The Time Machine* (1895). In Gissing's and
Wells's novels especially, the reader is faced with a frightening Other
that threatens to destabilise and undermine the security of a normal,
healthy society. And the threat is largely to do with genetic
deterioration. It is not surprising to find, therefore, that the implicit
desire in the fiction of the 1880s and 90s for a 'refill' of Scandinavian
genes coincides almost precisely with the development of the new
science called eugenics. Incidentally, this field of research was
founded by the anthropologist Sir Francis Galton, who was not only
Charles Darwin's cousin, but also the editor of travel books, one of
which contains an article from Norway by H. F. Tozer, with rather
detailed comparisons between the Norwegian upper classes and the
English middle classes (Galton 1861, 382-3). For Galton and many of

his contemporaries, the genetic deterioration that they were trying to counteract in Britain had still not reached Norway. Even when compared to the other Scandinavian countries, Norway appeared to be in a special position, presumably because its population had less contact with the deteriorating impulses of the modern world and was consequently even more closely connected with a pristine and natural innocence than people in Sweden and Denmark. Charles Loring Brace wonders 'what it was in the rocks, the air, or the sea, which made such a people of conquerors', and offers the following clue:

> Norway is fortunate in still possessing a people who are not degraded in the comparison of manhood with their unconquerable forefathers. In Denmark, one cannot, in the character of the people, trace the historic descent from the Danish Northmen. Among the Norwegians, one feels that the same stuff is still there, and the same essential elements of nature (Brace 1857, 82–83).

As Barczewski points out, however, the construction of a British national identity required a careful balancing act in the choice of ethnic impulses that were respectively rejected or accepted. The attempt throughout the eighteenth century to construct a common idea of what Barczewski calls 'Britishness' could easily be spoiled by elevating specific elements to a dominant position. This is precisely what happened to the term 'Anglo-Saxon': 'an elaborate racial hierarchy was erected which placed the Anglo-Saxon peoples at the top, a crude, biological determinism seemingly confirmed by Britain's pre-eminent political, economic, and military position' (Barczewski 2000, 124). Generally, this rather loosely defined category came to include not only the Angles and the Saxons, but also other subgroups of a not particularly clear-cut definition, such as the Teutons, the Vikings, the Scandinavians and the Germans. But some writers were in no mood to accept such broad generalisations, and thereby pointed to the potentially brittle fabric of the emergent national identity. In 1852 William and Mary Howitt published their work *The Literature and Romance of Northern Europe* – 'a popular work on both sides of the Atlantic' (Wawn 2000, 108) – the first chapter of which contains a persistent and not infrequently aggressive argument to the effect that it is essential to distinguish sharply between the Scandiavian element, on the one hand, and the Anglo-Saxon, on the other. The Howitts start their diatribe by pointing, with great gusto, to what they consider a fundamental flaw in British and indeed European historiography:

Amongst the many wonders of this world, there is none greater than the blindness of the writers of this and other countries to the transcendent influence of the blood and spirit of ancient Scandinavia on the English character. (...) Whenever the spirit, the progress, the expanding and onpouring populousness of the English race is mentioned, it is immediately designated the Anglo-Saxon family. It is to the Anglo-Saxon that we yield the palm of originating the undying vigour and impulsive qualities which mark the British people. It is the Anglo-Saxon blood, according to the chorus of modern writers of almost all countries, which is peopling the most distant climes, and the most gigantic continents. Is this true? On the contrary, we are persuaded that it is one of the greatest fallacies of the age. (...) The Saxons, during their period of dominion, so far from showing themselves an enterprising and progressive people, notoriously degenerated; became slothful and weak, and were overrun by the Danes, and soon after permanently subjected by the Normans, another branch of the Scandinavians (Howitt 1852, 1: 1–3).

A modern reader of these reflections may wonder what is the Howitts's hidden agenda. It is only after further sweeping statements that the authors gradually disclose their objective by quoting at length from Samuel Laing's influential introduction to his 1844 translation of *The Heimskringla; or, Chronicle of the Kings of Norway*, including the following passage:

'All that men hope for of good government and future improvement in their physical and moral condition – all that civilized men enjoy at this day of civil, religious, and political liberty – the British constitution, representative legislature, the trial by jury, security of property, freedom of mind and person, the influence of public opinion over the conduct of public affairs, the Reformation, the liberty of the press, the spirit of the age, – all that is or has been of value to man in modern times as a member of society, either in Europe or in the New World, may be traced to the spark left burning upon our shores by these northern barbarians' (ibid., 5).

Both Laing and the Howitts, in other words, are using the Scandinavians as early and powerful representatives of what they see as a liberal, democratic society, that is, in short, modern Victorian Britain. There is no doubt that this position at the same time sanctions a significant and disturbingly aggressive element of jingoistic nationalism. As has been suggested above, this nationalism is hardly all-inclusive, as the Howitts's conclusion shows:

Turn now from these old Scandinavians to the English. Though they
have lived now for eight centuries, under the influence of a religious
faith totally opposed to that of Odin – under the religion of peace and
love – it has not been able to quench the old Norse fire in their veins. The
same love of martial daring and fame; the same indomitable sea-faring
spirit, the same passion for discovery of new seas and new lands, the
same irresistible longing, when discovered, to seize and colonize them,
the same victorious strength in subduing the vastest, the most populous
or the most savage nations to their yoke, still distinguish them, and
distinguish them above all other people. America, Australia, the Indies
East and west, South Africa, Gibraltar, Malta, the Ionia Isles, and the
isles of many a distant sea bear testimony to the survival of the spirit of
the Vikings in the bosoms of the British. How is it possible any question
could ever have arisen on the subject? That for a moment we could trace
to the Saxon race these great and ineradicable traits of our own? We
repeat it, that it is not an Anglo-Saxon nor even a Scandinavian race,
which astonishes mankind by its domestic freedom and marvellous
activity of spirit, as well as by its prodigious foreign conquests, but the
English race. But while we are compounded of British, Roman, Saxon
and Scandinavian blood, had that of Germany predominated we should
have been now as Germany is, a country without colonies, without
conquests, without a fleet, and without political liberty (12–13).

The Howitts make a clever attempt to gather all the threads together
and iron out the differences, but even here a modern reader is struck
by the uncritical use of the word 'English' and of the open hostility
towards 'the Saxon race'. Furthermore, they show a surprisingly
sharp and condescending edge against a Germany which, in the
1850s, did not yet represent a serious challenge to Britain's
hegemony in Europe or in the rest of the world. On the contrary, it
could be seen as almost hopelessly old-fashioned – in parts almost
feudal – and fragmented. With the benefit of hindsight, however, one
may perhaps detect in the Howitts's tirade a certain fear of Germany's
future potential.
    Wawn mentions the Howitts as an example of the not insignificant
'trickle-down effect' from Laing's influential translation of, and his
'Preliminary Dissertation' to, the *Heimskringla* from 1844, which
expresses a profound admiration for 'the raw Viking spirit' (see
Wawn 2000, ch. 4). Another such example, not mentioned by Wawn
and with more specific reference to Norway, is a book cited in chapter
1, namely *Driftwood from Scandinavia*, by Lady Wilde. Although, as
the title indicates, the literary qualities of the work are rather limited,
it is still interesting to see how the author, clearly on the basis of
works by Laing and others, plays around with the ancient tribes of

northern Europe and eventually makes them all fall neatly into place, with the Norwegians – that is in Lady Wilde's terminology those representatives of the 'Norse' who are 'pure Goths' – as virtually the sole ancestors of the British aristocracy:

In Christiania one meets representatives of all the northern nations: Swedes, Danes, Norse, and Germans, all of the one Teuton race, yet with strongly marked differences. The characteristic of the Norse is strength; of the Swedes, refinement and culture; of the Danes, grace and gaiety. The Saxon is the lowest Teuton type, the Goth the highest. The Saxon lies at the base of all Germanic peoples, as in England, rude, uncouth, material, gross, without any sense of the beautiful. A people, as D'Israeli observed, of enormous appetites and infinite greed, made for a middle class, and fated never to rise above it, with flat, formless, typeless faces – the much-worn copper coinage of civilization, suitable only for the vulgar uses of commerce.

The Danes are a mixture of Celt and Teuton, and the Celtic blood has spiritualized the Teuton clay, and given to them that charm of manner which is so loveable and attractive. The Swedes are a mixture of Goth and Greek, for in old times constant intercourse was kept up between Sweden and Byzantium, and to this dash of the Orient and the Greek may be due the noble serenity and calm dignity of Swedish expression and manner. The Danes are a small people, with small round heads and fair complexion. The Swedes are tall and slight; they have oval heads, dark hair and refined intellectual features. The Swedish chin is particularly well formed; it is, indeed, the only well-cut chin in all North-western Europe.

The Norse are pure Goths, of Odin's race, the Æsar, or demi-gods, the highest of the Teuton tribes, without any admixture of the Celt, who made no settlements and never progressed beyond the south of Sweden. They are of lofty stature, with proud, erect bearing, and frank, fearless manner. The head is high and well arched, as in the best Norman-English type; the head of races born to rule. (...) As a people the Goths of the North are physically, perhaps, the finest in Europe. Tradition says they are descended of the sons of the giants; the children of the gods and the daughters of men. They live simply, disdain all luxury, have the strong, irrepressible instincts of freedom, and hold themselves the equal of kings. A race of warriors and heroes, fierce and cruel in the old time, but never weak, they ravaged and ruled all Europe, and made the name of Goth a thing of dread, plundering and conquering all peoples and lands, yet still laying the basis of organized law and government wherever they held sway. They founded the Norman dynasty in England, and English liberty, even while they crushed the Saxons, who are made to be crushed: and the Norman nobility of England still show their Scandinavian affinity by the strawberry leaf on the ducal coronet; for the strawberry, the vine of the North, was sacred to Odin, and significant of territorial right and power (Wilde 1884, 126–28).[19]

Lady Wilde, who in this passage airs virtually every stereotyped racial prejudice of the nineteenth century, was not the only British visitor to Norway who drew attention to the differences between the Scandinavian countries, and thereby singled out the British-Norwegian connection as especially strong and significant. William Hurton's breezy and intelligent account *A Voyage from Leith to Lapland* makes the same distinction. Having noticed that people in Christiania followed English fashion 'more closely than any other place in Scandinavia', he remarks:

> It is curious that the three Scandinavian capitals, each are [*sic*] influenced by as many different foreign countries. At Copenhagen, German is the foreign language generally spoken, and German manners and ideas have hitherto had most influence, at Christiania it has been the same with English; and at Stockholm, French. It would be a curious chapter in the history of the several cities, to trace the progress of these foreign influences (Hurton 1851, 51).

In a broader perspective, however, Scandinavia at large is often seen as a net contributor to European civilisation, frequently at the expense of the countries traditionally regarded as the cultural heavyweights of Europe. This broad shift of attention from the south to the north, which was instigated by the Romantic movement and which ran counter to the whole pre-Romantic tradition, is apparent in Isabella Frances Blundell, who in regarding the Norse pantheon clearly finds the origins of those solid, matter-of-fact virtues that have made Britain great:

> Nor in looking upon Odin and the gods who stand around him, can we fail to be struck by the infinite moral superiority they possess in contrast to those of Rome and Greece, who sat in laughing ease, mere spectators of the conflict going on between the powers of good and evil; the gods of our forefathers knew no such contemplative mood; they took part in the strife and were themselves ever on the watch against the attacks of the Jotuns, or giants, who were ready to disturb the order of the world (Blundell 1862, 215).

[19] This passage may, of course, also serve as a useful reminder of the fact that the racism of the 1930s and 40s had its origins in widely held and largely accepted sentiments of the nineteenth century.

Lord Dufferin reflects a similar attitude when comparing the great heroes of the Northern and Mediterranean worlds: 'The forms of those old Greeks and Romans whom we are taught to reverence, may project taller shadows on the world's stage; but though the scene be narrow here, and light be wanting, the interest is not less intense, nor are the passions less awful that inspired these ruder dramas' (Dufferin 1857, 353). Finally, in Edward Wilson Landor's novel *Lofoden*, Ellinor, the daughter of a Scottish pastor who has moved to Norway for religious reasons, explains in a discussion with her sister how the Scandinavians injected a 'new vitality' into all of Europe: 'The profound homage of their genius and of their devotion is testified by works that form the glory, not only of Germany and of France, but of Lombardy and even of Sicily. Europe from north to south has felt their power, and waxed great from the infusion (into a worn-out system) of their vigorous vitality'" (Landor 1849, 59).

In her discussion of Britain's 'suitable past', Stephanie Barczewski makes the following observation:

> By locating and rooting the community in a historic space, 'the land of the fathers', it provides the nation with a definite geographical location. By pointing to ancestral heroes from whom the nation's present inhabitants are purportedly descended, it suggests a degree of continuity between generations. By reminding the members of a community of its past greatness, it instills them with a sense of inner worth and collective dignity. And finally, by displaying the past as a mirror of the future, it points the community towards a glorious destiny (Barczewski 2000, 46).

In such a careful construction of a gallery of 'ancestral heroes', it is hardly surprising to find that some groups are included, whilst others are left out. There can be little doubt that Blundell, Lord Dufferin, Landor and others either consciously or unconsciously played the Scandinavian card, as opposed to the Mediterranean or the Celtic, because it was felt to be more genuinely part of the British tradition as they chose to define it, and thereby contributed to a national identity rooted in the home soil. Also, their general attitudes were of course products of the old truth that history is written by the conquerors rather than the conquered, and British society was still dominated by an essentially *English* elite whose ancestral myth was linked to the Normans and their spirited forefathers from the far North.[20] As will be seen in the following, however, the flexibility of

---

[20] A number of commentators even use the term 'cousin' about the Norwegians, emphasising even more strongly the familial ties between the two countries.

the Viking myth similarly provided an ideal vehicle for explaining and justifying the transition from domestic nationalism into global imperialism.

Heroes and Empire Builders

In his highly entertaining and satirical essay from 1928, 'Talking (and Singing) of the Nordic Man', Hilaire Belloc – born in France and of part-French ancestry – effectively and with devastating precision sums up a Victorian ideal which, after the First World War, looked painfully outdated. With respect to the Nordic Man's life story, Belloc remarks:

> The Nordic Man is born either in the West End of London or in a pleasant country house, standing in its own park-like grounds. That is the general rule; he is, however, sometimes born in a parsonage and rather more frequently in a Deanery or a Bishop's Palace, or a Canon's house in a Close. Some of this type have been born in North Oxford; but none (that I can discover) in the provincial manufacturing towns, and certainly none east of Charing Cross or south of the river (Belloc 1951, 254).

Born in 1870 and having witnessed the cataclysm of the War and the emergence of a different and more democratic society in the post-War years, Belloc was looking back on ideals which a few decades earlier had played a significant role in the building and justification of empire, and thus also in the formation of the British national identity. 'The Nordic Man', in other words, represented a somewhat old-fashioned and tattered version of the heroic Victorian Viking. Although the deliberate use of the Viking for what could be called propaganda purposes has already been touched upon, the following discussion will focus more explicitly on the connections between British imperialism and Vikingism. But first of all it is necessary to go back briefly to the diverse and frequently contradictory image of the Viking in Victorian Britain.

As will be remembered, Lady Wilde made a virtue of the fact that 'the Norse' were 'pure Goths'. This celebration of the primitive and the Gothic, however, was not primarily a Victorian phenomenon; it was a natural consequence of the Romantic scepticism against civilisation and sophistication, or as H. Arnold Barton puts it in his *Northern Arcadia: Foreign Travelers in Scandinavia 1765–1815*:

> Foreign visitors were (…) strongly attracted to the North by nostalgia for

a past removed from the Mediterranean origins of civilization. (...) This glorification of rude 'Gothic' virtues reveals, in turn, contemporary apprehensions of the degenerate and enervating effects [of] an overrefined and luxury-loving civilization, what James Thomson in his *Brittannia* from 1729 had called the 'soft penetrating plague' (Barton 1998, 153).

Thus, the Vikings, and to some extent their nineteenth-century Norwegian descendants, were associated with a rough and rude simplicity and naturalness that were in opposition to typical Enlightenment values, and at the same time in perfect harmony with fundamental Romantic ideas. According to Wawn, it is first and foremost Sir Walter Scott who 'lent lasting glamour to the nomadic life of the sea-borne Viking' (Wawn 2000, 73–74) by inspiring a whole school of followers, who peopled nineteenth-century art and literature with innumerable versions of this particular character.

The image of the sea-faring Viking, in other words, acquired in the course of the century a flexibility which made it into the perfect model for the imperial hero figure that played such an important role in Victorian culture and education. With a raised sword in the battlefield or in the prow of his ship, he is prepared for storm and action. In the sonnet 'The Norwegian' from as early as 1800, the Scottish poet Anne Bannerman (1765–1829) says about her hero that 'when the first faint ray / Shines on the billow's ice-encumber'd foam, / Fearless he launches on his trackless way, / And on the stormy ocean hails his home' (Mains 1989, 252). The poet Sir Edwin Arnold (1832–1904), who spent his entire professional life in the service of the Empire, clearly had a similar figure in mind in the poem 'March', from his 1885 collection *The Secret of Death*:

Welcome, North-wind! from the Norland;
Strike upon our foremost foreland,
Sweep away across the moorland,
Do thy lysty kind!
Thou and we were born together
In the black Norwegian weather;
Birds we be of one brave feather,
Welcome, bully wind!

In many of the texts from the period, the theme of imperial expansion is clearly visible between the lines. This is certainly the case in Henry Wheaton's *History of the Northmen*, which also adds to the image of the sea-king a halo of honour and glory:

Thus the practice of sea-roving became the favorite pursuit, and, it might almost be said, the most graceful accomplishment of princes and nobles, and was surrounded with all the lustre of chivalry. The younger sons of the kings and Jarls, who had no other inheritance but the ocean, naturally collected around their standards the youth of the inferior orders, who were equally destitute. Thus the best and bravest of the nation were launched upon the waves, and the chieftains who followed this mode of life are distinguished in the Sagas by the appropriate appellation of Sea-Kings (...). It is easy to see, that all these circumstances combined tended to give the national character a strong impulse to maritime enterprises, and to stimulate it by the desire of renown and wealth, which last was more precariously acquired by the peaceful pursuits of commerce. These were sometimes indeed mingled with those of sea-roving, and the strange and apparently incompatible union of the characters of king, merchant, and pirate, were seen united in one individual (Wheaton 1831, 135–36).

To the Victorian empire builders, however, the widespread celebration of the simple, rude and merciless man of action represented a certain dilemma; after all, the somewhat heavy-handed way in which Britain frequently added new dominions to the empire was only justifiable when presented as a project by which ignorance and barbarism were to be eradicated by the light of civilisation. As has been shown, to counteract this paradox a number of nineteenth-century travellers and writers on Norway evinced a considerable admiration for the sophistication of Norse culture, and commonly defended its qualities in a comparison with the culture of ancient Greece and Rome.

For a long time this image of the civilised Viking had trouble competing with the more established image of the barbaric pirate. However, some rather spectacular events in Norway contributed to a change of focus. In 1867, a Viking longship was found buried in a mound at Tune in Østfold. It was immediately taken to Christiania, where it was exhibited in the park behind the University. Then, in 1880, the impressive and far better preserved Gokstad ship was unearthed in Vestfold, taken to the capital, and exhibited next to the Tune ship. The importance of these and later excavations – especially the sensational Oseberg find in 1903 – should not be underestimated. Up until this point, drawings of Viking ships had largely been based on conjectures and speculations; no one really knew what they had looked like, how big they were or how well they performed at sea. The Gokstad ship, however, provided information which could hardly fail to impress: built around 890 AD, it was 24 metres long and

The Viking's Ship.

Both the political drama around 1814 and the excavations of several Viking ships later in the century contributed strongly to an increased interest in Norway and Norwegian history, and the country's heroic past became a recurring theme in a large number of British travelogues. This illustration from Richard Lovett's *Norwegian Pictures* (1885) shows the Gokstad ship, which was found in 1880 and exhibited in the garden behind the University in Christiania.

5 metres wide, had a sail of 110 square metres, could accommodate 32 oarsmen and was capable of doing more than 12 knots. Furthermore, the ship's excellent seaworthiness was proven when a copy was built and sailed across the Atlantic to the World Exhibition in Chicago in 1893.[21]

Thus the Gokstad find was in itself enough to cause a re-evaluation of the Vikings and of their contribution to European (and American) history, and from a British point of view the new information could not have been more pertinent to the imperial propaganda effort. The excavations showed beyond doubt that the Vikings, that is the alleged forefathers of contemporary British imperialists, had been in possession of advanced technological knowledge, and that they were indeed both capable of and willing to exploit it in order to branch out into the wide world. Thus, with a military and merchant navy which had for centuries been the pride of the British nation, the Viking ships in Christiania provided the perfect bridgehead between past and present greatness; in fact, these discoveries were reminiscent of the way in which the early eighteenth-century Augustan age in Britain had drawn deliberate parallels to the Romans. But whereas the Romans represented a foreign and relatively distant culture, the Vikings could justifiably be regarded as an integral part of British history. The nation, in other words, could boast her own proud maritime tradition and her own gallery of historical heroes by underlining the kinship between Britain and Norway. The historian James Anthony Froude saw clearly these parallels and connections, and so did Olivia M. Stone, who travelled in Norway in 1881, only a year after the Gokstad find. She spends more than twenty-five pages and a number of detailed illustrations on the Viking ships and their significance, and demonstrates a keen awareness of a change of focus:

> The people of the Viking period appear from this discovery [of the Viking ships] to have been in a much higher state of civilisation than has generally been supposed. (...) We have been so accustomed to regard these northern freebooters as rough, unkempt, irreligious barbarians, that it gives us somewhat of a mental wrench to find these ideas upset (Stone 1882, 35–36).[22]

[21] According to Mrs Alec Tweedie's *A Winter Jaunt* to Norway, the Americans had wanted to exhibit the real ship, and had 'offered any amount of money for it' (Tweedie 1894, 25).

[22] Her husband, John Harris Stone, similarly wrote an article entitled 'The Viking

LETTERS

FROM

HIGH LATITUDES;

BEING

SOME ACCOUNT OF A VOYAGE

IN

THE SCHOONER YACHT "FOAM," 85 O.M.

TO

ICELAND, JAN MAYEN, & SPITZBERGEN,

IN 1856.

BY 'LORD' DUFFERIN., *Frederick Temple Blackwood*

THIRD EDITION.

LONDON:

JOHN MURRAY, ALBEMARLE STREET.

1857.

Before the excavations of Viking ships, very little was known about their actual size and appearance. This highly imaginative example is from the title page of Lord Dufferin's book *Letters from High Latitudes*, which was published in 1857, ten years before the Tune ship was found.

And later on in the book, she asks a rhetorical question that may have been inspired by similar reflections: '[I]s not Norway, in the true meaning of the word, the most aristocratic country on the face of the earth?' (ibid., 97). Even well before the Viking ship finds, the Oxford don Frederick Metcalfe similarly credits the ancient Scandinavians with virtually every quality that has contributed to Britain's greatness, in the cultural as well as the military field. Between the lines there is an unmistakable streak of pride in a gene pool which – it is implied – has produced a perfect combination of talents:

> It is from them our Frobishers and Drakes, our Parrys and Franklins, and Rajah Brookes, are lineally descended. (...) With them to attempt was to succeed, in whatever line they chose, whether as navigators, colonists, legislators, conquerors, historians, poets. (...) [I]n England transfusing new blood into the body social and political, administering a tonic to a frame massive and strong, but lethargic and deficient in vital energy, thus leavening the torpid elements of the Saxon nature, and making a mark in the land never to be effaced (Metcalfe 1880, 193).

Among poets, there had been an interest in Norway and the Vikings from the late eighteenth century onwards. Since the poetry of Thomas Gray, James Macpherson and Thomas Percy in the 1760s, a number of poets had kept the fascination alive, including such major names as William Blake ('Gwin, King of Norway', 1783), Robert Southey ('The Race of Odin' and 'The Death of Odin', 1795), and Thomas Love Peacock ('Fiolfar, King of Norway', 1806). Mention should also be made of Anna Seward (the 'Swan of Lichfield'), whose poem 'Harold's Complaint: A Scandinavian Ode' was included in her *Poetical Works* (1810), edited by Sir Walter Scott. However, whereas the large majority of these poems were sentimental, backward-looking and thus mainly apolitical, the more explicitly imperialistic theme, frequently coupled with Viking imagery, became particularly evident in the public verse that from the middle of the century onwards was turning increasingly jingoistic and patriotic. Published in collections of poetry, in magazines and newspapers, these poems were everywhere visible, providing an image of the British Empire as closely connected with the Viking tradition. Karl Litzenberg even claims that the general significance of this fashion of the North has been underestimated:

Ship' in *Good Words* in November 1881, probably based on the same visit (ref. Schiötz 1970–1986, 1: 467).

The fact that hundreds of short Norse pieces – chiefly poems and essays
– were published anonymously in a large number of nineteenth-century
periodicals such as the *Westminster Review, Fraser's Magazine*, the
North British Review, the *Quarterly Review*, and others suggests that the
interest in Old Norse themes in the Victorian Age was more general than
the actual number of separate nineteenth-century Norse books and
treatises in the Anglo-Norse field might indicate (Litzenberg 1947, 3).

The poet Gerald Massey (1828–1907) included the poem 'Old King
Hake' in his collected poems, entitled *My Lyrical Life*, from 1889.
Hake is described thus: 'He was a hero in the old / blood-letting days;
/ An iron hero of Norse mould, / And warring ways' (ll. 5–8). And he
is, not surprisingly, a restless man of the sea: 'But Hake could never
bind at home / His spirit free; / It grew familiar with the foam / Of
many a sea' (ll. 73–76). In some texts, however, the imperialistic
theme takes on a blunter and more explicit character. The poet and
critic Richard Henry (or Hengist) Horne (1802–1884), a close friend
of William Howitt (see above), published in 1875 the poem 'Arctic
Heroes: A Fragment of Naval History', a title which clearly draws a
significant line between the ancient sea-kings and the current
greatness of the British Navy. The poem's prologue is spoken by the
'red-handed Eirek', a phantom of a sea-king and the son of
'Thorwald, Norway's chief'. Speaking 'through the long freezing
centuries', he celebrates 'The Scandinavian spirit of the brine, / That
sent us forth to conquest, plunder, fame!' (ll. 33–34).
     An even more direct statement, however, is found in a poem by
Frederick William Orde Ward (1843–1922), the majority of whose
works were published under a pseudonym containing an
unmistakably Scandinavian middle name: Frederick *Harald*
Williams. From 1865 to the end of the First World War, Ward
produced several collections of poems, thus carrying the Victorian
tradition of patriotic, public verse full of traditional imagery
connected with Vikings and knights in armour, into the inferno of the
first modern war. In 1894 he published the collection *Confessions of
a Poet*, which contains the aggressively jingoistic 'How I Won the
Victoria Cross'. The poem begins on a note of quiet sadness before
the impending battle, but soon escalates into a frenzied celebration of
the 'fever of the fight' and 'the savage thirst of slaughter', of sacrifice
pro patria, and of heroic death: 'Not for true love's sweet story, / Not
for a Prince's power, / Would I exchange the glory / Of this one
gallant hour' (ll. 57–60). And here the Viking blood, boiling and
brave, comes to the surface, transforming the civilised, Victorian

Briton into a berserker of the old school, mixing, in the process, the past and the present by including both 'sword and belching gun':

> I feel the ancient Viking
>   All blazing in my blood,
> The hungry wrath for striking
>   Through fiercest fire or flood;
> Why, 'tis a game for Princes,
>   With sword and belching gun,
> That the stout heart evinces,
>   When those poor vermin run;
> My steed her head has lowered
>   Prepared for worse than that,
> To seize yon creeping coward
>   And shake him like a rat;
> His stroke has lost its labour,
>   The swarthy visage pales,
> As through him shears my sabre,
>   And dead men tell no tales;
> What, faint? Think not of falling
>   So near the dazzling goal,
> With England's honour calling,
>   And here the waters roll (ll. 121–40).

This poetic glorification of violence may be seen as related to a widespread view not only of the Vikings but also of nineteenth-century Norwegians as tough, hardy and courageous. Accounts of the fiery temper of the Norwegians from as sober a source as the 1801–1810 edition of *Encyclopædia Britannica* reveal perhaps less condemnation than a kind of admiration that could easily be translated into a dubious sanctioning of the use of power in general:

> Even the farmers stand upon their punctilio, and challenge one another to single combat with their knives. On such occasions they hook themselves together by their belts, and fight until one of them is killed or mortally wounded. At weddings and public feasts they drink to intoxication, quarrel, fight, and murder generally ensues (s.v. 'Norway').

The political implications are equally obvious in the hero worship that forms such an integral part of nineteenth-century culture. It is no coincidence, for instance, that Walter E. Houghton, in his classic *The Victorian Frame of Mind* (1957), devotes an entire chapter to this phenomenon, claiming that at the beginning of the Victorian period, 'all the prerequisites for hero worship were present: the enthusiastic temper, the conception of the superior being, the revival of Homeric mythology and medieval ballad, (...) the popularity of Scott and Byron, and the living presence of Napoleonic soldiers and sailors' (Houghton 1975, 310). Thus, as has already been suggested, the hero worship of the period took many forms within such different areas as politics, religion, art and philosophy, and the celebration of violence and sacrifice was only one of them. Carlyle's hero figure, for instance, represented first of all through the god Odin, is not just a superhuman soldier; as Karl Litzenberg points out, Carlyle's main concern was 'to show that Odin was a man who became a Hero; a Hero who became a god' (Litzenberg 1947, 21).[23] In the lectures *On Heroes, Hero-Worship and the Heroic in History* (1841), this man-cum-god had been elevated to a Christ- or Messiah-like stature, that is a moral idol that would guide nations and individuals through Delectable Mountains and Sloughs of Despond, if necessary with sword in hand.[24] And towards the end of his career, in *The Early Kings of Norway*, Carlyle once again returns to the proud Scandinavian heritage:

> All readers will admit that there was something naturally royal in these Haarfagr [*sic*] Kings. A wildly great kind of kindred; counts in it two Heroes of a high, or almost highest, type: the first two Olafs, Tryggveson and the Saint. And the view of them, withal, as we chance to have it, I have often thought, how essentially Homeric it was: – indeed what is 'Homer' himself but the *Rhapsody* of five centuries of Greek Skalds and wandering Ballad-singers, dine (i.e. 'stitched together') by somebody more musical than Snorro was? Olaf Tryggveson and Olaf Saint please me quite as well in their prosaic form; offering me the truth of them as if seen in their real lineaments by some marvellous opening (through the art of Snorro) across the black strata of the ages (Carlyle 1875, 97).

This variant of the hero is not least prominent in children's literature. One example is Mary Howarth's *Stories of Norway in the Saga Days*, which contains four stories with a very obvious pedagogical objective. The first of these, 'The White Prince and King Olaf', is set in Gardariki or 'Russian Sweden', which is ruled by King Valdemar

---

[23] Shortly before his death in 2002, the Norwegian explorer and scientist Thor Heyerdahl revived this idea, causing considerable controversy, by claiming he had found archaeological evidence that Odin was a warlord from Azerbaijan who, together with his people, had emigrated to Northern Europe.

[24] For a discussion of Carlyle and Odin, see Anne Varty, 'Carlyle and Odin', in Ewbank et al. (1999), 60–70.

Legendary heroes appear to have a magnetic appeal to young people in all ages. Victorian children were brought up with Viking heroes who were frequently presented as embodying a combination of political, military and moral strength. This illustration is from the story 'The White Prince and King Olaf', in Mary Howarth's *Stories of Norway in the Saga Days* (1895).

and Queen Allogia. Before she dies, the old queen, Valdemar's mother, speaks the following prophecy: '"In Norway there has just been born (...) a man-child of a beauteous form and health most wonderful. He will be great; a king of our neighbour land, bringing light to all who will hearken to his teaching, and to one sore afflicted, life and joy eternal' (Howarth 1895, 5). The similarities between Olaf Tryggvason, the child in question, and Christ are beyond dispute, and when later on in the story Olaf becomes king, he emerges as the incarnation of the hero as a moral as well as a military force: 'Olaf's sovereignty was that of personality. He could not tell his ministers what to do and then leave the kingdom in safety, because he had no ministers. He ruled alone. Warriors were his assistants: men who fought. For the rest, he made the laws and saw them enforced. It was absolutely necessary that he should be on the spot' (ibid., 41). Similarly, in the final story, 'The Boy Who Would Be a Viking', the heroic deed does not consist in military feats, but rather in a young man's realisation that life demands an acceptance of mundane responsibilities and sacrifice. Again, the Viking hero is capable of encompassing a wide and apparently contradictory range of ideals, from the unique and powerful leader, who is both his own moral guide and the guide of others, to the man in the street, who humbly finds his place and does his duty.

Also in F. Robertson's collection *Torquil, or the Days of Olaf Tryggvason* (1870), several poems describe hardened Vikings who learn a moral lesson. One of them, 'Ballad: Magnus of Norway – 1098', tells the story of the half-drunk King Magnus who is jealous of 'Olave the sainted', who allegedly lies 'uncorrupt' in his grave. In his fury he forces his bishop to come with him and open Olave's grave, but when he sees the dead man looking as if alive, he falls down on his knees and prays for forgiveness. Later, having 'tossed upon his bed', the King realises he is not alone:

A glittering form stood by his bed,
    With helm and cross of gold,
His snowy robes of heavenly sheen
    Fell down in heavy fold.

'Magnus King of Norway,'
    'Twas thus saint Olave spake,
'Why hast thou dared my shrine to taint,
    'My rest to scoffing break?

'Magnus King of Norway,

'E'er thirty days roll by,
'If thou leavest not this kingdom
'Thou shalt most surely die' (ll. 73–84).

With the thirty days' deadline nicely echoing the treachery of Judas, the Norse setting of the poem is connected directly with the religious values of contemporary nineteenth-century British society.

As one would expect, however, Victorian travellers in Norway also saw the hero in historical figures other than the Vikings. One such figure was the Swedish King Charles XII, who was killed in Norway during a siege of the fortress at Frederiksten in 1718. The young and gifted king's death, the circumstances of which are still unclear, provided him with a posthumous fame which alone made Frederiksten into a shrine and a tourist attraction, more than a hundred years later. The twenty-one year old Lord Brougham, who later became the British Lord Chancellor, was only one of many visitors. Jean A. Mains connects this fascination directly with the hero worship of the period. Lady Wilde's description, she claims, 'panegyrised his career. Other travellers called him "the kingly Swede", "a truly brave man", "heroic and generous". Even his sword had "something heroic about it". His death was "a tragic catastrophe"' (Mains 1989, 48).[25]

At the end of the nineteenth century, there was also at least one contemporary hero who deserved to be compared with the greats of the past. This was the explorer, scientist and later statesman Frithjof Nansen (1861–1930), whose dramatic Arctic expedition of 1893–1896 was seen as a confirmation that Norwegians still possessed the mettle of their ancestors. In 1897 the English version of

---

[25] It is not quite true, however, that all the British visitors showed an unquestioning admiration for the king. Edward Wilson Landor, who visited the place of his death in 1835 and wrote a poem subtitled 'On the Spot Where He Fell', depicts him – very much along the lines of Shelley's poems about Napoleon – as a tyrant who reaped as he sowed:

Unmourned by man that warrior's fate shall be
Who only fought for self and victory.
He who for glory was content to fall,
Glory may well be his – but that be all;
No fond remembrance rises at the name
Of him who marched o'er misery unto fame,
Who only strove Oppression's sword to wave,
And sought for conquest only to enslave
(Landor 1836, 1: 227, ll. 13–20).

Nansen's own account of the expedition was published under the title *Farthest North*, and in November the same year Florence Earle Coates's poem 'Nansen' appeared in the prestigious *Harper's New Monthly Magazine*[26]:

> To drift with thee, not strive against thy tide,
>   All-powerful Nature! to pursue thy law,
>   Attentive, – with devout and childlike awe
> Heark'ning unto thy voice, and none beside:
> To drift with thee! With thee for friend and guide,
>   In fragile bark, careless of cold or thaw,
>   To brave the ice-pack and the dread sea-maw! –
> So are man's conquests won, so glorified.
> The truest compass is the seeing soul.
>   Oh, wond'ring Earth! did not thy spirit glow,
>   Calling to mind the deathless Genoese,
> As Nansen, pilot of the frozen Pole,
>   Like a young Viking rode the icy floe,
>   Wresting their secret from the Arctic Seas?

There was also another way in which the British tourists and travellers of the nineteenth century renewed their sense of kinship with what they regarded as their Viking ancestors. As will be discussed in more detail in chapter 4, the fjords and the coastline were perceived by the travellers and marketed by the travel agents as the very epitome of the Norwegian experience. Well-to-do travellers, in particular, frequently enjoyed this experience in their own private yachts, thus recreating a Viking sense of freedom and exploration, and, according to Wawn, showing what the British were made of: 'That Victorian gentlemen sailors, "modern Vikings" every one, were eager to voyage north and explore the coasts of Norway and Iceland was seen as a favourable reflection on the mettle of the nation's youth' (Wawn 2000, 284). Against this background, the trips along the coast by such influential figures as William Gladstone, Lord Tennyson and James Anthony Froude can be read not just as aimless relaxation but also to some extent as 'value statements' underlining both the seafaring traditions of the British and their historical connection with the Viking sea-kings.[27] Incidentally, the male

---

[26] Though published in New York (from 1850), *Harper's New Monthly Magazine* was closely connected with the British literary scene and was read on both sides of the Atlantic.

[27] By a strange coincidence, the writer Martin Farquhar Tupper (1810–1889), who in

members of the Norwegian royal family have until recently made a similar statement by pursuing sailing as their chosen sport.

It is hardly possible to discuss the Vikings and their contribution to Britain and the English-speaking world without also mentioning their expeditions to and settlements in North America. This spectacular colonisation was probably the result of a combination of foolhardy courage, an urge for discovery, and maritime skill, qualities that would have provided the young and energetic America with a direct share in the Vikings, and a useful set of national myths into the bargain. However, Leif Ericsson's discovery of Vinland was not supported by archaeological evidence until the 1960s and was therefore perceived in the 1800s as extravagant speculation rather than as historical fact. As a consequence, nineteenth-century Americans could only claim a credible share in the Vikings through the hundreds of thousands of contemporary Scandinavian immigrants. Nevertheless, there is a relatively pronounced attempt by both the British and the Americans to monopolise the Vikings for their own use. Thus the American traveller Charles Loring Brace, who published his Norwegian travelogue in London in 1857, tries to appropriate the Viking connection from the British and to transfer it to the Americans: 'To an American a visit to the home of the old Northmen is a visit back to his forefather's house. A thousand signs tell him he is at the cradle of the race which leads modern enterprise, and whose Viking-power on both hemispheres has not yet ceased to be felt' (Brace 1857, iii). Presenting a mixed bag of Viking virtues which, Brace suggests, find a more fertile soil in the United States than in Britain, he even expresses an element of American self-confidence that may have appeared both overbearing and somewhat arrogant to the British as early as the 1850s, when Britain was still in the far superior position:

> (...) England had stamped on her national character the traits of the Norwegian sea-kings; and the American progeny yet bears them even

---

his student days at Christ Church in Oxford won a prize for a theological essay immediately ahead of precisely Gladstone (*Encyclopædia Britannica*, 4th ed., s.v. 'Tupper, Martin Farquhar'), also wrote a poem, 'The Lost Arctic', about the loss of his private yacht. The poem's title, which refers to the name of the yacht, was published in the collection *Lyrics* from 1855, and may, between the lines, carry references to the disastrous Franklin expedition (see ch. 4), whose fate had become public knowledge a few years earlier. But it also makes use of the Viking as an image of the 'Destruction' which has befallen the yacht.

more distinctly. The boundless spirit of individual enterprise – the love of the perils of the sea (which the Saxons never showed) – the recklessness of life – the shrewdness and skill in technical law – the fondness for wassail and wine – the respect for woman, and, above all, the tendency to associated self-government (ibid., 88).

Brace's somewhat forced argumentation, which has to acknowledge the British as mediators of the Viking legacy in America, shows exactly how valuable this connection was felt to be in the political context of the period.

But also British commentators endowed nineteenth-century Norwegians – and especially contemporary emigrants to the United States – with the same qualities as their ancestors a thousand years earlier. The anonymous author of 'The British Tourist in Norway', in the July 1872 issue of *Blackwood's Edinburgh Magazine*, explains the old Viking wanderlust by referring to overpopulation in Norway, and then adds: 'Even yet they are on the move, drafting emigrants to the United States, where they will make about the best blood that America can boast of' (312). John Bradshaw, in *Norway: Its Fjords, Fjelds and Fields*, similarly remarks about Norwegian immigrants in America: 'Their hard exposed lives among the mountains eminently adapts them for colonising, and thoroughly fits them for the laborious task, and the difficulties they must of necessity overcome, if they must be successful in such undertakings' (Bradshaw 1896, 47). Finally, Franklin D. Roosevelt's famous statement 'Look to Norway!', given during the handing over of an American subchaser to the Norwegian Navy in September 1942, may have contained an under-current of admiration not just for the contemporary Norwegian war effort, especially that of the merchant navy, but also for the sea-faring Vikings of the old days, whose legacy was still very much kept alive in the twentieth century.

Old Norse Literature

No survey of the Viking heritage in Victorian Britain would be complete without an examination of the impact of Norse literature. This subject, however, has been extensively and impressively covered by Andrew Wawn in his recent book *The Vikings and the Victorians* (2000); in addition it is touched upon in a number of contexts throughout this book. Only a few points, therefore, need to be made here. As Wawn's book has a strong Icelandic focus, it is important to remember that the Norse culture of the Viking age was a culture common to several countries grouped around the Skagerak, the North Sea and the North Atlantic. This sense of cultural unity is also apparent in the material on Norway. The Oxford don Frederick Metcalfe, especially, who was well travelled in Iceland as well as Norway, sees this common culture as an essential key not just to an understanding of the Nordic countries themselves (except Finland), but perhaps more importantly, to an understanding of Britain. His struggle to become acquainted with the institutions, language and literature of the ancient Scandinavians is, in other words, more fundamentally an attempt to come to terms with his own identity as a Briton. Thus, having listed the ways in which British institutions and people have inherited 'some of the most pronounced and best features' from the Norsemen, he moves on to the question of language and literature: 'The two tongues [i.e. English and Norse] in their similarities and divergences illustrate English and also each other. Without a knowledge of the Northern literature nobody can be thoroughly furnished for the study of our mother tongue' (Metcalfe 1880, 486). He then concludes his book by quoting 'the great Danish philologer, Erasmus Rask', who in the early nineteenth century justified his academic interests in an even more elevated style:

'I was astonished to find that our forefathers had such a noble language. (...) I do not study Icelandic in order to learn statesmanship or the science of war, but in order to think like a man, in order to educate my soul to meet danger with contempt, and rather leave the world than budge a jot from principles of the truth of which I have once become thoroughly convinced' (ibid., 485–86).

This passage is particularly interesting because it expresses so strongly an eighteenth-century faith in the importance of knowledge and learning, but – and significantly – not in the classics. On the contrary, Rask – like Metcalfe – seeks wisdom and intellectual nourishment in a field which has until recently been regarded as being beyond the pale of civilisation. To the British, in other words, regarding themselves as definitely belonging to northern rather than southern Europe, Norse language and literature represented a new renaissance, that is a rediscovery of an old and long forgotten treasure. As has been touched upon already, in a complex process of nation- and empire-building, this could constitute a proud and, not least, home-based alternative to the dominant Mediterranean culture, which the British would never quite be justified in claiming for their own. Although this interest in the old Scandinavian literature had started as early as the middle of the eighteenth century, it did not gather momentum until the Victorian period. Thus it is interesting to see how many of the travellers to Norway show a familiarity with this literature, and regard it as an integral part of the Norwegian experience. Metcalfe, in particular, is clearly impressed when in the almost depopulated interior of Telemark he meets a farmer, Richard Aslackson Berge, who confirms the truth of the Oxford don's conviction that deep down in the apparently unkempt and primitive Norwegian farmer, there are hidden cultural gems whose value can compete with that of the classics:

> [This] grimy, ill-clad fellow, quite astounded me by the extent of his information. Catching sight of my wooden calendar [which Metcalfe had bought at a farm nearby], he immediately fetched an old almanack, which contained some explanation of the various signs upon the staff. Fancy one of your 'alternate ploughboys' (...) studying with interest an ancient Anglo-Saxon wooden calendar; and yet this man Berge, besides this, talked of the older and younger Edda, the poem of Gudrun, and, if my memory serves me, of the Nibelungenlied. He had also read the Heimskringla Saga. The promoter of book-hawking and village lending libraries will be interested to hear that this superior enlightenment was due to a small lending library, which had been established by a former clergyman of the district. There was a pithiness and simplicity about this man's talk which surprised me (Metcalfe 1858, 74).

Also Charles Elton, who later became a lawyer and archaeologist but who was only aged twenty-three and twenty-four during his two trips to Norway, shows a comprehensive familiarity with Norse literature, even in the original.

The poems of Ossian, though allegedly from ancient Scotland, were similarly associated with the old Norse culture. Thomas Malthus, during his journey in Norway in the summer of 1799, is impressed by the landlord at a house where he dines in Gudbrandsdalen: he 'was one of the stoutest & strongest-made men I ever saw. He had light long hair, & put us in mind of some of Ossian's heroes' (Malthus 1966, 138). The artist Edward Price, a quarter of a century later, is reminded of the same quasi-ancient poems when looking back on his Norwegian journey: 'Whenever I take up Ossian, I read simple and forcible descriptions of scenes and effects which fell under my own observation in Norway' (Forester 1853, 167). And Lord Garvagh, who in 1872 comes to a small stone cabin, built by his father, in the mountains above the Sognefjorden, finds an interesting selection of provisions:

> (…) here were on the shelf whole tins of soup, and meat preserved, besides lobsters hermetically sealed, and on the ground – a dozen of champagne! (…) Not to neglect the mind, here was also some *pabulum mentis*, in the shape of a Danish dictionary (very interesting, but sent me to sleep), a 'Life of Peter the Great,' and the 'Poems of Ossian' (…) (Garvagh 1875, 168).

As part of their own education, both Malthus, Price and Lord Garvagh may have read Hugh Blair's widely read and respected *A Critical Dissertation on the Poems of Ossian* from 1763, where the author not only defends the authenticity of the poems but also points out how poetry is connected with cultural simplicity, or even primitiveness:

> [P]oetry, which is the child of imagination, is frequently most glowing and animated in the first stages of society. As the ideas of our youth are remembered with a peculiar pleasure on account of their liveliness and vivacity; so the most ancient poems have often proved the greatest favourites of nations (Ashfield and de Bolla 1998, 208).

In Scandinavian *Themes in English Poetry, 1760–1800*, Margaret Omberg emphasises how these qualities were connected with the Gothic, which, merging with the sublime, was introduced as 'a legitimate source of poetic inspiration' (Omberg 1976, 64): 'From signifying barbarous, tasteless and unpolished, it became an epithet which conjured up the enchanted past and the realms of the imagination' (ibid., 86).[28]

Simplicity and primitiveness, then, were elevated by the pre-Romantic and Romantic movement into a quality to be admired rather than despised, and in Norway nineteenth-century travellers found evidence of close and vital connections with this historical heritage. Thus, from a Rousseauesque point of view, Norway had to a remarkable degree succeeded in avoiding the pitfalls of civilisation by remaining true to her ancient heritage. But as this chapter has shown, Norway in the nineteenth century was paradoxically both an old country and a young nation, and perhaps it was the youthful energy in combination with respect for ancient traditions which more than anything else appealed to the many British visitors, who in a rapidly changing world felt the need for innovation as well as

---

[28] For a more thorough discussion of the sublime, see ch. 4.

conservation. In his *Scenes of Travel in Norway*, Joseph Phythian expresses precisely this dual sympathy, which is backward- and forward-looking at the same time. His comment may also serve as a suitable transition from the mythical and somewhat nebulous Norway of the Vikings to the more down-to earth Norway of contemporary, nineteenth-century society, which will be discussed in the next chapter:

> We should be sorry to speak harshly of anything Norwegian, as to a child. For Old Norway is still young in many ways, and she suits us all the better for that. The poet Ossian, whose romantic lines have a Scandinavian character, says, 'Age is dark and unlovely, like the glimmering light of the moon when it shines through broken clouds, and the mist is on the hills.' He may be right, or he may be wrong. There is plenty of time for Norway to throw off her youth, her primitive nature, and grow old. We hope it will be long before, for improvement is not always with age. At present there is hospitality, kindness, honesty, and we would have these remain, for they are virtues which commend a people, being of higher import than an existence of a thousand years (Phythian 1877, 80).

3. 'Nature's Noblemen': People and Society

> [A] practical knowledge of the physical and social
> condition of Norway at the present time must be of
> great value to the student of English history and the
> progress of English civilization.
>
> *William Mattieu Williams*, 1876

British travellers and other commentators showed an intense interest
in the lives of the Norwegian people. As they traversed the country,
they also ranged across the fabric of Norwegian life, frequently
touching upon the key concerns of nineteenth-century society,
including the physical and psychological characteristics of the
people, issues of democracy and class relations, aspects of ethnicity,
the position of women, the diversity of religious belief and a variety
of social problems and their solutions. It might be suggested that the
selection of areas of society covered by those who wrote on Norway
is in itself indicative of the concerns of nineteenth-century Britain
and that in their effort to describe, assess and evaluate these areas, the
British were in effect analysing and ultimately helping to redefine
themselves. As we shall see, Norwegian society, whether deliberately
or inadvertently, was used as a gauge upon which the changes
brought about by industrialisation in Britain could be registered. In
general, British commentary is calculated to confirm the superiority
of all things British but this superiority was by no means monolithic.
As the travel critic Helen Angelomatis-Tsougarakis has recently
commented of nineteenth-century British travellers, 'living in a
society undergoing so many changes, they sometimes could not avoid
projecting their own contradictions into their travel books'
(Angelomatis-Tsougarakis 1990, 23). There are indeed contradictions

within the works of individual writers and even, as shall be demonstrated later in this chapter, contradictions within individual passages of text. On a larger scale, however, the texts are a contradictory group, representing the views of a number of different strands of British society, a fact that evidently requires further investigation.

Tracing the backgrounds of the travellers who wrote on Norway presents some difficulties. A few, such as the feminist Mary Wollstonecraft (1759–1797) and the Liberal Prime Minister William Ewart Gladstone (1809–1898) are well-known and well-documented, but the majority of the commentators are of minor significance historically and one or two, indeed, are not acknowledged by any of the major sources of biographical information on the nineteenth century. Moreover, the conclusions that can be drawn from an investigation of the backgrounds of individuals also need to be treated with some scepticism. An understanding of place of origin, class status and overt political and religious affiliations can be useful, but it is ultimately impossible to ascertain how far such criteria influenced the way people perceived the world around them. In addition, many of the travellers wrote with no obvious intellectual purpose. This does not, however, detract from the fact that important historical discourses – indicative of class, politics or religion – may be detected between the lines of what they wrote. Particular words, images, allusions, or the sheer juxtaposition of certain kinds of information can reveal much about the unwitting narrators.

Whilst the business of constructing an intellectual milieu for individual travellers is problematical, however, it has, nevertheless, been possible to identify distinct groupings among them. These groupings can provide useful clues about why the travellers chose Norway as a destination and how they reacted to what they observed. The majority of British travellers to Norway were members of the middle and upper-middle classes. By the late 1820s, it is fair to say that these individuals were aware of the need for a political recognition of the unprecedented metamorphosis that British society was undergoing as a result of industrialisation. The influence of a Burkean conservatism which emphasised the importance of historical tradition and precedent as an anchor for change rather than dramatic upheaval or revolution, led them to fear the popular radicalism inspired by the French Revolution, whilst often deploring the old ideals of aristocratic political power. Yet within this broad band of travellers, many shades of opinion were represented. These shades ranged from those who favoured an almost total adherence to the political and socio-economic status quo through to those who preferred a progress commensurate with the developments wrought by the new industrial capitalism.

Of a more conservative persuasion were those Anglicans who had received a traditional education at the English public schools and then at Oxford or Cambridge. These included aristocrats such as Lord Thomas Allnutt Brassey (1836–1918) and Lord Dufferin (1826–1902), and clerics such as the Rev. Mourdant Roger Barnard (dates unknown), who was British Consular Chaplain at Christiania from 1858–1862. Other products of Oxbridge included the scientist Edward Daniel Clarke (1769–1822), who was Professor of Mineralogy at Cambridge from 1808 and University Librarian from 1817; William Coxe (1747–1828); Charles Elton (1839–1900); and Frederick Metcalfe (1815–1885), to name but a few. A number of aristocratic women, including The Marchioness of Westminster (Elizabeth-Mary Leveson-Gower, 1797–1891); and Lady Diana de Vere di Beauclerk (1842–1905), daughter of the Duke of St Albans, may have shared the essentially conservative views of these writers. These men and women upheld the values of the establishment and greatly feared political radicalism. In the works of these writers, Norway could be portrayed as either a de-politicised haven outside the dangerous currents of British political change; or alternatively, as a model of the kind of classless, bland uniformity that Britain must seek to avoid.

But there were other more progressive shades of opinion among the travelling contingent: a considerable number, for example, were associated with the rational and enlightened circles of the Scottish universities; others came from nonconformist backgrounds within the provincial towns and cities of England. It is fair to assume that many of these people shared views of a more liberal persuasion than those discussed above, supporting the Whiggish insistence on the progressive reform of proven abuses in politics.

Certainly, there were among the commentators on Norway a number of educated men from the middle and upper classes who had associations with the Scottish universities. These included Andrew Swinton (pseud. William Thomson, 1746–1817), who studied theology at St Andrews and Edinburgh; James D. Forbes (1809–1868), educated at Edinburgh and later Professor of Natural History there; William Dawson Hooker (1816–1840), whose father was Regius Professor of Botany at Edinburgh; Thomas Brown (1778–1820), who taught philosophy at Edinburgh from 1808, and was appointed Professor of Moral Philosophy in 1810; J. F. Campbell

(1822–1885), writer on Highland folklore, geology and meteorology and educated at Edinburgh; and the better known Thomas Carlyle (1795–1881) and Lord Henry Brougham (1778–1868), both also educated at Edinburgh.

The distinctive 'Scotch approach' to knowledge consisted of a grounding in medicine, moral philosophy and political economy. Key to these studies was an investigation of the processes of political and economic development in other societies around the world. Of the men described above, at least three, Thomas Carlyle, Thomas Browne and Lord Brougham, wrote for the new periodical *The Edinburgh Review*, founded in 1802. As Anand C. Chitnis has commented: 'The Review might be considered a bridgehead permitting Enlightened ideas to invade (...) society' (Chitnis 1986, 66). Amongst many other matters *The Edinburgh Review* was well known for its discussion of recent travelogues to places far afield and its subsequent analysis of developing societies.

It might be imagined that some of the Scotsmen who visited Norway at the beginning of the nineteenth century knew each other and certainly that they read and commented on each others' works. Some of them shared interests in science including, geology, mineralogy and botany, and in hill walking and (later) mountaineering. As those educated in Scotland moved to London, their friendships brought about the establishment of sporting and scientific associations such as The Alpine Club, The Raleigh Club, The Travels Club and The Royal Geographical Society. Among this group of men, trips to other countries may have provided an entertaining way of cementing a more intellectual sense of kinship.[1]

In addition, there were a number of travellers from England who most definitely shared some of the nonconformist and progressive political views of their Scottish counterparts. An early traveller, and pioneer of women's rights, Mary Wollstonecraft, for example, had

[1] Liberal or progressive ways of thinking might have been shared by a number of other travellers who had Scotch (and predominantly Edinburgh) connections, though not necessarily with the universities. Robert Everest (1799–?), a graduate of Oxford, was a member of the Edinburgh Phrenological society, for example. Alexander Burnett (dates unknown) lectured in Aberdeenshire; Derwent Conway (pseud. for Henry David Inglis, 1795–1835) lived in Edinburgh; Robert Gilfillan (1798–1850) was a Scotch poet from Dunfermline; Samuel Laing (1780–1868) was from the Orkney Islands; James Logie Robertson (1846–1922) was the First English Master at Edinburgh Ladies' College; and William Rae Wilson (1772–1849) was a Scottish solicitor.

associations with dissenting circles in London. Wollstonecraft was sympathetic to the French Revolution and married the radical, William Godwin in 1797. Among other nonconformist travellers was William Allen (1770–1843), a supporter of the abolition of slavery who was interested in social, educational and legal reform, and who travelled across Europe to report on social institutions of all kinds. In addition, several Quakers, renowned for their philanthropic endeavour and commitment to social reform, were among the travellers. These included, the political satirist Sir Philip Francis (1740–1818), William Howitt (1797–1879) and Mary Howitt (1799–1888), and Sarah Backhouse (1803–1877). The novelists Harriet Martineau (1802–1876) and Edna Lyall (ref. ch. 1), who used Norway as a background for their works of fiction, came from Unitarian backgrounds. Among the Irish writers who wrote on Norway was the ardent anti-papist, Selina Bunbury (1802–1882).

As is to be expected, these various groups of writers responded in different ways to the political, social and religious issues in Norwegian society. But they were also in some respects united in their adherence – at least in part – to the common myths about Norway. To some extent this shortsightedness is excusable; there were, for example, few published history books on the country in the period.[2] As late as 1897, the Norwegian Hjalmar H. Boyesen, who had been asked to write a history of Norway in English for *The Story of the Nations Series* published by T. Fisher Unwin, commented in his preface: 'It has been my ambition for many years to write a history of Norway, chiefly because no such book, worthy of the name exists in the English Language' (Boyesen 1900, xiii). Even then, Boyesen's *History of Norway* focused largely on the ancient and medieval past. Boyesen died in 1897 and the book was republished in 1900 with a new chapter on the 'recent' history of Norway by C. F. Keary. It is hardly surprising, given this dearth of empirical material on Norway, that travellers of all persuasions espoused some rather ahistorical

---

[2] Some of these have been mentioned in ch. 2. In addition, *The Norwegian Invasion of Scotland*, which was a small part of the colossal work of the Norwegian historian P. A. Munch's *History of the Norwegian People*, appeared in English in 1862. There were also at least two other significant works on Norwegian history available in English. The earlier, translated from the Danish, was G. L. Baden's *The History of Norway from the Earliest Times* (1817); the other, S. A. Dunham's *History of Denmark, Sweden and Norway* (1839), ran to several editions. A book for children, entitled *The History of Denmark, Sweden and Norway from the Earliest Period to the Present Time* by Julia Corner, was published in 1841.

notions about the country that coloured their impressions of their visits and remained largely unchanged even on their return. These overarching beliefs need to be examined before we explore British impressions of some more specific aspects of Norwegian society.

The Primitive Norwegian

Observations on the physical appearance and temperament of the Norwegian people were a staple of the travel account genre, providing much of its anecdotal content and setting its largely approving tone. In general, the Norwegians are described as a distinctive people, recently discovered near neighbours who exhibit striking similarities with the British. The Teutonic characteristics of the Norwegians, which linked them genealogically to the British and which were the subject of warm treatment in Victorian literature, have been closely examined in chapter 2. According to R. Latham in *Norway and the Norwegians* (1840), the feeling of affinity between the British and the Norwegians was reciprocal: 'England should think well of Norway, for Norway thinks well of England' (1: 54). His views were echoed in the same year by the cleric and angling expert William Bilton in *Two Summers in Norway* (1840): 'In Norway (...) the English character stands very high: and it will be the Englishman's own fault, if he be not both respected and liked' (214–15). In this climate of mutual approval, it is not surprising that early travel accounts in particular are infused with a sense of serendipity, a note of surprise and pleasure from the British as they went about the business of documenting the lives of a people so physically akin and yet so apparently absent from the annals of history and literature.

In *Britons: Forging the Nation* (1996), the historian Linda Colley has described how Britain defined herself in relation to a series of other cultures and nations from the early eighteenth century onwards. In a sense the Norwegian people were simply one more 'Other' in this picture, but it would be a mistake to consider accounts of the Norwegians in such non-specific terms. In the first place, the travellers themselves were keen to point out the very definite physical and temperamental differences between the Norwegians and the other inhabitants of the Scandinavian peninsula, particularly the Swedes and the Danes. Arthur de Capell Brooke in *Travels through Sweden, Norway and Finmark* (1823) remarked that 'though we had but just crossed the frontiers, I could not avoid perceiving a sensible

difference between the two nations. Already was the humility and
courteous disposition of the Swede exchanged for the freer, bolder
manner of the Norwegians' (70). Less approvingly, perhaps, Andrew
Crichton and Henry Wheaton in *Scandinavia, Ancient and Modern*
(1860) commented: 'The tallest and stoutest peasants are from
Guldbrandsal [*sic*]; but they are less athletic and shorter in stature
than the Swedes; while from the Danes they differ in having hair of a
deeper yellow or brown, copious eyebrows, countenances full of
expression, and the ruddiness of health upon their cheeks' (288).
Travellers themselves, then, were keen to point out the specificity of
their observations of the Norwegians. As this section will show, this
insistence on the distinctive 'nature' or anthropological character of
the Norwegians was motivated by one of Britain's cultural preoccupations, namely a fascination with the lives of people in so-
called 'primitive' societies.

There was, in the period, a distinct British interest in a variety of
'natural societies' of which Norwegian society is perhaps one of the
more extreme. Norwegians were seen as a simple people living in
harmony with nature and blissfully uncorrupted by the wiles of
civilization. Many descriptions of the Norwegian people in travel
accounts of the period drew on the late eighteenth-century
philosophical ideas of Jean-Jacques Rousseau (1712–1778) and his
followers. These ideas included a fascination with and an idealisation
of primitive societies. Although Rousseau's own thinking ultimately
went far beyond this, moving on to imagine ideal societies of the
future, it was his descriptions of man in his 'natural state' and the
happiness attendant on that state which became popular and which
were taken up by other writers across Europe. In *Discourse on the
Origin of Inequality* (1755), Rousseau described modern Western
society as corrupt and exploitative, and harked back to the simple
societies of pre-history. Far from seeing the state of nature as a 'war
of all against all', as had the earlier English political theorist Thomas
Hobbes, Rousseau depicted the primitive state as peaceful, solitary
and ultimately innocent. In the late eighteenth and early nineteenth
centuries, European readers were enthralled by a succession of
'discoveries' of individuals who had been brought up outside
conventional society. As Ronald Grimsley suggests, 'the discovery of
a child brought up by bears and of another living in the forest of
Hannover, as well as a case of the girl found in the woods in France,
seemed to offer opportunities for observing the power of nature's
appetites and laying bare the "natural movements of the soul"'
(Grimsley 1983, 26). In addition, travellers offered tales of primitive

societies overseas. In fact none of these societies came close to embodying the ultimate primitive state described by Rousseau, a society without politics, property, the division of labour and even conjugal and paternal love, but this did not stop travellers praising or denouncing the unparalleled simplicity of the societies that they encountered.

Rousseau's *Nouvelle Heloise* (1761), an immensely popular novel, started a vogue in Europe for what was seen as the unspoiled Arcadia of Switzerland, but this delight in things Swiss was to dwindle as the eighteenth century drew to a close. As Arnold H. Barton points out in *Northern Arcadia: Foreign Travelers in Scandinavia, 1765–1815*, the intellectual shift away from Switzerland was to help invest in Scandinavia in general, and in Norway in particular, an unprecedented degree of attraction:

> The Swiss idyll faded during the 1790s with the French Revolution, the resulting European wars, Switzerland's invasion and reorganisation by republican France, and the growing disillusionment of pre-romantic enthusiasm for the progressive ideals of the Enlightenment. (…) In its nostalgic search for an unspoiled haven of peace, simplicity and innocence, pre-romantic sensibility now found a new Arcadia, still accessible to travellers in a time of revolution and war in Scandinavia (Barton 1998, 157).

In Norway, more so even than in Sweden and Denmark, travellers found a robust peasantry living close to nature and apparently exhibiting the virtues associated with the primitive state. In descriptions of some areas of Norway in particular, such as Setesdalen, Telemark and the far North, the idea of the 'noble savage' was liberally cited in travel accounts, investing the genre with an anthropological style and purpose. Of course, the impression of the Norwegian as a creature of nature was also emphasised by the choice of individuals who came under scrutiny: travel literature abounds in peasant girls, fishermen and farmers, whilst shopkeepers, administrative officials and clerks, and factory-based weavers, for example, are largely ignored. Some travel guides such as the one written in English by the Norwegian Chr. Tønsberg, entitled *Norway: Illustrated Handbook for Tourists* (1875), actively steered the travellers' interest away from the urban areas:

> There is also much that is characteristic in the life of those who toil in mines, smelting houses, dockyards, or the mills and factories erected of late years in the towns and their immediate vicinity. But these sections of

the people as compared with the corresponding classes in the great
industrial nations, are none of them calculated to strike the foreigner
either from their numbers or their mental development (xlv).

The depiction of the Norwegian as a primitive rural creature relied
upon the idea that there was a causal relationship between climate
and environment and national character. This idea, common among
the French philosophers of the eighteenth century, and later a key
strand in the nineteenth-century literary movements of realism and
naturalism, was frequently reiterated in small but telling
observations, although not all travellers were as aware of its
intellectual pedigree as the Cambridge graduate, John Milford. In
Norway and Her Laplanders in 1841 (1842), some lines (which are
in fact attributed to Milford's friend and travelling companion,
Richard Ford) remark that 'without going the whole length of
Montesquieu's theory of the influences of climate on national
character, the invigorating, elevating effect of a mountainous country
is undoubted. (...) The vast fastnesses of nature have ever been the
cradle of personal liberty and independence' (113–14). In rather less
elevated language, the American Charles Loring Brace made the
same point in *The Norse-Folk* (1857): 'It is a poor, hard country, that
is the strong impression left by the Norwegian journey. One does not
wonder that the people leave it, and yet it is such soil that grows men.
It has begotten the Northmen, and all that has sprung from them' (93).

Commentators derived much rhetorical energy from the
comparisons they devised between the supposed natural state of
Norwegian society and more developed societies. For instance, they
quickly worked out that the distinct differences between dress,
customs and even language across the length of Norway were
indicative of a society in which the regions had historically remained
separate due to geographical obstacles.[3] Nineteenth-century
communications by road and rail were far inferior to those in
industrial Britain from the 1830s onwards, and, therefore, the
travellers supposed that this regional distinction would be likely to
continue for some time into the future.

[3] This physical isolation of communities was more than a traveller's tale. In 1875,
the Norwegian travel guide writer Chr. Tønsberg commented: 'A few years since, ere
the innovating agency of steam had been called into operation, the inhabitants of
districts cut off from intercourse by some trackless range of fjeld, knew as little of
the daily life of their neighbours as though they had been aliens' (Tønsberg 1875,
xliii).

CARVED LINTEL, STABBUR AND TANKARDS.

Not surprisingly, traditional craftsmanship evoked nostalgia in an industrial age. The log houses of the Norwegian *bønder*, especially the *stabbur*, provided a startling contrast in terms of size, decoration and prospect, to the back-to-back terraces and small rural cottages of British society. Illustration from Lovett (1885).

Despite the sense of British superiority occasioned by this state of affairs, it was the colourful aspects of Norwegian rural life that drew some of the most enthusiastic commentary. Robert Bremner's detailed description of the local costume of Telemark in *Excursions in Denmark, Norway and Sweden* (1840) is a case in point:

> We were guided by two lads, whose good figures, and striking costume, reminded us that we were fairly within the bounds of Tellemarken. All the young men wear a white woollen jacket, with sundry cuttings and slashings behind, that would tempt one to term it an incipient coat; being open in front, it displays to due advantage the full glories of a green vest, intended to be amazingly gay, with its double rows of clear metal knobs, shining with a splendour which no maid in Tellemarken can resist. Tight, dark-coloured breeches, with copiously furnished rows of similar buttons on thigh and knee; well-gartered stockings, also of a dark colour, and light mountain shoes of rough leather, complete by far the handsomest costume to be seen from the Alps to Dovrefield (2: 114).

In Britain, such fascination for regional differences and the preservation of local customs was a familiar tendency in counter-industrial discourse, and is indeed reminiscent of the extensive Romantic interest in regional identity typified in the early nineteenth-century novels of such writers as Maria Edgeworth and Sir Walter Scott.

Travellers were impressed by those features of Norwegian life which most evidently indicated its pre-industrial status; they marvelled, for instance, at the gold and silver work, and the painted glass and wood carvings produced by local craftsmen not yet tainted by the values of mass-production that characterised the factory system in Britain. The Rev. Robert Everest, quoting the economist Adam Smith as a guide to 'people in this state of society,' remarked on the system of bartering and the non-specialisation of Norwegian labour still current in some areas:

> Everything here reminds us of what we read of the dawn of society. The division of labour has not yet taken place, and vogs [a footnote explains that 'a vog is equal to thirty-six pounds'] of rye meal are the usual currency of the country. Every man is a carpenter, a shoemaker, a tailor, or a smith (Everest 1829, 146).

John Barrow, in *Excursions in the North of Europe* (1834), commented on the same issue, admiring the self-sufficiency of the peasants near Lærdal:

> There is no trade in fact, that a Norwegian peasant cannot, and does not, when required, turn his hand to; he unites in his own person that of a carpenter, blacksmith, weaver, rope-maker, tailor, shoemaker, joiner and cabinet maker. (...) In fact, clocks and watches, and church organs even, have been constructed by the self-taught Norwegian peasantry (252–53).

In his many roles, the Norwegian peasant was the living embodiment of the 'primitive' stage of social development as defined by political economists. The Briton, on the other hand, had passed through the pastoral, agrarian and commercial stages and was far advanced by comparison. Paradoxically then, the Norwegian peasant is regarded either as an unenlightened object of compassion or as an enviable creature outside the historical trajectory, who stands for all the virtues lost by society in its selfish pursuit of profit. Very often he occupies both positions simultaneously as here in one of a series of sonnets on Norway by James Logie Robertson, the Scottish schoolmaster and ultimately High Master of Edinburgh Ladies' College, who also wrote under the pseudonym Hugh Haliburton. Robertson describes a miller at work in 'The Little Meal-Mill':

> Perched on its four grey cairns across the stream
> That tumbles down the cliff, secure it stands;
> An old possession, for on plank and beam
> Are Knuts and Oles carved by various hands.
> Its cubic measure, six by five by four;
> Yet in this compass, everything complete;
> And there he bent — his back was towards the door —
> While plashed the mill wheel merrily at his feet,
> And ground his rye, and sang with honest glee.
> — Be mine the knowledge that I now possess,
> And mine a heart, like his, of envy free,
> And I could don to-day the saeter dress,
> And bring my wishes docile to my will
> To moil content in this Norwegian mill.
> (Robertson 1881, 250)

Production here is seen as a quiet, selfless and natural pursuit in harmony with nature. This is a far cry from the clanking mills, exploitative conditions and child labour of the Lancashire factory system, for instance. Of course, there is a real lack of contemporary contextualisation in such descriptions of the self-sufficient primitive economy in Norway. By accident or by design, there is little mention of Norway's moves towards industrialisation in most British accounts. In fact, as Kristine Bruland has indicated, there was an interchange of technical knowledge between Norway and Britain in the mid-nineteenth century with significant numbers of Norwegian engineers visiting Britain in the mid-1840s in order to learn textile manufacture and to buy machines with which to stock the new water-powered weaving factories of Bergen and elsewhere.[4] The travellers would no doubt have been surprised to learn of Norway's presence at the Industrial Exhibition in 1862, at which methods of industrial production were demonstrated (Bruland, 42). In most travel accounts, intimations of 'progress' are carefully omitted in the service of the greater myth that time in Norway has stood still and that the Norwegians are a trenchantly primitive people with no aspirations to join the modern industrial world.

As has been explained, the Norwegians, inhabitants of a 'natural society', generally functioned in the travel accounts to remind the British of all that they had lost in their overweening desire for material advancement. But such accounts were often contradictory, functioning also to bolster Britain's pride in her industrial and commercial achievements. Robert Taylor Pritchett, a former gunsmith turned painter, in *Gamle Norge, Rambles and Scrambles in Norway* (1879), found that travelling through the Geiranger region threw the problems of his own working life in London into relief:

[H]ow happy in themselves are these poor folks in their simple belief and faith, their home, love and trust! How difficult it is to consider this kind of happiness, when the same family goes on in the same position in life for three or four hundred years, in the same costume, and with the same old silver ornaments! 'How bad for trade!' some would say. 'What stagnation! how slow!' yet how enviable when we have tasted the bitters of overstrained brain-work, and the furious competition of millions of people, all amassed and arrayed for the daily struggle of modern time! It is from this latter that men retire for awhile [*sic*] to take a refresher, a change of air and circumstance becoming a matter of necessity; and so London, after a season of gaiety and rush, is left in favour of outlandish places, simple fare, and, in fact, to get away from the daily jostle of life, to be ready for the next bout (97–98).

---

[4] Bruland describes for instance how 'Arne Fabrikker was established in 1846 by Peter Jebsen, who came from Schleswig to Bergen in 1842 and worked in textile retailing. He spent about six months in Manchester in 1845 and bought machines there with which he returned to Bergen. The factory began production as a water-powered weavery in 1846, with thirty-six looms; by the following year it had ninety-six, and a year later, 128' (Bruland 1989, 42).

With the dramatic licence of the travel writer rather than the serious historian, Pritchett compares an isolated rural region of Norway with one of the world's largest cities and includes, just for good measure, some imagined dialogue with the unenlightened Britons. His lively account ostensibly praises the timelessness of Norwegian society, and its flagrant disregard for the exigencies of 'trade'; and yet we are left also with a desire for the 'gaiety and rush' of the big city. The Londoner may visit Norway to get away for a while, but he will always return, for the 'next bout.'

If Norway is metaphorically characterised as a child who had yet to grow wise in the ways of the world, the Norwegians themselves are also considered to embody qualities admirably suited to the 'innocence' of their environment. These qualities are those required to sustain a natural life away from the miseries and contaminations of large, urban communities. The strength, resilience and independence of the Norwegians have been mentioned already. Here, it will be appropriate to deal with those 'softer' aspects of the Norwegian character, singled out by British observers for special comment, namely the triumvirate of *honesty, hospitality and simplicity.*

The selection of these three characteristics reveals insights into the British perception of their own identity in the period. In a useful recent work of cultural criticism, *Englishness Identified* (2000), Paul Langford shows how these three traits among others had particular meanings for British identity in the nineteenth century. *Honesty*, for example, was a characteristic upon which the British prided themselves and on the grounds of which they differentiated themselves from the nations of Southern Europe. In his section on honesty, Langford comments that, 'in any international table of sincerity, the English would have figured high in the eighteenth century' (88). In this imaginary moral table, British travellers found that the Norwegians occupied a similarly elevated position to themselves.

Tales of Norwegian honesty became a staple feature of the travellers' accounts with each traveller trying to outdo the last in his praise. It might be said that Norwegian honesty became a defining theme of the genre. The Rev. Robert Everest suggested 'that a child [in Norway] might walk about with a bag of gold and no-one would molest it' (Everest 1829, 257). By the middle of the nineteenth century, anecdotes of honesty such as this one by Charles Loring Brace in *The Norse-Folk* (1857) abounded:

An English gentleman, a year or two ago, in travelling from Trondhjem to Christiania, tied his *porte-monnaie* – which is a large leather bag for carrying the quantity of little silver money necessary – on the back of his carriole, and lost out fourteen or fifteen sovereigns on the road. He wrote on arrival at Christiania to the country judges, and in a few days had every one of the sovereigns returned to him. They had been picked up by the peasants, and handed to the magistrates, who sent them on to the owner (20).

Less dramatically, Isabella Frances Blundell wrote in *Gamle Norge* (1862) of the security she felt in Norway even with her satchel and knapsack constantly hanging open, and E. Lester Linden Arnold, in *A Summer Holiday in Scandinavia* (1877), enjoyed the fact that the cooking utensils that he left on the ground whilst he went sight-seeing, were on his return, 'all perfectly safe and untouched, although there had clearly been numerous visitors to see them' (51).

By 1890, the concept of Norwegian honesty was so well-recognised that it could be used as a key aspect of characterisation in the narrative in Edna Lyall's popular novel *A Hardy Norseman*, also discussed in chapter 2. The story charts the interconnections between a Norwegian and an English family. Its hero, Frithiof, a Norwegian working for a time in London, is accused of stealing a five-pound note from the till at his place of work. Lyall takes the opportunity here of ridiculing the English detective who does not appreciate Norwegian honesty:

> The detective could, of course, not understand this. He was a clever and a conscientious man, but his experience was, after all, limited. He had not travelled in Norway, or studied the character of its people; he did not know that you may leave all your luggage outside an inn in the public highway without the least fear that in the night any one will meddle with it; he did not know that if you give a Norse child a coin equal to sixpence in return for a great bowl of milk, it will refuse with real distress to keep it, because the milk was worth a little less; he had not heard the story of the lost chest of plate, which by good chance was washed up on the Norwegian coast – how the experts examined the crest on the spoons, and after infinite labor and pains succeeded in restoring it to its rightful owner in a far-away southern island (Lyall 1890, 219–20).

Lyall's points of reference here seem to be the works of travel writers, a fact which attests to some degree of intertextuality in writings on Norway in the period and to the certain 'fashionability' of the subject.

Seasoned readers of the many Norwegian travel books on sale were ready for this constant reiteration of Norwegian honesty, and

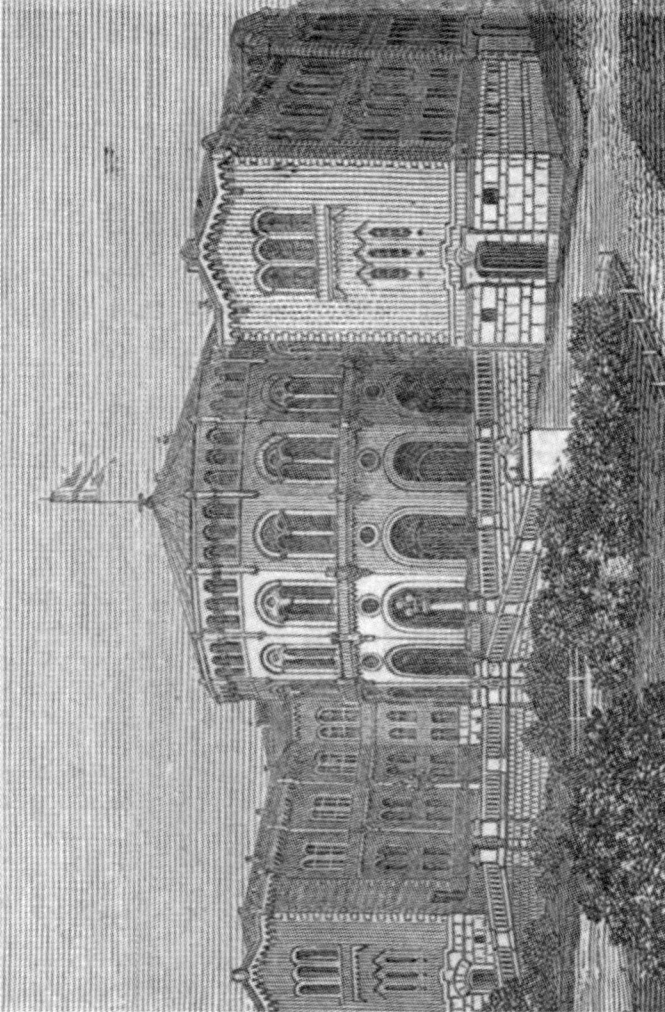

The Storthing Edifice.

As a potent symbol of Norway's independence within her union with Sweden, the Storting was a popular tourist venue. Illustration from Tønsberg (1875).

travel writers must have been aware that commentaries on the trustworthiness of the Norwegian people were well-worked and somewhat overdone. They also recognised the fact that honesty was perhaps not as marketable a subject as an analysis of the supposed characteristics of other more remote peoples such as the indigenous African or American might have been. Because of this, writers sought ever more outlandish comparisons with which to maintain the attention of the reader. J. A. Lees in *Peaks and Pines: Another Norway Book* (1899), a title which in itself indicates a certain weariness with the genre and its potential for parody, commented:

> Every traveller who publishes his experiences of this part of the world discovers as a new fact that the Norwegians are very honest. It is in fact probable that it is the identical country in which Alexander the Great went about with a lantern looking for a dishonest man. The story may not be in your history-book, but that does not prevent it from being true (19).

It is also worth noting that references to Norwegian honesty in any text, were part of the writer's own 'rating' of Norway as a holiday destination. When writers commented on this particular feature of the Norwegian peasant, or indeed on any of his other virtues, they were, in effect, advertising Norway as a holiday destination and helping to shape the discourse of holiday promotion itself.

Like their honesty, the *hospitality* of the Norwegian people became legendary in travel reports. Again this was seen as a characteristic of a less advanced society. By many accounts, the British themselves were not renowned for unstinting hospitality in the nineteenth century. Many travellers to Britain in the period noted that they were well treated in inns and hostelries only where they were prepared to pay for it. As Paul Langford states: 'The tendency to treat sociability in highly commercial terms had begun unusually early in Britain' (232). What amazed the British in Norway then was not so much the hospitality offered to them but the fact that it did not have to be paid for.

The Rev. R. M. Barnard found in Østerdalen 'many a cottage where I have asked for a drink of water, and have been presented with a bowl of fresh milk' (Barnard 1871, 208), and described how when a banquet was going on in the house 'persons are stationed along the roads in the neighbourhood, in order to see that no-one passes by without coming in to partake of the good cheer' (ibid.). Like honesty, hospitality was a characteristic that sold holidays. In its advertisement for excursions to Norway in 1886, the travel company

Thomas Cook made much of Norwegian hospitality: 'In no land is hospitality more open-handed and more unaffected than in Norway, and though these features are naturally becoming blunted along the beaten lines of travel, the genuine goodness of heart, fine "gentlemanly feeling", and entire absence of that sordidness that is so often seen even in the primitive regions, cannot fail to strike the unprejudiced observer' (Cook 1886, 5).

Of all the virtues of the Norwegians in the 'primitive' narrative, however, it was their *simplicity* which drew the most comment and debate. In the case of simplicity, British travellers drew significant parallels *and* differences between themselves and the Norwegians. On the one hand, the British had long admired in themselves a certain *plainness* of dress, manner and custom, which could be favourably compared to the artifices of Continental peoples. A history of Protestant simplicity had led to a public life in Britain in which ostentatious displays of ornamentation and wealth were generally frowned upon. In this sense, Norway's lack of affectation struck a familiar chord. On the other hand, the British did not, of course, see their own austerity as an expression of backwardness. Quite the contrary, it was considered a characteristic which had aided the British people in their ascent to the pinnacle of progress, by supposedly gaining them the trust of their imperial conquests. In this sense, the simplicity, or 'ignorance,' of the Norwegians was of a different order altogether.

Commentators might praise the unfussy manners and clothes of the Norwegians, but they were less complimentary about their simplicity in cultural matters. Many focused on the way in which the Norwegians seemed to be inhabiting a world less well versed, for example, in the possibilities of science and literature than their own. Mary Wollstonecraft's comments in *Letters Written During a Short Residence in Sweden, Norway and Denmark* (1796) place the Norwegians some way behind the British in terms of intellectual advancement: 'The Norwegians appear to me a sensible, shrewd people, with little scientific knowledge, and still less taste for literature: but they are arriving at the epoch which precedes the introduction of the arts and sciences' (103). Other accounts made cruder comparisons between the Norwegians and much more primitive peoples. In a passing, but telling, reference describing a stay among the Gudbrandsdalen peasants, the Rev. Robert Everest in *A Journey through Lapland, Norway and Sweden* (1829) imagined 'a rude likeness in the wooden bowls and cups, which they carve for themselves, to many of the Etruscan models' (51). Charles Kelsall, writing under the pseudonym Mela Britannicus, scoffed in *Horae Viaticae* (1836): 'In literary and scientific attainments, [Norway] has not even done so much as the desolate Iceland, which has not a fifteenth of the Norwegian population; which is rent asunder by volcanoes, and which scarcely sees the sun for half the year' (113–14).

The commentators found evidence of simplicity in almost every aspect of Norwegian cultural life. A significant number of accounts, however, exhibit an ambiguity of opinion in their descriptions which may or may not be intentional. Either way, such ambiguity can be unravelled to reveal insights into the fundamentally paradoxical nature of Britain's attitude to her own cultural development. Witness this comment from John Milford on the songs sung by Norwegian maidens, in *Norway and her Laplanders in 1841* (1842):

> It is quite clear that the songs of the Norwegian maidens are as old as their hills. All writers of music are agreed that in its early unsophisticated state, the airs were low, sad and devoid of ornament, flourishes and variations. It was the voluptuousness of taste in Italy, and the complicated intellect of Germany, which first corrupted pure and simple harmony, and introduced by degrees the present, forced, elaborate and scientific system. The Norwegians know nothing of all these novelties and niceties, nor have their ears ever been scarified by French performances (125–26).

Here we have once more the contradiction familiar to British travel works. Milford praises the Norwegians on the one hand, suggesting that the Italians and the Germans were responsible for complicating 'pure and simple harmony.' But the compliment is nullified by the earlier sentence which relegates such pure music to the realms of the 'unsophisticated'. The result is that we are unsure whether the 'novelties and niceties' of the last sentence are to be eschewed or embraced.

Similar contradictions are apparent in commentaries on Norwegian art. In 1873, the British art critic Joseph Beavington Atkinson published the book *An Art Tour to Northern Capitals of Europe*, based on a journey three years earlier. In the chapter on Christiania, he introduces the Norwegian art scene in a rather peculiar manner:

> Norway fortunately remains in a wild state of nature, and civilisation being elsewhere over-artificial, and the life in cities feverish to excess, travellers gladly plunge into cool pine forests, and track the stream which

dashes from the mountain to the fiord. Such regions, it may be hoped, will be long left intact, if only to serve as fishing, hunting or sketching-ground for the rest of Europe; at all events we scarcely deplore in Norway the paucity of art. Happily, the civilisation which in England has come with smoky chimneys is as yet distant from Scandinavia; the observer finds himself thrown back on primeval times ere art was thought of, on prehistoric periods when the flint was the only implement in use, and when the hardy Norseman trusted to the spear for his dinner. While other lands have passed through successive phases of civilisation, while the arts in the South and the West have attained maturity or fallen into *decadence*, it is curious to note how Northern territories lie still on the frontier which divided nature from art; how primitive peoples have not yet entered on *aesthetic existence*, and how art, when she does struggle into life, assumes only simple and elementary forms. Students of history will in Norway mark phases which lands more advanced passed through centuries ago. Observations thus made are like the notes of geologists on early strata of the earth still under mutation. I may add that, while primary rocks indicate that Norway was among the first of created lands, primitive art conditions show that she is one of the last in art development (82–83; italics added).

Here again is a position apparently wavering between scorn and admiration. It is difficult not to see an air of cultural if not imperialist condescension in the wish that such regions 'will be long left intact, if only to serve as fishing, hunting, or sketching-ground for the rest of Europe.' Furthermore, if Norway is 'fortunate' to remain in a state of wild nature, and if 'happily' civilisation is still distant in Scandinavia, it is an open question what Atkinson means by the value of 'aesthetic existence,' a state which, it seems, he assumes that the British have already attained. In this case, then, is 'aesthetic existence' nothing but a sign of decadence and moral degradation? When studying Adolph Tidemand's paintings of the lives of the Norwegian peasants in Oscar's Hall near Christiania, he is equally unclear as to whether the pictures are accomplished or not. As to Tidemand's technical performance, he is overtly critical: 'These truly national pictures by Tidemand, the most national of painters, are a little disappointing in execution; it is seldom indeed that these rude Northern schools gain mastery over the subtle technicalities of art. The pictures are poor in colour and in texture, and the lines of composition are devoid of harmony'. Still, there are qualities that compensate because

the strength of Tidemand lies in his loyalty to humanity; his characters are true to nature; his narratives have the charm of childrens' stories sold in the simplest words; his pictures are popular because they are pathetic; they come home to the human heart. Tidemand may be taken as the type of Northern schools. His character is individual and rugged, his spirit earnest (...). In these honest downright works we scarcely feel the intrusion of art between nature and the spectator (...) (ibid., 86–87).

Thus Norwegian art represents a problem, simply because artistic activity requires the kind of civilised merit, such as technical mastery, refinement, breeding and cultural sophistication, which are fundamentally contrary to the positive quality, that is to the intuitive naturalness, in Norwegian people and scenery. In effect, Atkinson is actually asking for a kind of anti-artistic art, a contradiction that underlies the very ideal of romantic and picturesque art, but he seems totally oblivious of his own prescriptive tone. Like most of his fellow travellers, in other words, he does not seriously raise the question as to what he really wants: progress or regress.

Not all accounts wrap their criticisms in such contradiction. The Rev. M. R. Barnard, in *Sketches of Life, Scenery and Sport in Norway* (1871), is blunt in his criticism of the unsophisticated nature of education in the Setesdalen region:

> As regards enlightenment, the Saetersdal peasantry stand remarkably low. Very few of them can read, and still fewer write. Their ideas are, naturally, primitive to a degree. The rotundity of the earth they still look on as a most doubtful matter. Like our venerable forefathers, they believe the world to be flat, like a pancake, in the middle of which the Almighty has placed Norway, and Saetersdal again in the middle of this; and that America, the sea, Jotunheim, are on its extreme limits (301).

Cultural simplicity was one area in which the Norwegians undoubtedly suffered in comparison with the British.

Another fruitful area for comment, which grew out of the idea of Norwegian simplicity, was the supposedly poor state of *hygiene* among the Norwegians. Whilst travellers generally agreed that Norwegian townsfolk exhibited exemplary cleanliness on a par with the imagined cleanliness of the British, accounts of rural life, particularly of those unfortunate areas of Telemark and Setesdalen, all too often tell a different story. The early traveller the Rev. Robert Everest, in A *Journey Through Lapland, Norway and Sweden* (1829), commented on the vermin harboured in Norwegian houses that caused the people to 'be as busy about their persons as a parcel of mangy dogs' (35). The class superiority of the visitor is implied by William Mattieu Williams in *Through Norway with a Knapsack*

(1876, first edition 1859) when he makes the frequent link between dirt and the unsavoury nature of Norwegian food in an account of a visit to a peasant's cottage in Telemark:

> My supper consisted of dirty fladbrod, good butter, and sour milk; this last the master brought me in a bowl, quite filled: he held the bowl with one hand, and his thumb was immersed in the sour milk, which exercised its solvent powers upon the film of dirt that overlaid the skin, so that by the time he placed the bowl before me his immersed thumb was surrounded by an aura, or dark halo of dirt particles, suspended in the beverage (296–97).

Charles Kelsall continued the equation between inedible food and filth in *Horae Viaticae* (1836):

> Enter a peasant's dwelling; and I grant you will often find an iron stove, in an apartment well-glazed; sour butter they will serve you with a fair admixture of hairs and dirt, though the finest springs are generally at hand. You will also find gritty and hard rye-cakes, a few watery potatoes, and a cream of a slimy quality; though with a moderate attention to the dairy, they might have cream and butter nearly as good as in England, and cheese equal to our Cottenham and Stilton; what you find is salt, as hard as a brick, and usually cemented with hairs and dirt (109–10).

Isabella Frances Blundell in *Gamle Norge* (1862) furthermore complained that 'the excessive neglect, visible in the appearance of every man, woman and child, was quite revolting' and reported that the peasant children 'looked as though they had never seen soap and water' (99).[5]

Vignettes of dirtiness added colour to what might otherwise have been somewhat pedestrian British accounts, exuding a realism that may borrow something from the mid-nineteenth century social novels of writers such as Charles Dickens and Mrs Gaskell, who revelled in depictions of the unhygienic living conditions of the working classes.

---

[5] It is interesting to note that even Norwegian accounts comment on the lack of cleanliness among their countrymen and women. Chr. Tønsberg, the Norwegian editor of the English travel guide, *Norway: Illustrated Handbook for Travellers* (1875) comments: 'The Norwegian fishermen are generally looked upon as uncleanly in their habits, and their avocation is considered injurious to health. (...) Cleanliness (...) is not as general as it might be in the rural districts, which is seen from the fact that the housewives of Osterdal and Gudbrandsdal, as compared with their sisters in other parts of the country, are renowned for their clean and well-kept dwellings, and for the care they bestow on their dairy produce' (xlviii).

As with accounts of other characteristics, travellers' depictions of dirtiness strive to entertain, and exaggerations abound. The Rev. R. M. Barnard indulges in a graphic portrayal of a peasant's cottage in Setesdalen:

> The Saetersdal peasant has an innate horror of water, and washes himself (properly) only every Christmas time! On his cottage floor, which has not undergone any cleaning process since it was laid down, his pig jumps cheerfully about; the hens sit on the shelf, between milkpan and cheeses; while the cock majestically struts about on the tester-bed. In the same room which serves as a dairy the Saetersdal peasant sleeps with his family and servants among pigs and goats, and other smaller and still more lively animals. (...) When a milkbowl is produced, especially in summer, it seldom fails to be covered with a thick coating of dust and smuts, which leaves the spectator in doubt as to what it really is. But the native Saetersdalian takes it down without even blowing the dust off, so little does it disturb his equanimity; for in the great vessels where he keeps his sour milk for a whole year, one can see worms and such other trifles running about as merrily as possible. It all goes down in enviable combination! (Barnard 1871, 296–97).

M. Paterson in *Mountaineering Below the Snow-line* (1886) outdid all the other travel commentators in an unapologetically racist depiction of the hygiene of the people of the same area. He recounted an anecdote told him by a German, Herr Seipel, living in Setesdalen: "'There are dirty people in all countries,' said he, 'but if you take a Saetersdal man and throw him against the wall, he will stick'" (209).

It is worth speculating on the implications of the frequent references to dirtiness in travel accounts. In general, as chapter 1 has demonstrated, British travellers were impressed by the purity and healthiness of Norwegian life, and doubtless the sanitation of British cities was far worse than anything seen in Norway. Yet the travellers appear to have an investment in reminding the reader that dirt is not the privilege of the industrial nations but rather a legacy of medieval backwardness. In addition, the removal of dirt has been associated with the formulation of ideas about class in nineteenth-century Britain. As G. M. Young comments in *Portrait of an Age: Victorian England* (1977), '[c]leanliness is next to godliness. The Victorian insistence, whenever the poor are the topic, on neatness, tidiness, the well-brushed frock and the well-swept room is significant' (21). Cleanliness was supposed to be one of the defining attributes of respectability, something which marked off the middle classes and later the respectable poor from those beneath them.

178 THE NORTHERN UTOPIA

In describing Norwegian dirtiness, the British visitors might be considered to be asserting both their own industrial ascendancy and their class superiority. Interestingly, a Norwegian traveller to Britain, A. O. Vinje, was moved to comment in 1863 upon the propensity of the British for cleanliness:

> This island climate, gives a fine skin, of course, when people are washed; and the upper classes lash themselves literally into a soap rage. People *must appear* civilized, and it has been *said* that the civilization of a country can be measured by its consumption of soap. This *soap civilization* has apparently originated among vapours, coal and smoke; for it would never do in a country with dry and pure air, where it would only crack the skin' (Vinje 1863, 19; italics added).

Vinje is evidently sceptical here of the common equation between soap and civilization, remarking that soap may give the appearance of civilization even where none exists and making the facetious, if practical, point that there is a greater necessity for soap in Britain where the air is dirty than in Norway where the air is 'dry and pure.'

Vinje's account, when seen alongside those of British travellers to Norway, indicates that the matter of cleanliness had come to highlight distinctions of nationality and class in the period. It is perhaps as good a point as any at which to move away from the rather ahistorical depictions of the Norwegians that characterised many of the travel accounts and to look at those features of nineteenth-century Norwegian society that brought some contemporary issues into more acute focus.

The Bonde, Class, Property, Representation and National Identity

Travellers were surprised to find an entirely different social and political landscape in Norway from that which existed in Britain. Though Norway herself was changing in social and political terms in this period, it is fair to say that the changes were slower and less dramatic than those witnessed by the travellers at home. On the whole, as we have seen, the travellers did not perceive Norway's own historical trajectory, but portrayed her ahistorically as static and unchanging. Over the course of the nineteenth century, however, their reflections on the different social and political systems operating in Norway were sometimes indicative of their attitudes towards the developing situation back in Britain.[6]

For the observer, the most immediately noticeable fact about the Norwegian population was its small size. Journeying, as they often did, from the major British cities, travellers marvelled at the tiny communities of Norwegians living at vast distances from each other, often separated by huge areas of uninhabited wilderness. The absence of villages and 'dissemination' of houses was a particularly distinctive feature (Ainsworth 1862, 46). The population of Norway in 1825 was roughly one million, about half that of Scotland at that time. Although this figure did increase in the early part of the nineteenth century, it was not until the late 1840s that Norway began to experience her Industrial Revolution with its attendant population growth. Indeed by 1882, the whole population of Norway was still only 1.9 million. Of these, almost 80 per cent still lived in rural areas. This might usefully be compared with the population of England and Wales in 1881, which numbered nearly 26 million. The largest town in Norway, Christiania, had only recently exceeded 100,000 residents and Bergen, the second largest, had only approximately 43,000. This compared with a population in London of 3.69 million in 1881. Most other Norwegian towns had populations of under 10,000. Given these statistics, it is easy to appreciate the statement of the linguist and ethnologist R. G. Latham in 1840 that 'if Norway is no desert, it is to a certain degree a solitude. No part of Europe is more thinly populated' (76).

To understand the British representation of Norwegian society and politics in the nineteenth century, it is useful to begin by considering those members of the community in whom the various commentators showed most interest. Travellers of the middle classes and above would perhaps have been introduced to the *embedsmenn*, responsible for civil, military and ecclesiastical matters in the large towns and here and there in the provinces, but these higher civil servants were few in number and elicit relatively little comment in the travel accounts. Of all the characters in the Norwegian panorama, the most notable, as far as the travellers were concerned, were the *bønder* or farmers, men who, from a British point of view, owned small farm holdings of a relatively equal size and who had a surprisingly

---

[6] According to Jeremy Black, travellers on the Grand Tour to Southern Europe tended to be more interested in the religious than in the social and political aspects of the countries they visited. The unfamiliar signs of Catholicism understandably provided endless fascination (Black 1985, 165). In Protestant Norway, by contrast, where a general religious sympathy with Britain was assumed, the travellers' attention was more easily drawn to social and political issues.

important stake in the political life of the nation.[7] These *bønder*, often confusingly translated as 'peasants' or 'peasant farmers,' were so strikingly different from the large landowners or – after 1832 – from members of the influential urban middle classes who dominated the social and political scene back in Britain, that many travellers felt duty bound to describe them.

To the British traveller well versed in the conventions and prejudices of the British class system, the *bonde* possessed one unexpected characteristic for one who worked so close to the earth: he was independent and free of any overlord. Samuel Laing, a member of a wealthy landowning family from the Orkneys, was a resident in Norway for three years in the 1830s and may be considered to be one of the more reliable sources on the characteristics of Norwegian society. He commented in his *Journal of a Residence in Norway During the Years 1834, 1835 and 1836* (1837) that, 'if there be a happy class of people in Europe, it is the Norwegian bonder [*sic*]. He is the owner of his little estate: he has no feu duty or feudal service to pay to any superior. He is king of his own land, and landlord as well as king' (331).

As a kind of antidote to this enviable independence, the *bønder* were often satirised in British accounts as simple and somewhat old-fashioned characters happily outside the hubbub of modern society. Of all the quaint characters who populated the Norwegian travel account, none seemed so definitively entrenched in the past as this particular group. Describing a journey to Hammerfest, William Dawson Hooker in *Notes on Norway* (1839) commented that '[a]ll the Norwegian peasants care for, is to get plenty to eat, and smoke, during the winter; if they have this and nothing to do, they are satisfied' (46). For the British, the *bønder* set the Romantic tone of the Norwegian social scene, typifying, as they did, the apparently timeless rural existence of the country as a whole. William Hurton found them 'so obstinately wedded to the customs of their progenitors, that they, in wilful defiance of their own most obvious interests, neglect all the scientific appliances and improvements which other countries have long gladly adopted. Their mode of living, manners and social observances, are also little different to what prevailed hundreds of years ago' (Hurton 1851, 83–84).

The *bønder* play the rustic comic role in the Norwegian social tableaux, but they also have a rather more serious significance in

---

[7] *Bonde* (sing.), *bønder* (pl.). Many commentators ignored the Norwegian ø (ö) and used the plural form in the singular.

some travel accounts. Their position in the class hierarchy, their entitlement to property and their political rights made them the locus of interest for those travellers who were concerned about such issues in Britain. In Norway, as in Britain, class, property and enfranchisement were closely connected. Traditionally, entitlement to vote depended, in each society, on the ownership of property, which was in turn an indicator of class. It is fair to say that the majority of travellers appear either ignorant of or simply not interested in the finer details of Norwegian political representation. Many, however, give impressionistic accounts of what they see as striking contrasts between the two societies and, at moments of particular political interest, there are sometimes powerful descriptions of the Norwegian political landscape which reveal much about the constitutional preoccupations of the British at the time.

A frequent theme of the travel writers was the apparently 'flattened' class structure of Norway. Travellers noted the prominence of the *bønder* and the almost entire absence of larger rural landowners. The kind of vast estate owned by great landlords (and later by prominent industrialists) such as those to be found in most counties in Britain hardly existed in Norway. After his visit to Norway in the summer of 1837 the famous geologist Sir Charles Lyell, in a letter to his sister from Copenhagen, claims that the Norwegians 'would be better off (...) if they had more than one single nobleman of fortune and independence like Count Wedel Jarlsberg (...) with whom dies out the last remnant of Norsk nobility' (Lyell 1881, 2: 20). The fact that the Constitution of 1814 had annulled the orders of nobility was undoubtedly a startling fact to a British readership. Only five years after Lyell, John Milford brings up the same topic, stating that the three remaining barons 'will be the last of their race' (Milford 1842, 20). Quoting a Norwegian traveller, he also goes on to remark that one of the three, Baron Wedel, 'is somewhat exposed to ridicule here, as we do not approve of orders of nobility' (ibid., 21). As soon as they set foot on Norwegian soil, travellers sensed this unfamiliar egalitarianism, and for those who stayed longer it seemed to infuse every aspect of life. Samuel Laing, cited earlier, comments in his *Journal* of 1837:

> There is no circumstance in the condition of the people of this country which strikes the observer more than the great equality of all the classes, not only in houses, furniture, diet and the enjoyment of the necessaries and comforts of life, but in manners, habits, and character: they all approach more nearly to one standard than in any other country; and the

standard is far from being a low one as to character, manners and habits (333).

Used to a social geography in Britain in which size of property tended to match levels of income, Laing is delighted to find few architectural or material indications of class. The aristocrat Thomas Allnutt Brassey is likewise surprised in Norway by 'the general uniformity of the houses, in respect of their size and the apparent wealth of their inhabitants: the bakers, for instance, and dealers in articles and food, inhabit houses, quite as large and good as those of drapers, who with us are *facile principe* among shopmen' (Brassey 1856, 42).

The absence of pronounced social distinctions pervaded the smallest nuances of social behaviour. Laing, for instance, suggests that good manners are to be found among every type of Norwegian: 'There seem none so uncultivated or rude, as not to know and observe among themselves the forms of politeness. The brutality and rough way of talking to and living with each other, characteristic of our lower classes, are not found here' (Laing 1837, 158–59), and W. Mattieu Williams, in *Through Norway with a Knapsack* (1876, first ed. 1859), uses a pleasingly concise image to make the same point: 'The Norwegians are remarkably polite, ceremoniously so in the matter of bowing: and the best feature of this bowing is, that the gentleman bows to the poor man in just the same way as the poor man to the gentleman'(15). These references, of course, are two-way mirrors which simultaneously reflect the Norwegian scene and demonstrate that the British were increasingly coming to measure social distinctions in terms of dress, demeanour and behaviour as much as in terms of overt signs of wealth, land and property.

Where they sought familiar indications of class, the British found instead an innate sense of pride and independence among the Norwegians that straddled and blurred hierarchies of status. W. Mattieu Williams, for one, described 'the great bulk of the people (...) as an aristocracy' (Williams 1876, 68), and in a similar vein William Hurton, in *A Voyage from Leith to Lapland* (1851), commented that

there is an entire absence of that exclusiveness which in England places an insurmountable barrier between the different classes. The poor mix with the rich, and feel themselves morally equal, without for one moment forgetting the difference of station, or failing in all due respect to superiors (...). In one grand respect all ranks of Norwegians are alike. They are emphatically the Sons of Freedom, and tread their native soil with the proud consciousness of this (82).

In such statements, though it is clear that a hierarchy of deference remains important in Norwegian society, it is acknowledged that it has been tempered by a sense of the moral parity between people in different bands of society. The implication in these comments by British travellers is that such mutual respect regrettably does not exist in Britain.

After the sense of social equality, the British are also struck by what appears to be the preponderance of property ownership among the Norwegian peasant farmers. In Britain, of course, there was no equivalent property-owning class in the rural counties and – as a generalisation – a large gap existed between large landowners and their tenants, and, in turn, between tenants and their landless labourers. Thomas Forester was one of several writers to focus on the legal reasons behind the extent of property ownership in Norway. His *Norway in 1848 and 1849* (1850), which is rare in the thoroughness of its examination of the country's military, political, ecclesiastical and social organisation, describes the absence of feudalism in Norway's past and the different laws of inheritance which obliged fathers to distribute their land fairly among their children. Under *Udal* law [Norw. *odelslov*] all sons were entitled to an equal share of property. Such a law prevented the accumulation of wealth by elder sons that might lead to a huge disparity in the incomes of members of the same family. This latter scenario, dependent on the law of primogeniture, was all too familiar in Britain and in other countries of Europe:

> The reader is probably aware that the feudal tenure, with its right of primogeniture, and all its burdensome incidents, was never introduced into Norway. Under the Udal law, which has here existed from the earliest ages, the immediate possessor of the soil holds of no superior. He is absolute owner, subject to no rent or duties, or vexatious interference of any description. Of the effects of that system, so different from that which has prevailed, and, in some shape or measure, still subsists, throughout the greatest part of Europe, it is needless to enlarge. They are visible in the character, habits and institutions, the sturdy, yet quiet feeling of independence, – the self-possessed, but mannerly, demeanour that distinguish this primitive people (Forester 1850, 77–78).

British reaction to the operation of Udal law was mixed. Some argued that if each man had just enough to live on, this would abnegate the necessity for younger sons to exert themselves to earn their own living. It was suggested that the spirit of enterprise and entrepreneurialism that so characterised British capitalism in the late nineteenth century, could not exist in Norway. Even E. Lester Linden Arnold, whose lighthearted *A Summer Holiday in Scandinavia* (1877) primarily offers shooting and fishing advice to the would-be traveller, was moved to reflect on the potentially stultifying effects of the Norwegian odelslov:

> The uniformity of social position is also very striking. The law of compulsory division of property equally among all the children of a family has apparently brought one and all to a dead level. Everybody in the country (country as distinct from town) seems to be a small farmer; and these little occupiers apparently cultivate such small holdings that they are in great part naturally their own labourers. It has been judiciously remarked that the chief cause, or one of the chief causes, of the lack of enterprise shown by Frenchmen in planting colonies or in 'striking out' new lines for themselves, is owing to the disastrous law above referred to. Where every citizen has just enough land given him to live upon in his own country, it is not likely that he will show much taste for emigration or anything, in fact, that tears him from the surrounding to which he has become accustomed. Thus, too, in the case of Norway, it may be safely concluded that much of her poverty and industrial languor is due to the law which stereotypes her people as a gradeless mass of agricultural labourers (91–92).

Whatever their attitude to the equable holding of property, British commentators could not ignore the fact that small rural Norwegian landowners had significant – some might say disproportionate – rights of political participation. With the birth of the Constitution in 1814, representation in the Storting was available to officials, townspeople who owned premises to the value of about £70, and farmers who owned their farms or held a lease for not less than twenty-five years. This last were a relatively large group and they dominated the Norwegian democratic chamber. T. K. Derry in *A Short History of Norway* (1973) comments that 'a seemingly democratic provision awarded the peasants who constituted four-fifths of the population, a minimum of two-thirds of the seats' (134). Although this provision for the *bønder* had been made as early as 1814, it was not until 1833 that they availed themselves of its true potential. Under the leadership of Ole Gabriel Ueland, the peasants not only occupied a considerable number of seats in the Storting, using their influence to campaign for a reduction of State expenditure on the activities of the official class, but also demanded and, in 1837, obtained full powers of local self-government. By the third decade of the nineteenth century, 'long before the equivalent class in other nonindustrial countries,' the *bønder* came, according to Derry, 'to be the controlling factor in the life of the nation' (Derry 1973, 148).

By contrast with this seemingly wide franchise, the British parliamentary system in the early part of the nineteenth century must have seemed to some travellers in need of reform. Although the British prided themselves on a limited monarchy (a fact which they believed had enabled them to avoid the horrors of a revolution similar to that in France in 1789), the British parliamentary system reflected the interests of a pre-industrial landed elite. Of the two Houses of Parliament, only the House of Commons was fully elected. Both Whig and Tory political groupings were dominated by wealthy landowners who, many believed, could by no means accurately represent the interests of a rapidly industrialising nation. Before the Great Reform Act of 1832, there were numerous inconsistencies in the system with some sectors such as the northern industrial towns being totally unrepresented. In addition, whilst each existing borough was entitled to elect two MPs, boroughs differed enormously in size, and the numbers and the kinds of people who could vote in each borough varied. Even very small boroughs known as 'rotten boroughs' were anachronistically entitled to two MPs. In 1832, some of these anomalies were corrected. New constituencies, such as those in Leeds, Birmingham and Manchester were created. Rotten boroughs disappeared, and in the remaining constituencies the vote was made dependent upon a single, uniform property qualification. In the boroughs, the franchise was awarded to the owners or occupiers of property rated at £10 a year or more, whereas in the county constituencies, 40 shilling freeholders kept the vote. Many individuals, however, – especially those who owned or rented smaller, cheaper properties together with all those who owned or rented no property at all – were still excluded from the franchise. Given this state of affairs, it is easy to see how, in the early part of the nineteenth century, the Norwegian system, with what appeared to be a fairer distribution of both property ownership and representation, was envied in some of the more progressive quarters of the British political arena. The very different circumstances of the Norwegian economy, the fact that it was rural rather than urban, for instance, was sometimes conveniently ignored in the furtherance of this argument. Commenting on the favourable reception in Britain of his book *Journal of a Residence in Norway*, Samuel Laing in 1836 gives a hint of the way the Norwegian political scene was viewed from the British perspective: 'The Liberal Party receive it [the book] with pleasure as Norway affords an example of good government and well being among a nation of which the legislation is in the hands of the people.'[8]

The success of the Norwegian system became all the more evident towards the middle of the century, as class tensions in Britain became more strained. The vast disparity between those who had accumulated wealth through capitalist enterprise and the working classes started to cause problems in the late 1830s when the Chartists, a group of working-class men and women, with some middle class support, mounted a campaign for universal male suffrage. The resulting uprisings after each of three petitions to the government in 1839, 1842 and 1848 provoked fear in the British establishment. The Chartist protests failed, but it is surely with the chastening memories of these recent insurgences in mind – not to mention similar and more bloody demonstrations across Europe – that the British commentator Thomas Forester reminds the reader in 1850 how Norway has cleverly avoided such horrors:

> While Norway looks to England, the wealthier, the more powerful, the more intelligent community, for the furtherance of her material prosperity – perhaps, in time of need, for the guarantee of her political independence – England may learn from Norway the great moral lesson which her social condition teaches. The absence of any marked disparity of wealth or position among the people of Norway is not only the source of her social welfare, but the basis on which the permanence of her political institutions rests.
>
> But the contemplation of the social state of Norway may do more than awaken those feelings of admiration, perhaps of envy, which it is calculated to excite. It may afford us a clue to the difficulties of our own position; and its pervading spirit, duly comprehended, and influencing our own acts, both individual and collective, may at least tend to alleviate the evils under which we labour. In a free country, property cannot be accumulated in a few hands and political power confined to certain privileged classes, without exciting envy in the masses daily growing in intelligence, and coveting material and political advancement. Nor can a state of society be considered healthy, in which the upper and middle ranks are enjoying, in the fruits of wealth, an exuberance of luxury and comfort such as perhaps has never fallen to the lot of any nation, while large sections of the population are either entirely destitute of the means of subsistence, or earn them by a degree of unremitting toil to which probably no other race of freemen has ever submitted.

[8] Laing Typescript, 93. A copy of this typescript of an apparently lost memoir of Samuel Laing was kindly lent to the authors by Alastair Laing, Adviser on Pictures and Sculpture at the National Trust, and a collateral descendant.

If the rights of property are to be preserved, and the claims of station respected, if the dangers that threaten our social and political organisation are to be averted, the crisis must be met by timely and voluntary concessions (Forester 1850, 457–58).

Here again, a commentary ostensibly focused on Norway has the effect of refracting important messages about contemporary Britain. Forester's tart acknowledgement of the failure of the British system must have sounded radical to the reading public in Britain in 1850. The suggestion that a revolution in Britain might be averted by an understanding of the Norwegian system, indicates the possible importance of the Scandinavian example in mid-nineteenth century politics.

Ironically, perceptions like Forester's of the apparent classlessness and attendant peacefulness of Norwegian society were to some extent figments of a collective imagination. Though the *bønder* and their families had a considerable influence on the political and social landscape in Norway, there was also a sizeable population of cottars, labourers and servants who were 'politically unrepresented and largely neglected' (Derry 1973, 31). The Norwegian sociologist Eilert Sundt (1817–1892) gave voice to some of the concerns of these 'lower class' people in the middle of the nineteenth century, but was faced with growing scepticism by many professional Norwegians, a fact which suggests that the Norwegians themselves were as complicit as the British travellers in promulgating the image of an egalitarian society. In fact, just as in other European nations, social division caused unrest in Norway in the middle of the nineteenth century. In 1845, 46,000 people were revealed by the Norwegian census as being supported either wholly or partly by public funds. Marcus Thrane, a radical socialist, who had spent time in France and Britain and who drew on the ideas of British Chartists, travelled throughout Norway from 1848 and in the course of two years founded 273 workers' unions comprising more than 20,000 members and constituting, 'the largest Labour party in the world looked at in relation to the population of the country, as Thrane himself remarked' (Drake 1969, 24). Thrane brought together the interests of Norway's few industrial workers with those of the cottars in the east and the impoverished small farmers of the west coast, and many local disturbances arose as a result of his activities. Together with several of his supporters, Thrane served some years in prison and, after his release in 1858 eventually emigrated to America. Whilst few political changes occurred immediately as a result of his activities, Thrane had recognised the discontents of a large sector of society and he remained an inspiration. 'Manhood suffrage', that is the acquisition of the franchise by all men over the age of twenty-five, was finally achieved in Norway only in 1898 and universal suffrage in 1913. With these considerations in mind, the rose-tinted accounts of Norway's democracy held by some travellers in the mid-nineteenth century appear to be wildly amiss and indicate the enormous degree of selectivity and the extraordinary manipulation of Norway in nineteenth-century British representations.

Even taken at face value, however, for the more intellectual of the travellers, Norway presented an interesting paradox. On the one hand, she seemed to be entrenched in the primitive stage of social development, producing little commercially and unencumbered by the ideals of profit, whilst enviably still exhibiting the 'social spirit' lost to more industrialised societies (Chitnis 1986, 5). On the other hand, the majority of the Norwegian rural population (or so it seemed to the travellers) owned property, a fact which entitled them to political representation and which was, in the eyes of many, an indicator of a high level of civilisation. According to these dictates then, Norway confusingly exhibited characteristics of both primitive and highly developed societies and, in such a way, provided an interesting case study for political debate. Through discussions of Norway, British thinkers of a progressive persuasion such as Samuel Laing and Thomas Forester could venture the idea that the government might safely extend the franchise to lesser property owners, an important reassurance for the political establishment in the years following the French Revolution and later the Chartist uprisings.

On the other hand, more conservative thinkers could argue that Norway's success was ultimately dependent on her special circumstances; her smaller population, pre-industrialised status and essentially rural economy. It was unrealistic, they would say, to expect Britain to follow suit. Most commentators, for example, would not have advocated the flattened class structure of Norway for Britain. The social levelling of a small population in a large land mass presented quite a different proposition to the major upheaval that would be required to achieve the same egalitarianism in Britain's crowded urban landscape. Thus, though many writers express admiration for Norway's unique situation, it is an admiration for the quaint or the eccentric, rather than a call for revolution at home; the political differences between the two countries provide literary fodder rather than polemic for the travellers. Social egalitarianism, for example, is seen as a delightful quality of the holiday experience, rather than a blueprint for political change. Mark Anthony Lower in *Wayside Notes in Scandinavia* (1874) suggests that the lack of emphasis on social status in Norway was the chief reason for the fact that 'a more friendly feeling seems to exist [there] than in many other parts of Europe' (25) and Lady Wilde remarks in *Driftwood from Scandinavia* (1884) that in Norway '[n]o one is born to live in idleness while others toil, but all classes live comfortably, and with a noble, honourable simplicity' (131). In 1893, Miss Vickers is moved to remind prospective British travellers of the practical consequences of Norwegian egalitarianism for their trip. In *Old Norway and Its Fjords* she quotes the then current *Baedeker* guidebook to Norway, which remarked that 'the democratic character of the people manifests itself in the freedom with which the peasant, the guide and the driver, seat themselves at the same table with the traveller'. She finishes by warning that snobbery of the British kind is simply not appropriate to the extent that 'persons who object to such demonstrations had better abstain from visiting Norway' (81).

Whilst most visitors romanticise and thus, perhaps, trivialise Norway's political freedoms there was at least one traveller of note who took them far more seriously. William Ewart Gladstone, British Liberal Prime Minister and towering figurehead of nineteenth-century politics was a voracious reader who had in his private collection six volumes of travels to Norway, some of which had been presented to him by their authors, together with a number of political pamphlets appertaining to the situation in Norway.[9]

Gladstone first visited Norway – without planning to – in September 1883. Accompanied by the Poet Laureate, Alfred Lord Tennyson, he made a cruise up the west coast of Scotland on the

[9] Patsy Williams, Librarian at St. Deiniol's Library at Gladstone's family seat in Hawarden, North Wales, comments in correspondence with the authors that the collection contains Richard Lovett, *Norwegian Pictures* (1885); W. L. Macfarlan, *Behind the Scenes in Norway* (1884); J. C. Phythian, *Scenes of Travel in Norway* (1877); Mrs Alec Tweedie, *A Winter Jaunt to Norway* (1894); Miss L. Vickers, *Old Norway and its Fjords* (1893); and W. M. Williams, *Through Norway with Ladies* (1877). She says that '[t]he first four of these definitely belonged to Gladstone. There is also a rather entertaining volume by George Brook entitled *Our Trip to Norway 1885*. This is a self-published book of notes and actual photographs, which he sent to 20 of his friends, including WEG (William Ewart Gladstone) whom he had never met but looked upon as a "friend." There is a letter attached, telling WEG that he (Brook) had preceded WEG to Norway by a couple of months, hence their mutual interest.'

Pembroke Castle, as a guest of its owner, Sir Donald Currie, MP for Perthshire.[10] They landed briefly at Kirkwall in the Orkneys where Gladstone, in keeping with the spirit of his times, made much of the ancient connection between Britain and Norway, remarking on Thursday 13 September 1883 that 'the aspect of the people bears testimony to their Scandinavian character' (Matthew 1990, 28). The decision to cross the North Sea to visit the south coast of Norway was taken on the spur of the moment with the Prime Minister and the poet 'as jovial as boys together' and the yacht put in briefly at Christiansand (now Kristiansand) on 14 September (Magnus 1954, 306). At Tennyson's suggestion, the cruise was extended to Denmark from where the group sailed for home. Gladstone's diary entry for Saturday 15 September 1883 evokes his simple enthusiasm for what he had seen on his short foray inland: 'We sighted Norway early. The working of the pilot boats was wonderful – in such a sea. We reached Christiansand before luncheon, went through the town and drove to Torrisdal Falls [i.e. Vigelandsfossen], returning by the steamer; splendid beauty and a most courteous, & apparently happy people. Re-embarked about seven and set off for Copenhagen' (Matthew 1990, 11: 28).[11]

But according to Gladstone's biographer, Philip Magnus, the trip to Norway engendered far more in the Prime Minister than a simple admiration for the scenery and people. Magnus suggests that Gladstone was fundamentally moved by his experience of the country to the extent that he became convinced of the need to extend the

[10] The 1883 trip to Norway was actually Tennyson's second trip to the country. Of his first trip, in 1858, Tennyson's biographer Robert Martin writes: 'There was a grand storm in the North Sea that broke the mast of the ship with a tremendous wave, and he looked at innumerable Norwegian waterfalls, but generally he kept away from the mountains because of the reputation of the inns. He sought out English society at the Consul's home in Christiania, and found it even less interesting than that in London. All in all, he said he could find little differences between Norway and Scotland' (Martin 1980, 431–32).

[11] Gladstone wrote to Queen Victoria to inform her of the excursion: 'Sept. 16th 1883. Mr Tennyson, who is one of the party, is an excellent sailor, and seems to enjoy himself much in the floating castle, as it may be termed in a wider sense than that of its appellation on the register. The weather has been variable with a heavy roll from the Atlantic at the points not sheltered; but the stormy North Sea has on the whole behaved extremely well as regards its two besetting liabilities to storm and fog' (Morley 1903, 115). Another biographer, Matthew, comments that Queen Victoria's rebuke to her Prime Minister for this unscheduled journey was sharp (Matthew 1990, 11: 28, n4).

franchise within the rural counties of Britain. The 1867 Reform Act
had given the vote to all rate-paying householders in urban areas who
owned or rented property. In the rural areas, the franchise was only
available to those ratepayers who paid £12 a year or more in rates and
to copyholders and leaseholders holding land valued at £5 per year.
The qualification remained high enough to prevent agricultural
labourers and other workers with small holdings of property or land
from voting. These men remained disenfranchised, though there were
many calls from Joseph Chamberlain and other radical members of
the Liberal Party to increase democracy in the rural areas. In Norway,
Gladstone had seen the power and the justice of the rural vote in the
hands of men with modest amounts of land and property. The
influence of Norway on Gladstone's thinking at this point must
remain a matter of conjecture. What is certain, however, is that on his
return to Britain, he supported the Parliamentary Reform Act of
1884.[12] This Act gave the counties of Britain the same franchise as the
towns and added about six million to the total number of people who
could vote in Parliamentary elections. In increasing the prominence
of the rural vote in Britain, the new Bill might be considered to have
brought Britain more into line with the Norwegian political model.[13]

In the summer of 1885, Gladstone, having been defeated at the
polls by the Conservative Lord Salisbury, made a second and more
prolonged trip to Norway. This time, he was suffering from a very
sore throat and was advised to rest on a sea voyage. He travelled on
Sir Thomas Brassey's yacht, *The Sunbeam*, from 8 August to 1
September 1885 and made the most of his journey by spending some
of it reading his host's published account of an earlier trip to Norway,
A Voyage in the Sunbeam (1883) (Matthew 1990, 11: 383). In his
diary, Gladstone describes the warm reception he enjoys at the many
places he visits, including Stavanger, the Hardangerfjorden, Vik,
Odde (now Odda), Bergen and the Sognefjorden. He is repeatedly
surprised by the way people in Norway recognise him and describes,

---

[12] In a speech made on May 6 1884, Gladstone told the House of Commons that
'there are questions concerned with the condition of the rural labouring population,
[…] with regard to which I may say that if it be not a blot, yet it is a defect in our
representative system that those persons have not a larger influence than they have
in this house for the representation of their particular interests' (*Hansard
Parliamentary Debates*, 3d ser., vol. 287 (1884), col. 1520).

[13] In fact some forty per cent of all adult males remained disenfranchised in
Britain until July 1918 when all males over twenty-one and all women over thirty
finally obtained the vote.

at one point, how a woman threw flowers over him, and a man brought him a photograph and 'was delighted with my writing on it' (ibid., 386). He also admires the majesty of the waterfalls and fjords and is as keenly aware of the cultural differences between the two nations as any of his fellow travellers. In particular, Gladstone praises the apparent lack of greed amongst the Norwegians recounting how, when he returned to the ship in a small Norwegian boat on one occasion, 'the man utterly refused money. This pleases me more than the approval of foreign cabinets and such' (ibid., 384).

The political issue that pre-occupied Gladstone at this time was the cause of Irish Home Rule. Just prior to his departure for Norway, he had been defeated at the polls largely because the Irish Nationalist leader, Charles Stewart Parnell, had switched allegiances from the Liberals to the Conservative Party under Lord Salisbury, in the mistaken belief that the latter was more likely to grant Irish Home Rule. But Gladstone's views were changing, and his visit to Norway was to play a part in developing his ideas. He had already been impressed in the 1850s and 1860s by Italian nationalism, and was growing convinced that nations ought to have the right to free themselves from foreign domination if they wished. In situations where countries belonged to a union of nations – such as Ireland and Britain – he hoped that each partner could enjoy independence without destroying greater historical ties. Gladstone saw similarities between Norway's relationship with Sweden and Ireland's relationship with Britain. Like Ireland, the Norway of the 1880s was a country of fierce national spirit struggling to preserve its equality with its larger, wealthier neighbour. In the early years of the decade, a group of radicals led by Johan Sverdrup aimed to free Norway from the controlling influence of the Swedish King by strengthening the powers of the Norwegian Storting. The overall union between Norway and Sweden remained intact at this point, though (unsuspected by Gladstone) the seeds had in fact been sown for the future severance of ties. Gladstone was following with interest the subtle shifts in power between the Swedish King and the Norwegian and Swedish parliaments. A pamphlet by H. L. Brækstad entitled 'The Constitutional Crisis in Norway', from *The Conservative Standard* of 4 October 1883 is to be found among Gladstone's private papers at Hawarden, and this was part of a larger debate in the British periodical press (Derry 1973, 179, n1). It was Gladstone's belief that Norway, through constitutional means, could retain the independence set out in the Constitution of 1814. At all costs war with Sweden must be averted. He believed that the strengthening of the Norwegian

Parliament would not only allow Norway to remain within the union with Sweden, but that it would also help to strengthen that union.[14]

It is possible that Gladstone's visit to Norway further convinced him of the success of the Norwegian system and helped him to formulate the link between the Irish and Norwegian situations. As one of Gladstone's biographers, Philip Magnus, puts it: 'Gladstone found in Norway a small people living happily in a spirit of democracy and the effect on his mind was comparable with that of his visit to Naples in the winter of 1850–1851. He loved what he found in Norway, for it touched one of the deepest chords in his nature' (Magnus 1954, 332). Fellow travellers of Gladstone record the fact that Norway seems to have had a profound effect on the former prime minister. Lady Brassey, for example, who kept her own diary of the visit comments that Gladstone read less avidly than usual and spent much time in 'meditation and review'. As she puts it: 'Not seldom a vision of the coming elections flitted before the mind's eye, and he made notes for what he calls an *abbozzo*, or sketch of his address to Midlothian' (Morley 1903, 218).[15]

On his return to Britain, Gladstone did not immediately reveal his conversion to Home Rule for Ireland, but in December 1885 his son Herbert leaked the news to the press. Gladstone threw in his lot with the Irish Nationalists and the combined Liberal and Irish votes defeated the Conservative government in January 1886 when Gladstone became Prime Minister for the third time. In April of that year, he attempted to convince Parliament to accept Irish Home Rule. The First Home Rule Bill suggested that Ireland should have its own Parliament in Dublin, that no Irish MPs should sit in Westminster and that the Dublin Parliament would control all the country's internal affairs, whilst foreign affairs, defence and trade would remain in the hands of Westminster. In an ambitious parliamentary speech Gladstone used numerous rhetorical strategies to convince fellow MPs that Home Rule for Ireland was the only just and reasonable

---

[14] For more on the intricacies of the shifting arrangements between Sweden and Norway and Norway's increasing independence in the period, see Derry 1973, 173–93 and Knaplund 1970, 254–61.

[15] Lady Brassey's account of Gladstone's visit to Norway appeared in *The Contemporary Review* (October 1885), 480–502. There are several other accounts of the visit. They include Gladstone's own account in *Punch* (22 August 1885), 217–18 (see also Schiötz 1970–1987, 176–77). As a result of all these different reports, Gladstone's is perhaps the best documented trip of any nineteenth-century Briton to Norway.

course of action. One of these strategies was his evocation of the fruitful relationship between Norway and Sweden, a union of independent nations flourishing close by:

> There are many cases to which I might refer to show how practicable it has been found by others whom we are not accustomed to look upon as our political superiors – how practicable it has been found by others to bring into existence what is termed local autonomy, and yet not to sacrifice but to confirm Imperial unity.
>
> Let us look to those two countries, neither of them very large, and yet countries which every Englishman and every Scotchman must rejoice to claim his kin – I mean the Scandinavian countries of Sweden and Norway. Immediately after the Great War, the Norwegians were ready to take sword in hand to prevent their coming under the domination of Sweden. But the powers of Europe undertook the settlement of that question, and they united those countries upon a footing of strict legislative independence and co-equality. Now, I am not quoting this as an exact precedent for us, but I am quoting it as a precedent, and as an argument a *fortiori*, because I say they confronted much greater difficulties, and they had to put a far greater strain upon the unity of their country, then we can ever be called upon to put upon the unity of ours. The legislatures of Sweden and Norway are absolutely independent. The law even forbids what I hope will never happen between England and Ireland – that a Swede, if I am correct in my impression, should bear office of any kind in the Norwegian Ministry. There is no sort of supremacy or superiority in the legislature of Sweden over the legislature of Norway. The legislature of Norway has had serious controversies, not with Sweden, but with the King of Sweden, and it has fought out those controversies successfully upon the strictest Constitutional and Parliamentary grounds. And yet, with two countries, so united, what has been the effect? Not discord, not convulsions, not danger to peace, not hatred, not aversion, but a constantly growing sympathy; and every man who knows their condition knows that I speak the truth when I say that, in every year that passes, the Norwegians and the Swedes are more and more feeling themselves to be the children of a common country, united by a tie which never is to be broken (*Hansard Parliamentary Debates*, 3d ser., vol. 304 (1886), col. 1046–47).

The Home Rule Bill was strongly opposed by other members of the Liberal party including the radical Joseph Chamberlain, who – among other reasons – believed that if Ireland became more separate from Britain, other countries within the Empire might demand the same independence. Gladstone's call for Home Rule was one of the factors that ultimately led to a split in the Liberal Party and to Gladstone's defeat at the polls in August 1886. He was, however, elected to office again in 1892 and remained loyal to the idea of Irish Home Rule. In the February of 1893, the Second Home Rule Bill was passed in the House of Commons but was defeated in the House of Lords.

Gladstone was ultimately unsuccessful in his bid to give Ireland her own parliament within his lifetime, yet his attempts to do so throw light on the importance of the Scandinavian example in nineteenth century British politics. Norway was certainly not the only influence on Gladstone's thinking in this difficult period, yet, as has been shown, there is significant evidence to suggest that she played her part. Paul Knaplund has commented that Gladstone's interest in Norway was rare among British politicians in this period: 'The Scandinavian disputes touched so few British interests that the prime minister seems to have stood practically alone in considering them worthy of attention' (Knaplund 1970, 261). Given the numbers of people of stature travelling to Norway by the 1880s, however, it seems likely that Gladstone's praise of the country in 1886 may well have fallen on the receptive ears of many others outside Parliament who had appreciated the country's political record.[16]

Gladstone was not the first to recognise that lessons could be learnt from this small nation across the North Sea; he was, however, in the unique position of being able to bring these lessons into the public arena of the British Parliament rather than simply record them in the pages of yet another travel work. What is clear from the current analysis is that, like many before him, Gladstone recognised a similarity of political outlook and possibility in Norway and Britain. His own words are perhaps the best attestation of this. On 6 February 1890, in a letter to Paul Du Chaillu, a French-American explorer who had travelled to Norway and was something of an authority on the country, he commented: 'When I have been in Norway, or Denmark, or among Scandinavians, I have felt something like a cry of nature from within, asserting (credibly or otherwise) my nearness to them. In Norway, I have never felt as if in a foreign country; and this, I have

---

[16] Evidence suggests that Gladstone's interest in Norway was reasonably well known. Certainly Thomas Cook used the information in a bid to advertise its holidays in Norway. In *Cook's Excursionist* of 1 November 1895 a subheading is entitled 'Mr Gladstone and Norway'. Commenting on the 'indefatigible reading habits' of the ex-Prime Minister, the item quotes from a postcard written by Gladstone to one of the authors of a recent book, *A Yachting Cruise to Norway*, by Edward Trustram (pseud. the Parson and the Lawyer). Gladstone remarks that he reads '"with pleasure all works relating to Norway as a country of rare beauty and varied interest"' (Cook 1895, 8).

learned, is a very common experience with British travellers.'[17]

Ironically, of course, Gladstone's high hopes that Norway could increase her powers of self government whilst still remaining united with Sweden 'by a tie which never is to be broken,' were proved to be naïve with the severance of the union in 1905.

The Sami

In their accounts of the Norwegian political scene, travellers might be accused of having sometimes treated all Norwegians without differentiation. They were never, however, under any illusion about the significant ethnic differences between the majority of the population and the minority Sami population (known to the British as the Lapps or Laplanders) living within Norway's northern extreme. As we have seen in chapter two, travellers' perceptions of all Norwegians were often interlaced with Victorian discourses of race. As Shearer West has commented: 'The English middle class did not simply see themselves as more civilized, more physically perfect, more morally correct than non-European peoples, but they defined themselves equally in opposition to the other Europeans, non-Protestant religions, the Irish, the Scots and even the working class (whether or not they were, by strict Victorian racial definition, of Anglo-Saxon stock)' (West 1996, 8–9). In such a scenario, the Caucasian Norwegian, with his Protestant religion, his Teutonic heritage and his apparent 'aristocracy', fared well; he was as genetically close to the Anglo-Saxon Briton as it was possible to be. Not so the Sami, who in appearance, religion and culture was very different. For the British traveller, the ethnographic interest of Norway lay precisely in this paradox; the discovery of two such distinct types, the one so similar, the other so different, living in close proximity.[18]

Some of the discourses that infused travellers' accounts of the Sami had a long heritage borne out of an apocryphal knowledge of

[17] The passage is cited by Schiötz 1970, 177, and is taken from Du Chaillu's *Ivar the Viking* (London 1893), which contains a facsimile of a four-page letter from Gladstone to the author. For further information about Du Chaillu, see Biographical Information.

[18] Chr. Tønsberg's travel guide *Norway: Illustrated Handbook for Travellers* (1875) draws the attention of the British travellers to two distinct races other than Caucasian Norwegians living within Norway: the Finns and the Lapps. According to

the harshness of the conditions in which they lived. Long before the popular age of travel to Norway, Samiland, or Lapland, as it was then known by the British, had been a familiar location in literature, a site imaginatively associated with difficult terrain, hardiness and natural strength. In the first half of the eighteenth century, James Thomson's topographical poem The Seasons (1726–1730) described the 'Sons of Lapland' as remarkably suited to their environment, peace loving and self-sufficient, devoid of European greed and at one with Nature:

> .... wisely They
> Despise th'insensate barbarous Trade of War;
> They ask no more than simple Nature gives,
> They love their Mountains and enjoy their Storms.
> No false desires, no Pride-created Wants,
> Disturb the peaceful Current of their Time;
> And thro' the restless ever-tortur'd Maze
> Of Pleasure, or Ambition, bid it rage.
> Their Rain-Deer [sic] form their Riches. These their Tents,
> Their Robes, their Beds, and all their homely Wealth
> Supply, their wholesome Fare, and chearful [sic] Cups.
> Obsequious at their Call, the docile Tribe
> Yield to the Sled their necks, and whirl them swift
> O'er Hill and Dale, heap'd into one Expanse
> Of marbled Snow, or far as Eye can sweep
> With a blue crust of ice unbounded glaz'd (ll. 843–58).

The Sami are the epitome of a natural people, but their relationship with Nature here is practical rather than Romantic. In John Dyer's pastoral poem The Fleece (1757), the tough life of the Sami in their frozen winters is directly contrasted with the softer lives of the British swains:

> With grateful heart, ye British swains, enjoy
> Your gentle seasons and indulgent clime.
> Lo, in the sprinkling clouds, your bleating hills
> Rejoice with herbage, while the horrid rage
> Of winter irresistible o'erwhelms
> Th' Hyperborean tracts: his arrowy frosts,

this book, the Finns (known as Quains by the Norwegian peasants), were believed to have emigrated into Norway from the Grand Duchy of Finland, their original home, and numbered from 8,000–10,000 in 1875. The Lapps (confusingly known as Finns by the Norwegian peasants) were regarded by most historians as 'an aboriginal people' and numbered 17,000. British travellers tended either to ignore the first group or to conflate it with the second (Tønsberg 1875, xlix).

That pierce through flinty rocks, the Lappian flies;
And burrows deep beneath the snowy world;
A drear abode, from rose-diffusing hours,
That dance before the wheels of radiant day
Far, far remote; where by the squalid light
Of foetid oil inflam'd, sea monsters spume,
Or fir-wood, glaring in the weeping vault,
Twice three slow gloomy months, with various ills
Sullen he struggles; such is the love of life!
(Dyer 1855, Book I, pp. 54–55)

The fact that the Northern latitudes were in darkness for 'twice three slow gloomy months', coupled with the persistence and abundance of the snow, created an aura of mystery and magic around the lives of the Sami. In this wild, inhospitable environment 'sea monsters' and other strange creatures could easily be imagined to flourish. This indeed was the land of old Norse legend, a body of mythology with which the British literati of the eighteenth century was familiar. Margaret Omberg in *Scandinavian Themes in English Poetry, 1760–1800* (1976) remarks that 'Northern necromancy was a fairly well-established tradition by the second half of the eighteenth century (...) and allusions to Lapland, in particular as the domain of the devilish arts, had appeared in literature from Marlowe onwards' (74).[19] In addition to literary representations, there were two key historical texts on the Sami in circulation by the mid-nineteenth century. The first was Johannes Sheffer's *History of Lapland* (1673), and the second an English translation of the *Treatise on the Situation, Manners and Inhabitants of Germany*, Vol. II (1777) by the Roman historian Tacitus. It is unlikely, however, that many travellers would have had access to these volumes, though there is occasional acknowledgement of their existence.

By the mid-nineteenth century the older natural and supernatural discourses on the Sami were increasingly augmented by more contemporary ideas about race. These were not necessarily specific to the Sami, but encompassed attitudes to the many different peoples across the world with whom Britons were increasingly coming into

---

[19] F. E. Farley comments that 'Lapland was thought of merely as an extension of Odin's domain, a gruesome, remote, ice-bound region where the Scandinavian gods had been worshipped and magic had been practised for centuries, and, in some literary circles, allusions to the barbarous North, to Odin, Thor and the cauldron of the Lapland witches, excited a peculiar kind of thrill which the effete "machinery" of the Homeric age had long since ceased to arouse' (Farley in Omberg 1976, 74).

contact through tourism, trade and conquest. The strands of this conflux of discourses are numerous, but they include an acknowledgement of the slave trade and its abolition, the racism inherent in British imperial conquests, and new understandings of class, education and literacy (West 1996, 2–3). In addition, British thinking on race borrowed much from the 'scientific' explanations provided by the French Count Arthur de Gobineau (1816–1882), whose *Essai sur L'Inégalité des Races Humaines* was first published in 1853. Gobineau's theories, which split humanity crudely into three distinct and unequal races – the White, the Yellow and the Black – and which preached the ultimate degeneration of European society as a result of inevitable racial mixing, were widely circulated.[20] As a result, whilst British accounts of the Sami depend almost entirely on empirical observation, they must nevertheless be read against the background of strongly held mid-nineteenth-century beliefs and prejudices about the characteristics and capabilities of other peoples.

For those British travellers who ventured to the Northern provinces of Finnmark and Troms, the Sami presented exciting new material for observation and discovery. The territory was, in itself, unfamiliar to British travellers. In the extreme north of Norway, they experienced a coastline exceptionally long in relation to its inland area, deeply scored with innumerable fjords and dotted with islands. Travellers were surprised to find a climate that was in places comparatively mild for such a northerly latitude and they witnessed a varied selection of flora including deciduous trees and forest undergrowth (Vorren and Manker 1962, 7). In this terrain lived several distinct groups of Sami pursuing varied lifestyles including fishing, agriculture, and hunting and gathering. Many of the Sami were nomadic, moving from one area to another and from one lifestyle to another according to the climate and the season. Their movement showed no regard for national boundaries, and Samiland encompassed parts of Norway, Sweden, Finland and Russia. By 1898 the number of Sami estimated to live within Norway was 18,500 (Hyne 1898, 172).

Though Alfred Elwes's *The Richmonds' Tour Through Europe* (1853) is an account from the middle of the nineteenth century, it gives a basic description of the Sami as they appeared to the British traveller, which might apply to the whole period:

---

[20] Appropriately enough for this study, Gobineau was appointed Minister to Sweden and Norway in 1872 and upon arrival was delighted by the purity of the Norwegian stock (Biddis 1970, 225).

At the northern extremity of the Peninsula lies the wild and forbidding region inhabited by the diminutive race of Laplanders. Their numbers are but small, probably not greater than twelve or fourteen thousand altogether, and their modes of living are peculiarly their own. The wealthier portion of the community possess rein-deer flocks, and come to the Norwegian and Swedish markets to sell frozen venison, rein-deer skins, and cheese, lodging meanwhile like gypsies, in outhouses and barns, and sometimes in the rudest tents. Others of this people follow the calling of fishermen, at which they are very expert, and the remainder are servants, herdsmen, and beggars. They are looked upon by the Norwegians as an altogether inferior race to themselves, and, indeed, their puny stature and peculiar formation stamp them as such; yet they are not wanting in intelligence, as their success as boat-builders will prove (...) (no pag.).

For those British travellers enchanted by the general backwardness of society in Norway, the Sami represented a yet more extraordinary extreme. In the first instance, the Sami could not be assessed on the same criteria as other European peoples of the travellers' acquaintance, because of their nomadic lifestyle, their more fluid social structures, lack of property and consequent absence from the European political scene. In essence they lacked that category of definition so vital to other nineteenth-century European societies, namely nationhood. More importantly, as far as those observing them at first-hand were concerned, the Sami were physically, linguistically and culturally very different from the rest of the Norwegian population and did not fit easily into any well-known ethnographic category. Whilst the scientist Carl von Linné (1707–1778) had categorized the Sami as Asiatic in 1755 and Johann Friedrich Blumenbach (1752–1840) had termed them Mongols a few decades later, many British travellers were unaware or unsure of these ethnographic categories and saw the Sami simply as different from and inferior to the Teutons, sometimes relegating them quite mistakenly to a branch of the Celtic family (Vorren and Manker 1962, 142). As Samuel Laing put it in his *Journal* (1837):

By the same instinctive operation which discovers at once what is called *blood* in horses, or the cast of countenance in families or nations, one is impressed, on seeing the Laplanders with the conviction that they are a branch of the great Celtic family which seems to have occupied Europe before the immigration of the Gothic people from Asia (...). Clothe a handsome Lapland girl in the Welsh costume, and place her with a basket on her arm in the market place of Chester, and the stranger would chuck her under the chin, and ask what she had got to sell, without suspecting

LAPPS IN TROMSÖDAL.
(From a photograph by Mr. G. H. Hoïges.)

Sami life appeared to bear little resemblance to that of any other European community. 'The Lapps are a peaceful and inoffensive people, untouched to any appreciable extent by modern influences. (...) They have been oppressed at various times in the past, but seem now free from the risk of that extinction which so often comes upon subject-races of a low type of civilisation' (Lovett 1885, 72). Illustration from the book.

that she was not a Cambrian (314–15).

This description of the Sami fits with the general tendency of British writers to equate what they considered to be 'fey and backward' with the Celtic (Pittock 1999, 42).

The Sami languages were a further problem for the British traveller since they had no overlap with either Norwegian or Finnish and belonged, in fact, to the Finno-Ugric branch of the Ural-Altaic family, having connections with languages spoken in Hungary and in northern and central Russia. These languages were completely unknown to most British travellers. Concomitantly, the Danish, German, English (and even Latin) which the traveller was often able to use with other Norwegians were useless in communication with the Sami. Alfred Elwes felt that 'had more pains been bestowed to acquire their language, and thus obtain a direct medium of communication with these diminutive beings, much more important results would, doubtless, have been gained than can at present be shown' (Elwes 1853, no pag.). Confronted, therefore, by a people with whom it was immensely difficult to hold a conversation, the British travel writer was freer than he had yet been with the Norwegian, to construct a version of Sami life that was often far from the truth.

Whilst the other Norwegians, as has been shown, engendered a mixture of responses from friendly condescension to outright admiration, the Sami could provoke the extremes of prejudice and disgust. The early traveller Andrew Swinton, in *Travels into Norway, Denmark and Russia* (1792), described them as 'an ignorant but harmless people' (34), but later accounts were still less tolerant. Edward Daniel Clarke's account in *Travels in Various Countries of Europe, Asia and Africa* (1824) of Sami living between Malmagen in Sweden and Trondheim, is typical in its focus on the physical appearance of the Sami, its tone of uncompromising revulsion, and its frequent recourse to bestial comparison. The title of Clarke's book reminds the reader of the way in which the Sami had been submitted to the same essentially racist discourse as the inhabitants of the dark continents:

> The Laplander is truly a pigmy: his voice, feeble and effeminate, accords with the softness of his language. When taken from his tent, he rolls his weak eyes about, like a bird or a beast of darkness suddenly exposed to the sun. The Lapps are said to be more cunning than the Swedes, who consider them as a crafty set of knaves; just as the Gipsies [sic] are regarded everywhere. (...) A person unaccustomed to their appearance,

meeting one of these creatures suddenly in the midst of a forest would, as we have said before, start from the revolting spectacle: the diminutive stature, the unusual tone of voice, the extraordinary dress, the leering, unsightly eyes, the wide mouth, nasty hair, and sallow shrivelled skin, 'the vellum of the pedigree they claim,' all appear, at first sight, out of the order of Nature, and dispose a stranger to turn out of their way (10: 169–70).

Science played its part in the construction of the Sami as an inferior being. The phrenologists found evidence for their prejudices in the distinctive short stature, short neck, broad head and low jawline. As usual, these physical characteristics were spuriously linked to imagined psychological characteristics. Travellers suggested that such a physiology could not service the higher powers of the intellect including reason; merely the baser animal instincts. As such the Sami emerge in the accounts as creatures somewhere between the animal and the human kingdom. Charles Boileau Elliott's second-hand account in *Journals from the North of Europe* (1832) begins fairly favourably. He describes in a letter dated 31 July 1830, how two of his travel companions spent some time with the Sami, and 'much did they enjoy the opportunity of observing the manners of a race who seem to form a link between the worlds of reason and of instinct (...). They were living in the uncivilized modes peculiar to that country, deriving subsistence, clothes and bedding, entirely from their deer' (100). But the romance of this picture becomes tainted. Elliott goes on to castigate the Sami, pretentiously throwing in a reference to Tacitus to remind the reader of his own academic superiority: 'Drinking and smoking form their chief sources of enjoyment. How pleasure can be derived from such habits is happily incomprehensible to us: but their ideas are few; their enjoyments still fewer. My friends left them with the impression they are as little as possible elevated above the brute creation; though they do not quite answer to the description which Tacitus quotes with ambiguous faith, that they have human faces with the bodies and limbs of wild beasts' (100–101). In *A Voyage from Leith to Lapland* (1851), William Hurton is vociferous in his denunciation of the Sami: 'They are exceedingly phlegmatic in temperament, greedy, avaricious, suspicious, very indolent and filthy, and by no means celebrated for strict adherence to truth (...). The countenances of most of the Laps [*sic*] present a combination of stolidity, low cunning and obstinacy, so as to be decidedly repulsive' (178–79). Such an account, which is deliberately constructed to contrast with the familiar favourable representation of the

MILKING THE REIN DEER AT THE LAPLANDER'S FOLD ON THE MOUNTAINS OF WHALE ISLAND.

Whilst the Sami practised many forms of livelihood, it was their husbandry of the reindeer that primarily gripped the imagination of the traveller. Arthur de Capell Brooke, who visited Finnmark in 1820 and spent a whole winter there two years later, gives a conventional description – by quoting Thomas Pennant's *Arctic Zoology* (1784) – of the physical and mental characteristics of the Sami: "'From use they run up rocks like goats, and climb trees like squirrels. They are so strong in their arms, that they can draw a bow, which a stout Norwegian can hardly bend; yet they are lazy even to torpidity, when not incited by necessity; nervous to an hysterical degree, and pusillani-mous. They are nearly a distinct species in mind and body, and not to be derived from the adjacent nations, or any of their better proportioned neighbours'" (Brooke 1823, 335). Illustration from the book.

Norwegians as hot and fiery in temperament, modest and honest, shows how the Sami and the Norwegians are sometimes used as binary opposites in the rhetorical structure of the travelogues.

In general, travellers had little knowledge or respect for the ancient history of the Sami, or for the enormous changes they were undergoing as a people over the course of the nineteenth century. In the West and South of the Northern provinces, the Sami were gradually moving from a nomadic existence to a more settled monetary economy, whilst in the East they retained a hunting-gathering subsistence until well into the century (Pareli 2000, 9).[21] Few travellers, however, did the Sami the justice of describing this transition or these differences. Cutcliffe Hyne pointed out that the lack of sensitivity towards the history of the Sami among British travellers was to some extent generated by the Norwegian who, 'does not regard him from the point of view of an interesting relic of the past. He merely looks on him [the Sami] in the light of the present, and finds him a thorn in the flesh' (Hyne 1898, 173). In addition to this ignorance, travellers misunderstood the operation of contemporary Sami life. Whilst the Sami were in fact eager participants in the European market economy, trading fur, hide and reindeer meat for other commodities at established market-places, the travellers' accounts tended to focus on those aspects of their lives that isolated and differentiated them from other European cultures (Pareli 2000, 21).

If British descriptions of other Norwegians often relegate (or paradoxically as we have seen, elevate) them to the role of primitive, those accounts of the Sami, riddled as they are with animal imagery and laced with evidence of his inability to rationalise, are more overwhelmingly negative. Late twentieth-century scholarship has suggested that some of the unpleasant characteristics attributed to the Sami in travellers' and other accounts, may well have been engendered by the activities of other Norwegians who had settled in Samiland. Nelson H. H. Graburn and B. Stephen Strong suggest that in gradually taking over the fishing industry in the nineteenth century, the Norwegians forced many Sami into farming or other disadvantageous positions in the trading market. They remark that, 'in response to these and other pressures, some Samek [sic] were described as indulging increasingly in drinking, petty crime, and

[21] Important events such as the closing of the frontier between Finland and Norway to the passage of all domesticated reindeer in 1852, which cut off the nomadic Mountain Sami from their traditional winter pastures, are largely ignored in travellers' accounts (Vorren and Manker 1962, 16).

reindeer rustling' (Graburn and Strong 1973, 28). Such recent scholarship reveals the narrowness and bias of the travellers' accounts.

Education and educability became key concerns of racial ideologies in the mid-nineteenth century and, perhaps surprisingly, through a consideration of these, the lot of the Sami improves somewhat in travellers' accounts. Charles Loring Brace, the American philanthropist, meets a 'Finn of the Mountain' in Hammerfest and decides, after some phrenological scrutiny, that he is a character capable of progress:

> I induced this man to take off his cap, and felt the shape of his head, much to his astonishment, no doubt. He had an exceedingly formed head; forehead strong and full, though not high; the frontal portions of the brain rising finely, perhaps highest in the phrenological organ of 'firmness,' and the backside of the head not too full in proportion. His hair was light and very long; eyes grey, and cheek-bones very high, the broadest part of the face being at that point; mouth large, and chin small, with a scanty mustache [sic] and imperial, as is usual. A face, I should say, showing some weakness but good capabilities of improvement (Brace 1857, 67).

Likewise, William Mattieu Williams in *Through Norway with a Knapsack* (1876, first ed. 1859) is forced to review his preconditioned opinions of the Sami. After a visit to a *sii'da* (group of Sami families) in the Tromsdalen, he treats them to an analysis similar to that which he has already bestowed on other Norwegians, investigating their religious, educational and industrial practices with enthusiasm:

> The more I see of these gentle savages, the more I become interested in them. They are quite an anomalous race. Here they live in direct contact with the high civilization of the Norwegians, in free communication and perfect harmony with them. They are converted to Christianity, and from all I can learn have a better claim to the title of Christian than many of our own church and chapel goers; for besides attending to the outward forms of devotion, they illustrate the reality of Christianity by their genuine unostentatious humility, their loving gentleness to each other and their neighbours, their contentment and their disregard of the ambitious struggles, the greed of wealth, and all the pomp and vanities of the civilized world. It is strange to see a people who can read and write, and who have family prayers morning and evening, still living as nomade [sic] pastoral savages; clinging in all particulars to the old habits of their forefathers, clothed in the skin of beasts, and with so much

contempt for Manchester, Birmingham, and Sheffield, as to still make
their own thread of the sinews of their own reindeer, their needles and
pins of the bones, and their spoons of the horns. (...) Whatever may have
been the moral effect of reading and writing, Christianity, and the
example of civilization, their influence on the industrial habits of these
people is almost nothing (125).

Literacy is at the heart of Williams's argument here. It is the fact that
the Sami can read and write that elevates him above 'brute creation'.
When Williams's book was first published in 1859, Britain was still
eleven years short of introducing a system of state education for the
working classes with Forster's Education Act of 1870. It was
therefore, presumably salutary for him to see the Sami engaged in
pursuits that were still beyond the majority of Britons. Thus whilst
the reference to Britain's manufacturing districts here is essentially
humorous, it is indicative of a great cultural irony of which the writer
cannot fail to be aware; a literate population still practising a pre-
industrial economy. As a salve to this rather embarrassing admission,
Williams reminds the reader of the Sami's lack of industrial
sophistication. He is also at pains to suggest the civilising influence
of Christianity, which is ultimately, of course, the gift of other
nations.
    Even in accounts which treat the Sami with greater humanity,
there remains a distance between observer and observed that is quite
simply not there in descriptions of the Norwegians themselves. Like
the Celts, the Gauls, the Latins, the Orientals and the Negroes as well
as all the other races who inhabited the far outreaches of the British
Empire in the nineteenth century, the Sami were very firmly 'Other'
and well outside the warm, if tentative, embrace which the travellers
extended to their fellow Teutons.

Women and Their Role in Society

The travel writers, male and female, took a healthy interest in the
female inhabitants of Norway. Discussions of women brought a touch
of romantic and sexual interest to the travel accounts but they also
brought to the fore ideas about the condition and role of women that
were of considerable importance in nineteenth-century British
thought. Reading countless anecdotes about pretty Norwegian
maidens, it is easy to forget, however, that female experience in
Norway has a history of its own. In fact, from the late 1830s onwards

changes in the law allowed some women to support themselves independently. The Craftsmanship Law of 1839 and the Commerce Law of 1842, for example, were instrumental in this respect (Derry 1973, 111). In the 1850s, there were changes in the laws of inheritance that were favourable to women, and the end of the century brought an opening up of educational and employment opportunities with admittance to university and, consequently, to professions requiring formal qualifications. All of these changes were to culminate in some (propertied) Norwegian women obtaining the vote in parliamentary elections as early as 1907, and the rest by 1913, some years before the first British women were enfranchised (Selid 1970, 10).[22]

Such developments, however, escape the attention of the British travel writers, whose remarks on Norwegian women tend to see their position as static. Comments range from a familiar objectification of the female form in descriptions of appearance, dress and manners, through puzzled expressions of distaste at what the travellers understood to be inappropriate aspects of female behaviour, to outright condemnation of the roles adopted by women in Norwegian society. The feminist historians Leonore Davidoff and Catherine Hall have argued that a separation of the public (male) sphere from the private (female) sphere, brought about by industrialisation, was instrumental in shaping middle-class identity in the period 1780–1850. Certainly, British commentators went to Norway armed with the view that women attained to middle-class status only by eschewing the public world and by occupying themselves with supervisory duties in the domestic environment.[23] What the travellers saw in Norway often ran against, or one might go so far as to say, clashed headlong, with their expectations. The difficulties encountered by the travellers in reading the Norwegian landscape of class described earlier, were further complicated by issues of gender. As this section will show, it was very difficult for the traveller to categorise the class status of some Norwegian women, including, for example, the wives of Norwegian government officials who, whilst they nominally appeared to belong to the middle class, acted in ways that ill-befitted that class as far as British commentators were

---

[22] For a concise summary of the changing position of Norwegian women through the nineteenth and early twentieth centuries, see Derry 1973, 110–11, 155, 173, 178 and 440. See also Selid 1970, ch. 1.

[23] For a full discussion of the gendered separation of the spheres among the middle classes in the nineteenth century, see Davidoff and Hall 1987.

During his stay at Dalen in Telemark, the painter Nico Jungman (1872-1935) produced a number of portraits of people from the area, usually dressed in the local costumes. One of his models was Andrea Fosli, the beautiful fifteen-year-old daughter of his host. Jungman's sister, Beatrix, who later published the book *Norway* (1905) with 75 colour illustrations by her brother, describes the girl as 'madonna-like'.

concerned. In such a situation, misunderstandings abounded and it is because of this that the travel accounts experience some of their lighter moments in their descriptions of Norwegian women.

To the large majority of travellers, young Norwegian women, both urban and rural, represented a simple and natural loveliness far superior to the kind of cultivated beauty that dominated fashionable circles in London and other nineteenth-century European capitals. Of course, this idea of female naturalness was in tune with the general view of Norway as a primitive and uncorrupted society. The merits of natural female beauty were already well understood by readers of British literature by the mid-nineteenth century. Romantic poetry deified it and in the nineteenth-century novel it was closely allied to moral superiority. In fiction, it is always the unadorned Jane Eyre or Elizabeth Bennett who gains her man whilst the Blanche Ingram of the piece, with her studied beauty and dubious morals, is ultimately rejected.

In general, male writers revelled in their praise of the voluptuousness, clear skin, good health and general air of physical well-being of Norwegian girls, features often linked to their apparent fertility. Andrew Swinton in *Travels into Norway, Denmark, and Russia* (1792) comments that 'Norwegian women are celebrated for their fecundity; and every inhabitable part of Norway swarms with people' (33), and Thomas Forester, in the middle of the century, remarked that the women amongst whom he and his party stayed at the parsonage at Land were 'extremely beautiful. There is a clearness and brilliancy in the complexion and a softness on the expressive features of many of the Norwegian women that is charming' (Forester 1850, 284).

In 1851, William Hurton composed the following song to celebrate the beauty of the girls of the capital city. References to health, nature and innocence abound, though the strains of physicality and sexuality are never far from the surface as the italicised lines below indicate:

THE GIRLS OF CHRISTIANIA!

O, the girls of Christiania! the merry, bonny girls!
Their eyes are bright as diamonds, their teeth are white as pearls!
Their necks are graceful as the swan's – *their lovely bosoms glow,*
Beneath the tight-laced bodice gay, as pure as Norway's snow!

O, the girls of Christiania! their smile how arch and sweet!
Their step how free on native hills – how sure their tiny feet!
They scale the dizzy mountain peaks, and clap their hands with glee,
To see how they can swift outstrip a rover e'en like me!

O, the girls of Christiania have tender hearts and warm;
They take you frankly by the hand, and think there is no harm,
In darting sunny glances, and whispering balmy words; –
I dread such winning gentleness more than their fathers' swords!

O, ye girls of Christiania! it never more may be
That your wee hands softly press mine, and your blue eyes beam on me!
But if e'er I yearn for home and wife – tho' to roam the world's my pride
– To Christiania I'll return, to woo and win my bride! (88–89; italics added)

The sheer naturalness of the Norwegian girls was reiterated right up until the end of the century. Miss L. Vickers in *Old Norway and its Fjords* (1893) commented that 'the Norwegian women, although for the most part plain featured, have blue eyes, and a quantity of nice fair hair. Probably this is because it is worn naturally, curling tongs and all such like hair torturers being unknown' (87). In popular British papers such as *The Girls' Realm*, Norwegian girls were held up as paragons described as having 'sweet, innocent faces, with a candid, open expression' (Turnbull 1899, 479).

The natural prettiness of Norwegian women was often mockingly contrasted with their lack of fashion sense, however. As might be expected, it is most often the women among the travellers who take time to note such details. Writers discovered that the common equation between quality of dress and social class that dominated descriptions of women in British society in the popular press, did not hold true in Norway. Some praised the lack of vanity and ostentation of Norwegian clothing, whilst others – notably here a lady of the British upper classes – were more scathing. In *Diary of a Tour in Sweden, Norway and Russia in 1827* (1879), the Marchioness of Westminster sneered that 'the women here dress horridly, like the English lower classes, with coloured prints, and they have a *mauvaise tournure*. The women among the peasants are hideous and dirty beyond description' (59). Olivia Stone complained that the holiday attire of the people of Christiania was 'in extreme bad taste' and speculated that 'all the unfashionable and unsaleable wares accumulated in English shops had been shipped to Christiania' to the effect that '[h]armony of colour was totally disregarded – red, green, blue, yellow, purple, and that awful majenta [*sic*], were scattered in wild but not artistic confusion over the person of each' (Stone 1882, 19–20). References to the national dress worn in rural areas for special occasions, whilst more complimentary, also function to remind us of the old-fashioned and uncosmopolitan nature of Norwegian fashion. Here is Miss Vickers again on the girls of the Hardanger region:

> Jolly Norwegian girls waited at table, dressed in true Hardanger costume. This consists of a full white muslin garibaldi, having wide, loose sleeves gathered at the wrist in a band; over this is worn a small waistcoat or low bodice of red or black cloth. A kind of breastplate and a waistband, both worked in bright-coloured beads is put over both. A full straight skirt of blue or black serge pleated at the waist, a wide muslin apron trimmed with lace or embroidery, and a huge gold or silver brooch fastened at the throat completes the costume (86).

Here the unfamiliarity of the Norwegian costume, free from all class connotations, allows Miss Vickers to write without prejudice.

British readers might have expected a somewhat more sophisticated account of the mores and manners of Norwegian females from Mary Wollstonecraft, the great proponent of women's rights in the late eighteenth century. They would have been rather disappointed. Wollstonecraft visited Norway in the summer of 1795, just three years after the publication of her groundbreaking *A Vindication of the Rights of Woman* (1792), in which she argued that women as well as men were entitled to liberty and equality by birthright and that the education of women ought to be primarily concerned with the cultivation of their reason. Having left her young daughter with her maid in Gothenburg, Wollstonecraft was experiencing the pangs of motherhood alongside a desperation to be reconciled with the child's father, the American Gilbert Imlay. Thus the background to her Norwegian trip was a maelstrom of emotion in which Wollstonecraft was exposed most forcibly to the trials of womanhood. Given this turbulent context, it is perhaps surprising that her comments on the women of Norway in the *Letters*, which she wrote for publication whilst undertaking the trip, are so brief and limited mainly to matters of dress and superficial manners. Wollstonecraft's lengthiest comments on Norwegian females concern the women of Tønsberg:

> These women seem a mixture of indolence and vivacity; they scarcely ever walk out, and were astonished that I should, for pleasure; yet they

are immoderately fond of dancing. Unaffected in their manners, if they
have no pretensions to elegance, simplicity often produces a gracefulness
of deportment, when they are animated by a particular desire to please –
which was the case at present. The solitariness of my situation, which
they thought terrible, interested them very much in my favour. They
gathered around me – sung to me – and one of the prettiest, to whom I
gave my hand, with some degree of cordiality, to meet the glance of her
eyes, kissed me very affectionately (Wollstonecraft 1987, 113).

Here the 'indolence' and 'immoderate' love of dancing are
reminiscent of those aspects of the lives of middle-class females in
Britain that Wollstonecraft criticised heavily in *A Vindication*. But in
Norway, these qualities are happily offset by the 'lack of pretensions
to elegance', the 'simplicity' and the 'desire to please'.
Wollstonecraft imagines that Norwegian women have somehow
bypassed the artificiality that contaminates more civilised circles. Of
her unhappy visit to the small town of Risør, therefore, whilst she
despises the women for 'having loaded themselves with finery, in the
style of sailors' girls of Hull or Portsmouth', she also comments with
optimism that she can feel 'the first steps of the improvement which
I am persuaded will make a very obvious progress in the course of
half a century' (ibid., 133). Wollstonecraft seems to suggest that this
progress will be reasonably straightforward because it is unimpeded
by the over-refinement of society. As if to bring her argument to a
conclusion, she is pleased to note in Christiania that the Grand
Bailiff's lady, whilst resembling English ladies 'in manners, dress
and even in beauty', has preserved her Norwegian simplicity (ibid.,
144).

The same simplicity is noted some years later by the Rev. Robert
Everest. *In A Journey Through Norway, Lapland and Sweden* (1829)
he attributes this simplicity specifically to the isolation of Norwegian
women from the influences of literature and art:

They are neither literary nor sentimental; and, if they have no
voluptuousness to learn in galleries of half-naked pictures by the best
masters, they are probably not the worse for it. If not gorgeously clad,
they are modest and retiring, without any of that masculine confidence
of manner which women who are much inured to society usually possess
(143–44).

By the majority of male commentators, Norwegian women are
praised simply for being outside the contaminating demands of high
society. Much later in the century, another reverend, M. R. Barnard,

comments that, '[i]t is quite impossible to help liking the young ladies. They are so simple, unreserved, conversational, well-informed and uncoquettish' (Barnard 1871, 3).

Whilst young women were admired for their artlessness and innocence, however, descriptions of older Norwegian women, who did not benefit from the artificial aids to beauty such as make-up, wigs or fashionable clothing available to their British counterparts, were often grotesque and highly derogatory. The sportsman Robert Bremner remarked of the women along the Tinnsjøen in Telemark that 'like all the females we have seen in the last few days, they have the horrid fashion of wearing their shapeless gown, or rather sack, of blue woollen, strapped tight up to the armpits, so that their breasts hang over the upper part of it in most unseemly size. In fact their appearance is frightful – they make one think of the misshapen creatures we read of in children's storybooks about Lapland' (Bremner 1840, 148). With the same recourse to supernatural imagery, John Milford in *Norway and her Laplanders* (1842) remarked of a visit to Trondheim in 1841 that 'some of the old women were absolutely hideous, and might have personated the witches in Macbeth without any stage embellishment' (51).

In descriptions of older Norwegian women, mythological comparisons continue to abound. M. Paterson in *Mountaineering Below the Snow-Line* (1886) writes of a woman at Moland in Fyresdal in language that is deliberately reminiscent of the sagas:

> She was a strongly built woman of fifty, with a face and head that commanded respect. Every feature was as perfect in symmetry as though modelled for a statue, which might well have been that of the *consort of some ancient sea-king*. The brow was almost *regal*, and certain strong horizontal wrinkles added to, rather than deducted from, the keen and intellectual expression of its broad, high, square mass (262; italics added).

The two contrasting figures of Norwegian womanhood, the young and the old, conform to a traditional polarity within Victorian artistic and literary representations of woman as angel or hag. This polarity, sometimes referred to as the 'madonna-harlot dichotomy,' tends in British art to pivot around degrees of sexual experience, with all women other than stainless virgins occupying the position of harlot (Logan 1998, 6–7). In accounts of Norwegian women, sexuality plays a relatively minor part, although as this section will show, it is not entirely absent from the travellers' narratives. The distinctions between Norwegian women, however, tend to pivot around age rather than virginity. A concise example of the rhetorical contrast provided by the two images of Norwegian womanhood is given by Lady Elgee Wilde in her honeymoon account, *Driftwood from Scandinavia* (1874). On the beauty of the maidens, she wistfully takes her favourite simile from nature, commenting that 'the serving maidens were tall and slender as young pine trees, dark-haired and exceedingly pretty, with splendid teeth flashing through merry smiles' (125). The natural comparisons turn sour, however, when she turns to the older Scandinavian women: '[I]t must be confessed that Nornas grow hard and corrugated, like rocks worn by the sea-wave, and seem more fitted for weird spells and fearful incantations than for playful smiles and maiden wiles. Indeed an old woman of the Cattegat is a true Rembrandt study for wrinkles and fearful corrugation of cheek and brow' (ibid.).

As has been noted in chapter 2, the Teutonic characteristics of the Norwegians in general were conceived as masculine. Writers thus often stumbled when they came to depict Norwegian women, because their oft-noted naturalness could be interpreted as hardiness or manliness. The size and strength of Norwegian women, for example, is frequently remarked upon. In his lively *Excursions in Denmark, Norway and Sweden* (1840), Robert Bremner complained of the unbecoming ladies of Christiania:

> We are compelled to admit, that the charms of the fair ladies who occasionally shew themselves in the streets, by no means give an idea of Norwegian beauty. In fact, both in look and manner, the ladies of Christiania are far inferior to those in Sweden. They are emphatically large, and dress in a way that would not be tolerated in a country town with us (2: 32).

Likewise when John F. Keane in *Three Years of a Wanderer's Life* (1887) became acquainted with the daughters of the 'master of the ice house' in Kragerø, he remarked:

> There were also two stalwart daughters of alarming physique, but with the prepossessing face sometimes accompanying Scandinavian blood and hard work. The elder was about twenty – as strong as a horse; but her sister – about two years younger, and not quite so robust – was the one under whose guidance I preferred to visit the striking natural beauties of the neighbourhood (199).

The masculinity of the Norwegian female, suggested in part by her outdoor lifestyle, clashed with British notions of the daintiness and fragility of the Victorian 'angel in the house,' first described by the poet Coventry Patmore (1823–1896) and later adopted as the abiding representation of British middle-class womanhood. The qualifier 'middle-class' is significant here. As Lynda Nead has commented in her analysis of representations of women in Victorian Britain, 'respectable women were inherently weak and delicate, and were in a perpetual state of sickness. This representation of middle-class femininity was set up in opposition to an image of working-class women who were defined as inherently healthy, hardy and robust' (Nead 1998, 171). The British traveller who witnessed the glowing health and physical vitality of the Norwegian woman could not, by virtue of that very robustness, be sure of her social standing. Physical well-being, so well-noted in travel accounts, contradicted ingrained British notions of what it meant to be middle-class. The confusion over status may, in part, account for the relative absence of sexual suggestiveness between male travellers and Norwegian women in the travel accounts. As will be shown in the following, the problems of defining the class of Norwegian women were also enhanced by their unfamiliar behaviour and roles.

In the nineteenth century, the dominant domestic ideology of the rising middle classes in Britain, aided by what amounted to a revolution in national morals, proscribed strict rules of propriety to which women ought to adhere. Many British travellers were therefore shocked by the apparent absence of such rules governing the conduct of females in Norway. The – to the British – peculiar Norwegian practice of delaying a marriage for up to a decade 'till circumstances favour[ed] it' meant that there was often a degree of familiarity between couples who were betrothed, but not married, which would have raised eyebrows in Britain. As George Matthew Jones remarked in *Travels in Norway, Sweden, Finland, Russia and Turkey* (1827) of the betrothed couples he witnessed at a party given by the viceroy in Christiania:

> During the whole of this time they are openly received in all company as lovers, and are never separated, nor is the lady allowed to bestow a smile on anyone else, and the gentleman is expected to devote himself to her. There is no impropriety in their driving out in the same carriage, or in their close and frequent association (108).

A more general lack of propriety exhibited by the female sex was evident when travellers were accommodated within the homes of Norwegian families – a regular occurrence in the first half of the nineteenth century before the development of hotels and inns. On these occasions, travellers often found that they were expected to sleep in the family's best room. Generous though this was, it was also inconvenient, for this was often the room to which the family required most access. A regular comic element of the narratives are the male travellers' complaints about being interrupted or disturbed by female members of the family entering their bedrooms to look for some article or other. For the British traveller, used to a far stricter separation of males and females, such intrusions into the bedroom by women were entirely inappropriate, providing much material for humour and sexual innuendo.

Inside the bedroom and out, male travellers found themselves the object of what they experienced to be an embarrassing degree of female attention. As John Milford noted: 'The stranger is indeed strange to them [i.e. the Norwegian ladies]; his sayings and doings are like nothing which they have ever heard or seen before; and therefore all that a traveller puts on or puts off, all that he does, and everything he uses, are to them matters of surprise, and elements of useful and entertaining knowledge. Nor are they content with merely feasting their eyes; they next proceed to touch and to try to rummage and turn over, being determined to ascertain whether all before them be not an unsubstantial vision' (Milford 1842, 130–31). Milford was not alone; numerous other travellers refer to having their bags searched in the night by the inquisitive ladies of the house.

Nowhere are the different codes of propriety so apparent as in an oft-recurring leitmotif of these travel accounts, the numerous anecdotes about young Norwegian girls serving their British visitors coffee in bed in the morning. Here a simple anecdote carries weighty and gendered cultural connotations, whilst simultaneously contributing to the shaping of the Norwegian travel account as a genre. William Dawson Hooker in *Notes on Norway* (1839) sets the ball rolling with an account of his trip to Bossikop in Finnmark:

> We were called from our *downy* slumbers by the entrance of a damsel, who offered to each of us a cup of strong coffee to sip in bed; not as a substitute for breakfast, but simply to serve as an awakening draught and to rouse us thoroughly. This custom we found to be universal in all Norske families (...). [T]he best looking girl in the house is selected to perform this office. It is certainly not unpleasant to see a fair-haired, blue-eyed child of the North, the first thing in the morning, before one is fairly awake, and to sip the refreshing coffee, which is proffered with such modest grace, as induced some of us to doze a little longer, in hopes of being favoured with a second visit. Having leaped from our couches

and commenced dressing, we who were strangers, felt not a little abashed at seeing our Hebe return for our empty cups before we were half-clad, and wished ourselves back in bed; but she walked quite unconcernedly past us, reminding me forcibly of the scripture expression, 'thinking no evil,' for it seemed to be a matter of no moment to her whether we were dressed or not, and when we said 'mony tak,' she quietly curtsied, and replying 'welbekommen,' went away with our cups (52–53).

Thomas Forester struggles to reconcile a similar event with his principles in *Norway in 1848 and 1849* (1850):

These damsels served the early dish of coffee before I rose in the morning, entering the chamber on all occasions without the slightest reserve; a custom on which I have before commented, and which argues either great innocence and simplicity, or great laxity of manners. I am inclined to attribute it to the former (297).

In another version, Charles Elton in *Norway, The Road and the Fell* (1864) is startled in waking up to find his hostess sitting on his bed:

I slept till I was awakened by the unfamiliar sound of a church bell and a buzz of Sunday-school children. My hostess, in the same dirty garment as yesterday, was sitting on my bed, not liking to wake me, and yet anxious to see the Englishman perform his toilette. She appeared to have forgotten that Saturday in Norsk is called 'Washing-day, Lordag, or Laur-dag,' from the plan of our common forefathers of taking their cleaning only once a week (215).

These frequent vignettes of coffee-drinking en *deshabille* provide a farcical flavour to the travelogues, reminding us of their almost fictional quality. Such saucy moments are laced with the same titillating innuendo common in many Victorian novelettes, though the *Frøken*, a good Teuton girl, always escapes with her honour unimpeached.

A second site of moral uneasiness as far as travellers were concerned were the Norwegian *seter* or mountain huts. These were rough wooden cabins in which young Norwegian girls might stay from the middle or end of June until the middle or end of September, tending the cattle. The *seters* enhanced the British view of the naturalness and simplicity of the Norwegian female, though there were also indications that they may have provided a romantic rendezvous for young lovers. As Miss Vickers in *Old Norway and its Fjords* (1893) pointed out:

COSTUMES AT HITTERDAL.

Whilst this picture ostensibly shows the traditional costumes of Heddal in Telemark, it also offers additional information. First of all, it shows a typical interior of a peasant house, with an earthen floor and the fireplace (the only source of heating) in the corner. Finally, it reveals the Norwegian *frøken* receiving her male visitor unchaperoned. Illustration from Ainsworth (1862).

The work is left mainly to the girls, two occupying each hut. During the day, whether it be wet or dry, they tend the herds, milk the cows and superintend the making of the butter and the cheese. Visits are few and far between. Provisions are brought up at stated intervals, and sometimes a friend, or a lover – most probably the latter – will make a call, involving a toilsome journey of many miles. Many of the Norwegian girls pass the summer, year after year in this toilsome laborious life (82).

Here there is a disjuncture between the apparent innocence of Norwegian girls and the strange independence of their lives. Such lack of supervision over such periods of time would not have been tolerated for young women of a certain status in Britain and the *seter* remained a dubious location in travel accounts, continuing to puzzle commentators who, in most other matters, saw themselves as clear moral arbiters between what they observed and the susceptible British reader.

Whilst many writers dallied with the superficial attractions and behaviour of Norwegian women, a few showed a far deeper engagement with the more fundamental issue of the role and status of Norwegian women in society. The status of women in societies was seen as an important issue by eighteenth- and nineteenth-century historians and anthropologists. The women's historian Jane Rendall has explained how the great historical works of the eighteenth century, including those by David Hume and William Robertson, attempted to formulate 'a putative hierarchy [of nations], a ladder of human societies, at the top of which was the apex of European civilization' (Rendall 1994, 3). On the lowest rungs of the ladder were the nomadic and hunting peoples of places such as Southern Africa; at the very top, as far as British historians were concerned, were the Britons themselves. In travel accounts, commentary on the position of women in other societies was common and, one might argue, crucial. By assessing the position of women in a certain society, travel writers had a measure by which they might gauge the overall degree of civilisation reached by that society. As William Alexander wrote in his *History of Women from the Earliest Antiquity to the Present Time* (1779), the condition of women marked 'the exact point in the scale of civil society, to which the people of such country [*sic*] have arrived' (103).

The business of constructing a hierarchy of societies was thus, in part, concerned with defining an ideal relationship between the sexes to which societies might aspire. Since no societies granted identical status to men and women, those countries at the top of the list were those in which relationships between the sexes could characteristically be seen to include such qualities as 'affection,' 'sympathy', 'companionship' and 'complementarity' (Rendall 1994, 4). Britain, with its apparent understanding of the different but equally important roles of men and women, was considered to be one such society. Relationships between males and females in Britain amongst the upper and upper middle classes and increasingly amongst large numbers of the middle class, were considered to embody the positive attributes mentioned above. By contrast, societies such as the Turkish Empire, in which women were considered to be treated with disrespect, or worse, as slaves, were marked out as 'uncivilised.'

There was then an assumption among British travellers, male and female, that nineteenth-century Britain stood at the pinnacle of civilisation and that this lofty position was deserved in part because of the way she treated her women. To a modern observer, this might seem an ironic statement. British women at all levels of society, but perhaps most obviously in the middle and upper classes, were by no means equal to British men. Women's legal status together with their opportunities in terms of education, employment and political representation were all limited. Given these inequalities it is hard to imagine just how British writers (male and female) justified the idea that the position of females in Britain was something to be desired. And yet, the British middle-class woman was seen as a model to be emulated, a woman in the happy economic position of being free from the necessity of earning a living herself and therefore able to focus her attention on the *supervision* and *organisation* of the domestic sphere. It was precisely this removal from menial tasks and the increased leisure time which attended it, which granted British women their status as middle or upper class. They had, it was argued, the time to pursue accomplishments, attend to their appearance and to the spiritual needs of their busy husbands. Such factors helped to guarantee the ascendant position of Britain on the great ladder of civilisation.

British travellers of both sexes went to Norway with high expectations of the position they were likely to find women occupying. This was due in part to a notion that fellow Protestant countries in general treated their womenfolk better than Catholic countries. It came as something of a shock, therefore, when travellers observed the women of Norway engaged in tasks that in Britain would always be reserved for men. As early as 1792, Andrew Swinton noted (and with some admiration) in *Travels into Norway,*

The Raft Boat : Thelemarken.

The sight of women rowing probably astonished many middle- and upper-class British travellers. Robert T. Pritchett comments on the peculiar vessel in this picture in the following way: 'On Sunday every variety is seen, and the additional interest of lake travelling is met with – namely the raft boats, consisting of seven stems of trees, the longest in the middle, the six cut shorter, like organ pipes; midships a seat for one; while the oars are tied in with green birch twigs with the leaves on. How suggestive of early lake habitation, and yet how like a modern outrigger; for there is only room for one and a *fine* [*tine*], or provision box, from which a Norwegian, male or female, is inseparable' (Pritchett 1879, 24).

Denmark and Russia that women were involved in the maritime business of Norway:

> The Norwegians are the most ingenious of all people, in the construction of their boats, which are the best calculated for safety in the world, and with which they venture out to sea, for the purpose of piloting ships into harbour, in the greatest tempests. I have even seen the women steering these boats, amidst the raging wind and sea, with the utmost composure and skill. They come off with their husbands, and having left them on board the ships for pilots, the wives take charge of the boats and bring them home (83–84).

Far from the 'affection,' 'sympathy' and 'complementarity' of the British middle-class ideal, travellers saw Norwegian women engaged in demeaning manual tasks, often ignored by their 'indolent' husbands. The Marchioness of Westminster in her *Diary of a Tour in Sweden, Norway, and Russia in 1827* (1879) was outraged to find that the Countess Wedel, 'who is the first lady in Norway, takes it as thing of course to step into the kitchen to see how the dinner is proceeding, and if the fish is come. Nor is this all; she equally looks to the washing, orders what beasts are to be killed and salted for the winter's provisions, and so on; makes all her own and her children's clothes with her own hands, even the gloves which she cuts out, and makes of reindeer skins' (75–76). The Rev. M. R. Barnard was also concerned about what he considered to be the unnatural duties of Norwegian women in some rural areas:

> It will strike the traveller painfully, not only in Saetersdal proper, but in the more Southern districts, and the whole western coast, on seeing the hardest and severest work imposed on the weaker sex. Whilst the husband, with a clay pipe in the corner of his mouth, is stretching himself at full length in true Oriental indolence, you may see the former weighed down under the roughest field work. The women hoe, thrash, plough, cut wood, and carry water, whilst the men, just for once in a way drive a load into town. The laziness of the Saetersdal peasant is so great, that he almost looks on it as something derogatory to put his hand to any farm work (Barnard 1871, 298).

For most British commentators, however, it was the role of those women who most closely approximated to the urban middle-classes that caused the most concern. In *A Personal Narrative* (1829), Derwent Conway undertook a lengthy and derogatory discussion of the domestic role of the women of what he considered to be the Norwegian upper middle classes, that is the wives of 'dignified clergymen, of doctors in medicine and of persons holding certain offices under government'(172). Conway reveals his surprise to find that even in these 'respectable' families, wives and daughters carried out much of the same menial work as the servants:

> I have mentioned elsewhere, that the duties of the ladies do not end with the cooking of dinner; the young ladies, (if there be any) carry in the dishes, and if there be none, the mistress of the house. They also change the plates, wipe the knives, and perform every other office that is performed elsewhere by servants; but, in Norway, a servant is seldom or ever seen in a dining-room. The Norwegians would, indeed, consider it disrespectful treatment, were they to employ servants to wait upon their guests. In one house, where we occasionally visited, and in which there were no young ladies, two farmer's daughters, neatly dressed, always assisted the lady of the mansion to wait upon the company. A Norwegian lady might, indeed, be cited as a pattern to any English servant in the waiting department. She is constantly walking round the table, observing the wants of the guests and supplying them. Nor does she, in general, partake of dinner with the party, but dines either before dinner is served, or after it is taken away. There is little of the comfort of an English dinner-table in this; but daily custom at length reconciles one to it (173).

Conway is not alone in remarking on the facility of Norwegian women for the practical skills of cooking, homekeeping and the rearing of children. Whilst there is some admiration for their skills and some recognition of different societal mores at play here, including, for example, the Norwegian idea that servants should not serve the guests directly in respectable homes, his comments are tinged with disapproval. There is the sense that the Norwegians have yet to reach the elevated status achieved by the British middle classes in which women are expected to supervise the production of a meal without getting their hands dirty.

Conway also describes how women helped not only in the dining room, but also in more basic culinary exercises such as the salting of meat, and the grating, beating and seasoning of meat for sausages and meat balls. He recounts with horror how on one visit to Norway he 'heard a young lady decline an invitation to pass a week with a friend, because *it was slaughter time*' (174). Many readers would have shared Conway's horrified exclamation: 'What should we think in England of a young lady who should make such an apology?' (ibid.) He goes on to point out that the necessity amongst Norwegian women 'for being so much in the society of servants' contributes 'in no small degree to blunt those refinements in thought and feeling which in

England, form the great charm of female society' (ibid., 176). The general ease with which the Norwegian 'middle classes' mixed with servants was a source of discomfort for the British travellers, but the particular closeness between *women* and servants was altogether distasteful to them. Conway's book reminds us that he for one is fully aware of the larger historical implications of his remarks:

> It has been usual to judge of the civilization of a country by the estimation in which the female character is held, and the accomplishments which it is thought necessary that females should possess. If by this test we judge of the civilization of Norway, we shall place it low indeed in the scale of nations (ibid., 175).

Once again, what appears to be a small matter in the travel accounts – the etiquette of serving a meal – has considerable cultural overtones. As has been discussed earlier in this section, the removal of women from the practical business of domesticity to a more supervisory position has been seen by recent historians as an important constituent in the construction of middle-class identity in Britain. The apparent absence of this phenomenon in Norway left travellers unsure about the comparability of their experiences in class terms.

The view of Norwegian women as downtrodden domestics is used in various ways in the travel accounts. On the one hand, it provides a convenient dramatic device allowing some male writers to wax lyrical on the supposed happiness attendant on this female subjugation. Edward Daniel Clarke, for instance, becomes poetic:

> It has been said that the women of *Norway* are domestic slaves, and their husbands domestic tyrants. Some truth, we are ready to allow, may be found in the former part of this sweeping assertion; although there be none whatsoever in the latter. But the slavery of a *Norwegian* wife is voluntary; she delights in her labour, because it is 'the labour of love;' and if this be 'domestic slavery,' it is well repaid by domestic happiness; by a full measure of reciprocal regard and affection in the fidelity and increasing attachment of her husband: for 'as the sun when it ariseth in the high heaven, so is the beauty of a good wife in the ordering of her house (Clarke 1824, 10: 398).

Others use the position of women to reinforce the notion of Norway as a backward country well behind others in Europe. Charles Boileau Elliott in *Letters from the North of Europe* (1832) includes an observation on what he considers to be the dangerous lack of polite

forms of address, which means that all Norwegian women are
reduced to the status of 'wife,' rather than 'lady':

> Norway is in a state of demi-civilization, a century behind Sweden,
> which is a century behind Denmark, and at least another century behind
> France and England. Nothing marks this more strongly than the degraded
> position of women, who are regarded as convenient appendages rather
> than as companions, to the men. Among the lower orders, they perform
> the hardest work. In the higher ranks their duty is to minister to their
> lords. The word lady is not known. When a gentleman introduces his
> wife, it is with the two words, 'my wife'. This unqualified brevity grates
> on an English ear; and the impression of severity thus conveyed is not
> diminished by observing the laconic speaker throw himself carelessly
> into his chair, with a pipe in his mouth, while his wife waits on her
> husband and his company (153–54).

On the whole, female writers were less impressed with the situation
of Norwegian women than were the men. Emily Lowe in her very
well-received *Unprotected Females in Norway* (1857) complained
that, 'the women are certainly rather too domestic, and look upon
their husbands with awe, as if they were another sort of creature: this
may sound too enchanting to the gentlemen, but, being the general
custom, it is not the least complimentary, and one wants a wife for a
companion, not a head servant' (158–59). The idea of the
'companionate' marriage was key to discussions about the role of
women in Britain in the mid-nineteenth century, and this remark
establishes Lowe as a participant in that debate.

Doubtless, many other British commentators accentuate the lowly
situation of Norwegian women as a means of boosting Britain's own
integrity on matters of sexual equality, but others point out that
British superiority is not so well-founded. R. G. Latham in *Norway
and the Norwegians* (1840) urges his readers to alter their perceptions
of Norwegian women:

> There is a good deal of sentiment thrown away upon the condition of
> ladies in Norway. Travellers should do in Rome as the Romans do. If, at
> the house of a respectable host, the wife and daughter wait at table, there
> is no occasion for being unnecessarily shocked. It is the custom of the
> country to do so. Similar things may be seen at home. There is just as
> much drudgery performed by the fair sex amongst ourselves (206).

The position of women is one issue upon which the travel writers
engage in debate with each other, and it provides good examples of
the intertextuality between Norwegian travelogues, a fact which

attests to the prevalence of discussions of the role of women within British nineteenth-century discourse. After making it clear that he judges Norway to have a high status among societies, Samuel Laing turns to the subject of women, acknowledging that the position of women in society must act as a guide to the status of that society. In 1837, whilst not denying the validity of the observations of Derwent Conway and others, Laing begs to correct their assumption that Norwegian women are in a more unhappy or degraded state than their English counterparts.

> [My] high estimate of the state of manners in this country may appear inconsistent with the statements of other travellers, representing females, even the highest classes, as holding a lower position than in other parts of Europe. Dr Clarke mentions, that they do much work, which with us, in any class of society above the lowest, would be considered servants' drudgery, such as not sitting down at entertainments, but waiting on the guests; and one lively traveller in Norway, Derwent Conway, reckons the life of a Norwegian froken, or young lady of rank, little better than that of an English chambermaid. He tells of one froken sending an apology for not accepting an invitation, as it was slaughter month, and she had to stay at home to make the black-puddings. If we inspect the arrangements in Norway with regard to *property*, this apparent inconsistency will disappear; and the female sex will be found to have in fact more to do with the real business of life, and with those concerns which require mental exertion and talent, than women of the same class in England (Laing 1837, 161–62; italics added).

Laing reminds us here of Norwegian women's rights to property, which in the period exceeded those of British women,[24] and he goes on to say that 'in the real business of life, in their influence on those concerns which occupy the male sex, the female sex in Norway stands on higher ground than among the upper ranks in Britain and has a more active and important role to perform' (164).

It is interesting, though perhaps not surprising, to note that possibly the most 'feminist' comment on Norwegian womanhood in the texts studied comes from a woman traveller, Isabella Blundell, who in *Gamle Norge* (1862) seconds Laing's views on the real influence of Norwegian women:

> It struck me, whether rightly so or not, that (...) women held a very influential position here; – they were constantly appealed to by the men

---

[24] Until the Married Women's Property Acts of 1870 and 1882, women in Britain handed over all rights to their own property to their husbands on marriage.

in whatever was going on, and in many stations it was quite clear that they reigned paramount. I often speculated as to whether any old influences, any remains of the respect once paid to the Alruna wives and maidens, the Scandinavian sybils of an age which now only lives in ancient saga and romance, has had any share in this state of things. I don't suppose it has, only one is carried back so many hundreds of years by the primitive life one meets here, that when on the spot the idea does not look so wild as it does in our practical, modern, English life (100).

Whilst it seems clear that Norwegian women were required to undertake more menial tasks than their counterparts in Britain, it seems probable that their engagement in 'the real business of life' (identified here by Laing and Blundell) coupled with better inheritance and property rights, actually meant that their influence in Norwegian society remained significant. Such a hypothesis might explain why some propertied Norwegian women obtained political enfranchisement as early as 1907 and the rest by 1913.[25] It is salutary to remember that in Britain, enfranchisement for women over the age of thirty was granted as late as 1918, and for women over the age of twenty-one as late as 1928.

Social Problems: Drinking, Poverty, and Prison Reform

With the industrialization of British society in the nineteenth century, the growth of towns and cities gave rise to a preoccupation with social degeneration and the possible resulting urban unrest. It was obvious to the travellers, of course, that a small, largely agrarian and pre-industrialised society such as Norway would hardly engender equivalent social disturbance and, as has been discussed previously, travellers found in Norway a society that, on the whole, seemed to have eluded the contaminations attendant upon industrialisation. But, as this chapter has also made plain, this view of Norway was, partly at least, an illusion. Norway, like all nineteenth-century societies, experienced social change and social unrest. From 1845 to 1900, the percentage of Norwegians living in urban areas increased from 15.6 per cent to 35.7 per cent, a fact which suggests that there was

---

[25] Women were given the Parliamentary vote in 1907 subject to the possession by themselves or their husbands of an income equivalent to £22 in the towns and £17 in rural areas (Derry 1973, 155 and 173).

considerable pressure on resources.[26] The sociologist Eilert Sundt investigated the problems of population, poverty, labour and the social environment from the late 1840s onwards. Through his writings, he also – for better or for worse – brought the life of the Norwegian peasant into the public arena. But nineteenth-century British visitors are unlikely to have known much about Sundt's findings.[27] Rather their interests in certain aspects of the social scene in Norway is, as usual, indicative of those matters which preoccupied them at home. From their selective accounts of the condition of Norway, it is relatively easy to deduce their chief concerns about the 'Condition of England'.

Derwent Conway commented in 1829 that, 'most people who have heard anything of the state of manners among the Northern nations, assign to them the vice of drunkenness. For my own part, I am constrained to admit, in a great degree the truth of this imputation. All ranks drink freely and the lower orders to excess' (39). Conway confirms the historical stereotype of the Scandinavian as a hard drinker. In the early nineteenth century, this long-held belief gained added credence in the case of Norway because of a change in the laws relating to alcohol distillation. Under Danish rule, Norway had been prevented from having any distilleries of her own and from importing alcohol from anywhere but Denmark (Pratt 1907, 10). Though some distilleries undoubtedly *did* exist in Norway before this period, it was only after the Constitution in 1814 and specifically after changes in the law in 1816, that every owner or occupier of land was authorised (and thereby encouraged) to distil from his own agricultural produce; distilleries were also allowed in towns. This relaxation of the distilling laws contributed, together with a number of other factors, to a massive expansion in the manufacture and consumption of alcohol in Norway in the first half of the century.

British travellers remarked on the vast amounts of alcohol consumed by the Norwegians, particularly at festivals such as weddings and at traditional midsummer celebrations such as the one witnessed at Kongsvinger by Arthur de Capell Brooke in *Travels Through Sweden, Norway and Finmark* (1823):

---

[26] Statistics obtained from *Official Statistics of Norway: Historical Statistics 1994* (1995).

[27] Sundt's work 'On Marriage in Norway' was translated into English by Michael Drake in 1980.

Their manner of celebrating this feast consisted chiefly in singing, and drinking most immoderately; and in the house where I was lodged, there were more than fifty persons of both sexes in a state of complete intoxication, yet still swallowing from time to time, large bumpers of brandy. No quarrels, however, or fighting, as is generally the case with us, attended their carousing; on the contrary, all was the most perfect mirth and good-humour (75).

According to Derwent Conway, as we have seen, excessive alcohol consumption was not simply confined to the rural poor in Norway. Indeed, all members of the community seemed to have had access to copious amounts of drink. The poor drank beer, *brennevin* (liquor) and, as the century progressed, a variety of cheap substitutes, including the sweet *laddevin* (a favourite with the women), and the lethal *politur* (the drink of hardened alcoholics), whilst the urban 'middle classes' drank large quantities of French wine as well as Madeira, Malaga and Burgundy (Conway 1829, 39).

Insobriety was one of the matters upon which travellers judged the relative merits of Norway and her nearest neighbour Sweden. Edward Daniel Clarke made the confident assertion that '[i]ntoxication, rare among the Swedes, is common in Norway. The Norwegians are a less virtuous, but they are a more lively people, and possess many amiable and valuable qualifications' (Clarke 1824, 10: 202). But five years later, the Rev. Robert Everest placed the heavier balance of insobriety firmly with the Swedes, stating that 'if drunkenness is prevalent in Norway, it is certainly much more so in Sweden' (Everest 1829, 258).

On the subject of drinking no less than any other matter, connections were made between climate and behaviour. Charles Boileau Elliott in *Letters from the North of Europe* (1832) commented of the lower orders in Norway: 'They are addicted to drinking; and the climate, rendering fermented liquor perhaps in some degree necessary, is pleaded in excuse for the indulgence of an odious vice' (191). The early twentieth-century historian Edwin Pratt describes how the drinking of home-produced *brennevin* became central to Norwegian culture in the early part of the nineteenth century and suggests that the act of drinking had cultural, patriotic and economic as well as climatic overtones:

When one peasant had a supply of liquor, he would summon his friends and neighbours to a drinking bout, and each of those friends and neighbours would do the same in succession. They indulged in the beverage on grounds that were alike personal and patriotic. They regarded brandy as an excellent tonic and a promoter of warmth in a cold

country, and they thought also that the more they drank the greater would
be the quantity of the grain and potatoes used, and the more prosperous
would agriculture become (Pratt 1907, 11–12).

In spite of the ready availability of alcohol, however, many British
commentators were sometimes surprised by the Norwegians' ability
to remain moderate in their drinking habits. John Barrow Jr. in
Excursions in the North of Europe (1834) commented: 'It is
surprising, indeed, and speaks much in their favour, that there is so
little drunkenness among these simple people, and the more so when
one reflects on the excessive cheapness of this corn-spirit' (327).
With an arch glance over his shoulder at the intemperance of the
British, Barrow comments that 'it is a remarkable fact that the only
man that I have seen tipsy since I left England was one of our own
countrymen, who was on board the steam-packet, on leaving the
tower Stairs, – and a Swede' (271).

Over the course of the nineteenth century, the drinking of alcohol
became closely related in the British consciousness to social
degeneration and immorality. As such it was seen predominantly as
an urban working-class issue, something from which the British
middle classes were supposedly proudly exempt. In the early part of
the century, intoxication among the Norwegians surprises the
travellers since it detracts from their clean, moral and essentially
middle-class image. It does, however, allow for the British assertion
of cultural superiority in the area of health and leisure.

In Britain, following the American example, the British and
Foreign Temperance society was established in 1831. Together with
other temperance societies, this was to play a key role in the
improvement of British manners and morals and in the formation of
the working-class 'culture of respectability' over the course of the
nineteenth century. From the inception of temperance onwards,
British comments on Norwegian alcoholism take on a distinctly
evangelical flavour. By the mid 1830s there were fears, even in
Norway herself, that the country could face 'a national disaster' if the
amount of alcohol produced and drunk was not curbed (Pratt 1907,
12). The British were puzzled by the fact that the drinking habits of
the Norwegians seemed to contradict the regularity of their church
attendance and other evidence of their piety. H. F. Tozer, in a
travelogue edited by the famous scientist Francis Galton, commented
that although the Norwegians were a religious people, 'they cannot be
considered a highly moral people. This arises partly from the large
consumption of corn-brandy, which causes not so much actual

drunkenness, as intemperance' (Galton 1861, 385). The sexual impropriety that might result from inebriation is never far from the surface, particularly as women were often observed drinking alongside men. Once again it was the Sami and the unfortunate people of Setesdalen who came in for particular criticism. The Rev. R. M. Barnard commented:

> The Saetersdal peasant (as with all uncivilized people) is greatly addicted to strong drink, and on particular occasions – at all events at marriages and Christmas feasts – there is nothing more common than to see men and women, like the Samoides, drinking together, till at last they roll down in a state of unconscious helplessness (Barnard 1871, 299).

M. Paterson compounded the insult in *Mountaineering Below the Snowline* (1886) by likening the Setesdalen peasant and his drinking to the stereotype of the Irish drunk:

> Looking on the forms and faces of these men, I first received the impression, striking in its distinctness, and afterwards confirmed by wider experience, of the strong resemblance of the Sætersdal men to the Irish farmer of better class. The full, bulky, powerful, and not ungraceful figure; the regular and intelligent features, peculiar grey eyes, and unwhiskered cheeks were identical; and even in their moral characteristics, the likeness holds good. Somewhat idle and dirty in his habits, impulsive, prone to strong drink, and quarrelsome in his potations; and finally, wedded to old and bad customs. In his drunken lusts, his hand goes straight to the knife, and a high feast rarely passed without bloodshed (203–4).

British accounts of drinking in Norway, however, were about to undergo a reversal in emphasis. Increasing moves towards prohibition over the course of the nineteenth century in Norway seem to have enjoyed fuller popular approval than they did in Britain where the Temperance Acts of 1853 (in Scotland), 1869 and 1904, which sought to control licensing laws, were bitterly opposed by many. In 1836, the Norwegian theological student and temperance pioneer K. N. G. Andresen set up an 'Association Against Brandy-drinking.' It was the first of many temperance societies in Norway. By 1844, these societies had gained government patronage and in 1845 and 1848 laws were introduced which virtually abolished rural home distilling. As a result the amount of brandy consumed per head of the population between 1833 and 1851 was reduced by about 60 per cent (Pratt 1907, 10). Finally, as a result of the so-called *Samlag* Laws of

1871 and, most importantly, 1894, spirits could only be sold through government shops or *Samlag*. These shops, however, were confined to the towns, and so in effect the countryside was left without any legal outlets of spirits.

It is rather amusing to note that the restrictions on alcohol consumption from the 1870s onwards became as worthy of comment among the travellers as its previous abundance had been. As an anonymous writer (describing himself as a Reverend) remarked in *Blackwood's Edinburgh Magazine* (vol. 112, no. 681, July 1872), 'police impediments in the way of obtaining intoxicants are very conspicuous to every one who travels in Norway' (317). W. Mattieu Williams in *Through Norway with Ladies* (1877), on his second trip to Norway (and this time accompanied by six women), found a welcome disparity between the warnings issued in a popular guide for travellers and the reality of the new temperate Norwegian society: 'In Murray's "Handbook" it is stated that "the vice of drunkenness prevails to a fearful extent among the lower classes of this place." During our stay of five days, we saw no evidence of this' (91).

On a practical level, the new rules meant that travellers arriving in Norway found it impossible to get an alcoholic drink in a hotel between 1 pm on Saturday and 8 am on Monday. Instead they were obliged to buy alcohol in advance from the local Samlag, a practice that inevitably meant that they had to buy a whole litre rather than any lesser amount. As Edwin A. Pratt points out:

> [T]his is done in the alleged interests of temperance; but the result is that the average tourist gets, and probably consumes, more than he wants, and he may, on his departure, leave the still partly-filled bottle behind in his room – in which case the hotel servants (to the risk of their own sobriety) help themselves to the remainder (Pratt 1907, 52).

Little wonder then that John Murray's Handbook for *Travellers in Norway* (1878) suggested that the prospective British traveller should carry a little brandy both as a provision for himself and as a present for his Norwegian hosts.

An interest in the Norwegian consumption of alcohol seems to have been retained throughout the nineteenth century and reflects Britain's own pre-occupation with the issue. Whether the Norwegians are criticised for over-indulgence or praised for abstinence, the message to the British audience back home is always a clear directive towards moderation. Drinking was in some senses the most thoroughly discussed of all Norway's social problems, perhaps because it was the issue that imposed most directly on the traveller's experience of Norwegian hospitality. But British commentary also turned its attention to the related issues of poverty and crime within the country.

Urban poverty of the Dickensian type, together with urban crime, seemed virtually non-existent in the slowly industrialising Norwegian landscape, and many writers ignore the issue altogether. In other accounts, the problems are mentioned but are softened through a more Romantic discourse; Norwegian criminals, like drunks, beggars, and other social oddities are portrayed poetically as lonely outcasts of society. Here is John Barrow in *Excursions to Europe* (1834) describing the 'imbecile' he encountered on the way from Trondheim to Christiania:

> In the course of the journey through the deep ravine, we met with a poor idiot by the road-side; but whether he had the goitre or not, I cannot say. His eyes were fixed steadily on the ground, but his countenance indicated a cheerful disposition: he seemed to be perfectly unaware of the carrioles passing him; the miserable hut, by the road side, in which the poor fellow lived, was close at hand; but no one appeared to take charge of him. This was the only imbecile we met with in Norway (353).

The tendency to idealise the criminal is also apparent in Robert Meason Laing's poem 'Meditations on the Ramparts of Agershuus Fortress, Christiania, November 1838', in *Hours in Norway: Poems* (1839). Here he imagines the thoughts and words of a 'slave' (criminal) who muses movingly on his own degraded position:

> (...) the man, degraded to a slave,
> Feeling unworthy of the name of man,
> Herdeth with miscreants, deeming them his peers.
> And in his mind if noble thoughts arise –
> Such thoughts as he was wont, in happier hours,
> To cherish, and delight in musing o'er –
> If one pure thought ariseth in his mind,
> He shrinketh from it, as the leper shrinks
> Before the healthy, and as he, doth cry:
> Avoid! avoid me! for I am unclean (56).

For those more interested in political economy than poetry, the comparative state of poverty in the different countries of Northern Europe became a point of debate in the periodical press in the last decades of the eighteenth and early decades of the nineteenth century. An early traveller to Norway, the economist and demographer

Thomas Malthus (1766–1834), kept a detailed travel diary of his observations of – among other things – the low population and apparent lack of poverty in the country.[28] The notes on Norway formed the basis for the chapter 'Of the Checks to Population in Norway', which appeared in the sixth and subsequent editions of his *Essay on the Principle of Population* (first published 1826). Here he claims:

> Even in Norway, notwithstanding the disadvantage of a severe and uncertain climate, from the little that I saw in a few weeks [*sic*] residence in the country, and the information that I could collect from others, I am inclined to think that the poor were, on the average, better off than in England. Their houses and clothing were superior and, though they had no white bread, they had much more meat, fish, and milk than our labourers; and I particularly remarked that the farmers' boys were much stouter and healthier looking lads than those of the same description in England (Malthus 1992, 270–71).

This is no idle commentary on the Norwegian peasant, but cleverly deployed evidence for Malthus's central thesis that smaller populations inevitably led to greater happiness, especially among the lower classes. In Norway he saw that, despite a lack of *positive* checks on population growth (such as war and epidemic), other *preventive* checks such as the social and economic obstacles to early marriage had fortuitously curbed population growth (McCleary 1953, 56–57).

Given the importance of the *Essay on the Principle of Population* to later thinkers such as Charles Darwin and John Stuart Mill, and indeed Eilert Sundt himself, it is possible to argue that Norway – through the accident of Malthus's early journey – became a strategic counter in the highest eschelons of nineteenth-century discourse. Despite their importance in this respect, however, Malthus's comments on Norway, conditioned by only one month's stay in the country, are in need of some qualification.

There is no doubt that the Norwegians went through periods of widespread suffering during the Napoleonic Wars. Edward Daniel Clarke, who accompanied Malthus on his journey in 1799, comments on the town of Kongsberg in terms which are reminiscent of the urban suffering of mid nineteenth-century London or Manchester:

---

[28] See Malthus 1966. Malthus travelled with the Rev. William Otter, Edward Daniel Clarke (*vid.*), and Clarke's young pupil, John Martens Cripps.

> The appearances of squalid poverty which disgrace the streets of
> Kongsberg were before alluded to: this place, like Christiania, swarms
> with beggars; who beset the door of the inn at which travellers arrive,
> forming together a mob of most disgusting objects (Clarke 1824, 10:
> 444–45).

It is important to remember, however, that Malthus and Clarke made
their observations well before the changes that followed after 1815,
and that, consequently, they do not give a representative picture of the
conditions thirty of forty years later. Although it is true that the
sudden rapid growth of the Norwegian population in the first half of
the nineteenth century, combined with the absence of any large-scale
industrial development, meant an increased pressure on the soil as a
means of livelihood, the fact remains that the widespread suffering of
the War years never returned. According to modern historians, the
number of holdings 'grew at about the same rate as the population',
and together with a steady growth in productivity, 'the agricultural
population as well as the nation as a whole was more self-sufficient
and better supplied with agricultural products by the middle of the
nineteenth century than it had ever been before' (Danielsen et al.
1995, 233).

Against this background, it may seem that some of the British
commentators, in comparing Britain and Norway, were basing their
arguments on information which was already dated. Responding to
comments made by the poet, dramatist and essayist Robert Southey
(1774–1843) about the terrible poverty in parts of Britain in 1830, the
historian Thomas Babington Macaulay (1800–1859) suggested in the
Edinburgh Review in January that year that the situation in
Scandinavia was worse: 'In Norway and Sweden, the peasantry are
constantly compelled to mix bark with their bread, and even this
expedient has not always preserved whole families and
neighbourhoods from perishing altogether of famine' (Levine 1967,
150-51).[29]

Still, to balance the picture, it should not be ignored that there are
observations from as late as the 1850s to the effect that Norway is not
exactly a land of milk and honey. John George Hollway in *A Month
in Norway* (1853) found that his first impressions of the glories of
nature in Norway were spoilt on his arrival in Gudbrandsdalen
(which he calls 'Guldebrandsdal'):

---

[29] The original article was first published in the *Edinburgh Review* 50 (January,
1830), 528–65.

The pleasure of looking on this fertile scene was entirely taken away
from me. I had fancied from our limited experience that the Norwegian
peasantry were such independent, noble, manly fellows, that the
discovery of this nest of beggars was a grievous disappointment - almost
the only one that Norway gave me (125).

The issue of poverty and the degree to which it should be addressed
by the state were important preoccupations of the British political
establishment by the 1830s. The writings of the moral and political
philosopher Jeremy Bentham (1748–1832), which included theories
about the nature and functions of government, motivated the Whig
administrations of the 1830s and 1840s to introduce a number of
measures based on the 'principle of utility'. Most notable of these
was the Poor Law Amendment Act of 1834, which abolished 'outdoor
relief' for the poor and provided instead workhouse accommodation
for those incapable of earning a living or unwilling to work. Seen by
some as indications of humanitarianism and progress and by others
merely as expedient measures designed to alleviate economic
problems and facilitate public order, the Poor Law Amendment Act
and the Poor Law Act of 1847, which followed it, were hotly debated
aspects of public policy. The degree to which these policies
constituted state intervention or – paradoxically – facilitated the
government's laissez-faire approach to social issues was equally a
subject of debate, and it is likely that such groundbreaking initiatives
were very much to the fore in the minds of those travellers who
strolled around Norwegian towns and cities in the middle years of the
century. In Norway, it seemed the state was taking a more
straightforwardly interventionist role in the management of poverty.
In fact, a system of poor relief was established which was fully
integrated into the system of local government by 1845. By the last
three decades of the century, it is possible that this system was much
more successful than its British counterpart and had really improved
the lot of the Norwegian beggar. Certainly, there seem to be fewer
references to poverty in later British accounts. W. Mattieu Williams
in *Through Norway with Ladies* (1877) eulogised on the situation of
the people in Tromsø. His repeated use of the word 'respectable' in
the extract below shows that he is participating in the class discourses
of late nineteenth-century Britain where the 'respectable' and
'unrespectable' poor were increasingly differentiated from one
another:

Using the term 'lower classes' in what I regard as its proper sense, I may say that there were no specimens of such classes visible in Tromsø – no roughs, no beggars, no slouching thriftless outcasts, and, above all, no powdered flunkies displaying, by their gaudy liveries, the ostentatious degradation of their vulgar-minded employers. A general tone of quiet respectability pervades the whole community. There are respectable boatmen, respectable fishermen, respectable artisans and labourers, respectable domestic servants, respectable shopkeepers, with respectable assistants, respectable merchants, bankers, &c., but scarcely any useless idlers are visible, either of the pampered or pauper class (91–92).

Likewise, Edith Rhodes commented of Bergen that 'the streets are cram full of people, all holiday-making. They look so nice and strong and well, all of them: I haven't seen one beggar since I came here' (Rhodes 1886, 40).

Alongside the alleviation of poverty were other reforms in the law.[30] In a number of respects, among them the treatment of criminals, the Norwegians adopted a Benthamite approach quickly recognised by the British travellers. The debate over prison reform raged on for years in Britain and explains the peculiar paradox in the travellers' accounts of a noticeable interest in prisons and prisoners in Norway despite the ostensible lack of crime in the country. Prison reform was an important issue in British politics from the late eighteenth century onwards. The Quaker philanthropists John Howard (1726–1790) and Elizabeth Fry (1780–1845), among others, had campaigned for more humanitarian conditions in those British prisons that were notorious for their lack of sanitation and order. As a result some improvements were made in the Gaol Act of 1823 by Sir Robert Peel, as Home Secretary in Lord Liverpool's administration. On the whole, however, the emphasis in British prisons was still on punitive measures designed to break the spirit of the convicts, rather than on rehabilitation.[31]

Some travellers of a conservative persuasion, such as the Rev. Robert Everest, believed that the Norwegian treatment of prisoners

[30] Derry comments that 'pioneering work of a broadly humanitarian character began gradually to establish [Norway's] claim to be a civilizing influence in the world' (Derry 1973, 162).

[31] The Gaol Act was one of several penal reforms introduced by Peel between 1823 and 1830. Though these reforms definitely improved law and order in the major British cities, some of them, such as the introduction of a thousand paid constables on to the streets of London, were considered repressive and reactionary in some quarters.

The lenient conditions of the Christiania Penetentiary (erected in 1857) helped to establish the reputation of Norway as a humanitarian society. Illustration from Tønsberg (1875).

(in this case in the prison in Bergen) was far too lenient:

> The number of criminals in slavery is sixty. The large room in which they were all working was light, clean, and well-aired, almost too much so to be as a punishment; and the treatment of the Tugt Huus is so mild, that, among the thirty-five there, are two or three old men who have petitioned the police to be allowed to remain in it. This is carrying humanity somewhat too far. Let us spare no pains to lead mankind by the worthiest of the two motives that influence them – the hope of reward. But whatever punishment must be had recourse to, should be known as such, and dreaded. However, it speaks in no small degree in favour of a population, over whom such slight coercion is necessary (Everest 1829, 219–20).

The Norwegian practice of parading convicted prisoners through the streets of the main cities in order that they might either undertake prison work or sell objects that they had made, drew some startled comment, chiefly because it was believed by Britons that prisoners should not be allowed to mix with non-offenders. Samuel Laing in his *Journal* (1837) remarked of the system in Christiania:

> One thing here is very revolting to good taste and good feeling. The convicts or galley slaves are employed, sometimes along with other labourers, in all parts of the town, and two or three times a day you meet a gang of them going to, or returning from, their work. (...) They are even speaking to the children and women in the streets. It is not wise and certainly not pleasant, to have these malefactors constantly before the public. They lose all sense of their disgrace, and perhaps the citizens do the same (14–15).

The treatment of prisoners remained a point of debate even for those British travellers who, unlike the resident Laing, were just passing through. For some, the Norwegian New Criminal Code of 1842 was considered too liberal as were the single cells provided in the new prison in Christiania in 1851 and, no doubt, the abolition of capital punishment in 1876. On the other hand, there were those travellers of a more progressive outlook who used the same examples as inspiration for possible reform of penal issues in Britain. By 1875, the Norwegian penal system had become a recognised feature of British interest to the extent that the travel book published in English by the Norwegian editor and publisher Chr. Tønsberg recommends that British tourists inspect the Penetentiary in Christiania as part of their visit. Among its other attractions, the penitentiary boasted baths, inspection rooms, cells for sick prisoners and depositories for working materials and finished products. It was also a masterpiece of modern construction, each of the four wings consisting of three tiers of cells which could be viewed from a central gallery girded by iron galleries. As Tønsberg indicates, the British might learn from an institution which successfully maintained the difficult balance between rehabilitation and surveillance.[32]

For some travellers, visits to such institutions as the Penetentiary give rise to musings on the key political issue of the day, that is the degree to which societies ought to depend on the state for certain key facilities. On the whole, however, the political issue is sublimated beneath the overarching Romantic myth that Norway has escaped most of the societal problems caused by industrialisation. As this section has shown, the discourse on society tends to blur over the unattractive features of Norwegian life: drunkenness is modified into abstinence; poverty conveniently disappears from the streets; criminality loses its stigma and social outcasts are romanticised rather than vilified. As always, Norwegian society is, in the end, configured as a haven of moral optimism untouched by the true concerns of the nineteenth century.

Religion

One of Norway's deepest sources of appeal, as far as British travellers were concerned, was its almost universal endorsement of Protestantism. The overall similarity of religious outlook between the two countries inevitably fostered a real sense of kinship between the visitor and the visited. To understand what Norway's Protestantism meant to its British visitors, it is necessary to consider the prevalence of anti-Catholic feeling in Britain in the late eighteenth and early nineteenth centuries. Even after Catholic Emancipation in 1829, and after the dramatic increase in the number of Catholics in Britain with the Irish immigrations of the 1840s, Catholicism continued to be very much a minority religion, regarded with suspicion by the Protestant community.

British anxiety about Catholicism had a long history in eighteenth-century travel accounts. Naturally, most of the countries of Southern Europe were Catholic. Many of these countries had historically been enemies of Britain, with the issue of religion playing a significant role

---

[32] For more detail of Norway's Criminal Code and the issue of Poor Relief, see Derry 1973, 38–40.

in the debacle. The response of British travellers to Catholic countries was often two-fold. Whilst they might be interested in the extravagant indications of the Catholic Church abroad – art, architecture and the relics of Popery – they also experienced and documented a certain relief and superiority in their own less ostentatious and, as they saw it, more morally upright, Protestant heritage. As Jeremy Black in *The British and the Grand Tour* (1985) puts it, 'Catholicism was equated with autocracy; it drew on credulity and superstition and led to misery, poverty, clerical rule and oppression' (189). By contrast, Protestantism, it would seem, was equated with freedom, democracy, rationality and ultimately prosperity.

In such a religious climate, Protestant Norway had distinct advantages as a venue for the British tourist. The vast majority of the Norwegian population including the Sami endorsed the state religion, Lutheranism, and, unlike in Britain, where the Anglican state religion was losing some ground to nonconformity in the nineteenth century, there continued in Norway to be close and mutually reciprocal support between Church and State. As Charles W. Wood in *Round About Norway* (1880) commented:

> The religion of Norway is Lutheran, and, perhaps, no country has less sympathy with Romanism, and in no country is Romanism making less progress. Its forms and ceremonials, appealing to the senses rather than to the spiritual part of man's nature, have few attractions for this honest, simple-minded people (16–17).

In this respect, Norway held an appeal for the majority of British visitors who, whether Anglican or nonconformist, tended to be united in their suspicion of and contempt for the Roman church.

Anglicans, who had witnessed the declining influence of the state church in Britain, admired Norway for still having one that flourished virtually unopposed. In the period from 1740 to 1830, Anglicanism had rapidly lost much of its national constituency. Though it started to revive from 1830 onwards, it remained seriously challenged by the growth of nonconformity. Anglicanism competed in particular with Methodism, a reform movement which had begun within its own walls, and with the resurgence of Catholicism itself. In addition, throughout the Victorian age, a plethora of nonconformist congregations were spawned in large urban centres such as Manchester, Birmingham and London. Anglicanism vied with the New Dissent, including Congregationalism and Particular Baptism, as well as the reformed groups of Old Dissent, including Baptists,

Unitarians, Quakers and Presbyterians (Gilbert 1988, vii–viii). It is hardly surprising then that to the British in the mid nineteenth century, Norway appeared by contrast a simple, homogenous country in terms of religious observance. William Wordsworth gestured to this uniformity in his poem 'By the Seaside' (1833). In a moment of thanksgiving for the beauties of nature, he imagines:

> A sea-born service through the mountains felt
> Till into one loved vision all things melt:
> Or like those hymns that soothe with graver sound
> The gulfy coast of Norway iron-bound;
> And, from the wide and open Baltic, rise
> With punctual care, Lutherian [*sic*] harmonies
> (Wordsworth 1994, 454, ll. 27–32).

These 'Lutherian harmonies' are very much uppermost in the mind of Thomas Forester, a staunch Anglican, who observed with relief in *Norway in 1848 and 1849* (1850) that:

> Sectarianism has no footing in Norway. If religious diversions are a great evil, contrary to the spirit and the literal injunctions of the Gospel, a snare to the doubting, a triumph to the unbeliever, and injurious to the frame of society, as I believe they are, (...) from such evil Norway is happily exempt (306).

But Forester's euphoria at Norway's religious uniformity was actually founded on a myth. It was convenient for British travellers, particularly those of the Anglican persuasion, to believe that the Norwegian church had experienced no dissension. In the early years of the nineteenth century, however, a reforming movement led by Hans Nielsen Hauge (1771–1824) had inveighed against the rationalism of the state church (Derry 1968, 122–24). By the 1830s, Hauge's followers numbered between 20,000 and 30,000. As Samuel Laing has remarked, however, the Haugeans '"were not dissenters or sectarians in the English sense. They were more like the evangelical part of the community of the Church of England (...) keen churchgoers and communicants"' (Laing 1837, 124 cited in Drake 1969, 10). Whether or not they were aware of the Haugean movement, Anglican commentators on the whole did not mention it, a fact that allowed them to imagine a utopian uniformity in the Norwegian church which could be strategically deployed in travel accounts as a means of criticising the plethora of religious viewpoints in Britain.[33]

There were those British travellers, however, who found the lack of religious diversity in Norway a cause for concern rather than for reassurance. Even Forester understood the 'advantages of religious controversy in quickening the intellect, stimulating inquiry, and awakening men from the passive state of mind produced by uninquiring conformity' (Forester 1850, 306). As has been discussed earlier, many visitors to Norway came from nonconformist backgrounds. Some were Presbyterians associated with the Scottish universities, others, such as William and Mary Howitt, were Quakers or Unitarians from England's provincial towns. Some of these people saw religious uniformity in Norway as a nullifying force which had given rise to religious apathy. On his visit to Norway made between May and August of 1799, the economist Thomas Malthus wrote in his diary of Trondheim: 'There are no sects in religion at Drontheim. Much *indifference* on religious subjects seems to prevail, & we were assured that the churches are by no means well attended' (Malthus 1966, 167; italics added). William Hurton in *A Voyage from Leith to Lapland* (1851) further described the lack of religious diversity as stultifying. By contrast with the intellectually vibrant atmosphere of religious controversy in Britain, Norway seemed dangerously passive:

> There is no dissent whatever in the Lutheran Church of Norway, nor in Scandinavia generally. *None would be tolerated*, and the power of the clergy is virtually as great as in any Catholic country. The conclusions forced upon me by a careful observation of this state of things is, that the very absence of dissent, although it precludes the painful polemical contests which schism often introduces, nevertheless is itself a great evil. The clergy have nothing to fear from the attacks of dissenting bodies, and they consequently have nothing to arouse them to vital exertion in support of their creed, or in correction of its errors and abuses; and the people, almost without exception, are lukewarm and apathetic on religious grounds (60–61).

John Milford in *Norway and her Laplanders in 1841* (1842) made a less common, but equally valid complaint:

[33] To some extent, travellers might be excused their simple view of Norwegian faith. In fact, due to an unexplained oversight in 1814, the Norwegian Constitution had not included a declaration of freedom for Christian religious bodies other than the State Church, the Jesuits and other Catholic orders. This anomaly was not fully rectified until 1845 and must account for the absence of any obvious signs of religious diversity in the early part of the century (Derry 1973, 38–39).

"THE CHURCH-GOING BELL."
SUNDAY MORNING, COAST OF NORWAY.
(By Our Yachting Artist.)

The satirical periodical *Punch* was no doubt attempting to prick some British consciences with this graphic description of Norwegian religious devotion: '"The Church-Going Bell". Sunday morning, coast of Norway'. From 2 August 1890.

Jews are not allowed to reside in any part of Norway; and I could not but feel that this want of religious toleration is not only illiberal, but totally inconsistent with that boasted liberality and independence in which the Norwegians considered themselves superior to all the rest of the world, but how often does practice belie the most specious theories (225).

As has been seen, some British travellers were interested in the different shades of religious belief – or lack of them – in Britain and Norway; for many others it was the general religiosity of the Norwegians that intrigued them more. Church attendance in Norway was high and one historian has noted how 'the church in Norway does not appear to have lost its hold on the people anything like to the same extent as it did in England during the eighteenth and nineteenth centuries' (Drake 1969, 12–13). This high rate of attendance seemed particularly impressive given the fjords, mountains and other geographical obstacles to church attendance that presented themselves to the Norwegian congregation. There was, of course, a notable comparison here with the English urban congregations who could find a church or chapel on every street corner. In 1873, the parson George Henry Hely-Hutchinson, who had spent long periods on the island of Lewes in the Hebrides and who wrote under the pseudonym 'Sixty-One', described in *A Trip to Norway* a typical Sunday in Bergen:

There were a good many of the peasantry in the town that day; for they come, like the Scotch, from a great distance to attend church. Not like our good English folk, who must have their churches brought to them, and thus not have far to go to worship God (17).

The implication here, of course, is that the proliferation of church building in England has actually induced a spiritual laziness.[34]

In Norway the situation was rather different. Whilst the population was increasing over the course of the nineteenth century, the number of parsons was not keeping pace. According to Michael Drake, in 1800 there was only one parson per 1,884 members of the population, and by 1855 only one parson per 3,164. In such a situation, the problems of attending a church were very real, particularly in the

[34] There was a general anxiety among the middle class in Britain from the 1830s onwards that a large part of the working class was not attending church regularly. In fact, as a national census of religious attendance in 1851 and further local censuses in 1881 showed, the pattern of church attendance differed widely according to region and denomination (McLeod 1989, 12–13).

rural regions (Drake 1969, 9). Of a visit in 1851, the Quaker Sarah Backhouse commented that:

> The people here (...) appeared to suffer from the want of a rallying point for social worship. Places for public worship are far between in this land; and a large part of the rural population rarely attend; a Minister being, in their view, essential for a religious congregation (181–182).

Backhouse's view may be coloured by her belief as a member of the Society of Friends that ministers were not necessary for the administration of religious services. Whatever the case, her belief that 'a large part of the rural population rarely attend' is unsupported in other accounts. For most travellers, especially those of an evangelical persuasion, the religious devotion of the Norwegians was highly admired. The Anglican Minister, the Rev. M. R. Barnard, marvelled in 1871 at the adventurous manner by which the Norwegians in (unspecified) mountainous districts got to church. 'It seems strange to speak of a congregation skating [i.e. skiing] in this manner to church; but such is often, nay, generally the case in winter-time when the snow lies at an incredible depth; and, stranger still, what is also of frequent occurrence, to think of the pastor, too, skating to the house of God' (135). John Bradshaw graphically illustrated the commitment of the Norwegian population to church attendance in Norway: *Its Fjords, Fjelds and Fields* (1896) by noting that:

> Away from important centres [the churches] are very far apart, nevertheless, natives travel long distances up the fjords, in their small boats to attend divine service. It is quite an interesting sight, on Sundays, to see the large number of boats, filled with people, chiefly women, paddling along the fjords, making their way to the nearest church. In these out-of-the-way places, services are not held every Sunday, but only at intervals to suit the clergymen who perform regular rounds, visiting each district in turn, and repeating the same in due course at stipulated periods (44).

In 1829, the Rev Robert Everest, in *A Journey through Lapland, Norway and Sweden*, remarked of the Telemark peasants that 'destitute as they were of every worldly comfort, we found two or three religious books in every house. The hope of the weary and heavy laden in every clime is not denied to these poor sojourners in the valley of tears' (36). There were of course those who remained sceptical about levels of Norwegian devotion despite the outward signs to the contrary. Charles Boileau Elliott, a contemporary of

Stave churches, such as this one in Heddal, provided a rare indication of Norway's medieval past. The illustration is taken from Alfred Smith's collection of plates from 1847, *Sketches in Norway and Sweden*, and is entitled 'Wooden Church in Hedersdal and a Wedding Dance'. According to the caption, the church 'is a pleasing evidence of the desire of this simple-minded people to devote their utmost skill to the house of God. The scene on [*sic*] the foreground is intended to represent a bridal party enjoying their nuptial festivities, which are very remarkable and for which preparation is made long before; feasting generally continues the whole week, and no expense which they can possibly afford is spared' (no pag.).

Everest's who visited the same region, remarked in *Letters from the North of Europe* (1832) that although every house had a Bible and psalter, 'the majority of the lower orders are very idle. They are addicted to cheating and falsehood; and, though more intelligent, are less interesting, because less moral, than their neighbours the Swedes' (108–9).

Whatever the degree of laxity in religious observance, one point seems clear: few Norwegians deviated from orthodox Lutheranism. The kinds of crises of faith arising from new scientific discoveries such as those experienced by British intellectuals including the poet Tennyson in the middle of the nineteenth century, were in Norway virtually unknown. As the church historian Einar Molland, quoting Thorvald Klaveness, a young liberal clergyman, has commented: 'Fifteen years after the publication of the *Origin of Species*, the author of an annual survey could claim that "the streams of unbelief which have passed over other countries have really not yet reached our fjords and valleys"' (Derry 1973, 40).

Those who commended Norwegian religiosity attributed that fact not simply to the straightforward nature of Norwegian Lutheranism, but to the character of the Norwegian people themselves. As ever, travellers considered this character to be dependent on environmental factors and the particular proximity of the Norwegian to nature and the elements. Robert Taylor Pritchett in *Gamle Norge: Rambles and Scrambles in Norway* (1879) described how the link between the ministers and the people was shown

> in the character of the sermons, the whole tone of which seems to aim at binding the parish together in Christian love and sympathy, bearing each other's burdens, caring for one another, and curbing self (...). The whole climate rather tends to develop this frame of mind: there is a certain sedate expression throughout the provinces; the long darkness of winter, extending its influence even into the continuous light of the northern summer, brings everyone into close and constant proximity (29).

This idea that the natural environment in some sense contributed to the strength of religion in Norway was frequently reiterated. After watching some small boys in a boat off the coast of Bergen, 'Sixty One' commented in *A Trip to Norway in 1873*:

> How these grand scenes of nature nerve the heart with confidence in Providence! And everywhere in this fine country, I have been struck by the great reliance upon the Power above, which is the essence of all true

religion. They have religion without fanaticism (21).

A straightforward account of the simplicity of the Norwegian church
service was made by William Ewart Gladstone during his trip down
the Hardangerfjorden in 1885. Having received Holy Communion
from the Bishop of Durham aboard his yacht at 8.30 on the morning
of Sunday 16 August, Gladstone was in a good position to note the
differences of the Norwegian situation. He records in his diary:
'11–1. Attended the Norwegian Service which gave much to observe.
Fine rain, the women came in black, with the white caps. Sitting
almost through the whole service. Luther's hymn tune. Vestment used
on celebrations: twice a year. Close attention especially from the
women. Service here once in three weeks.' (Matthew 1990, 11: 384).
The medieval appearance of Norwegian church architecture also
drew some fascination. John Bradshaw, among others, commented
with wonder in *Norway: Its Fjords, Fjelds and Fields* (1896) on the
eccentricity of the ancient Norwegian stave churches at Borgund and
Fantoft. He describes these churches, built as early as the twelfth
century, as 'singularly quaint in appearance, curious in design and
eminently unique in character,' and he comments that 'the general
appearance very much resembles a Norwegian pine tree, which, after
all, may have been the model as well as the material of their
construction' (45–46). Still, he finds them impractical in the extreme;
too small and too dark. In their favour, Bradshaw notes that these
churches were ill-suited to the form and ceremony of Popery and very
suitable for the simpler worship of Lutheranism.

For the British traveller, it was astounding to find thriving
religious communities in Norway despite the evident geographical
obstacles and the patent lack of resources. In such a scenario,
travellers recognised the superlative importance of the parish priests
– few though they evidently were. Many were the British travellers
who commented on the Norwegian parsonages and their inhabitants.
The visit of Edward Wilson Landor to the parsonage of the semi-
fictional pastor Ernest Vormensen somewhere in Østfold has been
discussed in depth in the Introduction. Visits to the homes of clerics
such as Landor's, of course, were not only the product of religious
curiosity. It can be assumed that many of the early British travellers
took refuge in these parsonages, seeing them as islands of culture and
civilisation in which they might be assured intelligent conversation
by men of similar background and education as themselves. Thomas
Forester commented on these Norwegian pastors and their homes:

A NORWEGIAN PASTOR.

The Lutheran pastor was fondly recognised as a fellow Protestant despite his sombre attire. Illustration from Lovett (1885).

In their residences, alone in the heart of wild and unfrequented districts, you meet with all the comforts and many of the elegancies of civilized life, agreeable and accomplished women, and in the praesten himself a highly educated and well-informed gentleman. Laborious in their pastoral duties, the calls of which, from the extent of the parishes, are extremely severe, they are looked up to as the centres of their several circles, familiar to all, and not disdaining friendly intercourse with the better classes of their parishioners. They thus enjoy a consideration in society, to which they are personally well-entitled (Forester 1850, 168).

Forester's view was echoed by W. Mattieu Williams, who tried to encapsulate the many roles of the pastor in a few words:

A Norwegian pastor is not merely a preacher; he is a clergyman, physician, magistrate, arbitrator, and general friend and father, to whom all his scattered friends and parishioners appeal. In a country where there are none but peasant farmers – no aristocracy, no gentry, no towns or villages, no shopkeepers, no professional class – a highly educated man must be strangely isolated, and, unless endowed with the true spirit of Christian benevolence, must be one of the most miserable of men; but if suited to his work, he may be one of the happiest, for his opportunities of doing unmistakable good, and of witnessing the full fruits of his good deeds, are almost unlimited. Most of these Norwegian pastors are, I believe, excellent men, and render great services to the people around (Williams 1876, 190–91).

An account from Miss Vickers in *Old Norway and its Fjords* (1893) of a service held at Trondheim cathedral gives an unusually clear physical picture of this Norwegian pastor figure:

'Martin Luther in the flesh,' I thought, getting a first glimpse of the preacher. Generally the Norwegians are fair, but he was very dark, with a pointed beard and a pleasant intelligent face. He wore a black cassock, with broad turned back collar, finished by a white linen frill or ruff around the neck (54).

It would be easy to leave an analysis of religion in Norway with an image of this memorable figure, a symbol of the simple, rational, Protestant religion which, even allowing for the travellers' exaggerations, undoubtedly characterised the country. But an examination of the spiritual aspects of Norway must not ignore what is a common subcurrent of commentary in the travel accounts. Many writers noted that a measure of superstition was prevalent amongst the peasantry alongside a commitment to the Norwegian church. This superstition conveniently supported the view of those commentators who saw Norway as only part- or semi-civilised. In *A Personal Narrative of a Journey Through Norway, Parts of Sweden and the Islands and States of Denmark* (1829), Derwent Conway pointed out why the people of Norway were so susceptible to superstition; again geographical and environmental factors were held responsible:

> The geographical position of Norway, and especially the character of its scenery, have contributed to render it, more than any other country, the fit habitation of local superstitions. The country is divided between mountains, forests, lakes and rivers; and to these the natives look for their means of subsistence. The snow-storm may bury their flocks and their habitations; the flood may sweep them away; a tempest may leave the inhabitants of the coast and the shores of the fiords without their daily bread; a too early frost destroys in one night the hopes of the husbandman, and, if protracted beyond the usual time of winter, it sends troops of famished wolves to prey upon their cattle. No wonder, then, that the traditions and superstitions of a mountain region have outlived the eras of knowledge, and still continue to have a firm hold upon the faith of the people. No wonder that their mountains, their forests and their rivers, are peopled with a race of controlling beings whose favour must be propitiated, and whose anger must be pacified or averted (220–21).

Whilst it was common knowledge that Norway had become Christianised in the eleventh century and had later undergone a Protestant Reformation, some travellers fancied that those Norwegians in the less accessible districts had never fully given up their pre-Christian, pagan beliefs. In his *Wayside Notes in Scandinavia* (1874), Mark Antony Lower remarked:

> I have elsewhere said that parts of Norway were but half-Protestantized at the Reformation; and I might have said not even Christianized; for, to this day, if a peasant finds one of these little bronze statuettes, he will not willingly part with it, because forsooth he thinks that it possesses some magical healing powers, and literally makes it *a household god*! In fact the Norsemen of the higher latitudes are nearly as idolatrous as the Ashantees or the inhabitants of Central Africa. Superstition, rather than Religion, has its hold on the uncultivated mind of these ignorant people (267–68).

Doubts about the true Christianity of the Norwegians were enhanced by travellers' accounts of the Sami. As has been mentioned earlier, many Sami became Christians after Danish-Norwegian missionary efforts starting in the eighteenth century (Beach 1981, 4). Nevertheless, the old religion of the Sami, an animistic faith based on natural powers and reliant on sacrifices made at the *seidi* (sacred stones or wooden images), persisted in some parts of Samiland (Pareli 2000, 45–46).

Both the devoutly rational and the superstitious elements of Norwegian spirituality had their attractions for British travellers. On the one hand, Norway was seen to embrace a simple and purified religion which threw into relief the complex theological controversies in Britain. On the other hand, in its association with paganism, Norway reminded the British of the powers of the irrational and of the imagination, qualities which in the pursuit of progress, she had pushed aside.

English and the Influence of Britain

Even in early travellers' accounts, there is a good deal of evidence that a knowledge of the English language was common in Norway throughout the nineteenth century. The evident similarities between Norwegian and English based on philological evidence, coupled with the facility of the Norwegians for speaking English were crucial factors in the whole business of establishing links, both real and imagined, between the two countries. The language issue was moreover a means of establishing Britain as the superior country; few Britons were prepared to learn Norwegian before travelling abroad, but most expected and were gratified to find that their hosts spoke a little of their language. After his journey of 1799, Edward Daniel Clarke commented that, 'a great number of the inhabitants speak the English language; and, as it is so nearly allied to their own, they learn it with ease and expedition; many words, and even whole sentences, being the same in both' (Clarke 1824, 10: 218).

Visitors to the major Norwegian towns of Christiania, Bergen, Trondheim and Tromsø, found that they had surprisingly few communication problems with the inhabitants. On a visit to Trondheim in 1820, Arthur de Capell Brooke remarked that 'English (...) is in general use; and there are very few of the merchants who do not speak it thoroughly' (Brooke 1823, 162). The residents of Christiania, with its commercial links with Britain, were observed to have a particular flair for the English language. This view is borne out by W. Mattieu Williams, who remarked that in Christiania, 'on making some purchases of books, maps, and minor matters of

THE SCHOOLMASTER CATECHISING IN HITTERDAL CHURCH.

(From a painting by Tidemand.)

This engraving, based on one of Adolph Tidemand's pictures, shows the schoolmaster administering the confirmation examination in the stave church in Heddal. Illustration from Lovett (1885).

clothing, I found in every shop some one who could speak English, and that it was generally well-spoken' (Williams 1876, 10).

Interest in the prevalence of the English language was, of course, allied to an interest in the Norwegian education system. Even those who might not have supported the wider dissemination of education in Britain were impressed by what appeared to be the almost uniform literacy and numeracy of the Norwegians. Compulsory schooling had been established in the towns for children between the ages of seven and confirmation as early as 1848, and in 1860 the principle was extended to the country districts. All this came ten years before Forster's Education Act introduced a state system of popular elementary education in Britain. As John Bowden, British Consular Chaplain at Christiania, remarked in *Norway, Its People, Products and Institutions* (1867), '[t]he lower orders in Norway are much better educated than they are in England, while the national schools system of education is simple and efficient. One very seldom meets with a poor person in this country who is unable to read and write' (78). In the same vein, the archaeologist Mark Antony Lower, who had himself founded a Mechanics' Institute and later a 'high-class' school at Lewes, waxed lyrical in *Wayside Notes in Scandinavia* (1874) on the high standard of qualifications among schoolteachers compared with those in England:

> I had not much opportunity, in my short visit, to look into the state of education in Scandinavia, but I believe there are few parts of it where all classes are not better educated than in England. A 'national school' in England is generally superintended by a person – often pretentious – who can teach the 'three R's,' and little besides. He is usually, so far as my observation goes, nothing of a scholar. In Scandinavia, however, the case is different, and the national schoolmaster is a graduate of one or other of the Universities (271–72).

So successful did the Norwegian system of state education seem that by 1885, Richard Lovett was able to boast in *Norwegian Pictures* that 'English is taught in all the Norwegian schools, and almost all educated Norwegians speak it thoroughly' (98).[35]

---

[35] The wide availability of elementary education in Norway is challenged by T. K. Derry, who points out that it was compulsory to build a school only where thirty children could be mustered together. There were many areas of Norway where, because of the inaccessibility of the environment, this was not possible (Derry 1973, 163).

To find English spoken in the cities was no real surprise, but the language was not only the provenance of urban dwellers or of the affluent. Travellers' accounts are peppered with references to obscure and isolated characters who reveal an extraordinary capacity for the English tongue. The presence of spoken English in distant parts of the country lends an air of romance and of serendipity to the travel account. Travelling up the west coast from Bergen, for example, John Barrow Jr. visited Vasenden [probably Vassendenseter] where he 'was surprised to find in this sequestered spot that the postmaster could speak a little, though very little, of our language' (Barrow 1834, 301) and the Rev. R. M. Barnard remarked of a visit to Romsdal that, '[w]e took up quarters in a farmer's house. He could speak English fluently' (Barnard 1871, 179). Such discovery of the rudiments of English in out-of-the way locations reinforced the colonialist flavour of travel accounts, helping to create the impression of the Norwegians as an educable nation on the verge of civilisation.

There were other less patronising reasons for the focus on language. Some travellers used the language issue as a means of bolstering their case for the notable sympathy, warmth and hospitality of their hosts. Olivia M. Stone in *Norway in June* (1882), on the other hand, used it to support her views on the intelligence of the females of Bergen:

> We were shown over the Museum by an exceedingly pretty, intelligent girl of about fourteen. She, like nearly every boy and girl in Norway, learns English at school, and with many blushes, she tried to speak to us. Once, in desperation at not being able to say what she wanted, she ran for a dictionary, which she consulted from time to time as she made up her sentences (...). This afternoon we went for a walk with two Norwegian ladies who speak English fluently (296).

The facility for English among Norwegian women, a sign surely of a kind of cultivation which might have jarred in the British mind with their apparent predilection for menial household tasks, is noted by other travellers including Mark Antony Lower: 'I can truly say that several educated Norwegian ladies whom we met spoke our language with the greatest purity and the best accent, though some of them had never been in England' (Lower 1874, 27).

Despite these many references to the comprehension of English among the Norwegians, an assured use of the language was by no means universal in Norway. There are many humorous moments in the travel accounts in which *lack* of understanding is the key note. Thomas Forester described how he ran through all the languages available to him in his attempt to change some English money into Norwegian currency at the parsonage at Ullensvang:

> We were very graciously received by a lady, who, begging us to be seated, retired to announce our arrival. A gentleman now appeared, whose address to us in the language of the country was met by an interrogatory whether he spoke English. Then we made the same experiment in French; and failing in both, as a last resort, I tried Latin. The challenge was accepted; and our new friend having stated that the praesten was absent at Christiania, and that he was his brother and *locum tenens*, I proceeded to make known our awkward predicament in the best manner I could, and to inquire, with such phrases of apology as I could muster, if it were in his power to assist us (Forester 1850, 164–65).

Some travellers found that their Norwegian hosts knew English only as a written rather than as a spoken language, a state of affairs that engendered some peculiar dialogues. R. G. Latham travelled with the poet Wergeland from Christiania to Eidsvold in 1833 and remarked on the oddity of his discourse: 'English he knew from having read it, so that when he spoke it, he spoke it as Byron would have written it. He talked *like a book*, as the common people say, and a very queer book too' (Latham 1840, 137). A similar phenomenon is mentioned by the Rev. M. R. Barnard in his description of his dance partner, the daughter of a pastor from the Lofoten isles:

> She was an uncommonly charming girl, the daughter of a pastor in the Loffoten [*sic*] isles, and had never been in Christiania before. She rejoiced in the name of Katinka. I naturally thought she might be shy, as this was the first time she had ever been in a town. Not a bit of it! She had plenty to say for herself; could talk English very well, though she had never heard it spoken by an Englishman before; and was thoroughly well up in English literature (Barnard 1871, 3).

A few British travellers did try their hand at a little Norwegian and their comments on this matter are revealing of other attitudes. Mary Wollstonecraft, a true woman of the Enlightenment, anxious to learn from all her experiences, remarked that 'the sound of the language is soft, a great proportion of the words ending in vowels; and there is a simplicity in the turn of some of the phrases which have been translated to me, that pleased and interested me' (Wollstonecraft 1987, 115). The bombastic Thomas Allnutt Brassey's account of his attempts in *Journal of a Voyage* (1857), on the other hand, is brusquely arrogant: 'As regards the necessities of travel-talk, some twenty-four words with gestures and a little common sense, quite suffice for "getting on"' (53). The traveller-scholar Charles Elton, a fellow of Queen's College Oxford, was perhaps exceptional in recording in detail the difficulties he had in matching Norwegian spellings and pronunciation (Elton 1864, 113–14).

Few Britons were able to differentiate between the Dano-Norwegian used in the urban areas and the rural dialects deriving from Old Norse, despite the fact that the differences between these two kinds of communication were the subject of intense debate in Norway towards the end of the century.[36] The political connotations of the two kinds of Norwegian – the one reminiscent of the old Danish occupiers and the other an expression of Norway's emergent national identity and independence – were somewhat lost on the majority of British travellers. Those travellers who did attempt to converse in the language of the country rather than in English generally used the urban Dano-Norwegian favoured by the guidebooks because it was traditionally the language of business and commerce, but their attempts probably fell well short of fluency.[37] Gladstone, on his second visit to Norway in 1885, no doubt impressed the locals by spending some time every day studying the helpful vocabulary lists in Murray's popular *Handbook for Travellers in Norway* alongside his other reading matter (Matthew 1990, 10: 383). For many others, conversation with the Norwegians often consisted of good-natured stumbling, as this humorous account by M. Paterson of his discourse with a 'slatternly, wild-haired woman' boiling potatoes beside a fire in Telemark testifies:

> In a very short and terse colloquy I travelled over the whole range of Norse cuisine so far as I knew it, receiving at any pause a checkmate in

---

[36] In 1800, 90 per cent of all Norwegians spoke the rural dialects, with urban dwellers, who spoke Dano-Norwegian, making up the remaining 10 per cent. Despite their small number, however, the Dano-Norwegian speakers held the vast majority of power. Later in the century, the rural dwellers sought to re-establish a true Norwegian culture. *Landsmål* was a combination of a number of rural dialects. For more on language use in Norway, see Haugen 1966 and Vikør 1975.

[37] Chr. Tønsberg advised British travellers to ignore the proliferation of dialects and reassured them that a little knowledge of Dano-Norwegian would suffice: 'The traveller in Norway is not incommoded by this manifold, and apparently confusing, diversity of speech to the extent he would imagine. The Norse dialects are one and all subordinated to the written or book language which, being the sole vehicle of religious and secular instruction in the schools, is understood by grown-up people all the country over' (Tønsberg 1875, xlviii).

the shape of an emphatic negative driven home by a shake of the head.

'Har de friske maelk?' (Have you fresh milk?)

'Ikke' (No)

'Flode?' (Cream?)

'Ikke'

'Fiske?' (Fish?)

'Ikke'

'Pandekager?' (Pancakes?)

'Ikke'

'Moltebaer?' (Cloudberries?)

'Ikke.'

Not caring to ask for the uneatable stuff they call bread, nor the abomination known as cheese, I asked, doubtfully, and with lively dread of the lamentable 'ikke.'

'Har de egg?' (Have you eggs?)

'Ya-ha, to egg.' (Aye! Aye! Two eggs.)

'Og petate?' (And potatoes?)

'Ya-ha, meget petate' (Aye, aye, plenty of potatoes.)

So I dined philosophically upon a fine dishful of smoking potatoes, redolent with what De Quincey would have called earthiness and raciness, and one small egg, smallness being the characteristic of eggs in this northern land as of most other animal productions. The remnant of the Siljord [now Seljord] biscuits and a dole of cheese enabled me to make a tolerable finish, after swallowing potatoes, dry and unlubricated, until they began to linger uncomfortably on the way (…) (Paterson 1886, 288–89).

On the whole, the ability and willingness of the Norwegians to speak English was much commended and fed into a larger British fantasy about their reverence for British culture as a whole. Even Samuel Laing, the great proponent of Norwegian life and culture, had to admit in his *Journal* (1837) that in terms of high culture, Norway had little to offer of her own:

From the end of the twelfth century, when Snorro Sturelson flourished – and he was a native of Iceland – down to the present day, Norwegian literature is almost a blank (...). It is evident (...) that no great literary effort has ever been made in Norway. It is possible that the state of society is not favourable to great mental exertion. There is nothing to be gained by it; and intellectual labour seems to follow the same law as bodily labour – where people are very much at their ease, not urged by want nor by ambition, they will make no violent exertion. They will neither build pyramids nor write Iliads (382–83).

As far as British commentators were concerned, the void left by this dearth of home-produced literature was filled by British works. There is no doubt that this must have been something of a distortion, since Norwegians would have read Danish and German works in at least equal proportion. To read the British travel accounts, however, is to partake of the myth that British literature was freely available to and eagerly devoured by the Norwegians. If we are to believe Isabella Blundell in *Gamle Norge* (1862) there was quite a prolific trade in Norway in the works of contemporary British authors:

> English literature is much sought after by the educated classes in Norway, and the works of some of our living writers are highly popular and well appreciated. I found Tennyson's 'Princess' and the 'Memoirs of Hedly Vicars' lying side by side in the drawing-room of a house where we called; with 'My Novel' translated into Danish, on the same table; and I was constantly assured, both in Bergen, Christiania, and Copenhagen, that the demand for English works, both in the original and as translations, was steadily increasing. We found also that English travels in Norway were much read, 'Through Norway with a Knapsack,' 'The Unprotected,' and others, being well known. We heard much concerning the authoress of the latter [i.e. Emily Lowe] in Bergen (123).

The lawyer and antiquary Charles Elton a couple of years later also gave an interesting resumé of Norwegian attitudes to some of the more famous British authors, revealing what appears to be a penchant for nineteenth-century regional and social novels as well as the better known Romantic and Victorian poets.

> I walked for a little while with some students on a holiday ramble, and talked about the state of literature in Norway. They said that English books were read far more than any others, and that people who do not know English read our books in translations, which I could well believe after seeing a circulating library at Bergen full of Walter Scott and Dickens. Most people of any education here speak or read a little English; many from visiting Hull and other places in the north of England to learn book-keeping, others because they must learn either English or German at school and college. These students were reading 'Bleak House,' which they seemed highly to enjoy. 'David Copperfield' they liked, 'because it was so funny;' but 'Pickwick' was 'much too dull.' (...) Thackeray's books are not nearly so popular. I was much surprised to find that they hardly knew their names. I met one Norwegian who had read 'Adam Bede,' and had the good sense to be very much struck by its extraordinary power. 'Jane Eyre' is still as popular in Norway as in all other European countries, being translated, reviewed, and acted upon the stage at Bergen and Christiania. A gentleman, with

whom I walked in Romsdal, said that English poetry is very much read
here, especially Scott and Byron; but that Tennyson had not yet
penetrated to the libraries. He promised to get the 'Idylls of the King'
from England, to see what 'this new poet might be like.' Also some of
Hallam's works, which he had not heard about. In the course of
conversation he praised Lord Macaulay's History, oddly enough, for its
great impartiality! (Elton 1864, 127–28).

In the same vein, Gladstone in 1885 was amazed to find on strolling
about the small town of Ålesund, a Norwegian translation of John
Mill's *Logic* (Morley 1903, 218).

The interest in British literature was an indication to the travellers,
wrongly or rightly, of a wider Norwegian fascination in all things
British. As befitted a powerful European nation, Britain inevitably
had a vested interest in believing that the Norwegians had a particular
respect for British political tradition and military strength. According
to Edward Daniel Clarke, who visited Norway during the Napoleonic
Wars in 1799, Norway evinced a reverence for the British from the
late eighteenth century onwards:

> Of all the nations to whom the *British* character is known, the
> *Norwegians* are the most sincerely attached to the inhabitants of our
> island. 'The welfare of *Great Britain*' was a toast which resounded in
> every company, and was never given but with reiterated cheers and the
> most heartfelt transports. Every *Englishman* was considered by the
> *Norwegians* as a brother: they partook even of our prejudices, and
> participated in all our triumphs. Whenever the Gazettes contained
> intelligence of a victory gained by the *English*, the glad tidings were
> hailed and echoed from one end of the country to the other; but
> especially in *Trönÿem* [i.e. Trondheim]. They sang '*Rule Britannia*' in
> every company. Their houses were furnished with English engravings,
> and English newspapers were lying upon their tables. The *Norwegians*
> would have fought for *England*, as for their native land; and there was
> nothing that an *Englishman*, as a sincere lover of his country, might more
> earnestly have wished for than to see *Norway* allied to *Britain* (Clarke
> 1824, 264–65).

Anglophilia, it seems, continued throughout the century. John
Barrow's comments on society in Trondheim in *Excursions in the
North of Europe* (1834) serve almost to suggest that Norway is a
province of Britain, such is the degree of interest taken there in the
British political scene:

> We were not prepared to meet in this northern city, in the latitude of

63°N., so many of the more respectable part of the inhabitants well acquainted with, and conversant in, the English language; and still less could we have expected to find how well-informed they were in regard to passing events in England, in which they appeared to take a more than common interest; they knew perfectly well who had spoken on such and such a question in the House of Commons, and which side he took in the debate. Both here and in Bergen, everything that relates to Britain seemed to create a deep interest (340).

J. C. Phythian in *Scenes of Travel to Norway* (1877) was amazed on his visit to the farm Berge in the remote region of Rauland in Telemark to hear English spoken, and admitted that the event was greatly enhanced by the enthusiasm of his host for all things English (46). As they rowed across the Totak lake, Phythian and Berge (for such was also the host's name) discussed current affairs in Britain:

> In the course of the conversation he requested me to send him some English newspapers, which I have done, so that copies of *The Manchester Guardian* and *The Daily Telegraph* would probably serve him for many a day. He asked about the Prince of Wales and his journey to India, evincing also considerable familiarity with matters connected with England. He knew the tunes of 'God Save the Queen' and 'The Marseillaise,' and finally gave us a Norwegian song, which, however, had lost the effect of earlier days. And thus passed a pleasant row of nearly an hour, when we reached the shore and walked up a path through the forest to Kosthweit [i.e. Kostveit] (ibid., 48).

It is impossible to know just how real or how prevalent this interest in British culture might have been in Norway.[38] No doubt, such moments of cultural overlap are given undue prominence in the travellers' accounts. As such they serve to contribute to the ever-growing imperialist discourse of British domination and superiority in Europe and the world, which was a feature of the latter decades of the nineteenth century. In accounts of cultural exchange, as in so many other ways, Norway was nearly always portrayed as a charming child keen to emulate her blood-sister across the North Sea. It is a connection that at once bound the two countries firmly together and yet relegated Norway to a position of simplicity and dependence.

***

[38] For a longer discussion of Norwegian interest in British culture in the nineteenth century, see Burchardt 1920.

The common theme of this chapter has been the representation of the Norwegians as a natural people, unsullied by the troubles of the modern age. This general picture reverberates through hundreds of travel accounts and other written sources for the better part of the nineteenth century, but it is not unchanging. As the tourist industry to Norway swelled in the last three decades of the century, one or two travellers started to note fissures in the utopian ideal and their accounts begin to voice caution. It was perhaps to be expected that after an influx of visitors from Britain, the local population in the big cities of Christiania and Bergen started to become a little more worldly-wise than before. The anonymous Reverend who contributes 'The British Tourist in Norway' to *Blackwood's Magazine* (vol. 112, no. 681, July 1872) comments:

> I noticed evil symptoms among the young, and it is on these only that the contamination of the tourist mob has had time to operate. (...) I saw enough among the boys at the post and steamboat stations to show that they are likely to grow, by reason of the temptations they are subject to, into vicious and dangerous men. They demand money, loudly and fiercely (...). On its being refused or ignored, I have heard on occasion an outburst of filth, ribaldry, and blasphemy uttered in the very purest English, and altogether with a style that would do credit to Whitechapel (313–14).

In the same vein, Robert Taylor Pritchett a few years later is concerned to discover that the beauty of Molde has become contaminated by modern fashion: '[T]he heads of the people are much more transformed, and soon become smiling victims to the first phases of the vile taste for artificial flowers, feathers and tawdry finery. If they only knew the dignity of simplicity and the charm of good silver ornaments handed down for generations, they would never so debase themselves' (Pritchett 1879, 106). Elsewhere in the book he also comments, with wry irony, that the Norwegians 'are a contented people, with no desire for change, or to have it thrust upon them, until they discover that they can make money of the delighted foreigner, who, elevated by the grandeur of the mountain scenery, grows more warm-hearted, kind, and generous than ever' (ibid., 6). Differentiating between the cities and the provinces he reiterates: 'There is no money greed amongst them [in the provinces], until spoilt by tasting the fruit of the tree of civilization, and then the reaction is all the worse' (ibid., 125).

Charles Wood also feared that the Norwegians would soon lose their enviable simplicity:

There is something very noble in their disposition, especially where it has been unspoilt by too much dealing with the outside world. For it is pretty certain that, as iron sharpeneth iron, so this people, coming into contact with the sharpness and cunning of other nations, will lose much of their native simplicity and integrity. Ten years hence, travelling in Norway will be as different from what it now is, as it is now unlike what it was ten years ago (Wood 1880, 23).[39]

It seems that by the 1870s, the view of the Norwegians as innocent primitives was fading away. This sea change, of course, was not simply the result of the increased contact between Norway and other 'more developed' societies. C. B. Burchardt points to other internal changes in Norway in the last decades of the century that contributed to the disintegration of the pre-industrial ideal. In *Norwegian Life and Literature* (1920) he comments that '[i]t must be regretfully stated that the sympathy once so keenly felt for [Norway's] national character in many instances shows a distinct falling off' (50). This 'falling off' in sympathy is attributed to Norway's growing nationalist and socialist movements. It is probable that as the British sensed the strength of the new Norwegian national spirit and witnessed new methods of organisation amongst the Norwegians, their condescending image of the 'noble savage' living peacefully in his natural state could no longer hold. It is fair to say that as Norway gained a visible history, she lost a part, at least, of the mythic status that had characterised her representation in the nineteenth century.

[39] There is a certain irony in the fact that Charles Wood, in particular, comments on the simplicity of the Norwegians. Seven years after the publication of his book, his famous mother, the writer of sensation novels Ellen Wood (Mrs. Henry Wood) was, at her death, to leave a personal estate valued at more than £36,000, and at his own death in 1919, Charles Wood would leave an estate valued at more than £88,000, based on his mother's copyrights (Flowers 2003).

4. 'A PECULIAR SAVAGE GRANDEUR': NATURE WORSHIP AND ESCAPE FROM CIVILISATION

> A grand and awful scene it was – so still,
> so calm; one seemed to have been
> transported to a region wholly
> unconnected with an inhabited world.
>
> *W. F. Ainsworth*, 1862

Nature and Civilisation

A taste for rural scenes, in the present state of society, appears to be very often an artificial sentiment, rather inspired by poetry and romances, than a real perception of the beauties of nature. But, as it is reckoned a proof of refined taste to praise the calm pleasures which the country affords, the theme is never exhausted. Yet it may be made a question, whether this romantic kind of declamation, has much effect on the conduct of those, who leave, for a season, the crowded cities in which they were bred (Wollstonecraft 1974, 159–60).

This passage from Mary Wollstonecraft's posthumously published essay 'On Poetry and Our Relish for the Beauties of Nature' (1798) might help contextualise the nineteenth-century fascination of Britons for Norwegian scenery. Herself a traveller to Norway, and one of the earliest at that, she realises with penetrating insight – a few years before the publication of *Lyrical Ballads* – that the appreciation of 'the beauties of nature' is largely a cultural construct, intimately connected with 'the present state of society', and not least with 'the crowded cities'.

Wollstonecraft wrote her essay at the time when the Enclosure Acts for some time had exerted a profound effect on the appearance and the use of the countryside in Britain.[1] Indirectly, they also set in motion a steadily growing exodus from the countryside to the increasingly industrialised cities. Thus a process of political change was closely accompanied by one of aesthetic change, or as Ann Bermingham puts it in her study *Landscape and Ideology: The English Rustic Tradition 1740–1860* (1986):

> It is a fact of history that in the eighteenth century, enclosure radically altered the English countryside, suiting it to the needs of the expanding city market. It is a fact of art history that in the eighteenth century, with the 'discovery of Britain', the English saw their landscape as a cultural and aesthetic object. This coincidence of a social transformation of the countryside with the rise of a cultural-aesthetic ideal of the countryside repeats a familiar pattern of actual loss and imaginative recovery. Precisely when the countryside – or at least large portions of it – was becoming unrecognizable, and dramatically marked by historical change, it was offered as the image of the homely, the stable, the ahistorical (9).

This, then, is the situation which Wollstonecraft envisages in the 1790s, and which, as the nineteenth century progresses, forms an important background to the vigorous search among city-dwellers for unspoilt scenery. For there is no doubt that the interest in Norway serves largely as a compensation both for the vanishing natural scenery itself and for the qualities that were perceived to go with it. However, with her customary clear-sightedness, Wollstonecraft also realises, and indeed reminds the reader, that not all who seek solace in nature know what they are looking for. Many have only acquired a stereotyped 'tourist gaze' and leave the city like mindless sheep. Probably, this could also be said of many of those who published their accounts after returning home from Norway. There are, indeed, few professional writers among them and on the whole their accounts are relatively predictable, but then again this predictability – this recurrence of common themes and modes of expression – is, from the point of view of the present discussion, precisely the area of interest. This sense of a common voice applies not only to those who wrote

---

[1] The majority of the Enclosure Acts were passed by Parliament during the period from 1760 to 1830, numbering several thousand altogether. The Acts divided up the 'common land'; redistributed plots into larger areas; revoked peasant farmers' traditional rights to use the land for grazing, gathering of fuel etc.; and required farmers to build a fence around their properties (http://www.cssd.ab.ca/tech/social/tut9/lesson_2.htm, accessed 03.12.02).

their own travel accounts after visiting Norway, but also to those non-visitors who wrote about the country, either in factual or fictional works, on the basis of written sources and a general impression of its landscape.

As has been pointed out earlier, the great majority of the British travellers who published on Norway seem to have come from the university-educated upper-middle class, which at the time was a small and relatively homogenous group. As the century progressed and the representatives of the landed gentry became even fewer, it would also increasingly have been a group whose predominantly urban background provided them with only rather vague ideas about life in rural communities. On the other hand, this group of educated readers was probably more likely than any other segment of the population to have acquired the aesthetic ideals of the age, and to show a degree of reflection around these very issues. As will appear from the following, the Norwegian landscape, which was after all the main goal of the journey, invariably led to interesting and frequently revealing discussions of its dialectic opposite, namely culture or civilisation. Furthermore, the encounter with the sheer majesty of the Norwegian scenery frequently forces the authors to go beyond the dominant aesthetic ideal of the age, namely the picturesque, and return to the more appropriate eighteenth-century tradition of the sublime. All in all, the comments on the Norwegian landscape, like those on Norwegian people and society, appear to have brought to the surface views, prejudices and reflections which are in effect comments – so to speak from abroad – on Romantic and Victorian Britain, and in particular echoes of the many aesthetic and even social conflicts that lay embedded in that society. Thus, the Norwegian experience, as expressed in travelogues, articles, novels and poetry, contributed to the general debate about nature and culture, tradition and progress, the country and the city.

Looking back, in 1928, on the golden years of nineteenth-century British travellers to Norway, S. C. Hammer, touches upon some of the reasons why Britons came in such numbers to see the 'rural scenes' of Norway:

> Until the last few decades of the eighteenth century Norway as a tourist country was practically unknown to European travellers.
>
> The juncture is no irrelevant one; it may rather be said to be intimately connected with the important epoch in the history of European culture when the gospel of Nature, which Rousseau had been preaching so fervently for a number of years, eventually began to prevail. A

generation of men and women who had become tired of the decadent civilisation of the large cities of Europe as well as of the tame scenery of ordinary travelling gradually took a fancy to wilder and more imposing aspects of Nature and longed to make solitary journeys through distant lands (Hammer 1928, 1).

And he adds:

A few details are sufficient to show how excellent Norway was adapted to meet the special requirements of the age. Her remoteness from England and the Continent, on the very outskirts of civilisation; her extensive area, her scanty population, of which the most extraordinary stories were told; her magnificent types of coast and inland scenery, so full of striking contrasts – all these make it easy to realise why the adventurous spirit of the age very early steered its course towards Norway, and why within a generation she became a favourite country for tourists, especially for those from Britain (ibid., 2).

Hammer thus intimates a twofold background, that is a push and a pull factor. To borrow one of Sigmund Freud's book titles, Britons were pushed – long before Freud – away from home because of 'civilisation and its discontents'. At the same time, they were pulled across the North Sea for the simple reason that Norway was perceived to be 'on the very outskirts of civilisation'. It was these two factors predominantly that lay behind the attraction of Norway at the time, and it is, therefore, necessary to take a closer look at how they worked and how they were related to the British cultural scene. These factors, then, will be recurrent themes in the following presentation.

First of all, in their descriptions of Norway several commentators turn to a terminology that virtually identifies civilisation with corruption, pollution and contamination. Not that this was a wholly new idea; in his book *Northern Arcadia: Foreign Travellers in Scandinavia 1765–1815*, H. Arnold Barton claims that it was a 'self-evident' truth in the eighteenth century

that nature and climate affected not only the emotions of the solitary viewer but the basic character of entire peoples, or 'nations,' as they were generally called at that time. (...) Deriving from this concept was the idea that those who lived in closest communion with nature, not least in its grander and more inspiring manifestations, preserved their virtue, as opposed to those who were removed from such natural surroundings and corrupted by the overrefinement and artificiality of civilization (Barton 1998, 149).

In the course of the nineteenth century, however, these attitudes take a somewhat sharper turn. As early as 1823, Arthur de Capell Brooke leaves no doubt that his journey north along the Norwegian coast is a journey away from contamination:

> As the traveller advances into the north, and gradually leaves behind him the good and evil, which arise in the civilized world from the frequent intercourse between man and man, he will be better able to judge, from the simplicity of the lives and manners of the inhabitants, and the state of happiness and contentment they appear to enjoy, of the effects which civilization, as it is termed, would produce among them; and whether in them the great purpose of life be not more truly answered, than in the crowded part of the community, where self, like a *contagion*, so surely *infects* every class, that it seems unfortunately and inseparably connected even with what appears fair, habitual, and guiltless (Brooke 1823, 73–74; italics added).

Similarly, he sees an intimate connection between the moral integrity of a nation and the degree to which it has been civilised. Paradoxically, however, he views this connection in a radically different way from that of the champions of progress: rather than seeing the one as the direct reflection of the other, he turns – Wordsworth-wise – the tables:

> As the traces of roads gradually disappeared, so in proportion did the manners of the inhabitants become more interesting; and when civilization would have been said by most to be left far behind, hospitality, candour, and simplicity became doubly conspicuous. (...) As society becomes more cultivated and polished, why does it lose these inestimable qualities? Does an intercourse with the world lead only to the knowledge of its vices and imperfections, and suspicion thus arise in the breast, to the exclusion of the virtues I have mentioned? (ibid., 224–25)

There is a considerable degree of doubt and uncertainty between the lines in this passage. Brooke's is as yet a cautious and wondering voice, however, compared to the more feverish sentiments of later and post-Darwinian decades, when the fear of degeneration in the industrial and civilised environment found wide expression both in novels, newspaper articles and scientific research. In his book *Faces of Degeneration* (1989), Daniel Pick shows precisely how phenomena such as crime, insanity, pollution and eugenics were discussed in the context of a predominantly urban environment: 'The "condition of England question" was re-formulated in medical language in *The Lancet and the Journal of Mental Science* (...)'

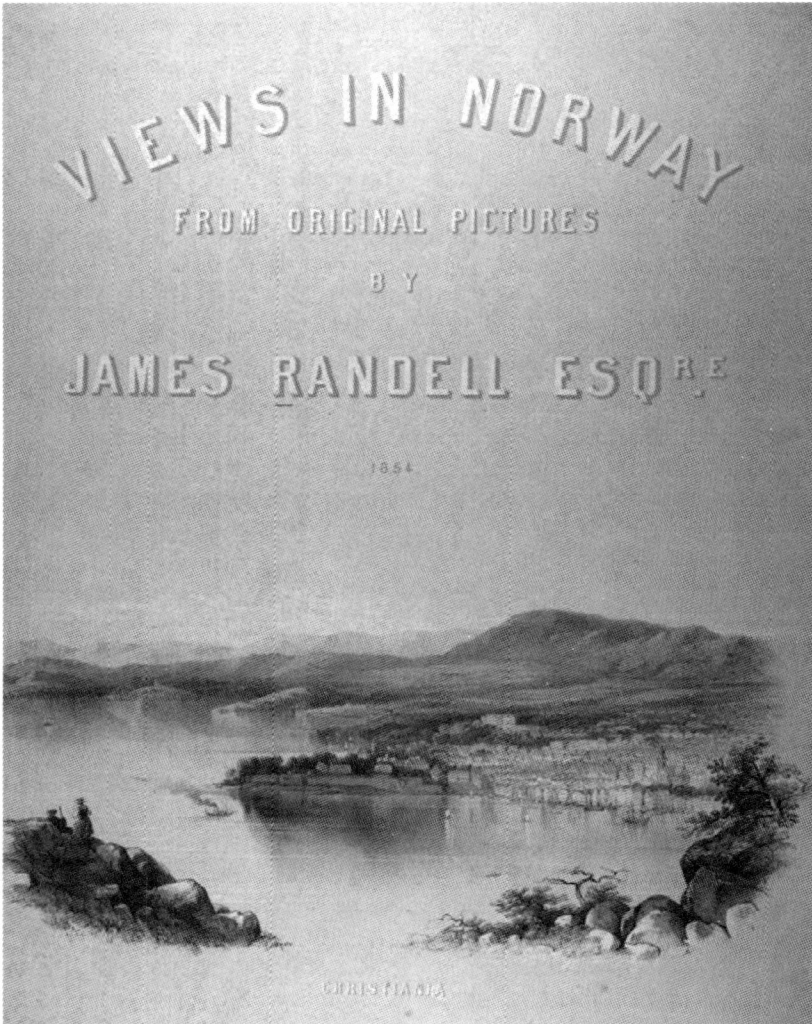

The title page of James Randell's *Views in Norway from Original Pictures* (1854), showing Christiania from the Ekeberg plateau. Like most commentators on Christiania, this illustration also emphasises the capital's setting in a rural, almost desolate landscape, rather than its urban qualities. Randell's work, which was published in London, Paris, Berlin and New York, contained twelve large plates showing natural scenery from various parts of Norway.

(178). With urban civilisation being regarded as a 'literal breeding ground of decay' (ibid., 190), the escape *from* the city was seen, by the late nineteenth century, as simultaneously an escape *to* health and recovery, both in mental and physical terms, and accounts of Norway throughout the century reflect this belief.

The Reverend M. R. Barnard gives a clear indication of this in 1871 when he claims that 'Norway is the safety-valve for all my ailments. Whether it is the air, or the sea-passage, or the "roughing," or the sharp exercise, certain is it, that when I get back to England, I feel better in body and in mind' (Barnard 1871, 65). Whether Barnard would have admitted to a fear of degeneration and an urge for escape as reasons for going to Norway is probably unlikely, but Norway is not the only place of great natural beauty described in these particular terms. Norman Nicholson, in his book on nineteenth-century tourism to the Lake District, makes the following observation:

> In spite of all the danger of the railways, the grasp and grab of trade, the grandiloquence of Empire, the flags, the dividends, the Harvest festivals, the brass bands, the gold watches and Prince Albert himself, there was hidden somewhere in every Victorian a tired, rather frightened, rather lost little dog that wanted to crawl under a table and sleep. So the Lake tour became a rest-cure rather than an adventure, and the hills became a refuge rather than a discovery (Nicholson 1995, 164).

Thus, Norway might be seen as a radicalised version of the Lake District, the place to which the most frightened dogs, or alternatively the most daring seekers of the wilderness, would go.

Regardless, however, of the actual push and pull factors, the widespread conclusion among most of the travellers is that Norway as a nation ought to remain an 'unsophisticated corner of the world' (Blundell 1862, 5), or a haven to which weary travellers from a busy modernity may seek refuge. Lady Wilde, Oscar Wilde's mother, who visited Christiania during a somewhat belated honeymoon in the summer of 1852, is similarly grateful that 'owing to the nature of the country, railroads can never be universal' in Norway, 'and this is fortunate, as Norway must remain sacred to nature and the picturesque, and to the painter and poet' (Wilde 1884, 132). This kind of wish also entails an explicit criticism of anything in Norway vaguely associated with progress or industrial development. As early as in the 1790s Mary Wollstonecraft complains during her visit to the falls outside Sarpsborg that 'I did not like to see a number of saw-mills crowded together close to the cataract; they destroyed the harmony of the prospect' (Wollstonecraft 1987, 153). Robert Everest, who may well have read Wollstonecraft, visits the same waterfall during his Norwegian journey in 1827–1828 and is equally critical of the visibly and audibly disturbing elements of civilisation: 'We cannot, then, help regretting that it should be profaned by hammering and sawing, and clattering of wheels, by piles of deals that shew their yellow faces a couple of leagues off, and the hum of men intent on worldly pursuits' (Everest 1829, 9). Both writers thus imply a wish to preserve their idea of Norway as essentially otherworldly. In the same way J. Ross Browne, whose 'Flying Trip Through Norway' appeared in *Harper's New Monthly Magazine* in the summer of 1862, is not pleased to see the sawmills along the river as he is leaving Lillehammer: 'The scene was pretty and picturesque, but rather disfigured by the progress of Norwegian civilization' (Browne 1862, 155).

Even the building of new and better roads is associated with a powerful nostalgia for the roadless tracts which are fast disappearing. When in 1848 Thomas Forester approaches the depths of the 'wild, rugged, half-civilised Thelemarken' (Wood 1886, 350) along a new road from the south coast, he envisages a future which does not appeal to him:

> Soon, then, the silence of those untrodden forests will be broken by the ringing stroke of the woodman's axe; and those passes, through which we toiled with so much difficulty, will be rapidly threaded by the light carriole. But if future tourists should find their progress through scenes which must always be eminently attractive thus facilitated, we, their pioneers, may perhaps rejoice in having drawn attention to them, and shall ourselves assuredly long retain the vivid impressions which our rambles in these wild districts, and our intercourse with the inhabitants, in their unfrequented and primitive state, are calculated to make (Forester 1850, 21).

And Frederick Metcalfe, the Fellow of Lincoln College in Oxford and writer on Old Norse language and literature, is full of enthusiasm when, arriving at Dalen in Telemark in 1856, he can safely claim to have left civilisation behind: 'In one sense we had come to the world's end; for there is no road for wheels beyond it. (…) Adieu to the "boppery bop" of civilization, with all its forms and ceremonies, and turnpikes and twaddle' (Metcalfe 1858, 51). Later on, however, any indication of social ills is immediately linked with a return to civilisation: 'We now get into an enclosed and more cultivated country, and see symptoms of civilization as we approached Vikersund, in the shape of a drunken man or two staggering homewards; and, at the merchant's, where I stop to make some small purchase, there is a crowd of peasants clustering round the counter, or sitting in corners, imbibing down brantviin [i.e. spirits]' (ibid., 251).

The Scottish poet James Logie Robertson (1846–1922) gives poetic expression to a similar attitude. In the sonnet 'The Voices of Norway', from his collection *Our Holiday Among the Hills* (1882), the contrast between Norway and civilisation is marked by the sharp divide between the octave and the sestet:

> The cataract thundering from the airy rock,
>   Or shouting through the forest wild and free;
>   The river roaring onward to the sea,
> Defiant of all craft to bind or block
> Its loose unshackled strength; the thunder-shock,
>   Echoed in silence, round the blasted tree;
>   And the black eagle screaming in his glee
> Above the storm, which his strong wings bemock:
>
> – These are old Norway's voices: not the shrill
>   Whistle of steam-car jarring down the street,
> Nor clang of factory-bell, nor clank of mill
>   Banging and beating to a fever-heat
> Of madness blood and brain; but Nature still
>   Inhabits here, and men sit at her feet!

Frequently, it is at the very end of the travel accounts, when the writer begins his or her mental preparations for the return to Britain, that these reflections come to the surface.[2] John Barrow Jr. leaves the country with these words:

> Farewell, then, to Norway! – a long farewell to her snow-capped mountains, her fir-clad hills, her lovely valleys, her clear and limpid streams, her clearer lakes and unfathomable fiords! – farewell, ye free and happy and contented sons of the mountains! May no intruder disturb your peaceful cottages with wild and pernicious theories, that lead only to confusion and ruin! (Barrow 1834, 378).

---

[2] This could even be seen as a characteristic of the travelogue as a genre. Whereas the main body of the accounts is usually characterised by a catalogue-like enumeration of more or less unconnected events and experiences, solely structured by a chronological progression, the conclusions – and sometimes introductions – make more of an attempt to reflect in more general terms on the impressions from the journey.

Even in the frequently humorous and sometimes hilarious classic *Three in Norway by Two of Them* (1882), which went through numerous editions both in Britain and in Norway, the concluding lines suddenly turn serious in an almost Lawrentian manner:

> 'Yes, I'm sorry to be leaving Norway, for, you know, there's something delightful to me about the simplicity of the people (...) ; they seem to place a childlike confidence in a stranger, which is quite incomprehensible to me. Then there is an unwordable calm, an indescribable tranquillity, which seems to cling both to the country and its inhabitants; even the houses seem to possess an imperturbable serenity of demeanor which you will not find on any other island in Europe. In fact, y'know, Esau, it's a country where one might live quietly and die in peace, where "moths do not corrupt, neither do worms break through and steal," don't you know, Esau? And I'm deuced sorry to have to count among past memories the time we have spent here, where the unbroken harmony of existence is that repose for which my soul has longed these many years; but never until now, no, by George! never, has it been able to discover the most uncertain tracings of its ideal. (...) A couple more days, and we shall be back in England, where, y'know, I think civilisation is overdone. My existence there is a perpetual state of toadying and being toadied: you see, it's a place where the serpent of social emulation creeps into our very beds, and hangs suspended over our heads by a mere thread when we least expect him (...)' (Lees and Clutterbuck 1995, 202–3).

Charles W. Wood, the son of the writer of popular bestsellers Ellen Wood, even draws a direct comparison between the 'small wooden tenements painted red, green and white, delightfully clean and fresh', which he can see from the ship, and the city of Hull, to which he will be returning:

> Who can forget his first impression, say of Hull and good old merry England when, landing after a month or two spent amidst the endless hills and valleys, woods and streams and rainbow atmospheres of Norway, he contrasts the horrible streets and heavy air, the gloom and grime of the houses with those glorious influences, those light and smiling tenements, which look as though built yesterday with pines fresh from the eternal forests? (Wood 1903, 12)

There is a distinct echo in these passages of Wordsworth's 'Tintern Abbey', in which the poet has returned from 'lonely rooms' and 'the din of towns and cities' to the banks of the Wye, to find 'life and food / For future years'. The Norwegian countryside, in other words, offered the greatest possible contrast to the crowded urban centres in which the majority of British visitors were accustomed to live. As a consequence, the travelogues, in an attempt characteristic of the genre to emphasise the contrast between the Other and the familiar, often tend towards a degree of exaggeration rather than objective description.

Norwegian Towns

With these various observations in mind, it is hardly surprising that the Norwegian towns (few Britons would call any of them a city), were something of a disappointment to sophisticated urban travellers. One of these, Charles Elton, who later in life became a distinguished lawyer, archaeologist and MP for West Somerset, gives a sweeping and general dismissal of Norwegian towns by simply stating that 'the best thing to do on arriving at a Norwegian town is to leave it as soon as possible' (Elton 1864, 7). A large majority of the roughly two hundred British travel accounts seem to agree with Elton's conclusion and, as would be expected, the capital of Christiania (Kristiania from 1877; Oslo from 1925) in particular comes in for a veritable bombardment of far from flattering characterisations, in which the word 'dull' occurs with almost embarrassing frequency: 'Christiania is the dullest capital we ever set foot in' (Bremner 1840, 2: 28); 'a place more dull or uninteresting I have rarely beheld' (Breton 1835, 49); '[s]tagnation broods in the very atmosphere' (Browne 1862, 150); '[w]e must always see Christiania to disadvantage' (Everest 1829, 245); '[t]here is no beauty in the mean little town' (Hare 1953, 126); 'it seems a miserably dull place' (Popplewell 1859, 9); 'this inanimate city (…) seems to have been visited by an asphaltic breeze' (Elliott 1832, 92); and it even 'wants the semi-barbarous picturesqueness of other Norwegian towns' (Galton 1861, 364).

Despite these unanimously unfavourable verdicts, however, Christiania also possesses for some a number of positive features. Brooke's description gives an intimation of the particular quality of these attractions:

> The view from the extremity of the fort is striking and beautiful: nothing is there seen to remind us of the neighbourhood of a large commercial city; and while the eye steals across the clear, calm waters of the *fiord*, and ascends the mountains of the opposite shore, backed in the distance by the snowy summits of others, we lose the recollection of the bustle of

the town, in the more pleasing contemplation of the surrounding scenery (Brooke 1823, 90).

'[N]othing is there seen to remind us (...)', and 'we lose the recollection of the bustle (...)': Brooke's admiration, in other words, is not at all associated with Christiania's urban qualities, but, on the contrary, with its rural situation. Lady Wilde, whose credibility, according to Jean A. Mains, should be taken with several grains of salt, similarly comments with considerable gusto on the view from the fjord: 'At length, on entering the great fiord of Christiania, we are in smooth water, and at peace to gaze upon the picturesque splendours of the panorama that opened [*sic*] out on all sides. (...) No city in the world could surpass Christiania for grandeur of position, and the scenery fills the soul with awe as well as admiration' (Wilde 1884, 121). What is only implied by Brooke and Wilde, however, is made more explicit by Charles W. Wood in his book *Under Northern Skies* (1886): 'There is nothing very attractive in Christiania itself. All its beauty lies in its neighbourhood, its drives and water excursions. These are sufficient to satisfy the most exacting and insatiable lover of nature and variety' (295). He then drives up to Frognerseteren above the town and has before him 'one of the finest panoramas in the world. Christiania lies sleeping in the sunshine, looking from this point a mere handful of houses. The noisy traffic of the streets is lost' (ibid.). Thus, a suitable distance has removed the urbanity of Christiania in a way similar to how Wordsworth, in his Westminster Bridge sonnet, views the city in a state of early morning calm and inactivity: 'Open unto the fields, and to the sky; / All bright and glittering in the smokeless air'.

There is of course a strange ambiguity about this overall attitude to the Norwegian attempts at city life, because it appears to contain simultaneously two rather contradictory positions. First, it reveals a sense of metropolitan condescension towards smaller and less sophisticated towns, and as such it represents an elitist and essentially urban set of values. Second, it expresses a wish that Norway had no towns or cities at all, simply because they represent a negative set of values. Mary Wollstonecraft is rare in her acknowledgement of the contradiction inherent in this position. In her *Short Residence* (1796), which according to Richard Holmes 'may be said to have entered into the literary mythology of Romanticism within a single generation' (Wollstonecraft 1987, 41), she reflects, during her stay in the coastal town of Tønsberg, precisely on the dilemma of a love both of the beauties of nature and of the benefits of urban life:

I am delighted with the romantic views I daily contemplate, animated by the purest air; and I am interested by the simplicity of manners which reigns around me. Still nothing so soon wearies out the feelings as unmarked simplicity. I am, therefore, half convinced, that I could not live very comfortably exiled from the countries where mankind are so much further advanced in knowledge, imperfect as it is, and unsatisfactory to the thinking mind. (...) My thoughts fly from this wilderness to the polished circles of the world, till recollecting its vices and follies, I bury myself in the woods, but find it necessary to emerge again, that I may not lose sight of the wisdom and virtue which exalts my nature (ibid., 122).

A few days later, in the small town of Risør, she continues on the same line of thought:

My present journey has given fresh force to my opinion, that no place is so disagreeable and unimproving as a country town. I should like to divide my time between the town and country; in a lone house, with the business of farming and planting, where my mind would gain strength by solitary musing; and in a metropolis to rub off the rust of thought, and polish the taste which the contemplation of nature had rendered just (ibid., 132).

Wollstonecraft here advocates precisely what later became the Victorian and the twentieth-century attempt to have the best of two worlds, namely the suburb, this 'abstraction of the rustic tradition, a utopian ideological construction that provided a refuge from the disappointing realities of both urban and rural life' (Bermingham 1986, 168).

Wollstonecraft also shows an awareness of the contemporary aesthetic debate (to be discussed shortly) when she comments on another phenomenon, namely that transitional stage between nature and civilisation called the garden. During her visit to Christiania, she is taken out of town to the villa of Peder Anker, who in accordance with the current vogue had created an English garden. But Wollstonecraft is not immediately impressed by her host's attempt to show himself up to date on continental fashion:

To a Norwegian both [that is the villa and the English garden] might have been objects of curiosity, and of use, by exciting to the comparison which leads to improvement. But whilst I gazed, I was employed in restoring the place to nature, or taste, by giving it the character of the surrounding scene. Serpentine walks, and flowering shrubs, looked trifling in a grand recess of the rocks, shaded by towering pines. Groves of lesser trees might have been sheltered under them, which would have melted into the landscape, displaying only the art which ought to point out the vicinity of a human abode, furnished with some elegance. But few people have sufficient taste to discern, that the art of embellishing, consists in interesting, not in astonishing (Wollstonecraft 1987, 146).

Here Wollstonecraft seems to imply, like many of her fellow travellers, that the Norwegian attempts at cultivation and refinement fail, because the surrounding scenery is so fundamentally uncultivated that even an English garden appears to be too artificial and pretentious next to the natural scenery. A similar attitude appears to lie behind E. J. Goodman's description, almost exactly a century later, of a private garden near the coastal town of Brevik. He concludes by commending the virtues of Norwegian gardening, which, in the course of the century, appears to have acquired precisely the qualities Wollstonecraft found missing:

> In Norwegian gardening there is little of the trim finish that we are accustomed to in England. It aims rather at interfering with nature as little as possible, and in this instance, as in others, a very picturesque effect was produced by merely cutting paths up the hill through the wild woods, and only pruning the trees here and there where an outlook was desired. Of course the ground in front of the house was well cleared, and the view from this point took in the whole area of the fjord for many miles, with its pleasant green banks to the rocky islands amidst which Brevik stands (Goodman 1896, 79).

Thus Goodman, with a late-Victorian nostalgia for days gone by, describes a garden which corresponds completely with the aims of the Romantic English landscape garden, as formulated by Ann Bermingham: 'Whereas the formal garden had stood between art and nature, the landscape garden tended to collapse the distinction altogether' (Bermingham 1986, 14). The garden Goodman describes peters unnoticeably into the surrounding countryside and loses itself – with no need of such artificial assistance as a ha-ha – into a borderless Mother Nature.

The Sublime and the Picturesque

Today the categories of the sublime and the picturesque are clearly perceived as belonging to a relatively distant past, but to the majority of nineteenth-century travellers they would be familiar labels and a natural part of the aesthetic vocabulary. Also, the variety of the

Norwegian landscape provided examples of both the sublime and the picturesque. The artist Edward Price, parts of whose diary were printed in Thomas Forester's *Norway and Its Scenery* (1853), even suggests that it is precisely the combination of these aesthetic categories which constitutes the main attraction of the Norwegian scenery:

> Norway, which surpasses every country of Europe in the depths of its fjords, the grandeur of its steeps, the blackness of its forests, and the angry savageness of its torrents, is interspersed with valleys and plains teeming with richness and beauty; even while the mountains are black with tempests, and are undergoing the ravages of continued storm, such stillness will prevail on the surface of the neighbouring lake, that the surrounding scenery will not cease to be faithfully reflected (Forester 1853, 168).

The sublime and the picturesque are both intimately connected with the visual experience. In their introduction to *The Sublime: A Reader in British Eighteenth-Century Aesthetic Theory* (1998), Andrew Ashfield and Peter de Bolla emphasise that within 'the mainstream of eighteenth-century discussion of the sublime[,] landscape-aesthetics were fundamentally preoccupied with the pleasures of the eye' (15). The same is also true of the picturesque. Furthermore, there is a close link between the interest in these aesthetic categories and the growth of tourism. According to Barbara Korte, 'travel for the enjoyment of the landscape may be regarded as a precursor of modern tourism, since the latter (...) is fundamentally dedicated to pleasure, and in particular to the pleasure of looking' (Korte 2000, 93). This pleasure of looking – not primarily for information but, as Norman Nicholson describes it, 'for sensation' – was achieved, before the arrival of the camera, either through the actual experience of travel, through the reading of written travelogues, or through pictures, the latter two frequently combined in the form of illustrated books. But pictures also had a market of their own. According to Donald A. Low's book *That Sunny Dome: A Portrait of Regency Britain*, 'prints and engravings, sold separately from books, were probably more popular than their modern pictorial equivalents, precisely because they formed the only visual record of geographical (and other) subjects which was available. It was fashionable to frequent print shops in the Regency, just as now the custom is to spend money on records and cassettes' (Low 1977, 174–75). Furthermore, he claims that the readers of the day 'were probably more skilled in visualizing scenes (albeit often in ignorance of what the originals were actually like) than subsequent generations who have been used to copiously illustrated books and magazines' (ibid., 175). This focus on the visual is also apparent in Mary Wollstonecraft, who describes how the 'poet contracts the prospect, and, [selects] the most picturesque part in his *camera*'[3] (Wollstonecraft 1974, 171); it plays a prominent role in the narrative structure of the travel accounts, where the leading principle appears to be an attempt to recount the visual sweep of the landscape, that is what the traveller actually sees 'on the road'; and it is present in many of the published titles, such as *Norwegian Pictures, Sketches in Norway* etc. Some of the travel writers even illustrated their own books, and the talent for drawing – often regarded as a feminine activity – was clearly also highly valued among male travellers, as appears from M. Paterson's *Mountaineering below the Snow-Line* (1886), where the author is overcome by the Telemark scenery and tries to capture it in a drawing:

> Sitting down, I essayed a sketch of the scene before me, but soon despaired of securing even a bare outline of so rich and varied a picture in the short half-hour, which was all I could spare. A sharp shower of rain resolved my doubts and reluctance, and with as bad a grace as ever I experienced on the like occasion, I put up my poor pencilled fragment, and once more drinking a deep draught of the beauty before me, I followed my stalwart leader (247).

In Britain, the sublime was made the subject of a long and lively debate, which carried on virtually throughout the eighteenth century and occupied a number of prominent writers and critics. It also had a profound effect on the Romantic and Victorian view of nature, and should therefore not be seen as an exclusively eighteenth-century phenomenon. In the context of British travellers to Norway, the importance of this aesthetic legacy can hardly be overestimated. Although the debate naturally brought to the fore a number of different approaches, there is still general agreement about its main characteristics. Edmund Burke, whose *A Philosophical Enquiry into the Origin of our Ideas of the Sublime and Beautiful* (1757) is central to the debate, states quite categorically: 'Indeed terror is in all cases whatsoever, either more openly or latently the ruling principle of the sublime' (Burke 1998, 102). A few pages later, he adds that 'I know

---

[3] The word *camera* here appears to be used as a metaphor for the eye, but ultimately it refers to the *camera obscura*, an optical instrument and precursor of the modern camera, known since ancient times but also used by artists in the seventeenth and eighteenth centuries.

BAKKE CHURCH.

In exaggerating the landscape into perfectly vertical walls, the artist here suggests –
consciously or subconsciously – the rather stereotyped Romantic connection between the
tiny church, nearly lost in the landscape, and the grand, sublime cathedral of nature.
Illustration from Ainsworth (1862).

of nothing sublime which is not some modification of power. And this branch rises as naturally as the other two branches, from terror, the common stock of every thing that is sublime' (ibid., 107). The origin and characteristics of the sublime are described in even more detail by James Beattie, in his *Dissertations Moral and Critical* (1783):

> The most perfect models of sublimity are seen in the works of nature. Pyramids, palaces, fireworks, temples, artificial lakes and canals, ships of war, fortifications, hills levelled and caves hollowed by human industry, are mighty efforts, no doubt, and awaken in every beholder a pleasing admiration; but appear as nothing, when we compare them, in respect of magnificence, with mountains, volcanoes, rivers, cataracts, oceans, the expanse of heaven, clouds and storms, thunder and lightning, the sun, moon, and stars. So that, without the study of nature, a true taste in the sublime is absolutely unattainable (quoted in Ashfield and de Bolla 1998, 186).

The sublime, in other words, is primarily associated with awesome natural phenomena which inspire a sense of terror and astonishment, the latter being 'that state of the soul, in which all its motions are suspended, with some degree of horror' (Burke 1998, 101). Naturally, these qualities are also essential ingredients in the wave of Gothic fiction, which drew nourishment from the aesthetic debates in the last decades of the eighteenth century.

A large number of descriptions of Norwegian scenery correspond closely with these definitions of the sublime. Charles B. Elliott claims, somewhat obscurely, that the Norwegian landscape is 'wild as beautiful, and beautiful as sublime' (Elliott 1832, 175). Furthermore, it is interesting to note the way in which this scenery is compared to that of other countries, as in Robert Bremner's two-volume work *Excursions in Denmark, Norway, and Sweden* (1840), based on his rather extensive journey in 1836:

> Among the lakes and mountains of Scotland, or among the wild vallies [*sic*] of Switzerland, may be found detached scenes, superior to any met with here; but still does Norway stand pre-eminent in attraction, by the combination of so many grand objects. Large mountains, large rivers, large forests – may all be found separately in other countries; here alone are they to be seen united and in such profusion. It is not one great mountain, or one great cluster of lofty rocks, that we pass in the course of a day's journey; – there are miles beyond miles of rock and mountain, stretching away till the fancy flags in attempting to follow them – a whole kingdom of grandeurs! It is also by their masses and extent, as well as by their frequency, that the sublimities of this wonderful land

surprise and overwhelm the soul (2: 158–59).

James Logie Robertson, the indefatigable sonneteer, makes explicit use of the very words frequently favoured by the theoreticians of the sublime, in 'A Terror of the Twilight':

Far in Norwegian *solitudes* we strayed:
  Behind us lay a long bright summer day,
  But evening now was stooping o'er our way,
When, at a sudden turn, *alarmed* we stayed.
It was a terror by the twilight made
  Of *river, cliff, and cloud,* and the weird play
  Of sunset's one live liberated ray
Piercing the *horror* of the pinewood shade.
Stood, like a charred cross, or a huge sword-hilt,
  Against the sky, above the cliff's black line,
That seemed a bastion by Harfager built,
  A solitary *thunder-blasted* pine;
On the dark *flood* below, the sunset spilt
  What now was blood and now was wassail-wine (italics added).[4]

Such observations, however, were not necessarily the result of a *personal* encounter with Norwegian scenery. As a matter of fact, without having visited the country, the philosopher of the picturesque, William Gilpin, himself draws attention to specifically sublime aspects of the Norwegian landscape in his *Observations on the Mountains and Lakes of Cumberland and Westmorland* (1786):

There is not an idea more tremendous, than that of riding along the edge of a precipice, unguarded by any parapet, under impending rocks, which threaten above; while the surges of a flood, or the whirlpools of a rapid river, terrify below:
  Many such roads there are in various parts of the world; particularly among the mountains of Norway and Sweden; where they are carried along precipices of such frightful height, that the trees at the bottom assume the azure tint of distance; and the cataracts which roar among them, cannot even be heard, unless the air be perfectly still. These tremendous roads are often not only without rail, or parapet of any kind; but so narrow, that travellers in opposite directions cannot pass, unless one of them draw himself up close to the rock (Gilpin 1973, 187–88).

---

[4] The poem appeared in the collection *Orellana and Other Poems* (1881), which contains altogether twenty-four 'Norwegian Sonnets'. It was also published in *Blackwood's Magazine* the same year together with five other sonnets from the same collection (vol. 129, June 1881, 750–52).

As there were hardly any British travel accounts on Norway published before Gilpin, it is difficult to establish which sources he may have had, but regardless of this, the passage shows that the late eighteenth-century aesthetic debate demonstrated at least an awareness of the Norwegian landscape.

As was reflected in the title of Burke's famous work, the category of the sublime was closely connected with that of the beautiful. Thus, with Gilpin's introduction into this debate in the 1780s and 1790s of the concept of the *picturesque*, travellers to Norway were equipped with at least three central aesthetic terms applicable to various types of landscape. In a simplified form the picturesque could be said to represent a compromise between the well-established categories of the sublime and the beautiful: 'Where the early eighteenth-century sublime is all blasting waterfalls and dizzying declevities, the picturesque softens the focus in its domestication of the landscape' (Ashfield and de Bolla 1998, 15). The picturesque, then, could be seen as a harmonious and sentimentalised version of the sublime, and a rough version of the beautiful; a scenery subjected and adjusted to man-made aesthetic ideals. Whereas the natural sublime is concerned with landscapes and phenomena which are totally beyond human control and overpowering in their awesomeness, the picturesque shows a landscape which has been subtly mastered and brought under man's will. This mastery is not least demonstrated in the use of the so called Claude glass – named after the French seventeenth-century landscape painter Claude Lorrain (1600–1682) – which actively frames and limits the scenery and adds a tint which is in line with the taste of the day: 'The primary effect of the glass was to reduce the landscape to the size of a postcard, so that the shape, balance, and perspective could be seen at a glance' (Nicholson 1995, 47). The picturesque is thus deeply concerned with the relationship between nature and art, involving the viewer in a creative process which to some extent places him or her in the role of the artist. There is something deeply attractive about this democratisation of the artistic process: assisted by aesthetic principles which serve almost as a recipe for a satisfactory experience, anyone can do what was previously reserved for a limited artistic or aesthetic elite. It follows from this that the whole idea of the picturesque is that it does not primarily require expert knowledge, but an intuitive sense of contact with the scenery, i.e. a kind of contact which is in principle available to all. According to Guglielmo Scaramellini, the picturesque is 'an understanding with the participation of the "spirit," the "idea," the "being," and the "mystery" that dwell in "nature"' (Scaramellini 1996, 53). This is an important part of the background for the change which took place at the end of the eighteenth century from the so called 'philosophic traveller', associated primarily with the Grand Tour and the topographical, fact-oriented account, to the sentimental or 'picturesque' traveller, inspired by such books as Sterne's *Sentimental Journey* (1768) and seeking the kind of communion with nature which developed into the Romantic sensibility.

As suggested earlier, few of the travelogues in question have been written by professional writers or aestheticians. Consequently, one cannot expect to find the kind of sharp and clear-cut distinctions between different aesthetic categories as are found in texts by such writers as Burke and Gilpin. As Scaramellini makes clear, the sublime, the picturesque and the beautiful are flexible categories on a scale between extremes:

> The *sublime* finds its most evident manifestations in the spectacle of nature in all its splendor, power and awesomeness. But, given the great variety of natural landscapes, between the *sublime* and its opposite, *rational beauty*, there is a vast array of intermediate gradations. The new conceptual perspective establishes other categories, such as *pleasant, friendly, pleasurable, gracious, attractive*, on one extreme of the scale, and, *grandiose, immense, awesome, frightening, horrible* on the other (ibid., 52).

It is not surprising, therefore, to find that several of the writers in question use the different categories rather inaccurately. The word 'picturesque' especially seems to have been used rather loosely, so that ultimately it came to mean little more than 'beautiful' or 'wonderful'. As a matter of fact, the cult of the picturesque was thoroughly ridiculed, according to Donald A. Low, as early as 1810, when William Combe and the illustrator Thomas Rawlandson published *The Tour of Doctor Syntax in Search of the Picturesque* in Ackermann's *Poetical Magazine*. Thus, by the time the great majority of British travellers were coming to Norway from the 1830s onwards, the term was already rather tattered and worn. A rather representative book from the period, *All Round the World: An Illustrated Record of Voyages, Travels and Adventures in All Parts of the World*, edited by W. F. Ainsworth, typically describes the valley of Romsdal as 'one of the most picturesque in the world', and quickly goes on to state – all on one and the same page – that the 'falls and cascades are highly picturesque'; that 'the outline of the mountains is more picturesque than in other parts of Norway'; that the scenery is 'increasing in grandeur and picturesque outline'; and finally that the river makes 'a picturesque fall' (Ainsworth 1862, 50). The picturesque, in other words, quickly became a catchphrase, the precise meaning of which was watered down with increasing use, and which was quickly turned into a cliché, associated with an approach to travel and landscape characteristic of the stereotyped tourist.

The Norwegian Landscape

A large majority of nineteenth-century travel accounts express an exuberant enthusiasm for Norway as a whole. The main component of this enthusiasm, however, is no doubt the country's scenery, which, according to another sonnet by James Logie Robertson, 'The Scenery – Go and See It!' (1881), can only be truly appreciated by being seen and felt:

> And speak ye may of grandeur and of gloom
>> And all the dread magnificence that lies
>> Where through the dale the foam-fleckt torrent flies,
> Or gorgeous sunsets o'er the mountains bloom.
> But who shall in the sonnet's scanty room
>> Set the majestic magnitude, the size,
>> The mighty mountains and the widening skies
> Up on Norwegian table-lands assume?
> This you must see to feel within your heart,
>> And cannot know from others: Nature still
> In this defies all imitative art,
>> Baffles all schools and soars beyond their skill:
> It is a joy she only shall impart,
>> But, once received, it ne'er can cease to thrill.

Similarly, Charles W. Wood goes into veritable raptures just as he is crossing the border between Sweden and Norway: 'Presently a change came over the face of Nature. We breathed Norway air, and were happy. Mountains uprose, hills and valleys laughed and sang, rivers and torrents frothed and foamed. We had left the tame and commonplace, and passed into the majestic and stupendous. It was exhilarating as a draught of wine' (Wood 1986, 292).

To blasé twenty-first-century travellers, who in addition to a wide-ranging travel experience have constant access via modern media to all the world's greatest attractions, it is perhaps difficult to understand the overwhelming sense of novelty which must have accompanied the travellers on their journeys. One point which needs to be kept in mind here and which has also been touched upon in previous chapters, is that up till the beginning of the nineteenth century there were very few books available in Britain about Norway, and hardly any with illustrations which gave any meaningful impression of the country's scenery. Probably this idea of the freshness of the visual impulse is also some of the background for William Gilpin's remark in his essay 'On Picturesque Travel', from 1794:

> The first source of amusement to the picturesque traveller, is the *pursuit* of his object – the expectation of new scenes continually opening, and arising to his view. We suppose the country to have been unexplored. Under this circumstance the mind is kept constantly in an agreeable suspense. The love of novelty is the foundation of this pleasure. Every distant horizon promises something new; and with this pleasing expectation we follow nature through all her walks. We pursue her from hill to dale; and hunt after those various beauties, with which she every where abounds (Gilpin 1794, 47–48).

This 'love of novelty', which in Gilpin's case referred primarily to a part of the British landscape which had so far received but little attention, that is the Lake District, applied to an even greater extent to foreign lands, and especially those which for centuries had been ignored by British travellers abroad. Thus, in some respects Norway fits into the same category as Africa, which was being explored at exactly the same time. As in accounts of that continent, several travellers found themselves trying to strike a balance in their interpretation of Norway between what could be called the 'tourist gaze' and the 'imperialist gaze'. An interesting example of this is the later linguist and ethnologist Robert Gordon Latham, who spent almost a year in Norway from 1832 to 1833, and who was also closely acquainted with the Wergeland family. In his two-volume work *Norway and the Norwegians* from 1840, he makes a direct connection between Norway and Africa: 'You may *discover* in Norway just as you may in the interior of Africa. The whole country has an aptitude for solitude, as some people have a talent for silence. There are whole tracts known only to the peasants in their neighbourhood. (…) There is no European country where you may go over new ground more than you can in Norway' (1: 88–89).

  As Latham is implying, Norway represents a nostalgic echo of a virginal, unblemished world. For educated Britons this conjures up a whole set of different, but closely related ideas, all rooted in the history of western civilisation. The story of the Garden of Eden is inseparably connected with the Christian heritage; the image of a peaceful and pastoral Arcadia echoes classical literature and mythology; and the more recent utopian tradition adds a political and indeed contemporary dimension.[5] Charles Francis Keary who, like Latham, wrote a book called *Norway and the Norwegians* (1892), says simply that in Norway 'man appears like a new comer; his civilisation, his cultivation of the soil, seem to be still only attempts, only a beginning' (2). The same attitude can be discerned in Joseph C. Phythian's *Scenes of Travel in Norway* (1877). 'Surely', he says,

> Norway has been made as a playground for the people of other countries, but especially for Englishmen. And in addition to the charms of the finest natural scenery, it possesses the distinctive character which recalls the first days of the world, the simplicity of the patriarchal order of society. Thought may wander down the vista of the past, and dwell upon those early times with pleasure, but in this northern land they seem to linger still (113–14).

Charles W. Wood, too, finds his Arcadia when he visits the Rjukan waterfall in the inaccessible interior of Telemark:

> Here and there portions had been cleared and cultivated, and small farms had established themselves. High up, one saw small cattle grazing, and still higher, probably, there were mountain saeters. A boat moored on the borders of the lake was the only means of communication with the outer world. Haymakers on the slopes, three or four of them just in one spot, were raking and gathering. What an ideal existence, if existence it can be called. Who would not renounce the pomps and vanities of this wicked world for such Arcadian bowers, where the shadows cast by the sun alone mark the passing hours, and the seasons are known by their fruits? (Wood 1886, 320–21).

In these passages by Phythian and Wood, there is present a dimension which Latham largely ignores, namely that of a savage, untamed primitiveness, and this is where the parallels to the imperialist view of Africa sometimes become evident. In the passage from Phythian's book, especially, there is an unmistakable possessiveness both about the word 'playground' and about the implication that it has been made

---

[5] Ref. for example Samuel T. Coleridge's and Robert Southey's plans of the mid-1790s to found a 'Pantisocracy' in Pennsylvania, and the utopian Socialism of Robert Owen in the early decades of the nineteenth century.

especially for Englishmen. From his journey in 1830, Charles Boileau Elliott gives an even more explicit example of this possessiveness. Having crossed the Hardangervidda on foot and arrived at a mountain above Ullensvang, he can look down on the Sørfjorden, a large inlet of the Hardangerfjorden:

> I am afraid to express what we felt when standing on the summit of the cliff, surveying the scene around: but each of us thought that our labors were more than repaid. We were probably the first, except a straggling unobservant huntsman, who had ever beheld this masterpiece of nature's works. We were assuredly the first who had ever dwelt on it at the end of such a journey, with minds so prepared to receive and contemplate its beauties. It is a bold assertion, but true – that I cannot recollect any view on the Alps or the Himala, which, uniting the minute beauties and grand outlines, the loveliness and sublimity, the varied objects, so numerous and so perfect of their kind, is altogether equal to this coup d'æil (Elliott 1832, 136).

Elliott's rather pompous insistence on the uniqueness of his experience gives the narrative a monumental pathos which would perhaps have seemed more appropriate if he had been a Captain Cook, or a Dr. Livingstone discovering – as the British so characteristically called it – the Victoria Falls. Furthermore, it is an interesting feature of his narrative, as with Latham's above, that he discusses the landscape as if it were devoid of human beings.[6] Somehow, Elliott's Norway is virtually depopulated: 'We were probably the first (...)' and '[w]e were assuredly the first (...)'. In addition to this, they were also the first 'so prepared to receive and contemplate its beauties', because a local huntsman would naturally be 'unobservant'. Thus, like a colonial conqueror, who chooses to

---

[6] In the children's book *Pug's Tour through Europe* (1824), which provides stereotyped descriptions of a large number of European countries, the two stanzas on Norway similarly suggest that the entire country is uninhabited:

> To Norway, then, our traveller went,
>   and o'er the mountains toil'd,
> Shuddering to view the steep descent,
>   The landscape rude and wild.
>
> There frowning woods and hills arise
>   Beyond the deep abyss;
> 'Save me,' cries Pug, and lifts his eyes,
>   'From such a place as this!' (quoted in Barfoot 1997, 12)

ignore the presence of a native population, Elliott enjoys the 'imperialist gaze', confident that he represents a superior culture and that, as a consequence, it is his duty to adopt the role of *Besserwisser*. Even in the relatively cultivated and populated area between Christiania and Drammen, he insists that the landscape is actually empty: 'No villages nor country-seats, no cultivated fields nor orchards, tell of the luxuries of the rich or the labors of the husbandman; but the whole is the monopoly of nature. Here she has planted her garden, and here she reigns supreme. The mountains her throne and the flowery valleys her footstool, she triumphs in the fulness of her charms' (ibid., 102). And when he cannot find the way across the Hardangervidda and is forced to seek assistance from the natives, they are described in much the same manner as African Blacks or American Indians in the same period: 'We learned that, some miles off, a mountaineer maintained a solitary, but friendly, communion with the winds and woods. He was believed to know something of the Alpine waste. A summons brought this wild child of nature' (ibid., 116).

A landscape devoid of humans, or alternatively one populated by humans who can safely be ignored, is an ideal prerequisite for the imperialist gaze, which could also be called the possessive gaze. This connects directly to another useful and more recent analytical framework, namely that of masculine and feminine landscapes. In *The Sublime and Beautiful* (1757), Edmund Burke draws attention to the quality of smoothness, and complains that 'none who have handled the subject have made any mention of the quality of smoothness, in the enumeration of those [qualities] that go to the forming of beauty. For indeed any ruggedness, any sudden projection, any sharp angle, is in the highest degree contrary to that idea' (Burke 1998, 148). He then goes on:

> Observe that part of a beautiful woman where she is perhaps the most beautiful, about the neck and the breasts; the smoothness; the softness; the easy and insensible swell; the variety of the surface, which is never for the smallest space the same; the deceitful maze, through which the unsteady eye slides giddily, without knowing where to fix or whither it is carried. Is not this a demonstration of that change of surface, continual, and yet hardly perceptible at any point, which forms one of the great constituents of beauty? (ibid., 149)

Thus, without mentioning it explicitly, Burke moves from a description of landscape to a description of a woman, applying the same characterisation to both of them and establishing a connection between female qualities and the beauty of the landscape. This makes an interesting comparison with Charles W. Wood's book from 1880, *Round About Norway*, where he opens his story not just with powerful echoes of Keats's 'Ode to a Nightingale', but also with an interesting contrast:

> Not a land flowing with milk and honey; not a land of olive-yards and vine-yards; of southern skies and effeminate luxuriance; of Spanish dances and Italian serenades; of soft intrigues and quick revenges that wait upon life itself. Not a land of fragrant breezes, where the nightingale sings to its mate, whilst the stately queen of night rises in the dark blue dome, bathing the earth in a silvery flood, the while lovers pace romantic ruins washed by a broad flowing Rhine, or a sterner Danube; or linger in bowers on the banks of the soft blue waters of a Moselle – lovers whose lips are silent for a bliss that is filling their hearts with an emotion for which an eternity would be too short, and life, alas! often proves but too long.
>   Not this. But a land of eternal snows, whose mountain heights are fraught with the mystery of a silence never broken, where the foot of man never falls; a land of gigantic icebergs, rushing streams, grand waterfalls and mighty cataracts, that seem to increase and multiply as you progress through the country. A land which owes everything to nature and nothing to man or to art; where ruins are not and the nightingale's song is unheard, and bowers of roses may be imagined but scarcely seen. (…) For such a land, one fine day – it was the 20th of June and a Friday – the good ship *Cameo* left the docks of Millwall (Wood 1880, 1–3).

Clearly, in Burke's terminology, Wood's continental and Mediterranean landscapes would be categorised as feminine (Wood himself uses the word 'effeminate'), and the Norwegian landscape as masculine. If, therefore, Wood may be regarded as representative of British travellers to Norway, the masculinity of the Norwegian landscape must be regarded as one of the country's main attractions. In that case, British tourists clearly sought something else in Norway than in most other countries and destinations.

   In James Buzard's book *The Beaten Track: European Tourism, Literature, and the Ways to Culture*, 1800–1918 (1993), he draws attention to the connection between the picturesque and femininity:

> The picturesque manner of viewing has been, from its inception, a practice culturally coded 'male' – and so, for that matter, has the Continental tour and the whole process of acculturation it represents. My work reflects and studies that coding. The picturesque retained the

assumptions of gender given to it by its founders, who imagined a male art of seeing that could correct and complete what a feminized landscape held forth. 'Nature', wrote William Gilpin, 'is always great in design; but unequal in composition. She is an admirable colourist; and can harmonize her tints with infinite variety, and inimitable beauty; but is seldom so correct in composition, as to produce an harmonious whole.' When, almost a century later, Anthony Trollope wrote that 'A landscape should always be partly veiled and display only half its charms', he was sustaining the ideas of male gaze and female landscape, in spite of his neuter pronoun (16).

Unfortunately, Buzard does not discuss British travellers in Scandinavia, but, as will emerge from the examination of various types of Norwegian landscape later in this chapter, femininity and picturesqueness could not be said to be dominant features. In other words, British tourists flocking to Norway were largely seeking other qualities than those offered by the 'picturesque manner of viewing'. Clearly, some of the reasons for this may also be found in the British appreciation of the heroic and masculine Viking past.

In chapter 1, the 1771 edition of *Encyclopædia Britannica* was quoted as stating curtly, in its four-line entry on Norway, that it was 'a cold and barren country, subject to Demark'. In the fourth edition (1801–1810), however, Norway is given nearly eight compact pages, suggesting not just a considerable extension of the encyclopedia, but also a considerably greater awareness of Norway. One of the interesting aspects of this entry is the way in which it describes natural conditions and phenomena. The coast is described as

> a natural barrier of rocks, which renders Norway inaccessible to the naval power of its enemies. Attempts of this kind are the more dangerous, as the shore is generally bold, steep, and impending; so that close to the rocks the depth of the sea amounts to 100, 200, or 300 fathoms. The perils of the north sea are moreover increased by sudden storms, sunk rocks, violent currents, and dreadful whirlpools (s.v. 'Norway').

As to conditions further inland, it is stated that

> from sudden thaws the inhabitants are sometimes exposed to terrible disasters. Vast masses of snow falling from precipices overwhelm men, cattle, boats, houses, nay even whole villages. About two centuries ago, a whole parish was covered and destroyed by an immense mass of snow; and several domestic utensils, as [*sic*] scissors, knives, and basons [*sic*],

The Rjukanfossen in Telemark, from Alfred Smith's *Sketches in Norway and Sweden* (1847). According to the work's subtitle, the illustrations have been 'Drawn on Stone from the Original Sketches by Henry Warren'. Not surprisingly, both the picture and the caption underline the barren wildness of the place: 'The Riuken Foss, which is situated in Westfjordal, in the district of Tellemarken, is perhaps the most picturesque and beautiful waterfall in Norway. The valley in which it is placed is wild, solitary, and inaccessible, seldom visited but by the eagle and the wolf' (no pag.).

have been at different times brought to light by a rivulet that runs under the snow, which has been gradually hardened and increased by repeated frosts and annual accessions (ibid.).[7]

There is, in other words, a focus on Norway as a country of what might be called 'extreme landscapes'. The main categories of these landscapes are mountains, wastes, waterfalls, seascapes, and the Arctic, all of which will be discussed separately in the following, and all of which are dominated by masculine rather than feminine features.

Communion with Nature

The sublime and the picturesque were eighteenth-century, that is pre-Romantic, terms which continued to be used throughout the following century. But the Romantic movement of the early decades of the nineteenth century also added to this stock vocabulary an additional set of ideas and concepts which, together with those of the 1700s, provided a surprisingly unified and highly influential vision of man's relationship with the natural world. One of the central ingredients of this vision was the pantheistic notion that nature and religion are essentially two sides of the same coin, and that, as a consequence of this, the chief ambition of religious worship is to achieve a sense of oneness between the individual and nature.[8] This in its turn had a powerful impact on the perception of the role of art and the artist, producing a frail and at the same time ambitious vision of a divinely endowed genius capable of healing the rift between man and the 'Other', in this case nature.

But there are also other Romantic features connected with the

---

[7] Interestingly, this particular incident is also mentioned by Joseph Cottle, the publisher of *Lyrical Ballads*, in Book 22 of his poem *The Fall of Cambria*, published in 1811, that is immediately after the publication of *Encyclopædia Britannica*. Mains (1989) also mentions the poem 'The Norwegian Hunter', published in Peter Bayley's *Poems* (1803), which describes how a hunter returns to find his home and family buried by an avalanche.

[8] This idea forms the key element in all Romantic nature poetry, but it is expressed with particular clarity in such poems as William Wordsworth's 'There Is an Active Principle', Robert Southey's 'Natural Religion' and Caroline Anne Bowles's 'There Is a Tongue in Every Leaf'.

travelogues in question. For instance, the perusal of just a few travel accounts will soon alert the reader to the fact that not many of the writers actually travelled alone. Most of them had a travel companion, virtually always of the same sex, sometimes a guide but just as frequently a friend or relative. As one would expect, the writer therefore generally uses the personal pronoun 'we'. This 'we', however, tends to be obscured by the fact that the travel companion is very rarely mentioned. He or she rather follows the writer as a largely ignored shadow, somewhat like the person 'who walks always beside you' in Eliot's *The Waste Land*. This phenomenon seems closely connected with the ideal of the solitary wanderer, who is an exile from the community of fellow citizens, partly out of choice, and partly from a sense of having been excluded. Typically, lack of human company is recompensed through a communion with nature. Joseph Phythian, who dedicates his book to 'the Lovers of Nature, with the hope that it may induce many to visit Old Norway' (Phythian 1877, no pag.), shows precisely how 'the world' – in a traditionally religious sense – is perceived almost as 'the valley of the shadow of death'. And so, by going to Norway, he escapes from people and society, but finds ample compensation by embracing Nature:

> The world may appear in deep shadow, and almost without hope, treading ignoble ways. And if, with flashing light, some phase of character reveals the near divine, another moment clips the wings of promise, and again is gloom. But who can weary of Nature? Her beauties never fade; her perfections are unique. Her finely-moulded form displays a faultless dress, and she has flowers for gems. The soul communes as with devotional instinct, walking by her side and listening to her voice, with all the happiness of love. She is wooed, and won. The presence of attractive worth makes life a brighter thing, and in the midst of gladness the Creator is revealed, for Nature tells of Him (ibid., 55).

Nature here is personified – in the Norwegian context quite unusually – in strongly female terms, as goddess, mother and mistress, and the mention of a masculine Creator appears, in the circumstances, as little more than lip-service to convention. In addition it is rather obvious that 'the world' also largely refers to the modern, urban civilisation of 1877, when the book was published. Thus, the source of salvation here is not a faith in a personal God, but in a pantheistic Mother Nature.

Another example of an overwhelming sense of communion generated by the traveller's encounter with Norwegian scenery, is found in William Hurton's racy and highly readable two-volume work *A Voyage from Leith to Lapland* from 1851. Having arrived in Norway in a terrible snow storm in the March of 1850, Hurton witnesses the explosive Norwegian spring and wallows in a rich Keatsean imagery of the senses:

> The Norwegian spring! oh, that unspeakably glorious season which links the winter and the summer of Norway so closely, that it seems an ecstatic state intervening between the death and resurrection of nature! (…) Day after day, and week after week, I did nothing but ramble amid the enchanting sylvan scenery which the Spring conjured into being. Ineffably exhilarating was every breath of air; nature and man seemed alike awakened from torpor to an all-pervading sense of delicious being. The evergreen pine woods gleamed brightly, diffusing aromatic fragrance through the transparent, voluptuous atmosphere; the vales were luxuriant with herbage of the freshest hue; the warm banks were one gleaming mass of beautiful scentless flowers; the prickly juniper bushes were loaded with green berries; the mountain streamlets joyously leaped, bubbled, and sparkled; the lark carolled in an ocean of blue sky; the mellow voice of the cuckoo echoed on every side; all Nature was one superb temple, and all things animate, one grateful choir attuned to harmony and love!
>
> Never before did I feel the life of life so absorbingly. I drank draughts of pure delight at every step, and lay for hours on grassy knolls gazing up in the heavens, indulging delicious dreams amid blissful realities. My very heart melted, and all the cares, pursuits, and fantastic artificial pleasures of mortals were as much forgotten as though I had never experienced them. Visions of the golden dawn of life, and forms of those dear beings who once made the sunlight of my existence, floated on every side. Ah, how sweet, and yet how sad were those precious hours!
>
> The Spring of Norway suggested vividly the Springs of England, and on the impulse of the moment I wrote the following lines: –

We have wander'd together, a glad youth and maiden,
　The newly-born stars, and rich flush'd sky beneath;
While the soft air of evening, with fragrance o'erladen,
　Came sweeping in gushes from the furze-blossom'd heath –
　　　　　　　　O, FLORA BELLAIR!

We have wander'd together where daisies were springing,
　'Mong cowslips and bluebells, and primroses sweet;
Where green boughs were waving, and blithe birds were singing,
　And dew-drops were glittering on the grass at our feet –
　　　　　　　　O, FLORA BELLAIR!

We have wander'd together by dell and by fountain,
   And wreathed the wild roses, and plaited the reeds;
We have forded the fairy stream, and climbed the steep mountain,
   The dark forest threaded, and tripp'd o'er the meads –
                              O, FLORA BELLAIR!

We have wander'd together 'long the shore of old ocean,
   Its bright shells to gather, and to dare its proud tide;
We have gazed, hand in hand, with speechless emotion,
   On the pure argent moon, array'd like a bride –
                              O, FLORA BELLAIR!

Years have sped by, and now rank, wealth, and glory,
   Bow to the sceptre thou wieldest, as beauty'd thron'd Queen,
But 'midst all the triumphs, will not sadness steal o'er thee,
   When my voice from afar sings o' times that have been
                              O, FLORA BELLAIR!
                                        (64–67)

Both the prose and the poetry suggest an almost total fusion and removal of boundaries: 'nature and man seemed alike awakened' so that there is a mutual joy and celebration; 'delicious dreams' and 'blissful realities' are two sides of the same coin; and in the poem it is difficult to establish whether Flora Bellair is Mother Nature in full bloom or a human lover of flesh and blood.

An account of even greater narrative power, which in a similar way describes the melting together – in a kind of Holy Trinity – of the author, the scenery and the divine presence, is found in Wollstonecraft's *A Short Residence*. On the way from Halden to Strömstad in the middle of the night, she gives a superb description of the way in which she opens herself up in an almost erotic embrace with everything that surrounds her:

My companions fell asleep: – fortunately they did not snore; and I contemplated, fearless of idle questions, a night such as I had never before seen or felt to charm the senses, and calm the heart. The very air was balmy, as it freshened into morn, producing the most voluptuous sensations. A vague pleasurable sentiment absorbed me, as I opened my bosom to the embraces of nature; and my soul rose to its author, with the chirping of the solitary birds, which began to feel, rather than see, advancing day. I had leisure to mark its progress. The grey morn, streaked with silvery rays, ushered in the orient beams, – how beautifully varying into purple! – yet, I was sorry to lose the soft watery clouds which preceeded them, exciting a kind of expectation that made me

almost afraid to breathe, lest I should break the charm. I saw the sun –
and sighed (Wollstonecraft 1987, 94).

And later, when she arrives in Tønsberg and wanders on her own on
what is presumably the small mountain in the centre of the town, she
produces a similar passage:

> Here I have frequently strayed, sovereign of the waste, I seldom met any
> human creature; and sometimes, reclining on the mossy down, under the
> shelter of a rock, the prattling of the sea amongst the pebbles has lulled
> me to sleep – no fear of any rude satyr's approaching to interrupt my
> repose. Balmy were the slumbers, and soft the gales, that refreshed me,
> when I awoke to follow, with an eye vaguely curious, the white sails, as
> they turned the cliffs, or seemed to take shelter under the pines which
> covered the little islands that so gracefully rose to render the terrific
> ocean beautiful. The fishermen were calmly casting their nets; whilst the
> seagulls hovered over the unruffled deep. Every thing seemed to
> harmonize into tranquillity – even the mournful call of the bittern was in
> cadence with the tinkling bells on the necks of the cows, that, pacing
> slowly one after the other, along an inviting path in the vale below, were
> repairing to the cottages to be milked. With what ineffable pleasure have
> I not gazed – and gazed again, losing my breath through my eyes – my
> very soul diffused itself in the scene – and, seeming to become all senses,
> glided in the scarcely-agitated waves, melted in the freshening breeze, or,
> taking its flight with fairy wing, to the misty mountains which bounded
> the prospect, fancy tript over new lawns, more beautiful even than the
> lovely slopes on the winding shore before me. – I pause, again
> breathless, to trace, with renewed delight, sentiments which entranced
> me, when, turning my humid eyes from the expanse below to the vault
> above, my sight pierced the fleecy clouds that softened the azure
> brightness; and, imperceptibly recalling the reveries of childhood, I
> bowed before the awful throne of my Creator, whilst I rested on its
> footstool (ibid., 110–11).

The result of this close encounter with divinity is not just a spiritual
revival; it also has a healing effect on the body, for a few lines later,
Wollstonecraft remarks in her letter that 'my constitution has been
renovated here' (ibid., 111). One does well to remember that this
epistolary travelogue is from 1796. It shows, in other words, a full-
fledged Romantic attitude two years before the publication of *Lyrical
Ballads*. It is also a reminder, as Richard Holmes indicates in his
introduction to the Penguin edition of the book, of the powerful
influence Wollstonecraft had on such writers as Wordsworth and
Coleridge.[9]

The travelogue as a genre also has another characteristic which is closely reminiscent of a poetic ideal formulated precisely by Wordsworth in his Preface to the 1802 edition of *Lyrical Ballads*. Here he formulates the famous statement that 'poetry takes its origin from emotion recollected in tranquillity' (Wu 1998, 263). Even though few travelogues are written in poetic form – Hurton represents a partial exception – most have been written down as an afterthought on the actual event. Furthermore, it is frequently in thus looking back that the traveller acquires the larger, divine perspective on what he or she has witnessed. Robert Bremner, having seen the Rjukan waterfall, even makes it clear that the 'beauties of such a scene (...) cannot be analysed at the moment when the mind is agitated by their effect.' And after once again having run through the most striking details of this spectacle of nature in his mind, he draws a conclusion concerning the essential divinity of the scene:

> The thoughts which occupied our minds while beholding this majestic exhibition, were among the most elevated – may we add, among the most edifying we have ever experienced. Who, with such a spectacle before him, would not have been driven to ask, Whose hand upholds these lasting bulwarks? Whose bounty feeds these ever-flowing springs? the heart must indeed be cold that does not here rise to a great Contriver (Bremner 1840, 154–55).

In a similar vein Bremner comments, during the same sojourn in Telemark, that '[o]ne hour of free intercourse with nature, amid such scenes, is worth years of ordinary life; its remembrance will be something to live on in after days' (Bremner 1840, 121). And by the time John Benjamin and his wife Sarah Popplewell went to Norway in 1858, the powerful impact of Wordsworth's poetry was clearly visible. Their book *Norway* in 1858, which was written – like Wollstonecraft's – as 'a diary, in letters', concludes with a quote from a certain 'Miss Bremer'.[10] Here the reader is confronted with some personal questions before being provided with a simple and straightforward answer:

[9] Holmes mentions in particular their 'verse landscape description' and 'the solitary, outcast woman dreaming of her faithless lover', exemplified respectively by such poems as Coleridge's 'This Lime Tree Bower My Prison' and Wordsworth's 'Ruth' (ibid., 38–39).

[10] Frederika Bremer (1801–1865), Swedish writer, whose book on Norway, *Strid och frid* (1840), was translated into several languages, including English (*Strife and Peace: or Scenes in Norway*, 1844).

> Is thy soul weary of the bustle of the world, the frivolities of daily life?
> is it oppressed by the confined air of rooms, the dust of books? or is it
> worn by deep, consuming passions? Fly, fly, then, to the heart of
> Norway; alone with these grand, silent, yet so eloquent scenes, listen to
> the beatings of the mighty heart of Nature, and win for thyself new
> strength, a new life (Popplewell 1859, 71).

Obviously Wordsworth's contempt for books in 'The Tables Turned'
and the 'mighty heart' of his Westminster bridge sonnet have been
closely associated by the authors with the naturally 'eloquent scenes'
of Norway, and their ability to provide 'new strength, a new life'.

It is now time to look more closely at some of the most
conspicuous features of the Norwegian landscape and the ways in
which the British travellers made sense of these within their aesthetic
framework.

Mountains, Wastes and Forests

> Here might be seen, built by the cunning hand of Nature in ten-fold
> magnitude, the massive donjon and the lofty tower, and here the more
> fantastic beauties of a Gothic ruin, the half-destroyed arch, or the
> traceried net-work of some time-worn spire, wrought out in a noble
> combination of rock, and snow, and sky. Again and again as we drove on,
> intoxicated with delight, and turned round to admire another detail of
> elegant change, the rocks seemed moulded in a new design of reverend
> cloister or time-shattered tower (Brassey 1857, 68).

This passage by Thomas Allnutt Brassey, or Lord Brassey (who was
later to accompany William Gladstone on his trip to Norway in 1885),
offers an interesting indication of the complex fabric that constituted
the Victorian view of nature. Brassey may himself have been unaware
of its rather multifarious history, but by describing the Romsdal
mountains as a 'Gothic ruin' and a 'time-shattered tower', he actually
points back to a seventeenth-century debate which is of some interest
in the present context. In her classic study from 1959, *Mountain
Gloom and Mountain Glory: The Development of the Aesthetics of
the Infinite*, Marjorie Hope Nicolson gives an account of the ways in
which perceptions of mountains have changed, particularly from the
1600s onwards, an account in which the image of ruins plays a central
role. In both Christian and Jewish tradition, mountains are in no way
seen as majestic specimens of God's creation. On the contrary, they

are closely associated with the story of the Fall and, according to Nicolson,

> Jewish and Christian expositors who held the theory that mountains emerged at some time after the Creation were in agreement in attributing the blemishes on Nature to human depravity. A majority of the Christian thinkers blamed mountains upon the sins of the generation of Enosh, but Jewish legend often chose an earlier date (82).

God, in other words, whose creation could only be governed by the rules of proportion, symmetry and beauty, designed the world as a smooth and even surface. As a consequence, the valleys and the low lands were associated with such virtues as humility and temperance, and – in a literal as well as a figurative sense – with the water of life. The mountains, on the other hand, being more or less a direct result of man's fall from grace, were essentially perceived as symbols of pride, hardness of heart, social superiority and other negative personal characteristics. From such a vantage point, a biblical story like that of Satan's temptation of Jesus at the top of a mountain (Luke 4: 2–13) would make perfect sense. Up to the seventeenth century, then, mountains were generally described as ruins, warts, blisters or other distortions and excrescences on the face of Nature, and as such they were generally avoided by civilised people. They constituted a dimension on the fringes, or even beyond the pale, of human society and habitation.

In the late seventeenth and early eighteenth centuries perceptions slowly began to change. The growth of science ensured a more rationalist approach, and there was also an increasing interest in exploiting natural resources. Gradually the mysterious and unapproachable mountains were made the subject of human inquiry. In addition, the Renaissance had to some extent brought to the fore an alternative tradition, namely the revitalised culture of the ancient Greeks, whose gods lived on a mountain. In her analysis of this gradual change, Nicolson puts particular emphasis on Thomas Burnet's book *The Sacred Theory of the Earth*, which was published in Latin in 1681 and in English three years later. Burnet, who was a theologian, had been to the Continent and had experienced the Alps at close range. The result was that '[a]ll his idols of proportion, symmetry, and decorum in Nature were suddenly shattered by Nature herself. Like the rude rocks, his ideals lay before him, ruins of a broken world (...)' (ibid., 209). In the end, Burnet's attempt to put together again the 'heap of broken images' that had been the result of his Continental experience did not primarily result, as he had hoped, in a theological position capable of incorporating Nature, including the Alps. Instead, his work, together with the considerable controversy that followed in the decades after its publication, contributed to the formation of the aesthetic category of the sublime, the general characteristics of which have been discussed earlier in this chapter.

According to Nicolson, 'Burnet's ruins became a persistent motif among minor poets of the eighteenth century' (ibid., 228), and: '[m]ountains and promontories, caves, caverns, and mines, exotic lands and rivers never seen by English eyes, the Ruins of Nature and the Ruins of Time – all are integral parts of the new Nature, filled with variety and diversity, majestic, magnificent, vast (…)' (ibid., 353). Similarly, this interest in natural and indeed in man-made ruins forms an essential part of the picturesque. In his essay 'On Picturesque Beauty', Gilpin admits that '[a] piece of Palladian architecture may be elegant in the last degree', but '[s]hould we wish to give it picturesque beauty, we must use the mallet, instead of the chisel: we must beat down one half of it, deface the other, and throw the mutilated members around in heaps. In short, from a *smooth* building we must turn it into a *rough* ruin' (Gilpin 1794, 7). An almost identical point is made by Uvedale Price, in his *Essay on the Picturesque, as Compared with the Sublime and the Beautiful*, published in 1794, the same year as Gilpin's essay. It is this fascination with naturally fractured surfaces that invades the poetry, the pictorial arts and, in their turn, the travelogues of the nineteenth century. Mountains, in other words, and especially in their most craggy and irregular form, found themselves in fashion. Charles Elton, who visited Norway in the early 1860s, shows an interesting awareness of the change of taste which has taken place over the last two generations: Perhaps, he says, we ought to 'take into account the fact that our grandfathers saw no more in the scenery of the Alps than did the Romans, and that even now, when it is the fashion to walk "with death and morning on the silver horns," there are still many of us who do not really care for mountains'.[11] Most nineteenth-century travellers, however, did indeed care for mountains. Frederick

---

[11] Elton 1864, 46–47. The quote is from Lord Tennyson's poem 'Come Down, O Maid', which forms part of the long narrative poem *The Princess* (1847) and which discusses precisely the relationship between the mountainous heights, on the one hand, and the valleys and lowlands, on the other. The poem was written during Tennyson's visit to the Alps in 1846.

Metcalfe is one example, and his remarks on the view down on the Sognefjorden are interesting, because they demonstrate the way in which the Romantic tradition adopted both the old and the new, both the pre-sublime, the sublime and the picturesque:

> The next two or three hours' travel presented the same scenes as before, savage in the extreme. Now snow, now ice, now rocks splintered, riven asunder, cast upon heaps, and ranged in fantastic groups, with now and then a delicate anemone, red or white, and other Alpine plants peeping modestly out of the ruins (Metcalfe 1858, 190).

In short, the Romantics and the Victorians made a potent aesthetic brew from just about any aspect of the landscape which might be construed as speaking powerfully to the human soul, as in Shelley's 'Mont Blanc', where the poet – like Moses at Mount Sinai – is overwhelmed by the divine presence: 'Thou hast a voice, great mountain, to repeal / Large codes of fraud and woe – not understood / By all, but which the wise, and great, and good / Interpret, or make felt, or deeply feel' (ll. 80-83).[12]

One of the central ingredients of this particular view of mountains was the obsession with what has been called 'the vertical landscape', an obsession clearly initiated by the philosophers of the sublime. From the early decades of the eighteenth century onwards, writers like Anthony Ashley Cooper (Third Earl of Shaftesbury), John Baillie and James Usher had been waxing lyrical on 'the narrow brink of the deep precipices' (Ashfield and de Bolla 1998, 76) and 'mountains piled upon mountains' (ibid., 88). And in *The Sublime and Beautiful*, Edmund Burke ventures on a lengthy discussion about the question of vastness, which brings him to the matter of extension in length, height and depth:

> Of these the length strikes least; an hundred yards of even ground will never work such an effect as a tower an hundred yards high, or a rock or mountain of that altitude. I am apt to imagine likewise, that height is less grand than depth; and that we are more struck at looking down from a

---

[12] In his letter to Thomas Love Peacock of 22 July 1816, Shelley elaborates on his and Mary's recent visit to the foot of Mont Blanc: 'I never knew, I never imagined what mountains were before. The immensity of these aerial summits excited, when they suddenly burst upon the sight, a sentiment of ecstatic wonder not unallied to madness. (…) One would think that Mont Blanc was a living being, and that the frozen blood forever circulated slowly through his stony veins' (Wu 1998, 844).

precipice, than looking up at an object of equal height; but of that I am not very positive. A perpendicular has more force in forming the sublime, than an inclined plane; and the effects of a rugged and broken surface seem stronger than where it is smooth and polished (Burke 1998, 114).

This kind of aesthetic debate, which had a direct impact on the way in which travellers approached the landscape, persisted not only during the Romantic period but throughout the nineteenth century. This is explicitly confirmed by a discussion in Charles W. Wood's *Norwegian By-ways* (1903) between the author and his travel companion. Looking into the black cauldron into which the Vøringsfossen falls, they disagree which is the more impressive: the Vøringsfossen or the Rjukanfossen. His companion favours the latter: 'Against this I argued that one could only see the Ruikanfos [*sic*] from the head of the fall, and the effect of looking up at 530 feet was more impressive than looking down upon 800 feet. Like the chameleon, possibly we were both right, both wrong. It was a mere matter of opinion, and each kept to his own' (39). The approach is very much the same in Wood and in Mary Wollstonecraft, who more than a hundred years before was similarly alert to the impact of the perpendicular landscape. While in Tønsberg, hardly a very mountainous place in the eyes of the Norwegians, she admits that 'when gazing on these tremendous cliffs, sublime emotions absorb my soul' (Wollstonecraft 1987, 100), and similarly in Risør, she explicitly addresses the question of rocks as a natural phenomenon: 'Before I came here, I could scarcely have imagined that a simple object, rocks, could have admitted of so many interesting combinations – always grand, and often sublime' (ibid., 134). It is this consciousness about rocks and mountains which is also present in the large number of Romantic poems such as Wordsworth's 'To – on Her First Ascent to the Summit of Helvellyn'; Coleridge's humble celebration of God's presence in 'Chamouny; the Hour Before Sunrise: A Hymn'; and Shelley's above-mentioned 'Mont Blanc'.

Another approach to the vertical landscape is found in Mrs I. M. Merrlees's *Jottings from Our Journal in Norway*. Merrlees, a Lutheran missionary, travelled around in southern Norway in the summer of 1871 together with the Norwegian pastor Peter L. Hærem, distributing Bibles, tracts and hymns. Crossing the Filefjeld, she gives her narrative a spiritual dimension which reflects the element of terror and awe associated with the sublime, and at the same time provides an interesting example of how, for many Victorians, Christian worship and nature worship were two sides of the same coin:

> [T]he road descends in a winding way, fearfully steep, like a spiral staircase. Majestic crags towering 3000 or 4000 feet, encompass us. We held the carriage behind, to prevent our good, patient horses from falling. Certainly, no scenery in the world can possibly surpass this. It preached a silent sermon to us all day long, telling us of God's 'eternal power and Godhead'. We scarcely dared to address one another, Nature was so imposing and impressive. We read Psalm civ (Merrlees 1871, 15).

Frederick Metcalfe also reminds us of the cultural specificity of the British perspective on the perpendicular landscape during his visit to the spectacular Ravnejuv (Raven's Gorge) in Eidsborg, Telemark:

> Where I stood, the cliff was perpendicular, or rather sloped inwards; and, by a singular freak of nature, a regular embrasured battlement had been projected forward, so as to permit of our approaching the giddy verge with perfect impunity. (…) What a pity a bit of scenery like this cannot be transported to England. The Norwegians look upon rocks as a perfect nuisance, while we sigh for them. Fancy the Ravne jüv [*sic*] in Derbyshire. Why, we should have Marcus' excursion-trains every week in the summer, and motley crowds of tourists thronging to have a peep into the dark profound (…) (Metcalfe 1858, 54–55).

The reason why the British 'sigh' for rocks is partly that they have been encouraged to appreciate them by both philosophers and artists. Thus Elizabeth Bennet in Jane Austen's *Pride and Prejudice* wants to go and see 'the celebrated beauties of Matlock, Chatsworth, Dovedale, [and] the Peak', i.e. landscapes which are as close as England can get to Gilpin's picturesque ideal.[13]

Another recurrent aspect of Romantic art – it could even be called a Romantic cliché – is the combination of a mountain setting and a sense of personal solitude and loneliness. As suggested earlier, the Romantic hero is frequently an exiled, solitary wanderer, pictured in a vast and threatening landscape. Against this background, it is hardly surprising that Caspar David Friedrich's famous painting *The Wanderer above the Mists* (ca. 1818) is a book cover favourite for virtually any aspect of the Romantic period. The solitary wanderer, with his back to the viewer and with misty and unpopulated mountains in front of him, is paradoxically both sharply separated

---

[13] Austen 1996, 196. In a note, the editor Vivien Jones refers to Austen's brother Henry, who in a biographical note on his sister claims that "'at a very early age she was enamoured of Gilpin on the Picturesque'" (ibid., 331).

from the scene and included in it, thus forming a perfect image of the Romantics' perpetual dilemma. In such paintings as 'The Upper Fall of the Reichenbach' by J. M. W. Turner, 'Near Chiavenna in the Grisons' by John Robert Cozens, and 'The Rocking Stone' by Thomas Girtin – not to mention the awesome canvases by John Martin – this ambivalent relationship between man and his natural surroundings is achieved by presenting human figures either as tiny specks almost lost in a colossal landscape, or as larger figures nearly melting together with the colours and formations of their surroundings. Another stock feature of these pictures is the presence of a solitary rock, which functions as a natural counterpart to the solitary wanderer, and which also echoes the tradition of mountains as ruins. Commenting on Girtin's 'The Rocking Stone', Jean Clay quotes Barbara Stafford as characterising these solitary rocks as '"ambiguous monuments": vague ruins whose stones are closely integrated with the vestiges of human constructions' (Clay 1981, 78). The best example of this setting from British literature is probably Byron's poetic drama *Manfred* (1817), where the landscape of the 'Higher Alps' and the summit of the Jungfrau form a perfect backdrop to the main character's lonely struggle with the demons and to his proud rejection of the abbot's offer of help.[14] Another classic from British literature, Charlotte Brontë's *Jane Eyre*, begins with Jane reading Bewick's *History of British Birds*. Here she moves straight from '"the solitary rocks and promontories" by [the birds] only inhabited' – thus clearly echoing her own loneliness – to 'the coast of Norway, studded with isles from its southern extremity, the Lindeness [*sic*], or Naze, to the North Cape' (Brontë 1985, 40).

A passage reflecting a very parallel setting, but far from the suicidal drama of *Manfred* or the heart-rending solitude of *Jane Eyre*, is found in Lord Garvagh's *The Pilgrim of Scandinavia* (1875). Charles John Spencer George Canning, Third Baron Garvagh, belonged to the Irish nobility and was the third generation visiting Norway. His grandfather had been one of the early salmon lords, and his father, an eager hunter of wild reindeer, had had three stone cabins built in the desolate mountains of the inner Sognefjorden area. It is in one of these cabins that Lord Garvagh stays for several months in the late autumn of 1872:

[14] The painter John Martin (1789–1854) showed a very similar scene in 'Manfred on the Jungfrau' (1837). He had also produced a similar picture twenty years earlier, namely 'The Bard' (1817), based on Thomas Gray's poem of the same title from 1757.

Oh! the delight of awaking on that morning after, in a region where time has assumed larger proportions and eternity appears to have commenced! I have lived here in anchoritic seclusion, and been absent from the world for months: and if the life of contemplation treated of by Aristotle is able to be realised on earth, I have realised it in that way. I have found it and enjoyed it alone among those mountains, like a heavenly calm, which none but those who have experienced it, can understand. But it is impossible, without some kind of being made expressly for the purpose to enjoy the tranquillity of that unbroken solitude [*sic*], for the soul seems to escape from its prison-house when upon those heights, and I re-enter from that hermitage upon the customs and usages of civilized life – possessing the secret of a happy dream (199–200).

And he adds: 'The *hermit* standeth out of strife, abiding in a contemplative calmness: what shall he contemplate, – himself? a meagre theme for musing; he hath cast off follies and kept aloof from cares; a man of simple wants; God and the soul, these are his excuse, a just excuse, for solitude' (ibid., 202). This overt celebration of a monastic life among the mountains is not equally attractive to Emily Lowe, the apparently gregarious author of *Unprotected Females in Norway* (1857), but passing the great mountains in the area where Lord Garvagh's cabin was situated, she and her mother felt 'that only in desolate Scandinavia could such a combination of savage loneliness exist. (...) Yes, traveller, if you have a soul devoted to nature's worship, and a heart which responds to her most powerful appeals, pass the Sógne-fjeld' (128–29).

Despite the Romantic interest, if not obsession, with mountains, most of the Romantics themselves remained in the role of observers: 'The ordinary Romantic sightseer, wishing to view the Mer de Glace, could ride a mule all the way to the Montanvert; but he preserved, as he looked upward, the sentiments of the wonderer at a distance' (Robertson 1977, 116). Even Lord Byron, when he pays the Alpine peaks his tribute in *Childe Harold's Pilgrimage*, clearly prefers the distant panorama: '(…) I have seen the soaring Jungfrau rear / Her never-trodden snow, and seen the hoar / Glaciers of bleak Mont Blanc both far and near (…)' (Canto IV, st. 73). It was only after the middle of the nineteenth century that British travellers abroad assumed a more material approach. According to David Robertson's article 'Mid-Victorians amongst the Alps', routes 'to a few high summits, including Mont Blanc (1786) and the Jungfrau (1811), had been discovered by continental chamois-hunters, priests, and savants motivated by curiosity and the spirit of adventure' (Robertson 1977, 116). But it was only in the 1840s and 50s that a more widespread

Raftsund, the Lofoten Islands. Sheltered hamlets and quiet inlets against a background of wild and craggy mountains provided the nineteenth-century traveller with a unique combination of sublime as well as picturesque landscape features. Lithograph from *Norway and Its Glaciers* (1853) by the famous Scottish glaciologist James David Forbes.

interest began to develop in mountaineering for pleasure, and in 1857 The Alpine Club was formed, largely recruiting Oxbridge men, a number of whom were prominent members of British intellectual and professional life.

As a result of this development, the fascination with mountains also became more differentiated than before. The great majority of visitors to the Alpine regions still preferred to admire the summits from a comfortable distance and limit their exertions to leisurely strolls around their hotel. But there was now also another group who preferred a far more direct contact with the elements. The contrast between the two groups is somewhat similar to that between tourists and travellers, which has been discussed in earlier chapters. As the century progressed and the tourist industry expanded, those who regarded themselves as travellers found less and less space unoccupied by queuing groups of tourists. The mountain peaks thus became a new kind of frontier, where they could still celebrate their experience of nature in comparative solitude. This so-called Golden Age of mountaineering lasted from the early 1850s till about 1880 (Keenlyside 1975, 26).[15] One could even say that the mountaineers of the second half of the nineteenth century were the first to make a reality of the Romantic ideal of the *Waldeinsamkeit*, or rather *Bergeinsamkeit*,[16] which Lord Garvagh represented in the quote above. But obviously there were other reasons, too. According to Robertson,

> both agnostics and believers took it for granted that exercise in the Alps cleansed and toned up the moral fibers. (...) To climb safely, a mere speck on a great mountain, was to gain some confidence in human strength, intelligence, and will; it was, at the same time, to undergo a salutary cutting-down to human size and quite possibly, as one member of a party literally roped together, to play down mere self-interest (Robertson 1977, 128–29).

Climbing was linked, in other words, to Victorian public school ideals, which were also closely connected with the success of British imperialism. As suggested above, the great majority of mid-Victorian mountaineers were the very people who had been taught to see themselves as prominent representatives of a global empire. Their

---

[15] According to Keenlyside, 51 out of 74 first ascents in the Alps were made during the Golden Age, including the Matterhorn in 1865.

[16] *Waldeinsamkeit*, meaning literally 'wood solitude' was coined by the German Romantic Ludwig Tieck (1773–1853) in his story 'Der blonde Eckbert' (publ. 1797).

mission was hard work, self-control, loyalty, conquest and supremacy. It is hardly possible to find a hobby whose qualities dovetail more smoothly with those required in the practical administration of imperial life. Very much like the uncharted parts of Africa, the great mountain peaks represented an irresistible temptation to conquer new territory. Mountaineering was thus a highly useful part of an education with a very specific purpose. In John Ruskin's *Frondes Agrestes*,[17] actually a book on aesthetics, any young man of the period would find, in the chapter on mountains, an heroic call to climb as well as to rule:

> Mountains are to the rest of the body of the earth, what violent muscular action is to the body of man. The muscles and tendons of its anatomy are, in the mountain, brought out with force and convulsive energy, full of expression, passion, and strength; the plains and the lower hills are the repose and the effortless motion of the frame, when its muscles lie dormant and concealed beneath the lines of its beauty, – yet ruling those lines in their every undulation. This then is the first grand principle of the truth of the earth. The spirit of the hills is action, that of the lowlands repose; and between these there is to be found every variety of motion and rest, from the inactive plain, sleeping like the firmament, with cities for stars, to the fiery peaks, which, with heaving bosoms and exulting limbs, with the clouds drifting like hair from their bright foreheads, lift up their Titan heads to Heaven, saying, 'I live for ever' (Ruskin 1904, 92–93).

Ruskin, who according to Norman Nicholson found consolation in 'masculine verticals of crags and trees' (Nicholson 1995, 164), then concludes with another bugle call: 'Where they [the mountains] are, they seem to form the world (...), one adamantine dominion and rigid authority of rock' (Ruskin 1904, 93–94).[18] Thus it is possible to read the Romantic and Victorian fascination with mountains as containing a barely concealed subtext on an empire which a few decades later

[17] The book was published in 1875 as an abbreviated version of the first volume of Ruskin's *magnum opus Modern Painters* (1843).

[18] With such an elevated view of mountains, it is not surprising to find that Ruskin had serious problems accepting the presence of increasing hordes of the vulgar masses invading his sanctuary. Barbara Korte claims that he 'found the summits littered with the leftovers of numerous tourists who held picnics while viewing the breathtaking panorama. As he complained in his chapter "Of Modern Landscape" in *Modern Painters*: "Our modern society in general goes to the mountains, not to fast, but to feast, and leaves their glaciers covered with chicken-bones and egg-shells"' (Korte 2000, 84).

would reach its peak, and from which its never-setting sun could be admired.

In Norway, the great pioneer of mountaineering as a sport and pastime is the Englishman William Cecil Slingsby (1849–1929), who first came to Norway in 1872, that is during the Golden Age in the Alps, but *after* the majority of peaks had been climbed for the first time. In the last decades of the century, Norway thus came to represent yet another frontier, with new opportunities for conquering *terrae incognitae*. Not that Slingsby was the first to take an interest in climbing Norwegian mountains. In his book, *Norway the Northern Playground* (1904), he himself pays tribute to some of his countrymen who were there before him. In particular he mentions Lieutenant William Henry Breton, who during his stay in 1834 climbed the Snøhetta; Thomas Forester and his travel companion the Lieutenant (later General) and artist Michael S. Biddulph; and not least the famous Scottish glaciologist James D. Forbes, the author of *Norway and Its Glaciers* (1853), which Slingsby unhesitatingly describes as 'one of the greatest mountain classics' and 'much the best book ever yet written on Norway' (Slingsby 1904, 8). The fact still remains that Slingsby himself made what are generally regarded to be first ascents of a number of the most difficult peaks both in the Jotunheimen and in the Lofoten area.

Given the political implications of Victorian mountaineering, it is interesting to note what a great importance Slingsby places on the intimate historical connections between the British and the Norwegians in this matter. In his preface he claims that the British have inherited from the Norwegians a 'sturdy independence, dogged endurance, and self-reliance' and, as was quoted in chapter 2, 'the best blood which we possess' (ibid., 14). In his account of the history of mountaineering in Norway he extends this explicitly Viking-age perspective:

It is (...) undoubtedly true that the sport of mountaineering was followed by the Vikings nine hundred years ago, as we can see by referring to 'King Olaf Tryggvesson's Saga' in the *Heimskringla*, where we read the following: – 'King Olaf was more expert in all exercises than any man in Norway whose memory is preserved to us in sagas; and he was stronger and more agile than most men, and many stories are written down about it. One is that he ascended the Smalsarhorn (Hornelen, or probably a spur of that grand sea-cliff) and fixed his shield on the very peak. Another is that one of his followers had climbed up the peak after him, until he came to where he could neither get up nor down, but the king came to his help, climbed up to him, took him under his arm, and bore him to the flat ground' (ibid., 6).

He then goes on to establish a triangle of mutual influence in which the British and the Norwegians are united in a common historical past:

> When the Viking days were ended, the spirit of active enterprise in great measure died out in Norway, and possibly lay dormant. (...) In the year 1820 there was a notable reawakening of the sport of mountaineering in the country. Two parties were afield, and Norse climbers have every reason to point to this year with especial pride. (...)
>
> After this, one would naturally have expected that the Norsemen would have continued to practise and to develop the sport up to the present day. Such, however, was not the case, and during the space of at least half a century ice-axes were not used by the natives as implements of snow craft, and practically the sport died out entirely. (...) [M]ountaineering, as a noble sport, was not recognised until it was reintroduced by our countrymen, upon whom the good fortune has fallen of ascending very many of the finest mountains in Norway, of making many new glacier passes, and of reopening others, which, though not new, were quite forgotten (ibid., 6–7).

Thus, by making mountaineering into an originally Norwegian sport, rooted in the Viking age, and then revived by modern Britons, Slingsby somehow weaves the destinies of the two nations together.[19] Despite these overtly Anglo-Norwegian elements, however, his conclusion at the end of the book returns to a more conventional celebration of nature, in which the mountains are imbued not only with the ability to produce men of physical strength and courage (women were rarely mentioned in this context) and to heal what a hundred years later would have been called the stress symptoms connected with modern life; they are also portrayed as moral teachers, reflecting Wordsworth's dictum about the vernal wood, that it 'May teach you more of man; / Of moral evil and of good, / Than all the sages can' (Wordsworth and Coleridge 1978, 105):

---

[19] In Edna Lyall's *A Hardy Norseman* (1890), the famous mountain Romsdalshorn is used in a similar way. Throughout the novel it represents to Frithiof, the young Norwegian eking out a meagre existence in London, a symbol of the home, love and moral values he will not give up. In a dream during a severe illness, the dangerous climb to its summit echoes this struggle, and at the end of the novel his happiness is complete when, under precisely the Romsdalshorn, Cecil [*sic*], the patient and faithful London girl, accepts his proposal of marriage.

The mountains of Norway – probably the oldest in Europe – invite us all. Let us go then and learn amongst them the wholesome lessons which Nature never withholds from those who really love her. (...) No man, however callous he may be by nature, can be much amongst the high mountains without gaining strength of character as well as physical strength. (...) Go then to the mountains for all that is best worth having in life. Learn again in the mountain solitudes the lessons which you learned on your mother's knee, and perhaps have forgotten in the bustle of this noisy world. (...) The high mountains are the natural playground of those who are endowed with health and strength. They are the resting-places for the weary. Then away to the mountains, away, away, and glean more health and strength of mind and body to enable you to combat the difficulties of life, and to lay up a rich store of happy memories from which you can always draw, yet can never exhaust (ibid., 421–22).

As has been emphasised in the preceding section, the Romantic landscape is frequently of a vertical or perpendicular nature. This does not mean, however, that horizontal landscapes cannot also exert a powerful or sublime impression. In *The Spectator* in 1712, Joseph Addison discusses the question of greatness, which Burke later calls 'vastness':

By *greatness*, I do not only mean the bulk of any single object, but the largeness of a whole view, considered as one entire piece. Such are the prospects of an open champian country, a vast uncultivated desert, of huge heaps of mountains, high rocks and precipices, or a wide expanse of waters, where we are not struck with the novelty or beauty of the sight, but with that rude kind of magnificence which appears in many of these stupendous works of nature (quoted in Ashfield and de Bolla 1998, 62).

And in an article only a week later, he gives a description of a literary landscape which could just as well have been Norwegian as Greek: 'Reading the *Iliad* is like travelling through a country uninhabited, where the fancy is entertained with a thousand savage prospects of vast deserts, wide uncultivated marshes, huge forests, misshapen rocks and precipices' (ibid., 66). Also such philosophers of the sublime as Hugh Blair and William Chambers underline the aesthetic effect produced by huge tracts of barren wastes and 'gloomy woods' (ibid., 214 and 268). Even William Gilpin, in his *Observations*, makes explicit mention of a Cumberland landscape characterised by desolation: 'We now approached the lake of Wyburn, or Thirlmer, as it is sometimes called; an object every way suited to the ideas of desolation, which surround it. No tufted verdure graces it's [*sic*] banks, nor hanging woods throw rich reflections on it's [*sic*] surface:

but every form, which it suggests, is savage, and desolate' (Gilpin 1973, 171).

As has been intimated earlier, it is obvious from several of the travel accounts that the empty, desolate landscape exists as an aesthetic category with which the travellers are already familiar from literature. When in 1856 the 'Two Unknown Quantities' John Willis Clark and Joseph W. Dunning cross the Hardangervidda, the central mountain plateau in the south of Norway, they experience a landscape whose solitude and barrenness are reminiscent of the tortuous 'field of thorns' from medieval vision literature:

> For six hours we traversed a vast and wild expanse of hideous barrenness. If there be upon earth a spot disregarded by its Creator, where conscience-stricken spirits roam, seeking in their unrest to escape themselves, surely on the Hardanger fjeld must be that spot! Oh, the monotony of that dreary ride! a monotony that crept into one's very vitals, stopped the flow of conversation, and thus increased seven-fold its own dismal horrors. It was not that calm and peaceful solitude in which man delights to commune with himself, and which calls forth oft-times the highest aspirations of his soul. It was a solitude where everything bore the blank aspect of desolation: even the humpy hills that rose above the plateau looked like the deformed excrescences of a neglected body, and possessed no beauty of form: the scattered rocks and withered herbage told only of ruin and despair. It was an almost colourless waste, relieved only by the presence of here and there a lake (Clark and Dunning 1857, 134–35).

This characterisation, which is far gloomier than that which a modern nature lover would give, is clearly indebted to the tradition mentioned earlier of regarding everything but the fertile plains and valleys as unfortunate consequences of the Fall. From the point of view of civilisation and culture, the landscape is perceived as a ruin. But these observations are also closely related to the Romantic idea of the solitary wanderer, who is exiled from society and who, in his uncompromising independence, chooses a life of splendid isolation. This Romantic ideal also serves to explain John George Hollway's description of the view from the Snøhetta, which for a long time was thought to be the highest mountain in Norway. First he assures the reader that 'it is impossible to give any idea of the peculiar effect of the desolation, complete and entire, which lay all around', and then he claims: 'I believe for a circle of fourteen or fifteen English miles radius from the spot where we stood there is not a single human habitation except one hunter's hut' (Hollway 1853, 120). Thus, there is almost an element of competition involved in the attitude to natural wastes: the further from civilisation, both literally and figuratively, the more genuine the experience. Thomas Forester's account shows clearly that even though the scenery seems dreary and depressing, it possesses precisely the required qualities:

> [D]esolate as all appeared, and difficult as was the progress, I had begun to experience those peculiar sensations which De Saussure[20] somewhere finely describes in his 'Voyages' in the Alps, and which I had previously felt in ascending high altitudes. In such situations, the great purity of the air, the unbounded solitude, and the grandeur of the scale of the objects presented, concur in affecting the mind with feelings of serenity, of freedom, and of awe. One seems to be lifted above the turbid atmosphere in which the cares and turmoils of the world unceasingly estuate; to be emancipated from the thraldom of passion and all gross and sordid influences; at the same time that the spirit is bowed, in the presence of the majesty of Nature, under a profound sense of one's own insignificance (Forester 1850, 136).

There is a powerful suggestion in this passage of a divine presence, even though it is not presented as a personal god. Arthur de Capell Brooke comes considerably closer to such an identification during his journey across the Dovrefjell, but still remains firmly in the tradition of the sublime:

> The scenery throughout the Dovrefield is of the sublimest and most imposing nature, though, in some parts, differing essentially in its distinguishing character. While ascending the first pass of the mountain, and when at the summit, a melancholy wildness prevails. (...) All is here majestic and sublime, though unattended with anything like beauty, or even what is generally termed fine scenery. The chief emotions felt are those of awe and reverence, not unmixed with silent pleasure. The mind, wandering from earth, fruitlessly endeavours to dive into futurity, and asks, what will be the end of these gigantic forms? and when will the time arrive, in which the mighty Dovrefield itself shall be split asunder, and its huge mountains, after becoming perhaps the instruments in the hands of an all powerful arm, to crush a guilty world, return again to chaos? Nature viewed with all these features has a strong tendency to elevate the mind, and divert it from the grovelling scenes of life; while the thoughts are irresistibly carried to the contemplation of that awful

---

[20] Horace Bénédict de Saussure (1740–1799), was a Swiss scientist and Alpine traveller. During most of his life he conducted important geological, chemical and meteorological investigations in the Alps, and he offered a prize to the first person to climb Mont Blanc.

Being, who, as he formed it with a nod, can as easily bid it dissolve and vanish into æther (Brooke 1823, 137–8).

As will become apparent from the next section, on waterfalls, the intensity of the individual experience is closely connected with the degree of divinity that the viewer finds in the scene.

The Norwegian forests seem to have had much of the same emotional impact on the traveller as the empty wastes. A representative text in this connection is the novel *Lofoden, or The Exiles of Norway* (1849) by Edward Wilson Landor, whose *Adventures in the North of Europe* (1835) was discussed in the Introduction. *The Exiles of Norway* is set in the 'Ranas-fjeld' (Ranafjellene) in the north of Norway, and the Anglo-Polish hero, with the unlikely name of Lofoden, braves both wolves and starvation in his attempt to cross the lonely wastes:

> What terrors lurk in that dark forest, from which the traveller cannot guard himself! They are everywhere about and around him. (…) He feels their presence, though he may behold nothing save the dark trunks of countless myriads of pine-trees, more gloomy from their superincumbent loads of snow. (…) Reader! I have passed alone, and on foot, through this dreary forest, and have learned, perhaps, some of its secrets – unless you, too, have done so, scoff not at the mysterious awe which weighs upon the heart during days of lonely travel (Landor 1849, 3).

Furthermore, the Beatles may not have been aware of historical connections when writing 'Norwegian Wood', but the fact remains that in the British consciousness the pine tree has for centuries been as closely connected with Norway as the bagpipe with Scotland. Due to the considerable export of timber from Norway to Britain – and until the arrival of steam ships particularly that of ships' masts – this was the primary point of reference concerning a country about which little else was known.[21] Thus, in the poem *Annus Mirabilis, or The Year of Wonders* (1666), John Dryden mentions Norway and fir trees precisely in connection with ships' masts, and so does John Milton the following year. When describing Satan's spear in Book I of *Paradise Lost*, he compares it to 'the tallest pine / Hewn on Norwegian hills to be the mast of some great Ammiral' (ll. 292–4). Shelley picks up the same image in *The Revolt of Islam* (1818), in

---

[21] Norwegian timber exports to Britain, which had been considerable before the Napoleonic Wars, reached a new peak in the 1860s and early 1870s, when the volume rose to more than 2 mill. cubic metres per year (Danielsen et al. 1995, 234).

which Laon trembles 'like one aspen pale / Among the gloomy pines of a Norwegian vale' (Canto XII, st. 6), and in 'Lines Written among the Euganean Hills' (ll. 269–70).[22] Shelley may well have had in mind a passage from a book that his wife Mary (then Godwin) brought with her when they eloped to France in 1814, namely her mother's *A Short Residence*. During her stay in Tønsberg, Mary Wollstonecraft visits a manor (which must be Jarlsberg), and gives a peculiarly striking description of the surrounding wood:

> Time had given a greyish cast to their ever-green foliage; and they stood, like sires of the forest, sheltered on all sides by a rising progeny. I had not ever seen so many oaks together in Norway, as in these woods, nor such large aspens as here were agitated by the breeze, rendering the wind audible – nay, musical; for melody seemed on the wing around me. How different was the fresh odour that re-animated me in the avenue, from the damp chillness of the apartments; and as little did the gloomy thoughtfulness excited by the dusty hangings, and worm-eaten pictures, resemble the reveries inspired by the soothing melancholy of their shade. In the winter, these august pines, towering above the snow, must relieve the eye beyond measure, and give life to the white waste.
>
> The continual recurrence of pine and fir groves, in the day, sometimes wearies the sight; but, in the evening, nothing can be more picturesque, or, more properly speaking, better calculated to produce poetical images. Passing through them, I have been struck with a mystic kind of reverence, and I did, as it were, homage to their venerable shadows. Not nymphs, but philosophers, seemed to inhabit them – ever musing; I could scarcely conceive that they were without some consciousness of existence – without a calm enjoyment of the pleasure they diffused (Wollstonecraft 1987, 118–19).

And she adds a passage pointing very strongly forward to Wordsworth's more famous reflections only a few years later: 'How often do my feelings produce ideas that remind me of the origin of many poetical fictions. In solitude, the imagination bodies forth its conceptions unrestrained, and stops enraptured to adore the beings of its own creation. These are moments of bliss; and the memory recalls them with delight' (ibid., 119). Precisely the same sense of a pantheistic communion informs Charles W. Wood's observation in *Under Northern Skies*, where an explicit identification is made

---

[22] Examples of other, less illustrious Romantic and Victorian poets who also connected Norway with the pine, were Bernard Barton (1784–1849), Richard Mant (1776–1848), Emmeline Stuart-Wortley (1806–1855), Sir Lewis Morris (1833–1907) and James Logie Robertson (1846–1922).

between nature and divinity. Driving through the deep pine forests, he claims that 'trees are pillars and branches are the aisles and fretted vaults of Nature's cathedrals: with these she [i.e. Norway] is independent of Gothic arches and crumbling walls' (Wood 1886, 301). The man-made evidence of religious worship, visible in other countries in the form of cathedrals, is in Norway substituted by God's own architecture.

A final and equally powerful indication of the pine being firmly connected with Norway in the British consciousness appears in Lady Wilde's account, published thirty-two years after her visit. Jean A. Mains's critical reading of the book reveals that Lady Wilde, probably without having seen much of the country, turns to descriptions which correspond to stereotyped ideas about the Norwegian scenery, including everywhere and in particular the pine. Her narrative shows her, Mains concludes, 'obsessed with the pine and oblivious of the birch, typical tree of the *fjells* she never saw' (Mains 1989, 81).

'The Sounding Cataracts'

'The sounding cataract / Haunted me like a passion'. If one were to look for the ultimate emblem of Romantic nature worship, waterfalls would seem to be the obvious choice. It is difficult to conceive of a natural phenomenon that during this period had a more magnetic attraction for travellers, writers, composers and painters alike. Even though Britain has relatively little to offer in the way of spectacular waterfalls, there is no doubt that Wordsworth's phrase from 'Tintern Abbey' is representative not just of the Romantic generation, but of the nineteenth century as a whole. Waterfalls echoed loudly in the art and writing of the period, and created an aesthetic taste which remained constant in succeeding centuries.

Behind this fascination lies of course the more timeless and universal fascination with water, and in particular the river, which could almost be regarded as an archetypal image. In *Rivermen: A Romantic Iconography of the River and the Source* (1989), Frederic S. Colwell gives some of the reasons why the river seems to have such a profound appeal for the artistic imagination:

> Unlike the rhythms of Ocean, rivers have direction and purposive flow. The river's will is always its own, not laid down by man, for whom the river passage demands a surrender to its will, its currents and eddies. To

move with the flow is to course with time and change; to stand astride or view it from a height offers the prophetic stance by which we contemplate its entire passage, its past, present, and the brightening waters or rippling shoals ahead (4).

And a few pages later he adds: 'Rivers baffled by shallows or circuiting through meanders, sinking into the earth and surfacing, rushing streams swelled by tributaries to a lordlier dimension and statelier pace, all serve as recurrent metaphors for the progress of the poetic sensibility and its chronicle' (ibid., 20). It is not surprising, therefore, to find that a poet such as Wordsworth figures prominently in Colwell's river study:

> The Wordsworthian source is a secluded, private, and generally secret place. To reach it requires some effort, but it lies almost, as it were, at hand. There is no eruption of demonic energy to overwhelm the seeker after sources; its emergence is epiphanic rather than apocalyptic, and it offers communion rather than terror. And yet the place is pervaded with the mystery of inexhaustible life welling from darkness into light, and we are invariably aware of an engaging presence, subtle, elusive, and pervasively feminine, whose charge it is (ibid., 47).

This 'pervasively feminine' presence, however, is nowhere to be found in the Alpine or Norwegian waterfalls, which are, on the contrary, characterised by overtly masculine qualities.[23] For like mountains, waterfalls are closely connected with the vertical landscape. Even though water is an element normally seen on the horizontal plane and, except in a stormy ocean, as relatively calm, the waterfall shows it in a state of considerable agitation and sometimes, as we shall see, breathtaking fury. Thus the waterfall also constitutes an important part of the inventory of the sublime. One of the late eighteenth-century writers on the sublime, William Marshall, claims in a review from 1795 that

> [a] giant precipice, frowning over its base, whether we view it from beneath, or look downward from its brink, is capable of producing sublime emotions. A river tumbling headlong over such a precipice, especially if it be viewed with difficulty and a degree of danger, real or

---

[23] It is hardly a coincidence that Frankenstein's masculine thirst for knowledge in Mary Shelley's novel – largely set in the Alpine region – is likened to a mountain river that rose 'from ignoble and almost forgotten sources; but, swelling as it proceeded, it became the torrent which, in its course, has swept away all my hopes and joys' (Shelley 1992, 38).

imaginary, still heightens those emotions (Ashfield and de Bolla 1998, 276).

Similarly Wollstonecraft's fellow feminist Helen Maria Williams, in her book *A Tour in Switzerland* (1798), struggles to find words after visiting the 24 metre high falls at Schaffhausen: '(…) the moments I have passed in contemplating thy sublimity will form an epoch in my short span!' (ibid., 304).

It is this quality that is reflected in Byron's and Shelley's waterfalls, which are inspired not by English streams but by Alpine torrents. In *Childe Harold's Pilgrimage* the waterfall comes across as an unstoppable force, in a sublime blend of the creative and the destructive. This is how the passage begins:

> The roar of waters! – from the headlong height
> Velino cleaves the wave-worn precipice;
> The fall of waters! rapid as the light
> The flashing mass foams shaking the abyss;
> The hell of waters! where they howl and hiss,
> And boil in endless torture; while the sweat
> Of their great agony, wrung out from this
> Their Phlegethon, curls round the rocks of jet
> That guard the gulf around (…) (Canto IV, st. 69)

Shelley is indebted to the same landscape when in *Alastor* he describes the rivulet which, akin to the composer Bedrich Smetana's majestic *Moldau* (1874), gathers volume and momentum on its way down the mountain side, transforming itself into a 'broad river, / Foaming and hurrying o'er its rugged path' before plunging 'into that immeasurable void / Scattering its waters to the passing winds' (ll. 567–70).[24]

The Victorians were no less occupied with waterfalls than the Romantics; it would be easy to collect an anthology of Victorian verse on waterfalls, cataracts, torrents and cascades. John Ruskin, previously quoted on mountains, for example, also wrote on waterfalls. In the first volume of *Modern Painters*, in the chapter 'Of the Foreground', he discusses at length Turner's engraving The

---

[24] Other Romantic poets who wrote poems specifically on waterfalls include John Clare ('Fragment: The Cataract Whirling to the Precipiece' [*sic*]); Samuel T. Coleridge ('On a Cataract from a Cavern Near the Summit of a Mountain Precipice'); William Wordsworth ('The Waterfall and the Eglantine'); and Robert Southey ('The Cataract of Lodore').

Upper Fall of Tees, and in *Frondes Agrestes* (1875) he comments, in the same way as Helen Maria Williams, on the falls at Schaffhausen:

> Stand for half an hour beside the fall of Schaffhausen, on the north side, where the rapids are long, and watch how the vault of water first bends unbroken, in pure polished velocity, over the arching rocks at the brow of the cataract, covering them with a dome of crystal twenty feet thick, so swift that its motion is unseen except when a foam globe from above darts over it like a falling star; and how the trees are lighted above it under all their leaves, at the instant that it breaks into foam (...) (Ruskin 1904, 66).

It is no coincidence, in other words, that Sir John Everett Millais's famous portrait of Ruskin, commissioned by Ruskin himself in 1853, shows him standing in front of a torrent in Scotland. He even wrote to his father that 'I am sure the foam of the torrent will be something quite new in art' (Wood 1983, 34). The popular fiction of the late nineteenth century, too, showed an awareness of the significance of waterfalls. In the story 'The Final Problem', which was an attempt by Sir Arthur Conan Doyle to bring an end to the adventures of Sherlock Holmes, he set the stage for his hero's final encounter with Professor Moriarty by the fall of Reichenbach, from which he never returned:

> It is, indeed, a fearful place. The torrent, swollen by the melting snow, plunges into a tremendous abyss, from which the spray rolls up like the smoke from a burning house. The shaft into which the river hurls itself is an immense chasm, lined by glistening, coal-black rock, and narrowing into a creaming, boiling pit of incalculable depth, which brims over and shoots the stream onward over its jagged lip. The long sweep of green water roaring for ever down, and the thick flickering curtain of spray hissing forever upwards, turn a man giddy with their constant whirl and clamour (Doyle 1993, 264).

Maybe this use of the waterfall as a place of death and destruction could also be seen as an expression of an increasingly bleak and pessimistic vision of nature, calling to mind 'the slime and ooze' of the Thames in the opening paragraphs of Dickens's *Our Mutual Friend* (1865), a novel in which the river of life and the river of death melt imperceptibly into one.

For British visitors to Norway, however, there is no doubt that waterfalls were the one landscape feature most generally sought after and admired. A number of writers appear to travel from one waterfall to another in an almost obsessive manner. Robert Latham says after his journey in 1833 that 'they are the *points* of the country, the pre-eminent lions, and those which if a traveller fail in seeing, he takes shame to himself for his incuriousness' (Latham 1840, 1: 75). Similarly, Charles Kelsall, an incurable classicist who published his book *Horae Viaticae* (1836) under the pseudonym Mela Britannicus, appears to have visited a dozen waterfalls during a short tour of southern Norway, continuously revelling in their sound, which 'assailed my auricular organs' (86).[25] This undisputable prominence of waterfalls as 'the thing to see' is further confirmed by a somewhat humorous passage in Charles Elton's *The Road and the Fell*, where he describes a boat trip into the Hardangerfjorden in order to see the Vøringsfossen. Besides the Rjukanfossen, this was undoubtedly the most famous of the Norwegian waterfalls, and on board was a Frenchman, who long before they arrived had worked himself into a frenzy of enthusiastic expectation: 'When we were opposite the entrance of the Hardanger Fjord he became very much excited, and cried: "I am coming near it! I am coming near! for thirty years I dream of Vöring Foss!"' (Elton 1864, 125).[26]

Naturally, to the large majority of travellers, the Norwegian waterfalls were simply a spectacular aesthetic experience, but there were also scientists among them. The famous geologist and glaciologist James David Forbes spends a whole chapter on waterfalls at the end of *Norway and Its Glaciers* (1853), offering scientific explanations for their vast numbers. According to Jean A. Mains, Forbes saw the waterfalls as 'the result of [Norway's] configuration, of its broad, flat mountains or fells and its deep, widely separated valleys combined with its excessive precipitation in the form of rain or snow. During autumn, winter and spring, this precipitation accumulated as snow on the high *plateaux* and, in consequence, the waterfalls then were reduced or dried up. But, during the long, warm days of summer, it thawed and in this, the tourist season, the falls were therefore at maximum volume' (Mains 1989, 184–85).

---

[25] At Tinnfoss (now Notodden) in Telemark, he even conjured up some self-made Latin verse: 'I took my farewell of the Tind-foss in the following extempore:

Cedite, Romani cataractes! Cedite, Graii!

Tinfosso cedat quicquid ubique ruit!' (Britannicus 1836, 99).

[Yield, O Roman cataracts! Yield, those of Greece!

Everything that rushes, wherever it be, must yield to the Tinnfoss!]

(The authors are indebted to Dr Jon Haarberg for the translation.)

[26] W. F. Ainsworth similarly claims that Vøringsfossen is 'a cataract of such sublimity, that a visit to Norway would be worse than incomplete without having contemplated and thereby identified oneself with its wonders' (Ainsworth 1862, 60).

The less scientifically minded traveller, however, paid attention to a different kind of quantity, because Norway possessed not merely a few spectacular falls; rather every leg of the journey was full of them. The historian James Anthony Froude, after a trip in a private yacht in the summer of 1881, claimed that 'I counted seventeen [waterfalls] all close about us when we anchored, any one of which would have made the fortune of a Scotch hotel, and would have been celebrated by Mr. Murray in pages of passionate eloquence' (Froude 1882, 206). In a Thomas Cook brochure from 1890, the traveller is similarly promised that 'you will pass waterfalls and cascades which would make a fortune to "proprietors" in Switzerland, and are not so much as mentioned in the Norwegian guide-books' (Cook 1890, 5). Charles Francis Keary, however, surpasses all his fellow travellers by insisting that '[y]ou may travel for days and yet the sound of them be never out of your ears. I have counted as many as four-and-twenty, standing in one spot' (Keary 1892, 27). Half a century earlier, on his way to Lærdal on the west coast, John Barrow Jr. even draws an analogy between various terms of musical expression and the many different waterfalls he passes along the road:

> Oft, as I sat musing in my little carriole, did I listen to the mingled sounds of cascades, cataracts, and waterfalls, of mountain-torrents, brawling brooks, and gurgling rills, with the sharper and sweeter notes of the feathered tribe, around and over head, 'harmoniously confused,' and even imagined I could arrange their diversified sounds into some kind of order like the notes of the musical scale. The deep and solemn tone of the waterfall was suited to the *Adagio*; the various sounds of the cascade, as it leaped from rock to rock, corresponded with the *Andante*; the rattling cataract, among the fragments of its rocky bed, resembled the *Allegretto*, and the trickling rill in its descent, emitting – 'A silver sound, that heavenly music seemed to make' – was a sort of *ad libitum*, – and, thus indulged in these freaks of the imagination, did I while away the time, and shorten the journey across this wild and highly romantic mountain passage (Barrow 1834, 251–52).

There is also evidence that those of the travellers who have seen waterfalls in other parts of the world prefer the Norwegian ones. William Mattieu Williams, in *Through Norway with Ladies* (1877), visits the Leirfoss falls outside Trondheim, and

> [a]lthough these are only classed with the ordinary waterfalls of Norway, we all agreed that they are finer than any in Switzerland. (…) This first and moderate experience of Norwegian waterfalls prepared those among our party who had travelled in Switzerland, to recant their scepticism

THE SKJÆGGEDALSFOS.

The Skjeggedalsfossen, near Odda in Hardanger. In accordance with the conventions of the sublime and of Romantic landscape painting, the forces of nature, here represented by the waterfall, are depicted as awesome and omnipotent, whereas the human beings, placed on a rock in the foreground, almost vanish from view. The main waterfall is more than 500 feet high.

concerning what I had stated respecting the great superiority of Scandinavian to Alpine waterfalls (15–16).

Similarly Charles W. Wood, having presented a quick survey of the world's greatest falls, dismisses them all in favour of the Norwegian ones, and for an interesting reason: '[T]he great waterfalls of Norway are different. They are remote and difficult to reach; they are amidst the mountains; they roar and thunder for ever in desert-like solitudes; you come upon them surrounded by all that is beautiful and wild and romantic in Nature' (Wood 1886, 341). Norway, in other words, gains a head on her competitors simply by offering attractions which are further away from civilisation than those in other countries, and which can therefore be enjoyed more intensely – and perhaps more genuinely – by the solitary traveller. Clearly, these are also qualities primarily connected with the sublime. Charles Elliott certainly conjures up all the familiar terms from his aesthetic vocabulary when he visits the Vøringsfossen in the July of 1830:

> We stood for some minutes contemplating with a mixture of surprise and terror this savage spectacle. In the gulf below was the blackness of darkness: a glimmering of light reflected through the sinuous valley just made the 'darkness visible,' and discovered 'shades' in which the ruins of some stony buttresses of the world lie mingled together in mighty fragments and in strange confusion. All is naked and abrupt. The common terms of language are lost in the description of a spot probably unrivalled in point of savage wildness and fearful sublimity. The surrounding country consorts with the impression this scene is calculated to inspire. All nature stands aghast. The very mountains seem petrified by the sight. The bare surfaces of gneiss are unvaried by a single tree or moss; and animals fly from a wild which may almost be said to terrify the vegetable creation (Elliott 1832, 168).

And Olivia Stone, whose book *Norway in June* (1882) went through three editions in seven years, even quotes Burke's *On the Sublime and Beautiful* while watching the Slettafossen in Romsdal: '"the noise of vast cataracts (...) awakes a great and awful sensation in the mind, though we can observe no nicety or artifice in those sorts of music"' (114). Earlier in the book she also reveals her fascination with waterfalls by discussing Coleridge's reflections on the same topic, and by quoting the following anonymous poem:

> And lo! two cataracts, from rival cliffs,
> Springing to meet and marry in mid air:
> Marry! it is the meeting of two wolves;

They foam, they tear, they wrestle in their ire,
Till spent they sink, and, cowering, roll in one
Their green and glimmering waters down the vale
Beyond (113).[27]

Here the two cataracts are personified – a typically pantheistic means
of establishing a connection between the animate and the inanimate
world – as two fighting wolves. Viewing the Vøringsfossen as a
monster, Frederic Metcalfe employs precisely the same device:

> Did not he writhe, and dart, and foam, and roar like some hideous
> projectile blazing across the dark sky at night. Such a sight I shall never
> behold again. It was truly terrific. It was well that the guide held me fast,
> for a strange feeling, such as Byron describes, as if of wishing to jump
> overboard, came over me in spite of myself (Metcalfe 1858, 148).

Another use of personification is found in James Logie Robertson's
'The Cataract' (1882), another of his Norwegian sonnets. But here the
cataract is not a wolf or a monster. On the contrary, Robertson reads
a distinctly erotic attraction into the contrast between the male
cataract and the female river (Norw. *elv*):

See where he bursts in beauty bar and lock
   In a fierce haste to wed with her below,
   The gentle Elv, that steals with rippling flow
Along the deep-sunk dale! With what a shock
His feet alight on this pink granite block!
   And how, half-stunned, he staggers to and fro,
   Compelled to pause, yet passionate to go,
Till, steadying all his strength, he shoots the rock!
The hazel coppice and a belt of pine
   Receive him next after his madman's bound;
Yet still I see his great eyes, questing, shine
   Between the branches; and I hear the sound
Of one whose lip is near some joy divine,
   Broken, and low, and last in rapture drowned.

---

[27] The poem, entitled 'Night', is written by the Scottish Dissenting minister,
literary critic, and editor George Gilfillan (1813–1878), who visited Norway in 1860.
It was published in 1867 and reflects his experience from the Romsdal area. Ref.
Mains 1989, 262. Stone here gives an interesting example of how many of the
travelogues find themselves in an intertextual dialogue with other writers, including
former travel writers on Norway as well as poets and aesthetic philosophers.

Arthur de Capell Brooke, too, sounds like a woeful, yearning lover when reluctantly he leaves a waterfall near Lillehammer:

> I have no hesitation in considering it to be by far the most beautiful and extraordinary cataract I saw during my tour in the north (...) . It was with reluctance I quitted this enchanting spot; and when on my descent I got to the bend of the torrent, I looked up with regret to its waters glistening at a distance through the dark shade of the pines, while fond expectation dwelt on the chances fortune might again throw in my way of revisiting them (Brooke 1823, 112–13).

As has been emphasised earlier, the typical nineteenth-century communion with nature is an individual, one-to-one experience; hence the striking absence of companions in most of the travelogues. This powerful sense of solitude also characterises Mary Wollstonecraft's visit to the falls at Sarpsborg, and in her case the overwhelming scene becomes an image of the emotional whirlpool in which the lonely traveller and abandoned lover finds herself:

> Reaching the cascade, or rather cataract, the roaring of which had a long time announced its vicinity, my soul was hurried by the falls into a train of reflections. The impetuous dashing of the rebounding torrent from the dark cavities which mocked the exploring eye, produced an equal activity in my mind: my thoughts darted from earth to heaven, and I asked myself why I was chained to life and its misery? Still the tumultuous emotions this sublime object excited, were pleasurable; and, viewing it, my soul rose, with renewed dignity, above its cares – grasping at immortality – it seemed as impossible to stop the current of my thoughts, as of the always varying, still the same, torrent before me – I stretched out my hand to eternity, bounding over the dark speck of life to come (Wollstonecraft 1987, 152–53).[28]

Wollstonecraft's outstretched hand is reminiscent of the despair in the passage from Tennyson's *In Memoriam*, where the poet, in section 55, stretches out 'lame hands of faith', and so it also points forward to the general tendency of Victorian travellers to combine Romantic nature worship with their own and more orthodox religiosity. The result is often a new kind of sublimity, in which a powerful and altogether rather gloomy Old Testament Jehova makes man even

---

[28] In his Introduction to the Penguin edition of Wollstonecraft's book, Richard Holmes offers some fascinating speculations on the possible connections between this passage and the description of the river in Coleridge's poem 'Kubla Khan' (ref. Wollstonecraft 1987, 39–40).

smaller and more victimised than in the eighteenth-century discussions of the sublime. Charles Elliott, who on more than one occasion shows a rather lively imagination, offers a good example of a writer who reads himself into the landscape and literally robes himself in apocalyptic, biblical images. He begins his account of the Rjukanfossen, which, according to Robert Bremner, 'by northern travellers, is pronounced the most magnificent waterfall in Europe' (Bremner 1840, 111), by employing the well-known terminology of the sublime:

> I do not remember to have seen a sight so calculated to inspire terror. The Moen [Måne-elven] rushes through a rock blackened by time, and falls from a height of four hundred and fifty feet perpendicularly into a caldron [*sic*] of the same dark material. The foam, or *riuken*, rises so high as to conceal from the distant spectator the depth of the fall, which we could duly appreciate only when lying on the ground and looking over the edge of the precipice at its highest point. Whether real or fancied, the earth seemed to tremble under the concussion of the continuous torrent (Elliott 1832, 111).

But then references to Genesis seem to gain the upper hand, including the majestic symbol of the Covenant:

> At this moment the sun burst from behind a cloud, and, shining upon the falling water and the playful spray, cast obliquely on the dark background a perfect double rainbow approaching nearly to a circle. The effect was exceedingly striking. Placed in the only point where the circumference was incomplete, we saw ourselves clothed with the rainbow. Unprepared as we were for so extraordinary a position, it was too sublime; and we almost shuddered at the glory of the vesture with which we were surrounded: while in the beauty and grandeur of this masterpiece of his hand, we recognized the power of Him who 'weigheth the mountains in scales,' and 'covereth himself with light as with a garment' (ibid., 111–12).

A related feature which becomes more apparent from the middle of the century onwards is the Tennysonian and angst-producing combination of religious doubt and cultural criticism, on the one hand, and the growth of the natural sciences and industrial progress, on the other. Even the observation of something as distant as Norwegian waterfalls seems to come under the influence of this persistent sense of uncertainty. Thus Thomas Forester's description from 1850 of the Rjukanfossen, which ought to have been a celebration of the wonder of creation, carries instead an atmosphere of existential unease. For a moment, the reader is even held in confusion as to the potential ambiguity of the word 'the Fall', with a capital F. But it is particularly towards the end of his long and dramatic description that Forester strikes a note in which the fusion of religion and science sounds discordant and threatening rather than edifying:

> The discharge of each successive wave of the mighty torrent was accompanied by a hissing sound, from which the fall derives its name of Rjukan, the steaming or *reeking* foss – the hoarse breathings of the mysterious spirit which, with unwearied energy, has worked since time was in that marvellous laboratory, and, with ceaseless throbs, will yet discharge those mingled volumes of steam and water, until that final catastrophe, when some yet mightier power of nature shall dissolve even the solid framework of those granite cliffs (Forester 1850, 99–100).

To a modern reader, at least, the combination of the 'hissing sound' of some laboratory and the 'final catastrophe' carries very little of the fundamental confidence in a benevolent nature that is visible in a poet like Wordsworth at the beginning of the century. Thus it seems that even the perceptions and 'readings' of Norwegian waterfalls are affected by the changing historical and cultural conditions of the visiting travellers.

The Fjords and the Arctic

Despite the fascination with mountains and waterfalls in the Norwegian interior, both Britain and Norway were first of all major maritime nations whose landscapes, histories and livelihoods had always been intimately connected with their coastlines. Also, before the arrival of aeroplanes, the coast most often provided the foreign traveller with a first and significant impression of the country. Thus, the Britons observing the Norwegian coast for the first time were natural connoisseurs of coastlines. It is not surprising, therefore, to find that a writer such as Francis M. Wyndham dwells on the impression of the coast as he approaches land to the south of Bergen. Initially, his description reveals a touch of disappointment: the view apparently does not quite live up to what 'my expectations had led me to anticipate' (Wyndham 1861, 2). But he then goes on: 'Still there was something sublime in the wide expanse of water being thus abruptly terminated by a stern wall of rock' (ibid., 3).

However, the more lively descriptions are reserved for the unique and distinguishing features that formed, and still form, the greatest natural attraction of the Norwegian landscape, namely the fjords. John Barrow Jr. says simply that 'I believe such deep and numerous inlets of the sea (...) are not to be met with in any other part of the world, accompanied with such romantic wildness and beauty, so well calculated to attract the admiration and rivet the attention of the traveller' (Barrow 1834, 318). The largest of them, the Sognefjorden, which is also the largest fjord in the world, penetrates more than 200 kilometres into the Scandinavian peninsula, and is surrounded by mountains more than 2,000 metres high. This dramatic combination of the horizontal sea and the perpendicular mountains produces a constellation of sublime landscape features that are hardly equalled anywhere. In the following, a selection of descriptions from the Norwegian coastline will be used to suggest various aspects of the voyage from the south and all the way up to the north, where the qualities associated with the Arctic will be given particular attention.

Once again it is tempting to begin with Mary Wollstonecraft, who strikes the rough and turbulent note that characterises most of these accounts. In the present context it is worth keeping in mind that the voyage in the small boats used by many of the travellers to Norway, at least before the middle of the nineteenth century, must have provided a very different first encounter from that experienced in the giant cruise and passenger ships of the twenty-first century. Wollstonecraft, crossing the outer part of the Oslofjorden, explains that '[w]rapping my great coat round me, I lay down on some sails at the bottom of the boat, its motion rocking me to rest, till a discourteous wave interrupted my slumbers' (Wollstonecraft 1987, 95), whereupon she describes the actual voyage:

> The sea was boisterous; but, as I had an experienced pilot, I did not apprehend any danger. Sometimes I was told, boats are driven far out and lost. However, I seldom calculate chances so nicely – sufficient for the day is the obvious evil!
> We had to steer amongst islands and huge rocks, rarely losing sight of the shore, though it now and then appeared only a mist that bordered the water's edge (ibid., 96).

In 1887, John Keane, clearly an experienced sailor, reports on a voyage from England to fetch a shipload of ice from Kragerø, a town further down the coast from Wollstonecraft's destination. His youthful enthusiasm conjures up a vivid picture of the sunny and windy spring morning and of the coast that is coming into view:

We were bound to a little port called Kraagero, and one glorious morning we hove-to off the bold Norwegian highlands to windward of the fiord we were to enter. It is a fearsome, forbidding coast, albeit one of the best lighted in the world, with the sea deep to the mighty fir-clad bluffs and capes. Sailing along it, close in, as may be done, one becomes oppressed with grandeur. Each minute opens up a new marvel in Nature's stupendous granite rockery. We become weary of variety, as wonder after wonder opens before us in precipice, fantastic mountain, forest-clad hill, and dark ravine. Gloomy frowning aspect as this land presents, the whole coast is one network of refuges from the sea. It is probable that all the harbours of Norway will never be known (Keane 1887, 181–82).

No less lively and articulate is William Hurton's wonderful account from a few decades earlier of his voyage round the Cape Lindesnes, in a small '*yægt*' or sea-sloop, together with a crew of five Norwegian sailors. The whole voyage from Christiania to Bergen took five and a half days, and Hurton paints the coastline in rough and sweeping brush strokes:

The view of the coast here is magnificent; vast rugged rocks uplift their hoary and fantastic heads among the clouds, while impotent breakers wreath their base in sheets of milky foam. The whole coast of Norway, hence to the extreme north, is one continuous chain of mighty rocks, varying from one thousand to four thousand feet in height, presenting a barrier to the ocean unparalleled for magnitude, length, and savage grandeur. The entire line of coast is also studded with innumerable isles of every size, from a few yards in diameter to as many miles – being in nearly every instance solid rocks, in a few cases inhabited by hardy fishermen and pilots. (…) We had now a rough angry sea, but a capital wind, and the residue of our voyage was extremely interesting; for the size of the craft, and the intimate knowledge the skipper had of the excessively dangerous coast, enabled him to run the gauntlet of the narrow channels between the islands. In several places we sailed at a mad rate, so near the cliffs that it seemed as though one could almost pluck the flowers blooming in their fissures, and sometimes the end of the mainsail boom, as it stretched over the quarter, nearly scraped the jutting crags. The roar of the waves on these occasions was deafening, and our position exciting enough, for had our boom split, or tiller broken, or a gust of wind made us broach to for a single moment – smash! the yægt would have gone, and been scattered to fragments in less time than a tar can box his compass! A poor swamped boat was helplessly eddying about in one place – perchance she belonged to some lost vessel! (Hurton 1851, 97–99).

Neither Keane nor Hurton should be regarded as tourists in the modern sense. They are rather individual travellers who choose their own way of enjoying the Norwegian experience. Miss 'Lizzie' Vickers, on the other hand, came from Harwich to Bergen in a group of fourteen, who later continued to Trondheim by boat. She is thus more of a representative of the package tours, which were becoming more common towards the end of the century. In her book, typically entitled *Old Norway and its Fjords, or A Holiday in Norseland* (1893), she describes the Nærøyfjorden, one of the narrow inlets far into the Sognefjorden:

> As evening advanced it brought magnificent cloud effects, far surpassing the power of painter or writer to describe. At times the vessel appeared to sail in a vast ravine or chasm, surrounded by rocky mountains, down whose dark *sides* could be seen the gleaming cataracts, but whose *heads* were hidden far above in masses of fleecy clouds.
>
> A minute later the bottom and sides of these grim cliffs would be blotted from sight among the mists, but huge granite peaks, apparently cut off from connection with the rocks below, shewed above through the soft rolling vapour, appearing to hang over the boat, as though ready to fall upon it and sink it.
>
> Soon these were blotted out, and still sailing on, peak after peak, in seemingly endless succession, with rounded or pointed cones, started from their vaporous beds, each in turn to be hidden by that floating curtain of snowy mist. (...)
>
> All on board were impressed with the weird and charming effects of this magical panorama, even the least imaginative feeling something of its charm, while more than one, with bared head, felt like Moses at the bush, that the place was indeed holy.
>
> A writer in *Great Thoughts* says, 'There is no fjord scenery in Norway to compare with the Naero for sublimity and that awful calm majesty – indeed, it is one of the most awful chasms to be met with in the whole world.' (...)
>
> Passing through the Naero Fjord will ever be one of the most wonderful memories of our lives. Seen in the evening's gloom, with its magical cloud effects, its precipitous grey rocks, its marvellous cataracts, and its unbroken solitude, it was one long grand poem and one could only wish for the pen of a Milton, or the brush of a Doré, to describe it (71–72).[29]

---

[29] In fact, the celebrated French illustrator Gustave Doré (1832–1883), who altogether produced about 10,000 illustrations, also signed a number of pictures from Norway, though probably based on sketches by other artists.

There is no doubt that for the great majority of British visitors to Norway in the nineteenth century, the fjords on the west coast were the main destination and, as one would expect, the travelogues contain innumerable descriptions both of their beauty and of their sublimity. Also, as was indicated in chapter 2, this part of Norway was closely connected with the Viking past, and thus acquired an historical aura that gave the landscape an additional, mythical quality.

To many travellers, however, the far North represented an even greater attraction. Admittedly, it could not boast the same Viking roots as the west coast, but on the other hand, it resonated with all the mystique of the Arctic, which represented the limits of civilisation and so, by virtue of being an area of extremes, exerted a powerful attraction in a period celebrating man's heroic struggle against the elements.[30] According to Barton, travelling in the Arctic 'represented the ultimate Nordic experience, expressing the most basic motives for travels in the North: exoticism, primitivism, and escape from Mediterranean classicism' (Barton 1998, 116). The late eighteenth-century traveller William Thompson (pseud. Andrew Swinton), confirms Barton's claim. In a letter from a crossing of the North Sea in October 1788, he admits that 'it is a strange whim to get in love with deserts, with ice and with snow', but adds with true relish: 'I delight to see Nature in her Winter uniform; to be surrounded with rugged rocks and frozen oceans' (Swinton 1792, 1).

Like other countries with imperial ambitions, Britain realised at an early stage that the Arctic represented a region of potentially enormous natural resources and of vital strategic importance. As a result, there was a considerable element of international rivalry involved. This rivalry only gained a further momentum from the fact that an exploration of the area required all the competitive skill and courage that could be mustered in order to ensure what could be called, at least in post-Darwinian Britain, the survival of the fittest. Chauncey C. Loomis, in his article 'The Arctic Sublime', shows how this obsession with the Arctic fed into the very life of the nation:

During the nineteenth century, Arctic exploration aroused national

---

[30] A modern comment on this nineteenth-century obsession is found in Tim Moore's travelogue *Frost on My Moustache* (1999), a humorous but also serious reflection on modern man's lack of great causes, and a description of the author's rather unsuccessful attempt to travel through the Arctic in the footprints of the heroic Lord Dufferin, who made the journey to Iceland, Jan Mayen, Spitzbergen and, briefly, Norway, in 1856 (see Biographical Information).

interest in England. Preparations for Arctic expeditions were discussed extensively by the press, and their departures were usually accompanied by great fanfare. (...) The return of an expedition usually generated articles, dioramas, lectures, and perhaps a book or two. Narratives about Arctic exploration became very popular indeed. In 1859, Mudie stocked 1,000 copies of *Idylls of the King*, 2,500 of *Adam Bede*, and 3,000 of Leopold McClintock's *Voyage of the 'Fox' in Arctic Seas* (Loomis 1977, 95).

One crucial element in the exploration of the Arctic was the attempt to find the so-called Northwest Passage, which would give access from the Atlantic, via northern Canada, to the Pacific. The first attempts had been made as early as the late 1500s, and after a period of about 200 years, in which little happened, the search again gathered momentum in the years after Napoleon's fall.[31] Obviously, such a discovery would have an enormous commercial potential, and as a consequence it turned into a race of major proportions: 'Many government officials, the press, and the public came to believe that somehow British manhood and British power were on the line in the continued search for a passage' (ibid., 95). It was against this background of national fervour that expeditions were launched from 1818 and for several decades onwards, involving such future national heroes as Edward Parry, John Ross and John Franklin. As a result, Britain gathered significant knowledge about the Arctic, but in many cases at a terrible price. Most famously, the Franklin Expedition, starting in 1845, gradually turned into a national disaster. The terrible truth about it, including evidence that the crew in despair had resorted to cannibalism, only became public knowledge several years later, after a series of search expeditions. The scale of its impact on the national consciousness can only be compared to the apocalyptic interpretations of Captain Scott's death on the South Pole in 1911 and the sinking of the Titanic in 1912.

These aspects of the Arctic form a necessary background to an understanding of the ways in which British travellers experienced the landscape of the far north in the course of the nineteenth century; the aesthetic outlook, in other words, cannot be seen as separate from the general political and cultural climate. And with the dramas mentioned above in mind, it is particularly interesting to find that the aesthetics of the Arctic are a relatively accurate reflection of the highly ambiguous popular view of the same phenomenon. Again, it is the category of the sublime that is brought to the fore, and nowhere is it

---

[31] For a useful survey of this race towards the Arctic, see 'A Review of Previous Arctic Expeditions', in Keely and Davis (1893), 489–517.

found in a purer form than in descriptions of this region:

> From earlier generations the Victorians inherited images of the Arctic
> that had already been conditioned by the growing English response to the
> Sublime. (...) Certainly sixteenth- and seventeenth-century explorers
> and chroniclers provided images that would impress later writers with a
> sense that in the Arctic Nature was somehow vaster, more mysterious,
> and more terrible than elsewhere on the globe – a region in which natural
> phenomena could take strange, almost supernatural, forms, sometimes
> stunningly beautiful, sometimes terrifying, often both (ibid., 96).

Thus, Victorian writers and explorers carried with them a legacy of
visions of the Arctic that came to exert a certain influence on the
views developed by themselves. Richard Savage's poem *The
Wanderer* (1729), for instance, describes a personified Winter and
how 'o'er *Norwegian* Hills he strides away':

> Beneath his Eye (that throws malignant Light
> Ten Times the measur'd Round of mortal Sight)
> A waste, pale-glimm'ring, like a Moon, that wanes,
> A wild Expanse of frozen Sea contains.
> It cracks! vast, floating Mountains beat the Shore!
> Far off he hears those icy Ruins roar,
> And from the hideous Crash distracted flies,
> Like One, who feels his dying Infant's Cries.
> (...)
> The late-dark *Pole* now feels unsetting Day:
> In Hurricanes of Wrath he whirls his Way;
> O'er many a polar *Alp* to Frost he goes,
> O'er crackling Vales, embrown'd with melting Snow ...
> (Canto IV, ll. 13–36)

Similarly, John Dyer's poem *The Fleece* (1757) contains passages on
the 'horrid rage / Of winter irresistible [which] o'erwhelms / Th'
Hyperborean tracts' (Book I, ll. 465–67).[32] And in an article by James
Sambrook on James Thomson's 'Winter' (from *The Seasons*,
1726–1730), it is emphasised that

> there is a twenty-line passage near the end of the poem describing a thaw
> in the Arctic Ocean, when the ice fields break up with an awesome noise,
> bringing danger and fear to the weary, hungry crew of a ship, 'lost amid

---

[32] See also the discussion of the Sami in ch. 3, where a lengthier passage from
the poem is quoted.

the floating Fragments',
    While Night o'erwhelms the Sea, and Horror looks
    More horrible (…) (McVeagh 1990, 141).

As to the literary use of the Arctic in the following century, Coleridge's 'The Ancient Mariner' and Mary Shelley's *Frankenstein* clearly mark a new and psychologically significant stage. According to Loomis, 'Coleridge anticipated one Victorian response to the polar world by making it an environment that provoked theological speculation and fear' (98-99), and Shelley 'anticipated the Victorian response to the Arctic by making it a setting within which human pride shows its folly in face of the immensity and inscrutability of Nature' (ibid., 99). Furthermore, it is an interesting coincidence that *Frankenstein* was published in the very year when the new wave of polar expeditions started, that is 1818. Not surprisingly, Marlow, the frame narrator in *Frankenstein*, who is on an expedition to the Arctic, has 'read with ardour the accounts of the various voyages which have been made in the prospects of arriving at the North Pacific Ocean through the seas which surround the pole' (Shelley 1992, 14).

The Arctic, in other words, increasingly comes to reflect the doubt and the uncertainty often associated with the period in question: it is a place where Nature shows herself as supreme and merciless, and where man is caught helplessly in her grip. Clearly, this is also the way in which Charlotte Brontë makes use of the Arctic in *Jane Eyre*. In the famous opening paragraphs, which have been discussed earlier in this chapter, she quotes not only from Bewick's *History of British Birds*, but also from 'Autumn', in Thomson's *The Seasons*. Furthermore, in chapter 26, when after the disastrous near-wedding Jane is in her room wondering what course to take, she returns to the same Arctic imagery, thus reminding the reader of the equally desperate situation from her childhood:

> A Christmas frost had come at midsummer; a white December storm had whirled over June; ice glazed the ripe apples, drifts crushed the blowing roses; on hayfield and cornfield lay a frozen shroud: lanes which last night blushed full of flowers, to-day were pathless with untrodden snow; and the woods, which twelve hours since waved leafy and fragrant as groves between the tropics, now spread, waste, wild, and white as pine-forests in wintry Norway (Brontë 1985, 323).

Finally, it is interesting to note that *Jane Eyre* (1847) was published in the same year that concern was seriously beginning to mount with respect to the fate of the Franklin Expedition. Thus, the use of the

Arctic in both *Frankenstein* and *Jane Eyre* can be seen as potentially inspired by public interest in the region due to events much discussed in journals and newspapers.

In the British travelogues, the north of Norway has one particular natural phenomenon which, together with the famous Norwegian sea monsters, tends to acquire mythical proportions, namely the maelstrom. There are at least two major maelstroms in the north of Norway, both of them in the County of Nordland, both among the most powerful and dangerous tidal currents in the world. One of them is Saltstraumen, which Arthur de Capell Brooke describes in his book from 1823:

> It is most violent in the spring, from the great increase of water brought down from the mountains by the Salten river, owing to the melting of the snow; and also when there is a strong westerly wind. The agitation of it is then so great, and the noise so loud, that the fishermen affirm it shakes their very huts. The depth of the whirlpool in some parts is as much as twenty-five fathoms; and in the centre a vacuity is formed to the very bottom, by the curling spiral motion of the waters. Numbers of fishermen have been lost, from their boats being drawn in by the current; and there is yet living at Hundholm one, who has been taken down with his boat twice, and has had the singular good fortune of escaping each time, by clinging fast to the boat, which was thrown up in another part (259).

The other is the Mokstraumen, at the southern tip of the Lofoten islands, along the main shipping channel to the north of Norway. This commercial aspect is also one of the reasons why it has attracted so much attention over the centuries. In the 1810 edition of *Encyclopædia Britannica*, the following dramatic account is given:

> In time of flood, the stream runs up between Lofoden and Moskoe with the most boisterous rapidity; but in its ebb to the sea, it roars like a thousand cataracts, so as to be heard at the distance of many leagues. The surface exhibits different vortices; and if in one of these any ship or vessel is absorbed, it is whirled down to the bottom, and dashed in pieces against the rocks. (...) When its fury is heightened by a storm, no vessel ought to venture within a league of it. Whales have been frequently absorbed within the vortex, and howled and bellowed hideously in their fruitless endeavours to disengage themselves. A bear, in attempting to swim from Lofoden to Moskoe, was once hurried into this whirlpool, from whence he struggled in vain for deliverance, soaring so loud as to be heard on shore; but notwithstanding all his efforts, he was borne down and destroyed. Large trees being absorbed by the current are sucked down, and rise again all shattered into splinters (59).[33]

The maelstrom is also mentioned in *The Botanic Garden* (1791) by Erasmus Darwin, Charles Darwin's grandfather who, together with the *Britannica*, must have been heavily inspired by the English translation from 1755 of *The Natural History of Norway* by the Bergen bishop Erik Pontoppidan.[34] However, the most famous literary uses of this motif are found in Edgar Allan Poe's short story 'The Descent into the Maelstrom', which was first published in 1841, and in Jules Verne's *20,000 Leagues Under the Sea* (1869), both of which concern the Moskstraumen. Poe's story is about an old man who tells the narrator how years ago he and two of his brothers were caught in the maelstrom while attempting to escape a terrible hurricane. The boat was sucked into a great whirling funnel in which his brothers were drowned and the boat broken to pieces, while he himself was miraculously brought back to the surface after the tide had turned. The man also tells the narrator that his hair, which had been raven black, turned white overnight. Poe clearly exaggerates the fury of the maelstrom, but the area remains dangerous even for modern ships, and there is no doubt that the stories about it have been spread far and wide for centuries.[35] Thus, even today the word maelstrom is so closely associated with Norway in the British consciousness that the BBC in the 1980s gave a mini-series, a psychological thriller set in Norway, the same title.

Despite this interest in the maelstrom, it is still difficult to imagine that the far north would have attracted such large numbers of

---

[33] This passage is a good example of how various writers on Norway, without a first-hand knowledge of the country or other trustworthy information, uncritically reproduce old and sometimes fantastic accounts. Several of the details from the *Britannica* seem to be taken from a work from as far back as 1589, *The First Voyage of Master Anthonie Jenkinson from the City of London* (quoted by Burchardt 1920, 8). Then, later, Agnes Strickland (see Biographical Information) includes the passage verbatim in her story 'Arthur Ridley; or, a Voyage to Norway' in *The Rival Crusoes* (1826).

[34] For further information on the Moskstraumen and historical descriptions of it, see Gjevik (1997).

[35] There have been many speculations concerning Poe's possible sources for the story. One which does not seem to have been mentioned in the critical discussions of the story is 'The Maelstrom: A Fragment', printed in *Fraser's Magazine for Town and Country* (vol. 10, no. 57, September 1834, 267–81). The fragment, which is signed 'L.' (most probably Edward Wilson Landor, author of the novel *Lofoden*), contains a peculiar, dream-like story about a nameless character (a Byronic-type hero called 'the exile') on board a ship that ultimately vanishes in the 'Moskoestrom'.

travellers, given its enormous distance from the southern part of the country, if it had not been for the North Cape and the Midnight Sun.[36] In other words, the fact that these attractions are situated so far from the beaten track gives a clear indication of their magnetic appeal. Some of the travelogues even give a distinct impression that for a worshipper of nature, the Midnight Sun and the view into the bleak Arctic Ocean from the extreme end of the European continent carried the same religious significance as a Muslim's pilgrimage to Mecca. William Hurton, who was quoted earlier on the subject of his windy voyage round the south coast, gives a powerful impression of his first view of the Midnight Sun in Hammerfest: "Twas a sublime night, and it drew my soul nigher my God that Sabbath morning, than a year spent in the noblest temple erected by the hands of man could possibly have done' (Hurton 1851, 217–18). Somewhat later he approaches the North Cape from the sea:

> The impression I experienced as I came within its shadow, and swept its bulk with eager eye, was one of thrilling awe, for its magnificently stern proportions, its colossal magnitude, its position as the solitary unchanging sentinel of Nature that for countless ages had stood forth as the termination of the European continent, frowning defiance to the maddening assaults of the Arctic Ocean – all combine to invest it with associations of overpowering majesty. My ideas of its sublimity were more than realized (…) (ibid., 245-46).

He then leaves the boat behind and climbs at considerable risk straight up the rock-face to the top of the plateau. What follows might provide an ideal caption to Caspar Friedrich's *The Wanderer above the Mists*:

> I cannot adequately describe the emotion which filled my soul as I stepped up to the dizzy verge. I only know that after standing a moment with folded arms, and beating heart, I knelt, and with lowly-bowed head, devoutly returned thanks to the Almighty for thus permitting me to realize one darling dream of my boyhood.
> My nerve is good, and despite the wind which here blew violently, and bitterly cold; I sat down close to the pole, and, wrapping my cloak around me, long contemplated the spectacle of Nature in one of her sublimest aspects. I was truly alone. Not a living object was in sight;

---

[36] With respect to British travellers, it should be mentioned that the very name 'North Cape' was given by an Englishman, Captain Richard Chancellor, who passed the place in 1553 on his search for the Northeast Passage to China (Skavhaug 1990, 7).

THE NORTH CAPE

London. Pub. by Rodwell and Martin. New Bond St. 1822

The North Cape, from *Travels through Sweden, Norway, and Finmark, to the North Cape* (1823) by Arthur de Capell Brooke, who gives the following account 'At six in the evening we at last reached it; and, advancing to the edge of the precipice, contemplated the fearful step between us and the ocean. Let the reader imagine a cliff exceeding in height that of Dover, and with Shakespeare's celebrated description of the latter, he may form a good idea of the North Cape, black from the polar storms, and proudly frowning upon the foaming element at its feet' (380).

beneath my feet was the boundless expanse of ocean, with a sail or two on its bosom at an immense distance; above me was the canopy of heaven, flecked with fleecy cloudlets; the sun was luridly gleaming above a broad belt of blood-red mist; the only sounds were the whistling of the wandering winds, and the occasional plaintive scream of the hovering sea-fowl (ibid., 250–51).

A very similar description, but taken from a work of fiction, appears in Marie Corelli's *Thelma: A Norwegian Princess*, which has also been mentioned in previous chapters. The novel's setting is the Altafjord area, a short distance to the south of the North Cape, and the opening paragraphs, which 'won more praise than any other she ever wrote' (Mains 1989, 128), are interesting because they offer a revealing and intensely sentimental description of the nineteenth-century cliché presented by Hurton above:

Midnight, – without darkness, without stars! Midnight, – and the unwearied sun stood, yet visible in the heavens, like a victorious king throned on a dais of royal purple bordered with gold. The sky above him, – his canopy, – gleamed with a cold yet lustrous blue, while across it slowly flitted a few wandering clouds of palest amber, deepening, as they sailed along, to a tawny orange. A broad stream of light, falling, as it were, from the centre of the magnificent orb, shot lengthwise across the Altenfjord, turning its waters to a mass of quivering and shifting colour that alternated from bronze to copper, – from copper to silver and azure. The surrounding hills glowed with a warm, deep violet tint, flecked here and there with touches of bright red, as though fairies were lighting tiny bonfires on their summits. Away in the distance a huge mass of rock stood out to view, its rugged lines transfigured into ethereal loveliness by a misty veil of tender rose pink, – a hue curiously suggestive of some other and smaller sun that might have just set. Absolute silence prevailed. Not even the cry of a sea-mew or kittiwake broke the almost deathlike stillness, – no breath of wind stirred a ripple of the glassy water. The whole scene might well have been the fantastic dream of some imaginative painter, whose ambition soared beyond the limits of human skill. Yet it was only one of those million wonderful effects of sky and sea which are common in Norway, especially on the Altenfjord, where, though beyond the Arctic circle, the climate in summer is that of another Italy, and the landscape a living poem fairer than the visions of Endymion.

There was one solitary watcher of the splendid spectacle. This was a man of refined features and aristocratic appearance, who, reclining on a large rug of skins which he had thrown down on the shore for that purpose, was gazing at the pageant of the midnight sun and all its stately surroundings with an earnest and rapt expression in his clear hazel eyes

(Corelli 1894, 1–2).

Corelli's narrative is particularly striking because the long opening paragraph makes a significant point of *not* mentioning the presence of a human being. Thus, nature comes across as pure and free of disturbing elements. It is only after the author has opened up to the reader this vast and sublime panorama that the 'solitary watcher' is very cautiously brought into the picture. And precisely by being silent and receptive to the 'splendid spectacle', he is in that state of 'wise passiveness' that Wordsworth recommends in 'Expostulation and Reply' (1798). Consequently, his aristocratic appearance, besides being socially significant, also serves as an external indication of the spiritual refinement infused by the natural surroundings. In fact, it is hardly an exaggeration to see the Midnight Sun as a religious manifestation of a divine presence, which fills the receptive individual with a state of grace.[37] This Romantic emphasis on silence in connection with the Midnight Sun is even present in one of Thomas Cook's guidebooks for trips to Norway from 1890. The anonymous writer turns first to such contemporary authorities as Carlyle and the American writer Bayard Taylor:

> The effect of the Midnight Sun has been variously described. Carlyle revels in the idea that while all the nations of the earth are sleeping, you here stand in the presence of that great power which will wake them all; Bayard Taylor delights in the gorgeous colouring; and each traveller has some new poetic thought to register. For myself, the Midnight Sun, has a solemnity which nothing else in Nature has. Midnight is solemn in the darkness; it is a hundredfold more solemn in the glare of sunlight; richer than ever it is seen under tropical skies. It is 'silence as of death'; not the hum of a bird, not the buzz of an insect, not the distant voice of a human being. Silence palpable. You do not feel drowsy, though it is midnight; you feel a strange fear creep over you as if in a nightmare, and dare not speak; you think what if it should be true that the world is in its last sleep, and you are the last living ones, yourselves on the verge of the Eternal Ocean? (Cook 1890, 6).

---

[37] This is not the place to discuss Corelli's literary merits, but at least two famous travellers to Norway, William Gladstone and Edmund Gosse, expressed radically different opinions about her. The former called her 'an earnest woman-thinker' (whatever qualities the word 'woman' might imply in this context) and the latter 'dismissed her as "that little milliner"' (Federico 2000, 1). In terms of sales, however, she was probably the most successful novelist at the turn of the century, taking over the position of Ellen Wood, the mother of Charles W. Wood (see Biographical Information).

But he enjoys, together with the entire group of tourists, not only Wordsworth's 'passiveness' and silence, but also a recollection 'in tranquillity' which, as many a poet has experienced, leads to a breakdown of language. Such 'hyperboles of indescribability' (Chard 1999, 85), paradoxically enhance the focus on the narrator's own unique experience, while at the same time underlining the fact that even the most detailed travel account can never rival the experience itself. Thus the North Cape, itself bordering, in its sublime majesty, on the eternity of the polar ocean, similarly brings the writer to the limits of words and language:

> It is amusing afterwards to think of the way in which you landed on your excursion to the North Cape; how everyone seemed impressed with the same idea that it was sacrilege to break the silence, and the party that set forth in high spirits had settled down into the gravity of a funeral cortege. And it is strange how the stillness and awfulness felt while in the little boat upon the silent sea held you spell-bound and entranced; and the spell could not be broken until you set to work on the difficult climb to the head of the North Cape. And when you reached the top you felt – well, I don't know how (Cook 1890, 6).

Biographical Information

The information below has been gathered from a wide register of sources and has been cross-checked whenever possible. As several of the writers are not dealt with in standard reference works, however, some of the information may be uncertain. Furthermore, names mentioned in the book but not in the list suggests either that no information has been found or that information is readily available elsewhere. We would like especially to acknowledge our debt to Schiötz (1970–1986); the 11th edition of *Encyclopædia Britannica*; *The New Cambridge Bibliography of English Literature*, edited by George Watson (1969); *The Dictionary of National Biography* (1885–1900), edited by Leslie Stephen et al.; *Burke's Peerage & Baronetage* (1999), edited by Charles Mosley; the online catalogues of the Bodleian Library, Oxford, and the COPAC union catalogue.

ALLEN, WILLIAM
(1770–1843) Philanthropist, man of science and Quaker, who supported the abolition of slavery and the slave trade. In the interest of social reform he visited schools, prisons and social institutions on the Continent. In 1814, he was part of a group of reformers who bought New Lanark mills with the reformer Robert Owen. Allen travelled in Norway and continued through Sweden and Finland to Russia in 1818.

ARNOLD, EDWIN LESTER LINDEN
(1857–1935) The son of the poet and journalist Sir Edwin Arnold (1832–1904). He travelled to Norway in the summer of 1876. He also published a number of novels and the collection of stories, *The Story of Ulla and Other Tales* (1895), set in the Viking age.

ATKINSON, J. BEAVINGTON
(1822–1886) He was associated with the Pre-Raphaelites and with *Blackwood's Edinburgh Magazine* – the organ of the Scottish Tory party. He visited Norway in the summer of 1870 and had an essay in *English Artists of the Present Day* (1872).

BACKHOUSE, SARAH
(1803–1877) The sister of the Quaker James Backhouse (1794–1869), who was the author of books based on visits to both Australia and Africa. Her *Hymns and Verses* were published posthumously in 1878.

BANNERMAN, ANNE
(1765–1829) Scottish poet, daughter of William Bannerman and Isobel Dick. William Bannerman was a 'running stationer,' a street ballad singer and merchant, and this early familiarity with the Scottish ballad tradition was an important influence on his daughter's literary career. After her death, Walter Scott praised her ballads in his important 'Essay on Imitations of the Ancient Ballad' (1830), noting her poetry's characteristic obscurity.

BARNARD, MOURDANT ROGER
Dates unknown. Graduated at Christ's College, Cambridge, in 1851 and was ordained the same year. He served as British Consular Chaplain at Christiania 1858–1862 and as Vicar of Margaretting, Essex, from 1863. He translated a number of works related to Scandinavia into English, and published an English blank-verse translation of Homer's *Odyssey* in 1876.

BARROW, JOHN JR.
(1808–1898) Son of the statesman and travel writer Sir John Barrow (1764–1848), who also wrote a history of modern Arctic voyages and proposed the foundation of the Royal Geographical Society in 1830. Barrow Jr. was the author of several travelogues and historical works, and visited Norway in 1833 and again, in 1834, in the 'Flower of Yarrow' yacht en route for Iceland.

BAYLY, ADA ELLEN: see Lyall, Edna

BENNETT, THOMAS
(1814–1898) Educated at Westminster School. Having travelled widely in Europe, he came to Norway in 1848, married and settled in Christiania. Here he established the first Norwegian travel agency in 1850 and became the great pioneer of modern Norwegian tourism.

BIDDULPH, SIR MICHAEL ANTHONY SHRAPNEL
(1823–1904) General, educated at Woolwich. He saw active service in all parts of the Empire from around 1850 until the mid 1880s. He was appointed general in 1886; president of the Ordnance Committee (1887–1890); and keeper of regalia at Tower of London (1891–1896). In 1895 he was awarded the GCB. Biddulph visited Norway in 1848, 1849, 1851 and 1887.

BILTON, WILLIAM
(1800–1883) Clergyman and an authority on angling. His visits to Norway took place in 1837 and 1839. The surname is frequently spelt 'Belton'.

BOWDEN, JOHN
Dates unknown. British Consular Chaplain at Christiania 1862–1863. He
also edited *Black's Guide to Norway* (1867) and wrote *The Naturalist in
Norway* (1869), in which he is also listed with the honorary title LL.D.

BRACE, CHARLES LORING
(1826–1890) American clergyman and social reformer. A pioneer advocate
for children, he founded Children's Aid Society of New York (1853). From
the Civil War onwards, he organised the 'orphan trains', helping orphans
from New York City get a better life in the rural Midwest. He wrote several
books, including *Short Sermons to Newsboys* (1866) and *Gesta Christi*
(1882). Before his sojourn in Norway in 1856, he had also written travel
works on other parts of Europe: *Home Life in Germany* (1853) and *Hungary
in 1851* (1852). He later wrote a travel work on America: *The New West; or,
California in 1867–1868* (1869).

BRASSEY, LADY (ANNA, 'ANNIE')
(1839–1887) Married Lord Brassey (*vid.*) in 1860 and had five children. In
1874 she went on a voyage in the private yacht 'Sunbeam' on the west coast
of Norway, and with Gladstone and others in August 1885. Dame chevalière
of the Order of St John of Jerusalem (1881). She died and was buried at sea
outside Australia.

BRASSEY, LORD (THOMAS ALLNUTT)
(1836–1918) Son of the famous railway contractor Thomas Brassey
(1805–1870), who was also involved in the first Norwegian railway. He was
educated at Rugby, and graduated from University College, Oxford, in 1859.
Later he became Liberal MP for Hastings (1868–1886); Parliamentary
Secretary to the Admiralty (1884–1885); and Governor of Victoria
(1895–1900). He became a baron in 1886 and an earl in 1911. Brassey
visited Norway in 1856 in the yacht 'Cymba'; in 1866 in the 'Meteor'; and
then in the 'Sunbeam' in 1874 and 1885, the latter visit with Gladstone and
others. The 'Sunbeam', carrying 43 persons, was the first steam yacht to
circumnavigate the world. After his wife's death, he remarried Sibyl de Vere
Capell in 1890.

BREMNER, ROBERT
Dates unknown. Travelled in Norway in 1836. He also wrote *Excursions in
the Interior of Russia* (1839).

BRETON, WILLIAM HENRY
Dates unknown. Lieutenant in the Royal Navy. He left the Navy in 1827, and
was for a while police magistrate in Tasmania, where he published
Excursions in New South Wales (1834). He travelled in Norway in the
summer of 1834.

BRITANNICUS, MELA (PSEUD. FOR KELSALL, CHARLES)
(1782–1857) Traveller, book collector, amateur architect and classicist. He
was born at Greenwich to wealthy parents, and was educated at Eton and
Cambridge, but took no degree. In the period 1805–1844 he visited sixteen
countries and travelled over 100,000 miles. He published several books,
often under a pseudonym, on various topics. His *Phantasm of an University*
(1814) described his plan for an ideal university. He left his book collection
to Morden College and £2,000 to build a library to house it.

BROOKE, SIR ARTHUR DE CAPELL
(1791–1858) Baronet and army major. He graduated with an MA from
Magdalen College, Oxford, in 1816. Brooke spent much of his early life
travelling through the North of Europe. He was an original member of the
Travels Club and an originator of the Raleigh Club, which later became
merged in the Royal Geographical Society. He also published *A Winter in
Lapland and Sweden* (1826) whose companion volume, *Winter Sketches in
Lapland* (1826), contains a number of splendid illustrative plates from
sketches by the author.

BROUGHAM, LORD HENRY PETER
(1778–1868) Politician and Lord Chancellor. Educated at Edinburgh
University, where he studied maths and physics. As a student he spent his
vacations making walking tours. In September 1799, he left for Scandinavia
and visited Norway in December 1799 and January 1800. He helped to set
up the *Edinburgh Review* and became a life-long contributor. Brougham was
Lord Chancellor from 1830–1834. As a radical in the Whig Cabinet, he
played an important role in the Reform Act debates. In general, he was
renowned for his interest in legal and educational reform and was a fervent
opponent of the slave trade. He is more popularly remembered for the type
of horse-drawn carriage that bears his name.

BROWN, THOMAS
(1778–1820) Scottish philosopher and poet, born in Kirkcudbright. An
infant prodigy, he was deeply read in religious and philosophical literature
at a very early age, fluent in several languages and a superb Latinist, and
became a medical doctor at twenty-five. He taught philosophy in the
University of Edinburgh from 1808 and was appointed Professor of Moral
Philosophy in 1810. He was one of the first reviewers for the *Edinburgh
Review*, and had a passion for walking and hill climbing. His philosophical
works achieved great popularity both in England and America. His *Poetical
Works* (4 vols.) were published in 1820.

BROWNE, J(OHN) ROSS
(1821–1875) Year of birth possibly 1817. American diplomat. He was the
official reporter for the California State Constitutional Convention of 1849,
and came to California in 1849 as an employee of the government revenue

service. He travelled widely in the next two decades, including a stay in China as U.S. minister (from 1868), before settling down in Oakland in 1870. He published various travel books from the Americas.

BUNBURY, SELINA
(1802–1882) Irish travel writer, novelist and ardent anti-papist, born in County Leith to a Methodist family. She had connections with Fanny Burney, on whom she modelled herself, and wrote travel books that show the county districts of Ireland before the Irish famine, including *A Visit to My Birthplace* (1820). She visited every country of Europe except Greece and Portugal, and travelled in Norway in 1851. Other travel works include *A Summer in Northern Europe* (1856) and *My First Travels* (1859).

BURNETT, ALEXANDER G.
Dates unknown. His published work covers the period 1852–1901 and includes books on religious issues and travel works on Russia, Italy and France. Burnett was associated with Kemnay Parish School and Chapel, Aberdeenshire. He visited Norway in 1886 and probably also in 1884.

CAMPBELL, JOHN FRANCIS
(1822–1885) Heir to the Isle of Islay, Argyllshire, which was sold before he could inherit it. Educated at Eton and Edinburgh University, Campbell wrote on Highland folklore, geology and meteorology. He is known for his collection of folklore tales, collected orally, from the Western Highlands, *Popular Tales of the West Highlands* (4 vols., 1860–1862). Campbell's interest in geology and meteorology is manifested in *Frost and Fire: Natural Engines, Tool-Marks and Chips Taken at Home and Abroad by a Traveller* (1865). He was the inventor of the sunshine recorder for indicating the varying intensity of the sun's rays.

CLARK, JOHN WILLIS
(1833–1910) Born in Cambridge, Fellow of Trinity College, Superintendent of the Museum of Zoology, and Registrary of the University. He was a keen supporter of the Cambridge Amateur Dramatic Club, and published several books on Cambridge and its colleges, including the four-volume *Architectural History of the University and Colleges of Cambridge* (with Robert Willis, 1886). He also published books on bibliography and libraries, notably the classic *The Care of Books* (1901), and edited texts by Aristophanes, Cervantes and Defoe. Clark travelled in Norway with Joseph William Dunning (*vid.*) in 1856.

CLARKE, EDWARD DANIEL
(1769–1822) Mineralogist and traveller, born in Sussex. He was educated at Tonbridge and Cambridge. As a private tutor to wealthy families, he travelled widely in Europe and Asia. He became Doctor of Law (LL.D.) in 1803, Professor of Mineralogy in Cambridge from 1808, and university

librarian from 1817. He sold the manuscripts from his travels to the Bodleian library for £1,000 and earned £6,595 from their publication. Clarke visited Norway in 1799.

CLUTTERBUCK, WALTER J.
(1853–1937) Keen angler and co-author with James A. Lees (*vid.*) on one of the most frequently reprinted travel accounts from Norway. Clutterbuck visited Norway in 1880 and on various occasions later. He also co-authored *B.C. 1887: A Ramble in British Columbia* (1887) with Lees, and published himself *The Skipper in Arctic Seas* (1890) and *About Ceylon and Borneo* (1891).

COATES, FLORENCE (VAN LEER EARLE NICHOLSON)
(1850–1927) Poet, born in Philadelphia, Pennsylvania, educated in New England and Paris. She married her second husband, Edward H. Coates, a Philadelphia financier, in 1879. For the next two decades she was a prominent member of various literary and historical organisations. She was profoundly influenced by Matthew Arnold, a visitor at the Coates home and a correspondent. Her own poems began appearing in various leading magazines during the 1890s, and her work received praise from William Butler Yeats and Thomas Hardy.

CONWAY, DERWENT (PSEUD. FOR INGLIS, HENRY DAVID)
(1795–1835) Traveller and miscellaneous writer from Edinburgh. He published a number of travel accounts from various parts of Europe, including *Solitary Walks through Many Lands* (1828) and *Spain in 1830* (1831). His book *Ireland in 1834* (1834) was quoted as an authority by speakers in Parliament on the Irish Question. He also published books on contemporary politics, religious questions and phrenology.

CORELLI, MARIE
(1855–1924) Novelist. Probably the illegitimate daughter of the Scottish journalist and song-writer Charles Mackay, who adopted her as Mary Mackay. She wrote enormously popular, moralistic books, including *A Romance of Two Worlds* (1886), *Barabbas* (1893), and *The Sorrows of Satan* (1895). Corelli is said to have been Queen Victoria's favourite novelist. She does not appear to have visited Norway.

COXE, WILLIAM
(1747–1828) Historian, born in London, son of William Coxe, Physician to the Royal Household. He was educated at Marylebone Grammar School, Eton and Cambridge, and was elected Fellow of King's College in 1768. He took holy orders in 1771, then travelled extensively in Europe as tutor to various noblemen. Coxe was appointed Archdeacon of Wiltshire in 1804. He produced numerous historical works in a style 'remarkably dull', and several travel accounts. He visited Norway in 1784.

DE VERE, SIR AUBREY
(1788–1846) Baronet of Curragh Chase, County Limerick. He published historical dramas and, in 1842, *The Song of Faith: Devout Exercises and Sonnets*. The *Dictionary of National Biography* comments that 'his modesty prevented him from publishing too much during his lifetime.' His sonnets, proclaimed by Wordsworth to be 'the most perfect of our age,' were known for their chivalrous sentiment.

DI BEAUCLERK, LADY DIANA DE VERE
(1842-1905) Elder daughter of William Aubrey de Vere, 9th Duke of St Albans, and Elizabeth Catherine (née Gubbins). She married the Honourable Sir Walter John Huddleston QC and MP in 1872. Di Beauclerk visited Norway with her widowed mother in the summer of 1867. The journey began as a tour, but the women ended up spending the winter in Christiania. Di Beauclerk also wrote the novel *True Love* (1869).

DUFFERIN, LORD (HAMILTON-TEMPLE-BLACKWOOD, FREDERICK TEMPLE)
(1826–1902) Diplomat, with large properties in County Down, Ireland. Son of Price Blackwood, fourth Baron Dufferin. His mother was Richard Sheridan's granddaughter. Educated at Eton and Christ Church, Oxford. He held a long series of important offices, including Governor General of Canada (1872), Ambassador to Russia (1878) and Turkey (1881), Viceroy of India (1884), Ambassador at Rome (1888) and Paris (1892). He also wrote *Lispings from Low Latitudes* (1863) and a work on Irish emigration, *Irish Emigration and the Tenure of Land in Ireland* (1867). He travelled to Iceland and Norway in 1856.

DUNNE, MARY CHAVELITA: see Egerton, George

DUNNING, JOSEPH WILLIAM
(1834–1897) Travelled in Norway in 1856 with John Willis Clark (*vid.*). He edited a book on wills which came out in several editions.

EDY, JOHN WILLIAM
(1760–1805) Some sources give year of birth 1762. Illustrator, water-colourist and aquatint etcher. In 1785 he was represented for the first time at the Royal Academy Exhibition. At the instigation of the publisher John Boydell (1719–1804), he visited Norway in the summer of 1800 together with another artist, William Fearnside (?–1807). Both artists showed Norwegian scenes at the Royal Academy Exhibition in 1801. The portfolio of eighty plates from Norway was not published until 1820.

EGERTON, GEORGE (PSEUD. FOR DUNNE, MARY CHAVELITA)
(1859–1945) Author of four collections of short stories, notably *Keynotes* (1893), and an epistolary novel. She was born in Australia, but grew up in Ireland, England and Germany. She lived in Norway from 1887 to 1889 and

visited the country on several later occasions until 1900, becoming acquainted with, among others, Knut Hamsun. In 1899 she published a translation of Hamsun's novel *Hunger*. The pseudonym George Egerton was composed of her mother's maiden name (George) and her second husband's first name (Egerton).

ELLIOTT, CHARLES BOILEAU
(1803–1875) Wrote an essay 'On The Effects of Climate on National Character' (1821) while a student at the East India College at Heylebury, Herts., and became a Fellow of the Royal Society in 1832. He was interested in the condition of the peoples of India, made some minor translation from the Persian, and also wrote *Travels in the Three Great Empires of Austria, Russia and Turkey* (1838). The British painter George Chinnery (1774–1852), who spent most of his life in China and the Far East, produced a painting of 'Captain Charles Boileau Elliott of the Bengal Horse Artillery' (date unknown). Elliott visited Norway in 1830.

ELTON, CHARLES ISAAC
(1839–1900) English lawyer and antiquary. He was born in Southampton and educated at Cheltenham and Balliol College, Oxford. In 1865 he was called to the bar at Lincoln's Inn, and became a QC in 1885. He was an expert on old real property law and served as MP for West Somerset 1884–1885. He wrote several works on historical, archaeological, legal and literary topics. His visits to Norway took place in the summers of 1862 and 1863.

ELWES, ALFRED
(1819?–1888) Writer and translator. He published grammars and dictionaries in Spanish, Portuguese, Italian and French; translated a number of books, including travelogues, from the same languages; and wrote a number of books for children and young people. He also published the novels *Ralph Seabrooke* (1860) and *Guy Rivers* (1861).

EVEREST, ROBERT
(1799–?) Clergyman. Probably the Robert Everest (of University College, Oxford) who is registered an ordinary member of the Edinburgh Phrenological Society in 1826.

FORBES, JAMES D.
(1809–1868) Geologist and glaciologist, educated at Edinburgh University. He was a member of the Royal Society of Edinburgh, later a Fellow of the Royal Society of London, and Professor of Natural History at Edinburgh. Forbes enjoyed Alpine travel and glacier investigations. He travelled to Norway in 1850–1851 to see the total eclipse of the sun and to examine the Norwegian glaciers. The journey was very tiring and on his return his health was seriously impaired. In 1858, Forbes was elected an honorary member of

the newly founded Alpine Club.

FORESTER, THOMAS
Dates unknown. He translated from the medieval Latin the twelfth century Henry of Huntingdon's *Historia Anglorum* (1853), a work based on the Anglo-Saxon Chronicle, and the *Historical Works* of Giraldus Cambrensis (1868). He also wrote the travel book *Rambles in the Islands of Corsica and Sardinia* (1858) and a handbook on Paris. He visited Norway in 1848 together with Michael Biddulph (*vid.*).

FRANCIS, SIR PHILIP
(1740–1818) Quaker and reformer, educated at St Paul's School. He was amanuensis to Pitt (1761–1762), first clerk at the War Office (1762–1772), councillor of the governor-general of India from 1774, and MP for the Isle of Wight from 1784. He was also the reputed author of the long series of satirical pamphlets entitled *Letters of Junius's*.

FROUDE, JAMES ANTHONY
(1818–1894) Historian and author of several travel books. He was educated at Westminster and Oxford. He resigned from a fellowship at Exeter College, Oxford and served as the editor of *Fraser's Magazine* 1860–1874. He wrote several major historical works and was especially concerned with the British seafaring tradition. In 1892 he was appointed Regius Professor of Modern History at Oxford. He visited Norway in 1881 and 1884.

GALTON, SIR FRANCIS
(1822–1911) Scientist ranging from anthropology and criminology to meteorology. He was the grandchild of Erasmus Darwin and cousin of Charles Darwin. His fame rests on his work on heredity, and he is regarded as the father of eugenics. His ideas informed thinking about race and national identity in Britain and Australia between 1860 and 1920. He is also the author of *The Narrative of an Explorer in Tropical South Africa* (1853) and *The Art of Travel* (1855).

GARVAGH, LORD (CANNING, CHARLES JOHN SPENCER GEORGE)
(1852–1915) Third Baron Garvagh, from Errigal (or Arrigale), a parish of Colraine, Londonderry, Ireland. He was educated at Christ Church, Oxford. His family had come to Norway for three generations, and his father had several mountain cabins built in the Sognefjorden area. He travelled to Iceland and Norway in the autumn of 1872, and built a stone cabin (which still exists) in the Hallingskarvet in 1880. In 1877 he married Florence Alice, daughter of Baron Joseph de Bretton, of Copenhagen, Denmark. He also had ornithological interests.

GILFILLAN, ROBERT
(1798–1850) Scotch poet from Dunfermline. Began his poetic career by

writing for local newspapers. Several of his 'songs' were set to music by
Peter M'Leod.

GOSSE, SIR EDMUND
(1849–1928) Librarian, first at the British Museum and later the House of
Commons. He devoted much attention to the history of northern languages.
In 1875 he published *Ethical Conditions of the Early Scandinavia Peoples*
and in 1879 *Northern Studies*, essays on Danish, Swedish, Norwegian and
Dutch poets. He wrote a life of Ibsen in 1908 and in 1911 published a
description of two visits to Denmark. He is best known for his
autobiography *Father and Son*, in which he describes his relationship with
his father Philip H. Gosse, an eminent zoologist and a Plymouth Brother.

GREENWELL, GEORGE CLEMENTSON
(1821–1900) Manager of Lady Waldegrave's Radistock collieries in
Somerset, and later important in Poynton Mines, near Stockport. Betweeen
1878 and 1881 he was President of the North of England Institute of Mining
and Mechanical Engineers. He was interested in trade unions, housing and
labour conditions. Besides books on mining, he also published an
autobiography, two travel books on Italy and a book on Roman bridges.

GRIFFITH, DURHAM
Dates unknown. Also published *Summer Days in the Lofoten Islands* (1893).

HABBERTON. JOHN
Dates unknown. He contributed to a group of essays put together by the
American Press Association in preparation for the World Fair in Chicago in
1893. The essays ran in newspapers across the country from March to May
that year and dealt with predictions of what American life might be like in
the 1990s.

HARE, AUGUSTUS JOHN CUTHBERT
(1834–1903) Born in Rome, educated at Harrow school and University
College, Oxford. He wrote several guidebooks, mostly for John Murray,
especially on Italian cities. He also wrote *Memorials of a Quiet Life* (1872)
and an autobiography in six volumes, *The Story of My Life*. Hare was an
accomplished water-colour artist, and book and art collector. He visited
Norway in 1878.

HELY-HUTCHINSON, GEORGE HENRY: see Sixty-One

HEMANS, FELICIA DOROTHEA
(1793–1835) Poet. Daughter of George Browne, a Liverpool merchant and
Felicity Wagner, the daughter of the Austrian and Tuscan consul to
Liverpool. She grew up in Wales, where she returned with her children after
separating from her husband, Captain Alfred Hemans, in 1818. She moved

to Dublin in 1831. She published her first poems at the age of fourteen, and achieved considerable popularity, especially in America.

HOOKER, WILLIAM DAWSON
(1816–1840) Doctor, son of Sir William Jackson Hooker, Regius Professor of Botany at Edinburgh University and later director of Kew Gardens. He formed a considerable ornithological collection, but published nothing on the subject. He visited Scandinavia in 1837.

HORNE, RICHARD HENRY (HENGIST)
(1802/1803–1884) Poet, playwright and critic. Born in London, he started his career as a soldier, and later as an editor of *The Monthly Repository* (1836–1837). He was commissioned by Parliament to inquire into the working conditions of children in the 1840s, and kept a close friendship, and correspondence, with Elizabeth Barrett until her marriage with Robert Browning. In 1852 he went to Australia with William Howitt (*vid.*) and remained there until 1869. In 1874 he received a civil list pension. He is best known for his epic poem *Orion* (1843).

HOWITT, MARY
(1799–1888) Miscellaneous writer. Born in Gloucestershire to a Quaker family. She married William Howitt (see below) in 1821 and began a career of joint authorship. She contributed to periodicals and wrote children's books. Whilst residing at Heidelberg in 1840, her attention was drawn to Scandinavian literature and she set about learning Danish and Swedish. She afterwards translated Frederika Bremer's novels (1842–1863) in 18 vols. She also translated many of Hans Christian Andersen's tales.

HOWITT, WILLIAM
(1792–1879) Miscellaneous writer. He was born in Derbyshire to a Quaker family. In 1821 he married Mary Howitt (*vid.*), and in 1823 they made a pedestrian tour through Scotland, at that time 'an unheard-of achievement'. He published books about Germany and Australia, and founded, in 1847, *Howitt's Journal*. He received a civil list pension in 1865.

HURTON, WILLIAM
Dates unknown. Also wrote *The Maniac Improvisatore and Other Poems* (1845); *The King's Daughter: or, Revelations of Our Own Times* (1847); *The Doomed Ship: or, The Wreck of the Arctic Regions* (1855); *Vonved the Dane* (2 vols., 1861); and *Hearts of Oak: or, Naval Yarns* (1862). He visited Norway in 1850.

HYNE, CHARLES JOHN CUTCLIFFE WRIGHT
(1865–1944) Known as Cutcliffe Hyne. He was famous for the 'Captain Kettle' series of short stories which was regularly featured in *Pearson's Magazine*. This series was intended to compete with Conan Doyle's

'Sherlock Holmes' series in *The Strand*. He also wrote detective fiction under the pseudonym Weatherby Chesney. He travelled in Norway in 1897.

INGLIS, HENRY DAVID: see Conway, Derwent.

JONES, GEORGE MATTHEW
(1785?–1831) Traveller and captain in the navy. He saw active service in the Adriatic. After 1818, he travelled in Europe with the object of examining the maritime resources of the different countries.

JUNGMAN, NICO
(1872–1935) Landscape and figure painter. He was born and educated in Amsterdam but became a British citizen and lived most of his life in London. The book *Norway* (1905), written by his sister Beatrix, was preceded by a similar book, *Holland*, from the previous year. He exhibited extensively in England and had seven pictures at the Royal Academy from 1897–1923.

KEANE, JOHN FRYER
(1854–1937) He also published four travel books from Arabia, where he travelled 'disguised as a Mohammedan'. He visited Norway in 1884.

KEARY, CHARLES FRANCIS
(1848–1917) Numismatist, historian, novelist, librettist and poet. He published books on Norway in particular, and on Scandinavian history and mythology. He wrote the libretto for Frederick Delius's opera *Koanga* (composed 1895–1897).

KELSALL, CHARLES: see Britannicus, Mela

KINGSLEY, CHARLES
(1819–1875) Clergyman, poet and novelist. He was born in Devonshire, educated at King's College, London and Magdalene College, Cambridge. He became chaplain to Queen Victoria 1859 and Professor of Modern History at Cambridge 1860–1869. He took a vigorous interest in the Chartist and Christian Socialist movements for social reform. He wrote several novels, including *Alton Locke* (1850), *Hypatia* (1853), *Westward Ho!* (1855) and *Two Years Ago* (1857). His children's books include the famous *The Water-Babies* (1863). He also produced a series of history lectures entitled *The Roman and the Teuton* (1864).

LAING, ROBERT MEASON
1815–1886. Scottish poet and officer, a relative of William Bilton (*vid.*) and nephew of Samuel Laing (*vid.*). He is also known as Robert de la Laing (Meason) and various other names. He came to Norway in 1838 and stayed for several years, hunting and angling. During the period 1842–1847 he

owned a property, with fishing rights in Numedalslågen, near Larvik. During his stay he became a friend of Peter Chr. Asbjørnsen, the Norwegian collector of fairy tales. In 1847 he moved to Denmark, where he spent the rest of his life, serving as a courier in the Danish Army and eventually being awarded the Ritter Cross of the Order of Dannebrog. Speaking fluent Danish, he resigned from the Army in 1865 and became a teacher. He is buried in Frederiksborg, Jutland.

LAING, SAMUEL
(1780–1868) Born into a wealthy landowning family in the Orkney Islands he studied law and enlisted as an officer in the Napoleonic Wars (1805–1809). After some years as manager for a mining company in southern Scotland, he returned to the Orkneys, where he organised a large herring industry and pioneered modern agriculture. He was Mayor of Kirkwall for fourteen years, but suffered major financial losses in the late 1820s and lost a parliamentary election. He came to Norway 1834 and stayed for nearly two years. He also published other travel books and translated Snorri Sturluson's *Heimskringla* (3 vols., 1844).

LANDOR, EDWARD WILSON (also Willson)
(1811–1878) Younger cousin of the writer Walter Savage Landor (1775–1864). From 1834, he was for a period a junior partner in his uncle's attorney's practice. He wanted to marry Walter Savage Landor's daughter Julia (b. 1820) but was firmly rejected by her father (see Introduction). In 1835 he visited Norway, and in 1841 he emigrated to Western Australia, together with two of his brothers, practising as a barrister in Perth. He returned to England in 1846, where he published *The Bushman; or, Life in a New Country* (1847). He also published the novel *Lofoden: or, The Exiles of Norway*, 2 vols. (1849), which is set in northern Norway. He married while back in England, and returned to Australia in 1859 with wife and three children, resuming his practise, now as a solicitor. He took a keen interest in local politics, was active as a journalist and lecturer, and served as a Police Magistrate for Perth from 1866 until his death.

LATHAM, ROBERT GORDON
(1812–1888) Linguist and ethnologist. He visited Norway in 1833, only twenty-one years old, and became closely acquainted with the Wergeland family. Later he became Professor of English Literature, University College, London, and published widely on linguistic and historical topics. He also translated Esaias Tegnér's *Frithiof, a Norwegian Story* (1838) and *Axel* (no year).

LEES, JAMES ARTHUR
(1852–1931) Lancashire barrister. He married Lucy Martyn, daughter of the Rector of Melford, in 1882. He served as barrister of the Inner Temple (1881–89), and later county magistrate for Lancashire and Staffordshire. He

wrote *B.C. 1887: A Ramble in British Columbia* (1887) together with Walter J. Clutterbuck (*vid.*). He visited Norway in 1880 together with Clutterbuck and C. Kennedy, then in 1898 together with C. Kennedy, his son Robin and a nephew, and finally in 1907.

LLOYD, LLEWELLYN
(1792–1876) Son of a wealthy London bankier. Inspired by Arthur de Capell Brooke's (*vid.*) account, he travelled widely in Norway and Sweden from 1823 onwards, hunting and fishing, and then settled in Sweden, where he lived till his death. He published several books on hunting and wildlife and is reported to have hunted 102 bears.

LOVETT, RICHARD
(1851–1904) Clergyman, Master of Arts. He published several books of travel from various parts of Europe and several on religious topics.

LOWE, EMILY (EMMELINE)
Dates unknown. She was the daughter of Atwell Lowe, a judge in India, and visited Norway with her mother in the summer of 1856. In 1859 she visited Sicily and wrote the book *Unprotected Females in Sicily, Calabria, and on the Top of Mount Etna* (1859). She married Sir Spencer Clifford in the same year and had three daughters.

LOWER, MARK ANTHONY
(1813–1876) Archaeologist, from Chiddingly, Sussex. Largely self-taught, he first founded a mechanics' institution, and then in 1835 a 'high-class' school at Lewes, where he lived for more than thirty years. He founded Sussex Archaeological Society in 1846, and published several works on British history. He visited Norway in 1873 in search of health.

LYALL, EDNA (PSEUD. FOR BAYLY, ADA ELLEN)
(1857–1903) Novelist, born in Brighton into a family of Unitarians. Her father was a barrister. She moved to Eastbourne in 1884 and spent the rest of her life there. She published eighteen novels pseudonomously between 1879 and 1902, but allowed her identity to be known in 1886 after rumours of atheism and madness. John Ruskin is said to have read her novel *In the Golden Days* (1885) on his deathbed. Her visits to Norway took place in the summers of 1886 and 1888.

MACGREGOR, JOHN
(1825–1892) Of Scottish origin, he grew up in Brighton, but also spent part of his youth in Halifax, Nova Scotia, where his father was stationed. He was educated at Trinity College, Cambridge, earned an MA and became a barrister-at-law in the Temple, London. His publications include numerous magazine articles on canoeing (or kayaking), a book on law, and various travel books from America and the Middle East. He formed and became

Captain of the Royal Canoe Club, and largely invented this sport as it is known today.

MARTINEAU, HARRIET
(1802–1876) Writer and social critic. She published fictional works for children and adults, and works on history, religion and philosophy. In 1845 she moved to the Lake District, and became a friend of the Wordsworths. She probably never visited Norway.

MASSEY, GERALD
(1828–1907) Poet, born in Hertfordshire in humble circumstances. Tennyson described him as 'a poet of fine lyrical impulse, and of a rich half-Oriental imagination'. He was the original of George Eliot's character Felix Holt, in the novel of that title. Massey also published works on spiritualism, the origin of religions and on Shakespeare's sonnets, but is now more famous for his works on ancient Egypt.

MERRLEES, I. M. (MRS)
Dates unknown. Scottish missionary, who travelled around Norway with the Norwegian pastor Peter Lorenzen Hærem (1840–1878) in 1871. She had been brought into contact with Hærem through the Rev. Johan C. H. Storjohann, who was central in the foundation of the Norwegian Seaman's Church in London in the same year. Both Merrlees and Hærem were associated with the Norwegian *Lutherstiftelsen*, to which, in 1871, Mrs Merrlees donated a sum of £800. For the money a plot of land was bought in Underhaugsveien 15 in Christiania, on which a student home was built in 1876.

METCALFE, FREDERICK
(1815–1885) Graduated from St John's College, Cambridge, in 1838, and served as a Fellow of Lincoln College, Oxford, from 1844 until his death. He was ordained deacon in 1845, was bursar of Lincoln College and incumbent of St Michael's, Oxford, a living in the gift of his college. In 1851 he became sub-rector and in 1853 Greek lecturer at Lincoln. He was an acknowledged authority on Icelandic and on Norse language and literature, which he also taught at Oxford. His academic publications include works on Greek and Roman history. He travelled in Norway for several summers in the 1850s and in Iceland in 1860, and reportedly died in Norway.

MILFORD, JOHN
Dates unknown. He also published a travel account from the Continent in 1818, and a book on 'country bankers' in 1826. He travelled in Norway in 1841.

PHYTHIAN, JOSEPH COLLIER
(1844–?) Born in Manchester, where he ran a 'smallware' clothing

manufacturing business. He was an enthusiastic traveller, for business and pleasure, and a keen early amateur photographer. He travelled in Norway in 1876 but also appears to have visited the country earlier. He returned in 1879, whereupon he published the book *Three Years After* (1880).

POPPLEWELL, JOHN BENJAMIN & SARAH
John Benjamin (1830–1907) and his wife Sarah (b. Ward) ran a pub in Market Street, Bradford. They travelled in Norway in 1858.

PRICE, EDWARD
Dates unknown. Artist. He visited Norway in 1826, and he also published two books of illustrations from Dovedale, Derbyshire.

PRITCHETT, ROBERT TAYLOR
(1828–1907) He was originally a gunsmith, but turned to drawing and water-colours. He travelled in Norway in 1874 and 1875, and returned with Lord and Lady Brassey (*vid.*) in their yacht in 1885.

RHODES, EDITH CAROLINE
(1848–1905) The third child of Francis Rhodes, the Vicar of Bishop's Stortford in Hertfordshire, and his wife Louisa. She travelled widely and lived for some time in South Africa, where she acted as the principle hostess at Groote Schuur for her bachelor brother, the famous Cecil Rhodes (1853–1902). She also published some children's books and novels. Her visit to Norway probably took place in the summer of 1885.

ROBERTSON, JAMES LOGIE
(1846–1922) His pen-name was Hugh Haliburton. Being First English Master at Edinburgh Ladies' College, he published several collections of poetry, edited the works of Chaucer, Milton, Thomson, Scott and Burns, and wrote text books for schools, especially in literary history. He travelled in Norway and Sweden around 1880.

SEWARD, ANNA
(1747–1809) Writer, born at Eyam in Derbyshire, the daughter of Thomas Seward, the canon of Lichfield and of Salisbury, and Elizabeth Hunter. She started writing poetry at an early age, partly at the instigation of Erasmus Darwin. In addition to her poetry, consisting primarily of elegies and sonnets, she also published a poetical novel, *Louisa* (1784), which went through five editions, and a biography of Erasmus Darwin. She never married, and several of her poems were written in celebration of female friendship. After her death, Sir Walter Scott edited a three-volume edition of her poems.

SIXTY-ONE (PSEUD. FOR HELY-HUTCHINSON, GEORGE HENRY)
(1799–1883) Parson and sportsman. He came from a well-known Irish

family and was educated at Westminster and at Gonville and Caius College, Cambridge. He was ordained in 1829 and spent long periods in the island of Lewis on the Hebrides, shooting and fishing. He visited Norway in 1873, at the age of 74, and resigned his livings in 1876.

SLINGSBY, WILLIAM CECIL
(1849–1929) Born into a wealthy Yorkshire family of Scandinavian descent, he owned a textile factory and served as organist for Carlton Parish, Wakefield. Partly inspired by Harriet Martineau's (*vid.*) *Feats on the Fiord*, he visited Norway for the first time in 1872, made first ascents of a number of Norwegian summits, and became the pioneer of Norwegian mountaineering. During a thirty-year period he conducted about twenty expeditions to Norway.

SMITH, ALFRED
(1799?–1877) Curate of Poulshot, Wiltshire.

STONE, OLIVIA M.
Dates unknown. In a review in *The Atheneum* she was described as 'a pioneer of picnic travel.' Jane Robinson describes Stone's hefty tomes as providing 'touring gentlefolk with everything they needed to know in order to spend as comfortable and picturesque a time as possible in what were in the 1880s still rather outlandish holiday destinations'. She also published another travel book, *Tenerife and Its Six Satellites* (1887). She visited Norway in 1881 together with her husband John Harris Stone.

STRICKLAND, AGNES
(1796–1874) Born in Suffolk, she started writing historical romances and poetry, and later became a respected historical writer. Her works include *The Lives of the Queens of England* (12 vols., 1840–1849) and *Lives of the Queens of Scotland* (8 vols., 1850–1859), and she obtained a civil-list pension of £100 in 1871. Her book about Norway appeared in a sixth edition in 1851, and in a French translation in 1858.

STUART-WORTLEY, LADY EMMELINE (CHARLOTTE ELIZABETH)
(1806–1855) Poet, and the second daughter of John Henry Manners, fifth Duke of Rutland. She published numerous collections of poetry and some plays, and edited the annual the *Keepsake* in 1837 and 1840. An intrepid traveller, her books include *Travels in the United States* (3 vols., 1851).

SWINTON, ANDREW (PSEUD. FOR THOMSON, WILLIAM)
(1746–1817) Miscellaneous writer, born in Perthshire, Scotland. He studied theology at St Andrews and Edinburgh Universities, had an honorary degree in law from Glasgow University, and wrote pamphlets, memoirs, biographies, travelogues, commentaries on Scriptures, treatises, novels and dramas. He owned *The English Review* from 1794 to 1796. Other travel

works include *Travels in Europe, Asia and Africa from 1780–1784* (1788); *A Tour in England and Scotland by an English Gentleman* (1798), which was enlarged into *Prospects and Observations on a Tour in England and Scotland* (1791), written under the pseudonym 'Thomas Newte'; and *Travels in Scotland, 1805* (1807), under the pseudonym James Hall. He also wrote under the pseudonyms 'Harrison' and 'John Gabriel Stedman'.

TAYLOR, BAYARD
(1825–1878) American poet, novelist, travel writer and diplomat, whose books were published on both sides of the Atlantic. He was an acquaintance of Poe, Thoreau, Emerson, Lowell and Hawthorne, and is most famous for his book from California, *Eldorado: Or Adventures in the Path of Empire* (1850). He travelled in Norway and Sweden in the winter and summer of 1857, and married a Swedish woman, Marie Hansen, that year. From 1869 he taught German literature at Cornell and was appointed American Minister to Germany in 1878, but died shortly after arrival.

THOMSON, WILLIAM: see Swinton, Andrew

TUPPER, MARTIN FARQUHAR
(1810–1889) Writer, born in London of a Huguenot family. He was educated at Charterhouse and Christ Church, Oxford, and was later called to the bar, but never practised. He is most famous for his *Proverbial Philosophy* (1838–1867), a 'long series of didactic moralizings in blank verse', which was very popular at the time, but now the subject of satire.

TWEEDIE, MRS ALEC (ETHEL BRILLIANA)
(?–1940) Appearing also as Mrs. Ethel Alec-Tweedie, she was a writer of journalistic articles, biographies, autobiography and books on etiquette. Described as a pillar of Edwardian womanhood, she also wrote *A Girl's Ride in Iceland* (1889) and *Through Finland in Carts* (1897). She visited Norway several times during the 1890s and had a brother living in Christiania.

WADE, MARY HAZELTON
(1860–1936) Author of children's books. She lived in Hartford, Connecticut, and wrote a series of books in the 'Little Cousin' series about children of Eskimo, African, Indian, Russian, Japanese and Norwegian backgrounds, and frequently reprinted books for children about William Penn, James Cook, Henri Fabre and Thomas Jefferson.

WARD, FREDERICK WILLIAM ORDE
(1843–1922) Clergyman. He published several collections of poetry, frequently under the pseudonym Frederick Harald Williams, some works on religious questions, and a study of Shelley. His *Selected Poems* was published posthumously in 1924.

WARDLE, CHARLOTTE
Dates unknown. Welsh poet, daughter of the controversial radical MP
Colonel Gwyllym Lloyd Wardle and Ellen Elizabeth Parry, heiress of an old
North Welsh family. Her father was at various periods sheriff of Anglesey
and of Caernarvon. In 1809 he led an attack on corruption in the army which
forced the king's second son, the Duke of York, to resign as commander.
Ensuing law suits and financial problems forced him to give up his estates
and retire to Florence. Charlotte's other published poem, 'St. Aelian's: or,
The Cursing Well' (1814), shows a common combination of republican
sympathies and romantic localism. She remained in North Wales, marrying
Edward Morgan, but produced no further literary works.

WESTMINSTER, MARCHIONESS OF (GROSVENOR, ELIZABETH-MARY
LEVESON-GOWER)
(1797–1891) Her father was George Granville Leveson-Gower, Second
Marquis of Stafford and Duke of Sutherland (1758–1833), who was 'a
leviathan of wealth', owning most of the county of Sutherland, through his
wife. Her mother was Elizabeth, Countess of Sutherland (1765–1839). She
was married to Richard Grosvenor, Viscount Belgrave, later Marquis of
Westminster (1795–1869). She visited Norway, staying with the Jarlsbergs,
in 1827, and later also published *Narrative of a Yacht Voyage in the
Mediterranean during the Years 1840–1841* (1842).

WHEATON, HENRY
(1785–1848) American lawyer and diplomat. He was Chargé d'affaires in
Denmark (1827–1837), Minister to Prussia (1837–1846), a major authority
on international law and author of *A History of the Law of Nations in Europe
and America* (1842; originally published in French in 1838). His book on
Scandinavian history was coauthored with Andrew Crichton.

WILDE, LADY (JANE FRANCESCA ELGEE)
(1821–1896) Oscar Wilde's mother. She was married to the Irish surgeon Sir
William Wilde, and published several books of poetry under the pseudonym
'Speranza', in addition to books on Irish myth and superstition. She also did
some translations, especially of French novels. She visited Norway during
her honeymoon, in the summer of 1852. H. Wyndham published *Speranza:
A Biography of Lady Wilde* in 1951.

WILLIAMS, WILLIAM MATTIEU
(1820–1892) Chemist, who appears to have lived in Twickenham. He
published several books on chemistry, and articles on such diverse topics as
clothing, short-hand and electricity. He was also interested in Theosophy,
and his *A Vindication of Phrenology* was published posthumously, in 1894.
The book contains a memoir by his son G. C. Williams.

WILLSON, THOMAS B(ENJAMIN)
(1851–1932) Pastor. He wrote a large number of articles on Norway, in addition to the books *The Handy Guide to Norway* (1886; 6th ed. 1911); *History of the Church and State in Norway from the Tenth to the Sixteenth Century* (1903); and *Norway at Home* (1908). He was Secretary for the Norwegian Club in London from its foundation in 1894 until 1929.

WILSON, WILLIAM RAE
(1772–1849) Scottish solicitor, traveller and writer. Having inherited a fortune from his uncle, he travelled in Norway in 1824 and also published travel books on France and Italy, Russia and the Middle East. Especially *Travels in Egypt and the Holy Land* (1823) ran through several editions. He received the honorary degree of LL.D. from the University of Glasgow in 1844.

WOOD, CHARLES W(ILLIAM)
(1850?–1919) The son of the extremely successful writer of sensation novels Ellen Wood (Mrs Henry Wood; 1814–1887), who also owned the periodical *The Argosy*. For a number of years he contributed to and edited *The Argosy* together with his mother. He also published a biography, *Memorials of Mrs. Henry Wood* (1894), together with travel books on Germany, Holland and Spain. He visited Norway in 1877, 1885 and 1899, publishing one book from each visit.

WYNDHAM, FRANCIS MERRIK
(1839–?) Son of Lt. Col. Charles Wyndham of Rogate and Elizabeth, nee Scott, daughter of Baron Polwarth. His father was the brother of George, 1st Baron Leconfield, to whom his book is dedicated. Wyndham gained a BA at Merton College, Oxford, in 1861, and an MA in 1864. He was ordained a clergyman in the Church of England and became a curate in Kington, Herefordshire (1862–1866) and later in the parish of St. George in East London. Some time after 1866 he converted to Catholicism and became Canon of Westminster Cathedral. His later career is unclear, but he resided as a boarder at St. Charles College, Kensington, London, in the 1881 census, and in Brighton in 1882. He also published a genealogy of the Wyndham family. His visit to Norway took place in 1859.

REFERENCES

The list contains works consulted but not necessarily quoted. Authors whose names are uncertain are marked by a question mark after the name. Names and other information not mentioned on the work's title page are given in parenthesis.

Primary sources:

Ainsworth, W. F., ed. 1862. *All Round the World: An Illustrated Record of Voyages, Travels and Adventures in All Parts of the World.* Vol. 4. London: W. Kent & Co.

Alexander, William. 1779. *The History of Women from the Earliest Antiquity to the Present Time: Giving Some Account of Almost Every Interesting Particular Concerning that Sex, Among All Nations, Ancient and Modern.* 2 vols. London: W. Strahan and T. Cadell.

Allen, William. 1846–47. *Life of William Allen: With Selections from his Correspondence.* London: Charles Gilpin.

Anderson, Sir C. 1853. *An Eight Weeks' Journal in Norway &c. in 1852.* London: Francis & John Rivington.

Anglers' Evenings: Papers by Members of the Manchester Anglers' Association. 1880. Manchester: Abel Heywood & Son.

Arnold, E. Lester Linden. 1877. *A Summer Holiday in Scandinavia: With a Preface by Edwin Arnold.* London: Sampson Low.

Atkinson, J. Beavington. 1873. *An Art Tour to Northern Capitals of Europe.* New York: Macmillan and Co.

Austen, Jane. 1996. *Pride and Prejudice*, edited by Vivien Jones. 1813; Harmondsworth: Penguin Books.

Babington, Thomas: see Macaulay, Lord

Backhouse, Sarah. 1870. *Memoir of James Backhouse: By His Sister.* York: William Sessions, and London: F. Bowyer Kitto.

Baden, Gustav Ludvig. 1817. *The History of Norway: From the Earliest Times Continued from the Union of Calmar by Baron Holdberg.* Translated from the Danish by A. Andersen Feldborg. London: Printed for J. Bumpus by Hamblin and Seyfang.

Barnard, M(ordaunt) R(oger). 1864. *Sport in Norway, and Where to Find It; together with a Short Account of the Vegetable Productions of the Country, to Which Is Added, a List of the Alpine Flora of the Dovre Fjeld and of the Norwegian Ferns, &c.* London: Chapman and Hall.

————. 1871. *Sketches of Life, Scenery, and Sport in Norway.* London: Horace Cox.

Barrow, John Jr. 1834. *Excursions in the North of Europe, Through Parts of Russia, Finland, Sweden, Denmark, and Norway, in the Years 1830 & 1833.* London: John Murray.

Bates, H. W., ed. 1873. *Illustrated Travels: A Record of Discovery, Geography, and Adventure, With Engravings from Original Drawings by Celebrated Artists.* London: Cassell, Petter & Galpin.

Bayly, Ada Ellen: see Lyall, Edna

Beauclerk: see De Beauclerk, Lady

Belloc, Hilaire. 1951. 'Talking (and Singing) of the Nordic Man'. *Hilaire Belloc: An Anthology of His Prose and Verse.* Selected by W. N. Roughead. London: Ruper Hart-Davis.

Bennett, T(homas). 1881. *A Selection of Phrases for Tourists Travelling in Norway.* Fourth edition. Christiania: H. Tønsberg's Printing-office.

Bilton, William. 1840. *Two Summers in Norway.* 2 vols. London: Saunders and Otley.

Blacklock, W. J.: see Skinner, Bruce

Blackwood, Frederick Temple: see Dufferin, Lord

Blakeney, E. H., ed. 1926. *Peaks, Passes & Glaciers.* London: J. M. Dent.

(Blundell, Isabella Frances). 1862. *Gamle Norge (Old Norway) or, Our Holiday in Scandinavia.* London: Hamilton, Adams & Co.

Bowden, John. 1867. *Norway: Its People, Products and Institutions.* London: Chapman and Hall.

Bowden, Rev. J(ohn). 1869. *The Naturalist in Norway: or, Notes on the Wild Animals, Birds, Fishes, and Plants, of That Country, with Some Account of the Principal Salmon Rivers.* London: L. Reeve & Co.

Boydell's Picturesque Scenery of Norway: see Edy, John William

Boyesen, Hjalmar H. 1900. *A History of Norway from the Earliest Times.* With a New Chapter on the Recent History of Norway by C. F. Keary. London: T. Fisher Unwin.

Brace, Charles Loring. 1857. *The Norse-Folk; or, A Visit to the Homes of Norway and Sweden.* London: Richard Bentley.

Bradshaw, John. 1896. *Norway: Its Fjords, Fjelds and Fields*, London: Digby, Long and Co.

Braithwaite, Cecil. No year. *Fishing Here & There: Being Extracts from a Diary and Other Fragments.* London: Home Words Printing & Publishing Co.

Brassey, Lady. 1885. 'Mr. Gladstone in Norway'. *The Contemporary Review* (October): 480–502.

Brassey, Thomas Allnutt. 1857. *Journal of a Voyage through the Western Isles of Scotland and along the Coast of Norway, in the Yacht "Cymba," in the Summer of 1856.* London: Mann Nephews.

Bremner, Robert. 1840. *Excursions in Denmark, Norway and Sweden; Including Notices of the State of Public Opinion in Those Countries and Anecdotes of Their Courts.* 2 vols. London: Henry Colburn.

Breton, William Henry. 1835. *Scandinavian Sketches, or a Tour in Norway.* London: J. Bohn.

Britannicus, Mela (pseud. for Charles Kelsall). 1836. *Horae Viaticae.* London: Printed for the author.

'British Tourist in Norway, The'. 1872. *Blackwood's Edinburgh Magazine* 112, no. 681 (July): 31–48, 306–26.

Bromley-Davenport, Lenette. 1974. *The History of Capesthorne, Cheshire.* No publ.

Bromley-Davenport, W(illiam). 1885. *Sport: Fox-Hunting, Covert-Shooting, Salmon-Fishing, Deer-Stalking.* Illustrated by Lt.- General Henry Hope Crealocke. London: Chapman and Hall, Ltd.

Brontë, Charlotte. 1985. *Jane Eyre.* Edited by Q. D. Leavis. 1847; Harmondsworth: Penguin Books.

Brooke, Arthur de Capell. 1823. *Travels through Sweden, Norway and Finmark, to the North Cape in the Summer of 1820.* London: Rodwell and Martin.

Brougham, Lord Henry. 1871. *The Life and Times of Henry Lord Brougham, Written by Himself.* 3 vols. Edinburgh: William Blackwood & Sons.

Brown, Thomas. 1816. *The Wanderer in Norway, with Other Poems.* 1815; London: J. Murray.

Browne, J. Ross. 1862. 'A Flying Trip Through Norway'. *Harper's New Monthly Magazine* 25, no. 146 (July): 145–61, and vol. 25, no. 147 (August): 289–306.

Buch, Leopold von. 1813. *Travels through Norway and Lapland, During the Years 1806, 1807, and 1808.* Transl. John Black. With notes and illustrations, chiefly mineralogical, and some account of the author, by Robert Jameson. London: Henry Colburn.

Bunbury, Selina. 1853. *Life in Sweden: With Excursions in Norway and Denmark.* 2 vols. London: Hurst and Blackett.

Bunsen, Theodor von. 1888. 'Home Rule in Norway'. *The Nineteenth Century*, no. 131 (January): 54–70.

Burnett, Alexander G. 1887. *A Trip to Norway in the St. Rognvald.* Aberdeen: James Murray.

Burnett, Frances Hodgson. 1993. *The Secret Garden.* 1911; Bristol: Parragon Book Service.

Byron, Lord. 1970. *Poetical Works.* Ed. by Frederick Page. Oxford: Oxford University Press.

Campbell, J. F. 1865. *Frost and Fire: Natural Engines, Tool-Marks and Chips with Sketches Taken at Home and Abroad by a Traveller.* 2 vols. Edinburgh: Edmonston & Douglas.

Campbell, John R. 1871. *How to See Norway.* London: Longmans, Green, and Co.

Campion, William Winter. 1892. *Through Northern Seas: A Trip to the Land of the Midnight Sun.* London: Jarrold & Sons.

Canning, Charles John Spencer: see Garvagh, Lord

Carlyle, Thomas. 1889. *The Early Kings of Norway.* 1875; London: Chapman & Hall.

Chapman, Abel. 1897. *Wild Norway: With Chapters on Spitsbergen, Denmark Etc.* London: Edward Arnold.

(Clark, John Willis & Joseph W. Dunning). 1857. *A Long Vacation Ramble in Norway and Sweden, by X and Y (Two Unknown Quantities).* Cambridge: Macmillan and Co.

Clarke, Edward Daniel. 1824. *Travels in Various Countries of Europe, Asia and Africa.* Part the Third: Scandinavia. Vol. 10. London: T. Cadell.

Coates, Florence Earle. 1897. 'Nansen'. *Harper's New Monthly Magazine* 95 (November): 924.

Cobbett, William. 1967. *Rural Rides.* Edited by George Woodcock. 1830; Harmondsworth: Penguin Books.

Conway, Derwent (pseud. for Inglis, Henry David). 1829. *A Personal Narrative of a Journey through Norway, Parts of Sweden and the Islands and States of Denmark.* Edinburgh: Constable and Co; London: Hurst Chance and Co.

Cook, Thomas. 1866. *Supplement to Cook's Excursionist and Home and Foreign Tourist Advertiser* (1 May).

———. 1880. *Cook's Excursionist and Home and Foreign Tourist Advertiser* 30, no. 1 (2 February).

———. 1886. *Cook's Excursionist and Home and Foreign Tourist Advertiser* 36, no. 10 (11 October).

———. 1890. *Programme of Cook's Conducted Tours to Denmark, Sweden and Norway, the Land of Fjord, Fjeld and Fos, the North Cape and Land of the Midnight Sun.* London: Thos. Cook and Son Chief Office.

———. 1891. *Cook's Tourist's Handbook: Norway, Sweden and Denmark.* New York: Thomas Cook and Son.

———. 1892. *Cook's Excursionist and Home and Foreign Tourist Advertiser* 42, no. 6 (13 June).

———. 1895. *Cook's Excursionist and Home and Foreign Tourist Advertiser* 45, no. 11 (1 November).

———. 1897. *Cook's Tourist Handbook: Norway, Sweden and Denmark, Including Iceland.* 3rd ed. London: Thomas Cook and Son.

Corelli, Marie. 1894. *Thelma: A Norwegian Princess.* 1887; London: Richard Bentley and Son.

Corner, Julia. 1841. *The History of Denmark, Sweden and Norway from the Earliest Period to the Present Time: Adapted for Youth, Schools and Families.* London: Dean and Munday.

Cottle, Joseph. 1978. *The Fall of Cambria.* Introd. by Donald H. Reiman. 1808; New York & London: Garland Publishing.

Coxe, William. 1802. *Travels in Poland, Russia, Sweden, and Denmark: Illustrated with Charts and Engravings.* Vol. 5. 5th edition. London: T.

Cadell, Jun. and W. Davies.

Crichton, Andrew and Henry Wheaton. 1860. *Scandinavia, Ancient and Modern; Being a History of Denmark, Sweden and Norway: Comprehending Description of These Countries; an Account of the Mythology, Government, Laws, Manners, and Institutions of the Early Inhabitants; and of the Present State of Society, Religion, Literature, Arts, and Commerce; with Illustrations of Their Natural History.* 2 vols. New York: Harper & Brothers, Publishers.

Crompton-Roberts, Violet: see Three Girls.

Davy, Sir Humphry. 1968(?). *Scandinavia Assessed in 1824.* London: (Stockwell). Reprint from John Davy. 1836. *Memoirs of the Life of Sir Humphry Davy.* London.

De Vere, Sir Aubrey. 1842. 'The Fate of Norway'. *A Song of Faith: Devout Exercises, and Sonnets.* London.

Di Beauclerk, Lady (Diane de Vere). 1868. *A Summer and Winter in Norway.* London: John Murray.

Dickens, Charles. 1997. *Our Mutual Friend.* Edited by Adrian Poole. 1864–65; Harmondsworth: Penguin Books.

Downes, George. 1839. *Three Months in the North, including Excursions in Tellemark and Ringerige with an Itinerary.* Edinburgh: William Blackwood and Sons; London: T. Cadell; Dublin: J. Cumming.

Doyle, Sir Arthur Conan. 1993. *The Memoirs of Sherlock Holmes.* Ed. by Christopher Roden. 1894; Oxford: Oxford University Press.

Dufferin, Lord (Blackwood, Frederick Temple). 1857. *Letters from High Latitudes: Being Some Account of a Voyage in the Schooner Yacht 'Foam', 85 O.M. to Iceland, Jan Mayen, & Spitzbergen, in 1856.* London: John Murray.

Dunham, S. A. 1839. *History of Denmark, Sweden and Norway.* London: Longman.

Dunne, Mary Chavelita: see Egerton, George

Dyer, John. 1855. *The Fleece,* in *The Poetical Works of Mark Akenside and John Dyer.* Edited by Robert Aris Willmott. London: George Routledge.

(Edy, John William. 1820). *Boydell's Picturesque Scenery of Norway with the Principal Towns from the Naze, by the Route of Christiania to the Magnificent Pass of the Swinesund from Original Drawings Made on the Spot and Engraved by John William Edy with Remarks and Observations Made in a Tour through the Country, and Revised and Corrected by William Tooke, F. R. S.* 2 vols. Vol. 1. London: Hurst, Robinson and Co.

Egerton, George (pseud. for Mary Chavelita Dunne). 1894. *Discords.* London: John Lane.

———. 1898. *Fantasias.* London: John Lane, The Bodley Head.

———. 1977. *Keynotes.* 1893; New York: Garland Publishing, Inc.

———. 1897. *Symphonies.* London: John Lane, The Bodley Head.

———. 1901. *Rosa Amorosa: The Love-Letters of a Woman.* London: Grant

Richards.

Either and Both (pseud. for Scargill-Bird, S. R.). 1885. *One and a Half in Norway: A Chronicle of Small Beer*. London: Kegan Paul, Trench & Co.

Elliott, Charles Boileau. 1832. *Letters from the North of Europe, or a Journal of Travels in Holland, Denmark, Norway, Sweden, Finland, Russia, Prussia, and Saxony*. London: Henry Colburn and Richard Bentley.

Elton, Charles. 1864. *Norway: The Road and the Fell*. London & Oxford: John Henry and James Parker.

Elwes, Alfred. 1853. *The Richmonds' Tour Through Europe: With Seventeen Illustrations*. London: Addy and Co.

Everest, Rev. Robert. 1829. *A Journey through Norway, Lapland, and Sweden: With Some Remarks on the Geology of the Country; Its Climate and Scenery; the Ascent of Some of Its Principal Mountains – the Present Political Relations of the Two Countries – Statistical Tables, Meteorological Observations, &c.* London: Thomas & George Underwood.

Forbes, James D. 1853. *Norway and Its Glaciers Visited in 1851: Followed by Journals of Excursions in the High Alps of Dauphiné, Berne, and Savoy*. Edinburgh: Adam and Charles Black.

Forester, Thomas. 1850. *Norway in 1848 and 1849: Containing Rambles among the Fjelds and Fjords of The Central and Western Districts; and Including Remarks on Its Political, Military, Ecclesiastical, and Social Organisation, with Extracts from the Journals of Lieut. M. S. Biddulph, Royal Artillery*. London: Longman, Brown, Green, and Longmans.

Forester, Thomas, ed. 1853. *Norway and Its Scenery: Comprising the Journal of a Tour by Edward Price, Esq. with Considerable Additions and a Road-Book for Tourists with Hints to Anglers and Sportsmen*. London: Henry G. Bohn.

Francis, Sir Philip. 1814. 'Letter from Sir Philip Francis, Knight of the most Honorable Order of the Bath, to Earl Gray, on the Policy of Great Britain and the Allies towards Norway'. *The Pamphleteer* 4, no. 7 (August): 67–85.

Froude, J(ames) A(nthony). 1882. 'The Norway Fjords'. *Longman's Magazine* (December): 195–222.

Froude, James Anthony. 1884. 'Norway Once More'. *Longman's Magazine* (October): 588–608.

Galton, Francis, ed. 1861. *Vacation Tourists and Notes of Travel in 1860*. Cambridge: Macmillan and Co.

Garvagh, Lord. 1875. *The Pilgrim of Scandinavia*. London: Sampson Low, Marston, Low, & Searle.

Gilfillan, Robert. 1839. 'Norwegian Smuggler's Song'. *Poems and Songs*. 3rd ed. Edinburgh: Smith, Elder and Co.

Golder, S. 1888. *A Tandem Tour in Norway*. London: Iliffe & Son.

Goodman, E. J. 1892. *The Best Tour in Norway*. London: Sampson Low, Marston & Company.

————. 1896. *New Ground in Norway: Ringerike – Telemarken – Sæters-dalen. With Fifty-Six Illustrations, from Original Photographs by Paul Lange, Late President of the Liverpool Amateur Photographic Association.* London: George Newnes.

Gosse, Edmund W. 1874. 'The Present Condition of Norway'. *Fraser's Magazine* (New Series) 9 (February): 174–85.

————. 1879. *Studies in the Literature of Northern Europe.* London: C. Kegan Paul & Co.

Greenwell, George Clementson. 1892. *To Christiania, Stockholm, and Gothenburg.* Newcastle-on-Tyne: Andrew Reid, Sons & Co.

Grellet, Stephen: see Seebohm, Benjamin

Griffith, Durham. 1892. *An Arctic Eden: A Tale of Norway.* London: Skeffington & Son.

Grosvenor, Elizabeth Mary: see Westminster, Marchioness of

Habberton, John. 1881. 'The Land of the Midnight Sun'. *Harper's New Monthly Magazine* 63, no. 378 (November): 882–94.

Haggard, H. Rider. 1891. *Eric Brighteyes.* London: Longmans, Green, and Co.

Half Hours in the Far North: Life amid Snow and Ice. 1881. (The Half Hour Library of Travel, Nature and Science for Young Readers). London: Wm. Isbister Ltd.

Haliburton, Hugh (pseud.): see Robertson, James Logie

Hammer, S. C. 1928. *Norway.* With Illustrations by A. Heaton Cooper. London: A. & C. Black Ltd.

Handbook for Travellers in Norway. 1874. Fifth edition revised. London: John Murray.

Hansen-Taylor, Marie and Horace E. Scudder, eds. 1885. *Life and Letters of Bayard Taylor.* 2 vols. Boston: Houghton, Mifflin and Company.

Hare, Augustus J. C. 1885. *Sketches in Holland and Scandinavia.* London: Smith, Elder, & Co.

————. 1953. *In My Solitary Life: Being an Abridgement of the Last Three Volumes of The Story of My Life.* Edited with Notes and Introduction by Malcolm Barnes. London: George Allen & Unwin Ltd.

Hemans, Felicia Dorothea. 1839. 'Old Norway: A Mountain War-Song'. *The Works of Mrs. Hemans: With a Memoir of Her Life, by Her Sister*, vol. 7. 1834; Edinburgh, 100.

Heywood Jr., Abel. 1880. 'Trout Fishing in Norway'. *Anglers' Evenings: Papers by Members of the Manchester Anglers' Association.* Manchester: Abel Heywood & Son.

Hollway, John George. 1853. *A Month in Norway.* London: John Murray.

Hooker, William Dawson. 1839. *Notes on Norway; or A Brief Journal of a Tour Made to the Northern Parts of Norway, in the Summer of MDCCCXXXVI.* 1837; Glasgow: George Richardson.

Horne, Richard Henry (Hengist). 1875. 'Arctic Heroes. A Fragment of Naval History. Prologue'. *Poems.* Chadwyck-Healey Ltd.: English Poetry Data Base.

Howarth, Mary. 1895. *Stories of Norway in the Saga Days*. Ill. by F. Hamilton Jackson. London: Gay and Bird.

Howitt, William and Mary. 1852. *The Literature and Romance of Northern Europe: Constituting a Complete History of the Literature of Sweden, Denmark, Norway and Iceland, with Copious Specimens of the Most Celebrated Histories, Romances, Popular Legends and Tales, Old Chivalrous Ballads, Tragic and Comic Dramas, National and Favourite Songs, Novels, and Scenes from the Life of the Present Day*. 2 vols. London: Colburn and Co.

Hughes, Molly. 1935. *Vivians: A Family in Victorian Cornwall*. Oxford: Oxford University Press.

Hurton, William. 1851. *A Voyage from Leith to Lapland; or, Pictures of Scandinavia in 1850*. Vol. 2. London: Richard Bentley.

――――. (1856). *The Doomed Ship: or The Wreck in the Arctic Regions*. 1855; London: William Andrews & Co.

Hyne, Cutcliffe. 1898. *Through Arctic Lapland*. London: Adam and Charles Black.

Illustrated London News (26 September 1885): 317, 324, 326.

Inglis, Henry David: see Conway, Derwent

Jones, George Matthew. 1827. *Travels in Norway, Sweden, Finland, Russia, and Turkey; also on the Coasts of Azof and of the Black Sea: with a Review of the Trade in Those Seas, and of the Systems Adopted to Man the Fleets of the Different Powers of Europe, Compared with that of England*. Vol. 2. London: John Murray.

Jungman, Nico. 1905. *Norway*. London: A. & C. Black.

Keane, John F. 1887. *Three Years of a Wanderer's Life*. 2 vols. London.

Keary, C(harles) F(rancis). 1892. *Norway and the Norwegians*. London: Percival & Co.

Keely, Robert N. and G. G. Davis. 1893. *In Arctic Seas: The Voyage of the 'Kite' with the Peary Expedition together with a Transcript of the Log of the 'Kite'*. Philadelphia: Rufus C. Hartranft.

Kelsall, Charles: see Britannicus, Mela

Kent, S. H. 1877. *Within the Arctic Circle: Experiences of Travel Through Norway, to the North Cape, Sweden, and Lapland*. 2 vols. (bound in one). London: Richard Bentley and Son.

Kingsley, Charles. 1906. *The Roman and the Teuton: A Series of Lectures Delivered before the University of Cambridge*. London: Macmillan and Co.

Kinross, John. 1871. *A Holiday in Scandinavia*. Glasgow.

Laing, Robert Meason. 1841. *Hours in Norway: Poems. To Which Is Added a Version of Oehlenschläger's* Axel and Valborg, A Tragedy. London: Thomas Hookham.

――――. 1842. *A Bard's Last Dream: A Poem; in Three Fits*. Christiania: Printed by Guldberg & Dzwonkowski as Manuscript, for the Author.

Laing, Samuel. 1837. *Journal of a Residence in Norway During the Years 1834, 1835, & 1836, Made with a View to Enquire into the*

Moral and Political Economy of That Country, and the Conditions of Its Inhabitants. 2nd ed. London: Longman, Orme, Brown, Green, and Longmans.

———— (transl.). 1844. *The Heimskringla, or Chronicle of the Kings of Norway*. London: Longman, Grown, Green, and Longmans.

————. 1997. *Dagbok frå eit opphald i Norge i åra 1834, 1835 og 1836: Med det formål å undersøke den moralske tilstand og samfunns-økonomiske forhold i landet, og levekåra for innbyggarane*. Trans. and Introd. Kåre Snekkvik. Oppdal: Snøfugl.

————. Photocopy of typescript of Samuel Laing's unpublished diary for March 1834–December 1856, lent to the authors by Andrew Laing.

Landor, Edward Wilson. 1836. *Adventures in the North of Europe: Illustrative of the Poetry and Philosophy of Travel*. 2 vols. London: Saunders and Otley.

————. 1849. *Lofoden; or, The Exiles of Norway*. London: Smith, Elder & Co.

————. Warwickshire County Record Office. CR 1908 /276/1-4.

Latham, R. G. 1840. *Norway and the Norwegians*. 2 vols. London: Richard Bentley.

(Lees, James A. & Walter J. Clutterbuck). 1995. *Three in Norway by Two of Them*. 1882; Oslo: Aschehoug.

Lees, J. A. 1899. *Peaks and Pines: Another Norway Book*, with 63 Illustrations and Photographs by the Author. Longmans, Green, and Co.

Lloyd, L(lewellyn). 1854. *Scandinavian Adventures, During a Residence of Upwards of Twenty Years: Presenting Sporting Incidents, and Subjects of Natural History, and Devices for Entrapping Wild Animals. With Some Account of the Northern Fauna*. 2 vols. London: Richard Bentley.

————. 1885. *The Field Sports of the North of Europe: A Narrative of Angling, Hunting, and Shooting in Sweden and Norway*. Enlarged and revised edition. 1830; London: Hamilton Adams & Co.

Lovett, Richard. 1885. *Norwegian Pictures: Drawn with Pen and Pencil, Containing also a Glance at Sweden and the Gotha Canal, With a Map and One Hundred and Twenty-Seven Illustrations from Sketches and Photographs, Engraved by E. Whymper, R. & E. Taylor, Pearson, and Others*. London: The Religious Tract Society.

Lowe, Emily. 1857. *Unprotected Females in Norway, or The Pleasantest Way of Travelling There, Passing through Denmark and Sweden. With Scandinavian Sketches from Nature*. London: G. Routledge & Co.

————. 1987. *Reise i Norge 1856*. Edited by Åse Enerstvedt. Bergen: J. W. Eides forlag.

Lower, Mark Antony. 1874. *Wayside Notes in Scandinavia*. London: Henry S. King and Co.

Lyall, Edna, (pseud. for Bayly, Ada Ellen). No year. *A Hardy Norseman*. 1890; New York: George Munro.

Lyell, Charles. 1881. *Life, Letters and Journals of Sir Charles Lyell, Bart*. Edited by his sister-in-law, Mrs. Lyell. 2 vols. London: John

Murray.

(Macfarlane, K.?). 1884. *Behind the Scenes in Norway, by a Special Correspondent*. Glasgow: David Bryce and Son.

MacGregor, J. 1867. *The Rob Roy on the Baltic: A Canoe Cruise through Norway, Sweden, Denmark, Sleswig, Holstein, the North Sea, and the Baltic*. London: Sampson Low, Son, and Marston.

'Maelstrom: A Fragment, The'. 1834. *Fraser's Magazine for Town and Country* 10, no. 57 (September): 267–81.

Mallet, M.[1] 1847. *Northern Antiquities: Or an Historical Account of the Manners, Customs, Religions and Laws, Maritime Expeditions and Discoveries, Language and Literature of the Ancient Scandinavians (Danes, Swedes, Norwegians and Icelanders) With incidental notices respecting our Saxon ancestors*. Translated from the French of M. Mallet by Bishop Percy. New Edition, revised throughout, and considerably enlarged; with a translation of the prose EDDA from the original Old Norse Text; and notes critical and explanatory, by I. A. Blackwell, Esq. 1770; London: Henry G. Bohn.

Malthus, Thomas Robert. 1992. *An Essay on the Principle of Population, or A View of its past and present Effects on Human Happiness; With an Inquiery into our Prospects respecting the future Removal or Mitigation of the Evils which it occasions*. Selected and introduced by Donald Winch. Cambridge: Cambridge University Press.

———. 1966. *The Travel Diaries of Thomas Robert Malthus*. Ed. by Patricia James. Cambridge: Cambridge University Press.

Martineau, Harriet. 1894. *Feats on the Fiord*. 1841; Boston: Joseph Knight Company.

Massey, Gerald. 1889. 'Old King Hake'. *My Lyrical Life: Poems Old and New*. London.

Merrlees, Mrs. I. M. 1871. *Jottings from Our Journal in Norway*. Clifton: E. Austin.

Metcalfe, Frederick. 1857. *The Oxonian in Norway; or Notes of Excursions in that Country*. Second edition, revised. 1856; London: Hurst and Blackett.

———. 1858. *The Oxonian in Thelemarken; or, Notes of Travel in South-Western Norway in the Summers of 1856 and 1857. With Glances at the Legendary Lore of That District*. 2 vols. London: Hurst and Blackett.

———. 1880. *The Englishman and the Scandinavian; or A Comparison of Anglo-Saxon and Old Norse Literature*. London: Trübner & Co.

Milford, John. 1842. *Norway, and Her Laplanders, in 1841: With a Few Hints to the Salmon Fisher*. London: John Murray.

Milton, John. 1989. *Paradise Lost*. Ed. by Christopher Ricks. 1667; Harmondsworth: Penguin Books.

Morgan, Nicholas. 1871. *Phrenology and How to Use it in Analyzing*

[1] His first name was Paul Henry, but he is usually listed as 'Mallet, M' (for Monsieur).

Character. London, Longmans, Green and Co.

Mourey, Gabriel. 1897. 'Fritz Thaulow – The Man and the Artist'. *The Studio, An Illustrated Magazine of Fine & Applied Art* 11, no. 51 (15 June): 3–16.

Munch, P. A. 1862. *The Norwegian Invasion of Scotland: A Translation from Det Norske Folks Historie, Communicated to the Archaeological Society of Glasgow by Hugh Tennent*. Glasgow: Bell and Bain.

Murray, John. 1878. *Handbook for Travellers in Norway*. 6th ed. London: John Murray.

Naylor, Robert Anderton. 1887. *Letters on Sweden and Norway*. London.

'New Norwegian Highway, A'. 1893. *The Graphic* (23 September): 400, 402.

Newland, Henry (The Rev.). 1854. *Forest Scenes in Norway and Sweden: Being Extracts from the Journal of a Fisherman*. London: G. Routledge & Co.

Ogilvie, Alice. 1891. *A Visit to the Summer Home in the Saetersdal and Southern Norway, with an Introduction by R. M. Ballantyne*. Edinburgh: Macniven and Wallace.

'Our Tour in Norway. The Diary of Two London Girls'. 1885. *The Girl's Own Paper* 6, no. 266 (31 January): 284–6.

Parr, Mrs. 1833. 'A Northman's Story'. *Longman's Magazine* (April): 628–43.

Parson and the Lawyer, the (pseud. for Edward Trustram). 1895. *A Yachting Cruise to Norway*. London: T. Fisher Unwin.

Paterson, M. 1886. *Mountaineering below the Snow-Line, or The Solitary Pedestrian in Snowdonia and Elsewhere*. With etchings by Mackaness. London: G. Redway.

Peacock, Thomas Love. 1906. 'Fiolfar, King of Norway'. *The Poems of Thomas Love Peacock*. 1806; London: George Routledge & Sons.

Pease, George Card. 1894. 'Up the Norway Coast'. *Harper's New Monthly Magazine* 89, no. 531 (August): 375–83.

Philip, George Ernest. 1896. *Holiday Fortnights at Home and Abroad, with 38 Illustrations*. London: Houlston and Sons.

Phythian, J(oseph) C. 1877. *Scenes of Travel in Norway*. London: Cassell, Petter & Galpin.

Poe, Edgar Allan. 1986. 'The Descent into the Maelstrom'. *The Fall of the House of Usher and Other Writings*. Ed. David Galloway. 1841; Harmondsworth: Penguin Books.

(Popplewell, John Benjamin and Sarah). 1859. *Norway in 1858, Lindesnæs to Midnight Sun: And Nordkap to Christiania*. Printed for Private Circulation by Wm. Byles, Observer Office, Bradford.

Price, Edward. 1834. *Norway. Views of Wild Scenery: and Journal*. London: Hamilton, Adams, and Company.

———: see Forester, Thomas (1853)

Pritchett, Robert Taylor. 1879. *'Gamle Norge': Rambles and Scrambles in Norway, With More than a Hundred and Twenty Illustrations*. London:

Virtue & Co.

Randell, James. 1854. *Views in Norway, from Original Pictures*. London: Colnaghi & Co.

Rhodes, Edith. 1886. *The Adventures of Five Spinsters in Norway*. London: John and Robert Maxwell.

Richardson, George. 1849. *The Rise and Progress of the Society of Friends in Norway*. London: Charles Gilpin.

Robertson, F. 1870. *Torquil, or the Days of Olaf Tryggvason, with Legends, Ballads, Dreams, etc.* Edinburgh: Adam & Charles Black.

Robertson, James Logie. 1881. 'Norwegian Sonnets'. *Blackwood's Magazine* 129 (June): 750–52.

———. 1881. *Orellana and Other Poems*. Edinburgh: Blackwood and Sons.

———. 1889. *New Songs of Innocence*. Edinburgh: Macniven and Wallace.

Robertson, James Logie and Janet L. Robertson. 1882. *Our Holiday among the Hills*. Edinburgh: Blackwood and Sons.

Savage, Richard. 1962. 'The Wanderer'. *The Poetical Works of Richard Savage*. Ed. by Clarence Tracy. 1729; Cambridge: Cambridge University Press.

Scargill-Bird, S. R.: see Either and Both

Seebohm, Benjamin, ed. 1861. *Memoirs of the Life and Gospel Labours of Stephen Grellet*. 2 vols. London: A. W. Bennett.

Sheffer, John. 1674. *The History of Lapland Wherein Are Shewed the Original Manners, Habits, Marriages, Conjurations of that People*. Oxford.

Shelley, Mary. 1992. *Frankenstein: Or The Modern Prometheus*. Penguin Classics. Ed. by Maurice Hindle. 1818; Harmondsworth: Penguin Books.

Shelley, Percy Bysshe. 1966. *Selected Poetry*. Ed. by Harold Bloom. New York: New American Library (Signet Classic Poetry Series).

Shephard, J. S. 1873. *Over the Dovrefjelds*. London: Henry S. King & Co.

Shore, Charles John: see Teignmouth, Lord

Sixty-One (pseud. for Hely-Hutchinson, George Henry). 1874. *A Trip to Norway in 1873 by 'Sixty-One' with Illustrations by Fredrick Milbank, Esq., M. P. and Miss Alice Milbank*, London: Bickers and Son.

Skinner, Bruce. 1841. *Sketches in Norway: Etched by W. J. Blacklock, from Drawings Made During the Long Vacation, by Bruce Skinner, Esq. B. A. Trin. Coll. Cam.* London: J.Robinson.

Slingsby, William Cecil. 1904. *Norway the Northern Playground: Sketches of Climbing and Mountain Exploration in Norway Between 1872 and 1903*. Edinburgh: David Douglas.

Smith, Alfred. 1847. *Sketches in Norway and Sweden: Drawn on Stone from the Original Sketches by Henry Warren*. London: Thomas MacLean.

Smith, Alfred Charles. 1893. *The Autobiography of an old Passport*. London: Digby, Long and Co.

Smith, Hubert. 1873. *Tent Life with English Gipsies in Norway*. Henry S.

King & Co.

Smith, W. Alexander. 1864. 'Earl Eirek's Voyage: A Norse Ballad'. *Once a Week* 11, no. 280 (5 November): 545–46.

Snow, W. Parker. 1851. *Voyage of the Prince Albert in Search of Sir John Franklin: A Narrative of Every-Day Life in the Arctic Seas.* London: Longman, Brown, Green, and Longmans.

(Somerville, D. M. M). 1898. *Winter Life in Norway Descriptive of Sports and Pastimes on Ice and Snow.* Ed. by The Norwegian Winter Tourist Association. Christiania.

Stone, Olivia M. 1882. *Norway in June.* London: Marcus Ward & Co.

(Strickland, Agnes). (1826). *The Rival Crusoes, or The Shipwreck. Also A Voyage to Norway; and The Fisherman's Cottage. Founded on Facts.* London: J. Harris.

Stuart-Wortley, Emmeline Charlotte Elizabeth. 1838. 'Old Norway'. *Lays of Leisure Hours.* 2 vols. London: Thomas Hookham.

Sundt, Eilert. 1980. *On Marriage in Norway.* Translated and introduced by Michael Drake. 1855; Cambridge: Cambridge University Press.

Swinton, Andrew (pseud. for William Thomson). 1792. *Travels into Norway, Denmark, and Russia in the Years 1788, 1789,1790, and 1791.* Dublin: W. Jones.

Taylor, Bayard. 1873. *Lars: A Pastoral of Norway.* London: Strahan & Co.

———. 1858. *Northern Travel: Summer and Winter Pictures of Sweden, Lapland, and Norway.* London: Sampson Low, Son and Co.

———. 1907. *The Poems of Bayard Taylor.* With an Introduction by Albert H. Smyth. New York: Thomas Y. Crowell & Co.

Teignmouth, Lord (Shore, Charles John). 1878. *Reminiscences of Many Years.* 2 vols. Edinburgh: David Douglas.

Tennyson, Hallam Lord. 1897. *Alfred Lord Tennyson: A Memoir by His Son.* 2 vols. London: Macmillan and Co.

Thomas-Stanford, Charles. 1903. *A River of Norway: Being the Notes and Reflections of an Angler.* London: Longmans, Green, and Co.

Thomson, James: *The Seasons.* 1981. Ed. by James Sambrook. 1726–30; Oxford: Clarendon Press.

Thomson, William: see Swinton, Andrew

Three Girls (Crompton-Roberts, Violet): 1888. *A Jubilee Jaunt to Norway.* London: Griffith, Farran, Okeden & Welsh.

Times, The. 17 March 1814.

Tønsberg, Chr., ed. 1875. *Norway: Illustrated Handbook for Travellers.* Christiania: Chr. Tønsberg Publisher.

Tourist-Guide 1895 (no publisher).

Trip to Norway in 1873 by 'Sixty-One', A: With Illustrations by Fredrick Milbank, Esq., M.P. and Miss Alice Milbank. 1874. London: Bickers and Son.

Trustram, Edward: see Parson and the Lawyer, the

Turnbull, E. George. 1899. 'The Girls of Norway'. *The Girl's Realm*

1 (March): 479–83.

Tweedie, Mrs. Alec. 1894. *A Winter Jaunt to Norway: With Accounts of Nansen, Ibsen, Björnson, Brandes, and Many Others*. 1893; London: Bliss, Sands and Foster.

United Kingdom. *Hansard's Parliamentary Debates*, 3rd series, vol. 287 (1884) and vol. 304 (1886).

Usher, Frank: see Bates, H. W., ed.

Vere, Diana de: see Di Beauclerk.

Vickers, L. (Miss). 1893. *Old Norway and its Fjords or A Holiday in Norseland*. Lincoln: Arkihill, Ruddock and Keyworth.

Vinje, Aasmund Olavsson. 1863. *A Norseman's Views of Britain and the British*. Edinburgh: William P. Nimmo.

'Visit to the North Cape, A'. 1851. *Harper's New Monthly Magazine* 3, no. 13 (June): 102–5.

Vivians, Tony, Mary & Joe: see Hughes, Mary Vivian

Wade, Mary Hazelton. 1904. *The Little Norwegian Girl*. London: Ward, Lock & Co.

Ward, Frederick William Orde: see Williams, F. Harald (pseud.)

Wardle, Charlotte. 1814. *Norway: A Poem*. London: J. Ridgway.

Wemyss, R. Erskine. 1895. *The Maid of Norway and Other Poems*. Privately printed for the author by Messrs. Hatchard, Piccadilly.

Westminster, Marchioness of (Grosvenor, Elizabeth Mary). 1879. *Diary of a Tour in Sweden, Norway, and Russia, in 1827, with Letters*. London: Jurst and Blackett.

Wheaton, Henry. 1831. *History of the Northmen, or Danes and Normans, from the Earliest Times to The Conquest of England by William of Normandy*. London: John Murray.

Whitling, H. J. 1850. 'The Architect in Search of the Picturesque, in Norway'. *Bentley's Miscellany* 27 (London: Richard Bentley): 457–64.

Wilde, Lady (Jane Francesca Elgee). 1884. *Driftwood from Scandinavia*. London: Richard Bentley and Son.

Williams, F. Harald (pseud. for Ward, Frederick William Orde). 1894. 'How I Won the Victoria Cross'. *Confessions of a Poet*. London: Hutchinson.

Williams, W. Mattieu. 1876. *Through Norway with a Knapsack*. 1859; London: Edward Stanford.

———. 1877. *Through Norway with Ladies*. London: Edward Stanford.

Willson, Thomas B. 1886. *The Handy Guide to Norway*. With Maps and an Appendix on the Flora and Lepidoptera of Norway by R. C. R. Jordan, M. D. London: Edward Stanford.

———. 1887. 'Some Norwegian Characteristics'. *The Girl's Own Paper* 8, no. 386 (21 May): 529–32.

Wilson, William Rae. 1826. *Travels in Norway, Sweden, Denmark, Hanover, Germany, Netherlands &c*. London: Longman, Rees, Orme, Brown, and Green.

Wollstonecraft, Mary. 1987. *Letters Written During a Short Residence in*

Sweden, Norway, and Denmark. Edited with an Introduction and Notes by Richard Holmes. 1796; Harmondsworth: Penguin Books.

———. 1974. 'On Poetry and Our Relish for the Beauties of Nature'. *Posthumous Works*. Ed. by William Godwin. Vol. 4. 1798; New York: Garland Publishing, Inc.

Wood, Charles W(illiam). 1880. *Round About Norway: With Sixty Three Illustrations*. London: Richard Bentley and Son.

———. 1886. *Under Northern Skies: With Sixty-Eight Illustrations*. London: Richard Bentley & Son.

———. 1903. *Norwegian By-ways: With Nine Illustrations*. London: Macmillan and Co.

Wordsworth, William. 1994. *The Works of William Wordsworth*. Ware, Herts.: Wordsworth Editions Ltd.

———. 1995. *The Prelude: The Four Texts (1798, 1799, 1805, 1850)*. Penguin Classics. Edited by Jonathan Wordsworth. Harmondsworth: Penguin Books.

Wordsworth, William and Samuel T. Coleridge. 1978. *Lyrical Ballads*, ed. W. J. B. Owen. 1798; Oxford: Oxford University Press.

Wu, Duncan, ed. 1998. *Romanticism: An Anthology*. 2nd ed. Oxford: Blackwell.

Wyndham, Francis M. 1861. *Wild Life on the Fjelds of Norway*. London: Longman, Green, Longman, and Roberts.

Secondary sources:

Adams, Eric. 1973. *Francis Danby: Varieties of Poetic Landscape*. New Haven: Yale University Press.

Adams, Percy G. 1983. *Travel Literature and the Evolution of the Novel*. Lexington, Ky.: The University Press of Kentucky.

Allen, Ralph Bergen. 1933. *Old Icelandic Sources in the English Novel*. Doctoral thesis, University of Pennsylvania. Philadelphia.

Angelomatis-Tsougarakis, Helen. 1990. *The Eve of the Greek Revival: British Travellers' Perceptions of Early Nineteenth-Century Greece*. London: Routledge.

Ashfield, Andrew and Peter de Bolla, eds. 1998. *The Sublime: A Reader in British Eighteenth-Century Aesthetic Theory*. 1996; Cambridge: Cambridge University Press.

Barczewski, Stephanie L. 2000. *Myth and National Identity in Nineteenth-Century Britain: The Legends of King Arthur and Robin Hood*. Oxford: Oxford University Press.

Barfoot, C. C., ed. 1997. *Beyond Pug's Tour: National and Ethnic Stereotyping in Theory and Literary Practice*. Amsterdam: Rodopi.

Barfoot, C. C. 1997. 'Beyond Pug's Tour: Stereotyping Our "Fellow-Creatures"'. In *Beyond Pug's Tour: National and Ethnic Stereotyping in Theory and Literary Practice*, ed. C. C. Barfoot, 5–36. Amsterdam:

Rodopi.

Barton, H. Arnold. 1996. '*Iter Scandinavicum*: Foreign Travelers' Views of the Late Eighteenth-Century North'. *Scandinavian Studies* 68, no. 1 (Winter): 1–18.

―――. 1998. *Northern Arcadia: Foreign Travelers in Scandinavia, 1765–1815*. Carbondale: Southern Illinois University Press.

Beach, Hugh. 1981. *Reindeer Herd Management in Transition: The Case of Tuorpan Saameby in Northern Sweden*. Uppsala: Almqvist & Wiksell International.

Berggren, Brit, Arne Emil Christensen and Bård Kolltveit. 1989. *Norsk sjøfart*. Vol. 1. Oslo: Dreyers Forlag A/S.

Bermingham, Ann. 1986. *Landscape and Ideology: The English Rustic Tradition, 1740–1860*. Berkeley: University of California Press.

Bewick, Thomas. 1962. *1800 Woodcuts by Thomas Bewick and His School*, eds. Blanche Cirker et al. Introd. Robert Hutchinson. New York: Dover Publications.

Biddis, Michael D. 1970. *Father of Racist Ideology: The Social and Political Thought of Count Gobineau*. London: Weidenfeld and Nicholson.

―――. 1978. *The Age of the Masses: Ideas and Society in Europe since 1870*. New York: Harper Colophon Books.

Bjørhovde, Gerd. 1987. *Rebellious Structures: Women Writers and the Crisis of the Novel 1880–1900*. Oslo: Norwegian University Press.

Black, Jeremy. 1985. *The British and the Grand Tour*. London: Croom Helm.

―――. 1990. 'Tourism and Cultural Change: The Changing Scene of the Eighteenth Century'. In *All Before Them, 1660–1780* (English Literature and the Wider World), ed. John McVeagh. London: The Ashfield Press.

Bolt, Christine. 1971. *Victorian Attitudes to Race*. London: Routledge & Kegan Paul.

Bourdieu, Pierre. 1999. *The Field of Cultural Production: Essays on Art and Literature*. Edited and introduced by Randal Johnson. 1993; Cambridge: Polity Press.

Bradbury, Malcolm and James McFarlane, eds. 1986. *Modernism 1890–1930*. 1976; Harmondsworth: Penguin Books.

Bring, Samuel E. 1954. *Itineraria Svecana: Bibliografisk förteckning över resor i Sverige fram till 1950*. Stockholm: Almqvist & Wiksell.

Bruland, Kristine. 1989. *British Technology and European Industrialisation: The Norwegian Textile Industry in the Mid Nineteenth Century*. Cambridge: Cambridge University Press.

Burchardt, C. B. 1920. *Norwegian Life and Literature: English Accounts and Views Especially in the Nineteenth Century*. London: Oxford University Press.

Burkart, A. J. and S. Medlik. 1981. *Tourism: Past, Present and Future*. 1974;

London: Heinemann.

Burke, Edmund. 1998. *A Philosophical Enquiry into the Origin of our Ideas of the Sublime and Beautiful and Other Pre-Revolutionary Writings*. Edited by David Womersley. 1757; Harmondsworth: Penguin Books.

Burke's Peerage & Baronetage. 1999. Edited by Charles Mosley. Craus-sur-Céligny: Burke's Peerage.

Butenschøn, B. A., ed. 1968. *Travellers Discovering Norway in the Last Century: An Anthology*. Oslo: Dreyers Forlag.

Buzard, James. 1993. *The Beaten Track: European Tourism, Literature, and the Ways to 'Culture' 1800–1918*. Oxford: Clarendon Press.

Campbell, Colin. 1987. *The Romantic Ethic and the Spirit of Modern Consumerism*. Oxford: Basil Blackwell.

Chard, Chloe. 1999. *Pleasure and Guilt on the Grand Tour: Travel Writing and Imaginative Geography 1600–1830*. Manchester: Manchester University Press.

Chitnis, Anand C. 1986. *The Scottish Enlightenment and Early Victorian English Society*. London: Croom Helm.

Clay, Jean. 1981. *Romanticism*. Trans. Daniel Wheeler and Craig Owen. New York: The Vendome Press.

Cocker, Mark. 1992. *Loneliness and Time: The Story of British Travel Writing*. New York: Pantheon Books.

Colley, Linda. 1996. *Britons: Forging the Nation 1707–1837*. 1992; London: Vintage Books.

Collinder, Björn. 1949. *The Lapps*. New York: Princeton University Press.

Colwell, Frederic S. 1989. *Rivermen: A Romantic Iconography of the River and the Source*. Kingston: McGill-Queen's University Press.

Conradi, G. 1937. *Den Norske Klub i London: 17. mai 1887–17.mai 1937*. London: Den Norske Klub Ltd.

Crocker, Lester G. 1973. *Jean-Jacques Rousseau*. Vol. 2: *The Prophetic Voice, 1758–1778*. New York: Macmillan.

Damiani, Anita. 1979. *Enlightened Observers: British Travellers to the Near East, 1715–1850*. Beirut: American University of Beirut.

Danielsen, Rolf et al. 1995. *Norway: A History from the Vikings to Our Own Times*. Trans. Michael Drake. Oslo: Scandinavian University Press.

Davidoff, Leonore and Catherine Hall. 1987. *Family Fortunes: Men and Women of the English Middle Class, 1780–1850*. London: Hutchinson Education.

Davies, Mark. 2000. *A Perambulating Paradox: British Travel Literature and the Image of Sweden c. 1770–1865*. Lund: Lunds Universitet.

Derry, T. K. 1973. *A History of Modern Norway 1814–1972*. Oxford: Clarendon Press.

Dictionary of National Biography. 1885–1903. Edited by Leslie Stephen and Sidney Lee. London: Smith, Elder and Co.

Dolan, Brian. 2001. *Ladies of the Grand Tour*. London: Flamingo.

Downs, Brian W. 1952. 'Anglo-Norwegian Literary Relations 1867–1900'. *The Modern Language Review* 47, no. 4 (October): 449–94.

Drake, Michael. 1969. *Population and Society in Norway, 1735–1865.* Cambridge: Cambridge University Press.

Duncan, James and Derek Gregory. 1999. *Writes of Passage: Reading Travel Writing.* London: Routledge.

Dyserinck, Hugo. 1966. 'Zum Problem der "Images" und "Mirages" und ihrer Untersuchung im Rahmen der Vergleichenden Literaturwissenschaft'. *Arcadia* 1, 107–120.

———. 1982. 'Komparatistische Imagologie jenseits von "Werkimmanenz" und "Werktranszendenz"'. *Synthesis* 9, 27–40.

———. 1991. *Komparatistik: Eine Einführung* (Aachener Beiträge zur Komparatistik, no. 1). 1979; Bonn: Bouvier.

Dyserinck, Hugo and Karl Ulrich Syndram, eds. 1988. *Europa und das nationale Selbstverständnis: Imagologische Probleme in Literatur, Kunst und Kultur des 19. und 20. Jahrhunderts* (Aachener Beiträge zur Komparatistik, no. 8). Bonn: Bouvier.

———. 1992. *Komparatistik und Europaforschung: Perspektiven vergleichender Literatur- und Kulturwissenschaft* (Aachener Beiträge zur Komparatistik, no. 9). Bonn and Berlin: Bouvier.

Elwin, Malcolm. 1958. *Landor, A Replevin.* London: MacDonald.

Encyclopædia Britannica, 1st ed. (1768–1771).

———, 4th ed. (1801–1810).

———, 11th ed. (1910–1911).

Escreet, J. M. 1904. *The Life of Edna Lyall (Ada Ellen Bayly).* London: Longmans, Green, and Co.

Ewbank, Inga-Stina, Olav Lausund and Bjørn Tysdahl, eds. 1999. *Anglo-Scandinavian Cross-Currents.* Norwich: Norvik Press.

Farley, Frank Edgar. 1903. *Scandinavian Influences in the English Romantic Movement.* Studies and Notes in Philology and Literature, vol. 9. Boston: Harvard University.

Feaver, William. 1975. *The Art of John Martin.* Oxford: Clarendon Press.

Federico, Annette R. 2000. *Idol of Suburbia: Marie Corelli and Late-Victorian Literary Culture.* Charlottesville: University Press of Virginia.

Field, Jean. 2000. *Landor: A Biography of the Writer Walter Savage Landor, Plus a Selection of His Works.* Studley, Warwickshire: Brewin Books.

Fjågesund, Peter. 2002. 'Knut Hamsun and George Egerton: Factual and Fictional Encounters'. In *English and Nordic Modernisms*, eds. Bjørn Tysdahl, M. Jansson, J. Lothe, and S. Klitgård Povlsen, 41–59. Norwich: Norvik Press.

Flowers, Michael. 3 January 2003. 'The Ellen Wood (Mrs. Henry Wood) Website'. Available from World Wide Web: (http://www.mrshenrywood.co.uk/).

Forster, John. 1876. *Walter Savage Landor: A Biography.* London:

Chapman and Hall.

Foster, Shirley. 1990. *Across New Worlds: Nineteenth-Century Women Travellers and their Writings*. London: Harvester Wheatsheaf.

Frawley, Maria H. 1994. *A Wider Range: Travel Writing by Women in Victorian England*. London and Toronto: Associated University Presses.

Gardåsen, Tor Kjetil. 1994. *Gamle Telemark*. Skien: Fylkesmuseet for Telemark og Grenland.

———. 1997. *A Historical Journey on the Telemark Canal*. Trans.: Harry T. Cleven & Andrew Smith. Skien: Society for the Preservation of Norwegian Ancient Monuments & Telemark County Council.

Gaskill, Howard, ed. 1996. *The Poems of Ossian and Related Works: James Macpherson*. Edinburg: Edinburgh University Press.

Gathorne-Hardy, G. 1925. *Norway*. London: Ernest Benn.

Gierløff, Chr. No year. *Thomas Bennett: Bennett Reisebureau, markedsleder i 145 år 1850–1995*. Facsimile of MS from 1925.

Gilbert, Alan D. Gilbert. 1988. *Religion and Society in Industrial England: Church, Chapel and Social Change 1740–1914*. 1976; London: Longman.

Gilpin, William. 1973. *Observations on the Mountains and Lakes of Cumberland and Westmorland*. A facsimile of *Observations, Relative Chiefly to Picturesque Beauty, Made in the Year 1772, On several Parts of England; Particularly the Mountains, and Lakes of Cumberland, and Westmoreland*, London: R. Blamire, 1786. Richmond, Surrey: The Richmond Publishing Co.

———. 1794. *Three Essays: on Picturesque Beauty; on Picturesque Travel; and on Sketching Landscape: to Which Is Added a Poem, on Landscape Painting*. London: R. Blamires.

Gjerset, Knut. 1932. *History of the Norwegian People*. New York: Macmillan.

Gjevik, Bjørn N. 1997. 'Moskstraumen Myter, Diktning og Virkelighet'. In *Annual Proceedings from the Norwegian Academy of Science and Letters*. Oslo: Norwegian Academy of Science and Letters, 157–69.

Graburn, Nelson H. H. and Stephen B. Strong. 1973. *Circumpolar Peoples: An Anthropological Perspective*. Pacific Palisades, Calif.: Goodyear Publishing.

Greenacre, Francis. 1973. *The Bristol School of Artists: Francis Danby and Painting in Bristol 1810–1840*. Bristol: City Art Gallery.

Grimsley, Ronald. 1983. *Jean-Jacques Rousseau*. Sussex: Harvester.

Hansen, Trond Børrehaug, Håkon Gundersen and Svein Sando. 1980. *Jernbanen i Norge*. Oslo: Pax forlag AS.

Haugen, Einar. 1966. *Language Conflict and Language Planning: The Case of Modern Norwegian*. Cambridge, Mass.: Harvard University Press.

Haugstøl, Henrik. 1950. *Hundre år for Norge: Glimt av reiselivet før og nu*. Oslo: Bennetts Reisebureau A/S.

Houghton, Walter E. 1975. *The Victorian Frame of Mind 1830–1870*.

1957; New Haven: Yale University Press.

Huitfeldt, Carl. 1932. *Norge i andres øine: Utdrag av utenlandske reisebeskrivelser gjennom 2000 år*. Oslo: Gyldendal.

Hussey, Christopher. 1927. *The Picturesque: Studies in a Point of View*. London: G. P. Putnam's Sons.

Islam, Syed Manzurul. 1996. *The Ethics of Travel, from Marco Polo to Kafka*. Manchester: Manchester University Press.

Itineraria Svecana: see Bring, Samuel E.

Janowitz, Anne. 1990. *England's Ruins: Poetic Purpose and the National Landscape*. Oxford: Basil Blackwell.

Keenlyside, Francis. 1975. *Peaks and Pioneers: The Story of Mountaineering*. London: Elek.

Knaplund, Paul. 1970. *Gladstone's Foreign Policy*. London: Frank Cass.

Korte, Barbara. 2000. *English Travel Writing from Pilgrimages to Postcolonial Explorations*. Trans. Catherine Matthias. London: Macmillan.

Langford, Paul. 2000. *Englishness Identified: Manner and Character, 1650–1850*. Oxford: Oxford University Press.

Leerssen, Joep. 2000. 'The Rhetoric of National Character: A Programmatic Survey'. *Poetics Today* 21, no. 2, 267–92.

―――. 15 May 2002. 'National Identity and National Stereotype'. Available from World Wide Web: (http://www.hum.uva.nl/images/info/leers.html).

Leiren, Terje I. 1975. 'Norwegian Independence and British Opinion: January to August 1814'. *Scandinavian Studies* 47, no. 3, 364–82.

Levine, George, ed. 1967. *The Emergence of Victorian Consciousness: The Spirit of the Age*. New York: Free Press.

Lieberman, Sima. 1970. *The Industrialisation of Norway, 1800–1920*. Oslo: Universitetsforlaget.

Litzenberg, Karl. 1947. 'The Victorians and the Vikings: A Bibliographical Essay on Anglo-Norse Literary Relations'. *Contributions in Modern Philology*, no. 3 (April): 1–27.

Logan, Deborah Anna. 1998. *Fallenness in Victorian Women's Writing: Marry, Stitch, Die or Do Worse*. Columbia, Mo.: University of Missouri Press.

Low, Donald A. 1977. *That Sunny Dome: A Portrait of Regency Britain*. London: Dent.

Loomis, Chauncey C. 1977. 'The Arctic Sublime'. In *Nature and the Victorian Imagination*, eds. U. C. Knoepfelmacher and G. B. Tennyson. Berkeley: University of California Press.

Lucas, Colin. 1990. 'Great Britain and the Union of Norway and Sweden'. *Scandinavian Journal of History* 15, no. 4, 269–78.

MacDougall, Hugh A. 1982. *Racial Myth in English History: Trojans, Teutons and Anglo-Saxons*. Montreal: Harvest House.

Magnus, Philip. 1954. *Gladstone: A Biography*. London: John Murray.

Magnusson, Magnus. 1990. 'The Viking Road'. In *Scotland and*

Scandinavia 800–1800, ed. Grant G. Simpson (University of Aberdeen: The Mackie Monographs, no. 1), 1–12. Edinburgh: John Donald Publishers Ltd.

Mains, Jean A. 1989. *British Travellers in Norway During the Nineteenth Century*. Unpublished M. Litt. thesis, University of Edinburgh.

Markhus, Knut. 2000. *Ein Edens hage: Utlendingar opplever Hordaland*. Oslo: Det Norske Samlaget.

Martin, Robert Bernard. 1980. *Tennyson: The Unquiet Heart*. Oxford: Clarendon Press.

Matthew, H. C. G., ed. 1990. *The Gladstone Diaries with Cabinet Minutes and Prime Ministerial Correspondence*. Vol. 10 (Jan 1881–June 1883) and vol. 11 (July 1883–Dec 1886). Oxford: Clarendon Press.

———. 1997. *Gladstone: 1809-1892*. Oxford: Clarendon Press.

McCleary, G. F. 1953. *The Malthusian Population Theory*. London: Faber and Faber.

McLeod, Hugh. 1989. *Religion and the Working Class in Nineteenth-Century Britain*. Basingstoke: Macmillan.

McVeagh, John, ed. 1990. *All Before Them, 1660–1780* (English Literature and the Wider World). London: The Ashfield Press.

Moberg, Arvid. 1968. *Kopparverket i Kåfjord: Ett bidrag till Nordkalottens historia*. Nordbottens museum.

Molland, Einar. 1957. *Church Life in Norway 1800–1950*. Translated by Hans Kaasa. Minneapolis: Augsburg Publishing House.

Moore, Tim. 2000. *Frost On My Moustache: The Arctic Exploits of a Lord and a Loafer*. 1999; London: Abacus.

Morgan, Marjorie. 2001. *National Identities and Travel in Victorian Britain* (Studies in Modern History). New York: Palgrave.

Morgan, Thaïs, ed. 1990. *Victorian Sages & Cultural Discourse: Renegotiating Gender and Power*. New Brunswick: Rutgers University Press.

Morley, John. 1903. *The Life of William Ewart Gladstone*. Vol. 3. New York: Macmillan.

Nature's Way: Romantic Landscapes from Norway: Oil Studies, Watercolours and Drawings by Johan Christian Dahl (1788–1857) and Thomas Fearnley (1802–1842). Manchester: The Whitworth Art Gallery, 1993.

Nead, Lynda. 1988. *Myths of Sexuality: Representations of Women in Victorian Britain*. Oxford: Basil Blackwell.

Nicholson, Norman. 1995. *The Lakers: The Adventures of the First Tourists*. Milnthorpe, Cumbria: Cicerone.

Nicolson, Marjorie Hope. 1959. *Mountain Gloom and Mountain Glory: The Development of the Aesthetics of the Infinite*. Ithaca, New York: Cornell University Press.

Nielsen, Jens Petter. 1987. *I kopperverkets tid: Kåfjord kirke 150 år*. Elvebakken.

Norway's Official Statistics: Historical Statistics 1994. 1995. Oslo:

Central Bureau of Statistics of Norway.

Omberg, Margaret. 1976. *Scandinavian Themes in English Poetry, 1760–1800*. Uppsala: Almqvist & Wiksell International.

Østvedt, Einar. 1968. 'Storbritannia og den norske frihetskampen i 1814'. In *Strandhugg: Artikler og essays*, 5–11. Skien: Selskapet for Skien bys vel.

Parek, Bhikhu. 1973. *Bentham's Political Thought*. London: Croom Helm.

Pareli, Leif. 2000. *Samisk kultur*. Oslo: Norsk folkemuseum.

Pettersen, Hjalmar. 1973. *Norge og nordmænd i udlandets literatur (Norway and the Norwegians in Foreign Literature)*. Bibliotheca Norvegica, vol. 2. Copenhagen: Rosenkilde og Bagger.

Pick, Daniel. 1989. *Faces of Degeneration: A European Disorder, c. 1848–c. 1918*. Cambridge: Cambridge University Press.

Pittock, Murray G. H. 1999. *Celtic Identity and the British Image*. Manchester: Manchester University Press.

Porter, Dennis. 1991. *Haunted Journeys: Desire and Transgression in European Travel Writing*. Princeton: Princeton University Press.

Pratt, Edwin A. 1907. *Licensing and Temperance in Sweden, Norway and Denmark*. London: John Murray

Pratt, Mary Louise. 1992. *Imperial Eyes: Travel Writing and Transculturation*. London: Routledge.

Pryser, Tore. 1985. *Norsk historie 1800–1870*. Oslo: Det Norske Samlaget.

Rem, Tore. 2002. 'The Englishing of *Hunger*: Knut Hamsun, George Egerton and Leonard Smithers'. In *English and Nordic Modernisms*, eds. Bjørn Tysdahl, M. Jansson, J. Lothe, and S. Klitgård Povlsen, 61–76. Norwich: Norvik Press.

Rendall, Jane. 1994. 'Does History Speak: Writing a National History for British Women (c. 1780–1810)'. Paper given at University of York, 1994.

Riste, Olav. 2001. *Norway's Foreign Relations – A History*. Oslo: Universitetsforlaget.

Robertson, David. 1977. 'Mid-Victorians amongst the Alps'. In *Nature and the Victorian Imagination*, eds. U. C. Knoepfelmacher and G. B. Tennyson. Berkeley: University of California Press.

Robinson, Jane. 1990. *Wayward Women: A Guide to Women Travellers*. Oxford: Oxford University Press.

Roughead, W. N., ed. 1951. *Hilaire Belloc: An Anthology of his Prose and Verse*. London: Rupert Hart-Davis.

Ruskin, John. 1904. *Frondes Agrestes*. 1856; London: George Allen.

Ryall, Anka. 1997. 'A Vindication of Struggling Nature: Mary Wollstonecraft's Scandinavia'. *Nordlit* (Arbeidsskrift i litteratur, Universitetet i Tromsø), no. 1, Spring, 127–49.

Ryle, Martin. 1999. *Journeys in Ireland: Literary Travellers, Rural Landscapes, Cultural Relations*. Aldershot: Ashgate.

Said, Edward W. 1995. *Orientalism: Western Conceptions of the Orient*. 1978; Harmondsworth: Penguin Books.

Sambrook, James. 1990. 'Thomson Abroad: Traversing Realms Unknown'. In *All Before Them, 1660–1780* (English Literature and the Wider World), ed. John McVeagh. London: The Ashfield Press.

Sartre, Jean Paul. 1971. *L'Idiot de la famille. Gustave Flaubert de 1821 à 1857.* Vol. 2. Paris: Gallimard.

Scaramellini, Guglielmo. 1996. 'The Picturesque and the Sublime in Nature and the Landscape: Writing and Iconography in the Romantic Voyaging in the Alps'. *Geojournal* 38, no. 1, 49–57.

Scheen, Erland. 1956. *Bidrag til Norges turisthistorie.* Printed for private circulation. Oslo.

Schiötz, Eiler H. 1970–1986. *Itineraria Norvegica: A Bibliography on Foreigners' Travels in Norway until 1900.* 2 vols. Oslo: Universitetsforlaget.

Seaton, Ethel. 1935. *Literary Relations of England and Scandinavia in the Seventeenth Century.* Oxford: Clarendon Press.

Selid, Betty. 1970. *Women in Norway: Their Position in Family Life, Employment and Society.* Oslo: The Norwegian Joint Committee on International Social Policy in Association with The Department of Cultural Relations, Royal Ministry of Foreign Affairs.

Skavhaug, Kjersti. 1990. *Til Nordkapp: Berømte reiser fra vikingtid til 1800.* Honningsvåg: Nordkapplitteratur.

Solnit, Rebecca. 2001. *Wanderlust: A History of Walking.* London: Verso.

Stepan, Nancy. 1985. 'Biological Degeneration: Races and Proper Places'. In *Degeneration: The Dark Side of Progress*, eds. J. Edward Chamberlin and Sander L. Gilman, 97–120. New York: Columbia University Press.

Stetz, Margaret Diane. 1982. *'George Egerton': Woman and Writer of the Eighteen-Nineties.* Unpublished Ph.D. dissertation, Harvard University.

Super, R. H. 1954. *Walter Savage Landor: A Biography.* New York: New York University Press.

Symes, Ruth A. 1995. *Educating Women: The Preceptress and Her Pen, 1789–1820.* Unpubl. doctoral thesis, University of York.

Taylor, Ronald Lee. 1974. *The Swedish Acquisition of Norway: Anglo-Swedish Diplomacy, 1810–1814.* Ph. D. dissertation. Case Western Reserve University.

Theakstone, John. 2002. *Victorian and Edwardian Women Travellers: A Bibliography of Books Published Between 1837 and 1910.*

Vikør, Lars S. 1975. *The New Norse Language Movement.* Oslo: Novus.

Vorren, Ørnulv and Ernst Manker. 1962. *Lapp Life and Customs: A Survey.* Trans. Kathleen McFarlane. London: Oxford University Press.

Wallace, Anne D. 1993. *Walking, Literature, and English Culture: The Origins and Uses of Peripatetic in the Nineteenth Century.* Oxford: Clarendon Press.

Watson, George, ed. 1969. *The New Cambridge Bibliography of English Literature.* Vol. 3. Cambridge: Cambridge University Press.

Wawn, Andrew. 2000. *The Vikings and the Victorians: Inventing the Old North in Nineteenth-Century Britain.* Cambridge: D.S. Brewer.

Wergeland, Henrik. 1897. *Norges Konstitutions Historie.* 1841; Kristiania: Olaf Husebys Forlag.

West, Shearer, ed. 1996. *The Victorians and Race.* Aldershot, Hants: Scolar Press.

Wood, Christopher. 1983. *The Pre-Raphaelites.* London: Weidenfeld and Nicolson.

Wykes, Alan. 1973. *Abroad: A Miscellany of English Travel Writing, 1700–1914.* London: Macdonald.

Young, G. M. 1977. *Portrait of an Age: Victorian England.* 1936; Oxford: Oxford University Press.

Youngs, Tim. 1994. *Travellers in Africa: British Travelogues, 1850–1900.* Manchester: Manchester University Press.

INDEX

Nineteenth-century and modern spelling of several Norwegian place names varies considerably. In addition many foreign travellers had major problems spelling Norwegian names correctly. Here the modern Norwegian spelling is used (except with such established English versions as North Cape); nineteenth-century variants are referred to the main entry. For the benefit of readers not familiar with the map of Norway, the present county has been given in parenthesis after minor place names. The Norwegian letters *æ*, *ø* and *å* are alphabetised as if they were ae, oe and a respectively. In the nineteenth century, the *å* did not exist, and was spelt *aa*. The titles of medieval and other texts without a known author have been included (such as *Frithiof's Saga*); otherwise only the authors have been included (thus Charlotte Brontë, but not *Jane Eyre*). Fictional characters have also been omitted. The name of a country includes all references to its language, people etc.

Måbødalen (Hordaland) 85
Måne-elven (Telemark) 330
McAdam, John 85
Macaulay, Lord Thomas Babington
    236, 262
McCleary, G. F. 235
McClintock, Leopold 336
MacDougall, Hugh A. 113, 120
M'Donough (Captain) 43
Mcfarlan, W. L. 189
McFarlane, James 76
MacGregor, J. 67, 360
Mackay, Charles 352
Mackay, Mary: see Corelli, Marie
McLeod, Hugh 246
Macpherson, James 141
maelstrom 339-40
Magdalen College (Oxford) 350
Magdalene College (Cambridge)
    358
Magnus 'Barefoot', King of Norway
    146
Magnus, Philip 190-93
Magnusson, Magnus 11
Mains, Jean A. 55, 67, 74, 78, 107,
    122, 136, 147, 278, 296, 320,
    324, 328, 343
male gaze 292-94
Mallet, Paul Henri (M.) 114-15, 117
Malmagen (Sweden) 202
Malta 131
Malthus, Thomas Robert 86, 103,
    152-53, 235-36, 244
Manchester 71, 167, 185, 207, 235,
    242, 361
Måne-elven (Telemark)
Manker, Ernst 205
Manners, John Henry 363
Mant, Richard 319
Margaretting 348
market for travelogues: see
    travelogues, market for
marriage (see also intermarriage)
    126, 211, 216, 225-27, 229, 235,
    314
Married Women's Property Act 227
Marshall, William 321
Marstrand (Sweden) 43
Martin, John 73-74, 308
Martin, Robert 190

Martineau, Harriet 18, 74, 159, 361,
    363
Marylebone Grammar School 352
masculinity 119, 215, 297, 312, 321,
    328
Massey, Gerald 142, 361
Matlock 307
Matterhorn 311
Matthew, H. C. G. 190-91, 250, 259
Maud, Queen of Norway 101
Mayfair 54
Mayo, Rev. M. W. 65
medieval: see Middle Ages
Mediterranean: see Southern Europe
Melford 359
merchant navy: see British merchant
    navy; Norwegian merchant navy
merchants: see trade
Mer de Glace 309
Merrlees, Mrs I. M. 306-7, 361
Merry England: see England, Merry
Merton College (Oxford) 366
Metcalfe, Frederick 15, 34, 68, 82,
    85, 141, 151-52, 157, 274, 305,
    307, 328, 361
Methodism 242
Middle Ages 88, 159, 177, 316
middle class: see class
Midlothian 193
Midnight Sun 20, 38, 62, 341, 343-
    44
Midwest 349
Milford, John 163, 173, 181, 214,
    217, 244, 361
military 11, 22, 55, 66, 109, 129,
    139, 141, 145-46, 179, 183, 262,
    357, 358, 359
Mill, John Stuart 235, 262
Millais, Sir John Everett 323
Milton, John 318, 334, 362
minister: see clergy
Mjøsa 91
Mjosen: see Mjøsa
Modernist movement 75-76
Moen: see Måne-elven
Moland (Telemark) 214
Molde (Møre og Romsdal) 64, 264
Molland, Einar 249
Montanvert 43, 309
Mont Blanc 39, 305, 309, 317

About the Authors

Peter Fjågesund (b. 1959) is Senior Lecturer in British literature and civilisation at Telemark University College, Norway. After receiving his DPhil from the University of Oxford, he worked in publishing and as Director of the Norwegian Study Centre at the University of York. His publications include *The Apocalyptic World of D. H. Lawrence* (1991) and a number of articles on nineteenth- and twentieth-century British writers. In 2001, in connection with the present research project, he published a book in Norwegian on foreign travellers in the county of Telemark in the nineteenth century.

Ruth A. Symes (b. 1966) studied English Literature as an undergraduate at the University of Cambridge and received her PhD from the University of York. As a lecturer in British Culture at the Norwegian Study Centre, University of York (1995-1998) she lectured extensively on nineteenth-century literature, history and women's studies. Her publications include *The Governess: An Anthology* (1997, with Dr Trev Broughton) and a number of articles on nineteenth-century women's history. She is now Editorial Team Leader at Manchester Open Learning, Manchester College of Arts and Technology.